Great Family Vacations

Midwest and Rocky Mountain Region

Second Edition

Candyce H. Stapen

Guilford, Connecticut

Photo credits: page 8 courtesy Alberta Economic Development and Tourism; page 25 courtesy Calgary Convention and Visitors Bureau; page 30 courtesy Edmonton Tourism; page 79 by Ron Schramm, courtesy Chicago Tourism Council; page 95, courtesy Indianapolis Project; page 123 courtesy Henry Ford Museum and Greenfield Museum, Dearborn, Michigan; page 176 courtesy St. Louis Convention and Visitors Commission; page 217 courtesy South Dakota Tourism; page 231 by Jim Marie/courtesy Utah Travel Council; page 240 courtesy Salt Lake City Convention and Visitor Bureau; page 253 courtesy Utah Travel Council; page 291 courtesy Wyoming Travel Commission; page 309 courtesy Wyoming Travel Commission.

Cover photo background: Bill Backman/©1996 PhotoDisc, Inc.
Cover inset photographs: Lori Adamski Peek/©Tony Stone Images; Ken Fisher/©Tony Stone Images; Jess Stock/©Tony Stone Images
Cover design by Schwartzman Design

Library of Congress Cataloging-in-Publication Data
Stapen, Candyce H.
Great family vacations. Midwest and Rocky Mountain region / Candyce H. Stapen – 2nd ed.
p. cm. – (Great family vacations series)
Includes index.
ISBN 0-7627-0385-7
1. Middle West Guidebooks. 2. Rocky Mountains Region Guidebooks. 3. Family recreation – Middle West Guidebooks. 4. Family recreation – Rocky Mountains Region Guidebooks. I. Title. II. Title: Midwest and Rocky Mountain region. III. Series: Stapen, Candyce H. Great family vacations series.
F350.3.S73 1999 99-16324
917.704'33–dc21 CIP

Manufactured in the United States of America
Second Edition/First Printing

To my favorite traveling companions
Alissa, Matt, and David

Acknowledgments

I want to thank my agent, Carol Mann, for her assistance. I appreciate the hard work of Diane Ney, Katy Saldarini, and Luisa Frey Gaynor, who also contributed to this volume.

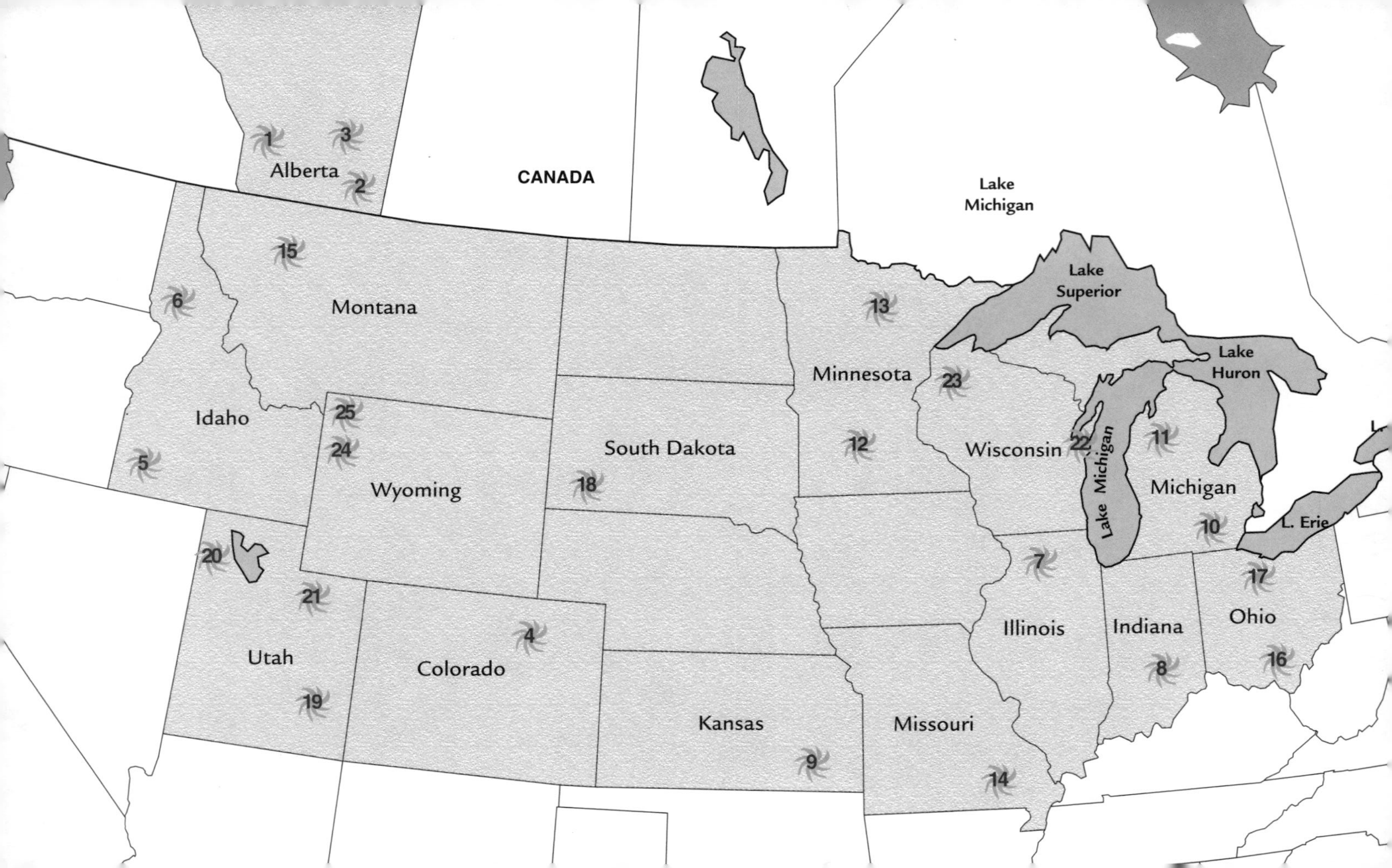
CANADA
Alberta
1
3
2
Lake
Michigan
Lake
Superior
Lake
Huron
L. Erie
Montana
15
6
Idaho
5
25
24
Wyoming
South Dakota
18
Minnesota
13
12
23
Wisconsin
22
Lake Michigan
11
Michigan
10
20
21
Utah
19
Colorado
4
Kansas
9
Missouri
14
Illinois
7
Indiana
8
Ohio
17
16

Contents

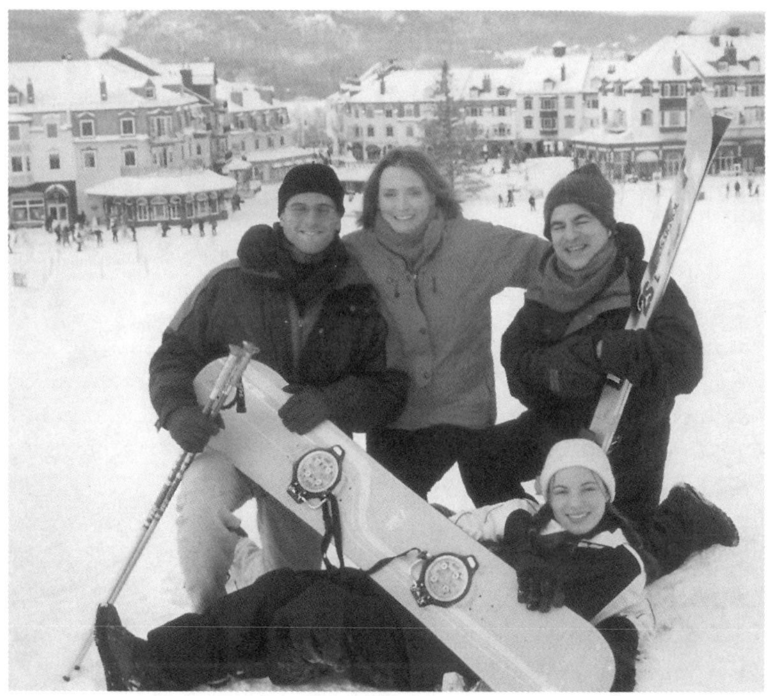

About the Author

Candyce H. Stapen is an expert on family travel. She has appeared on many television, cable, and radio shows, including *Good Morning America,* CBS *This Morning,* WUSA-TV, D.C., and National Public Radio. A member of the Society of American Travel Writers and the Travel Journalists Guild, she is a contributing editor/columnist for *National Geographic Traveler, FamilyFun,* the *Washington Times,* and *Vacations.*

Her articles about family travel appear in a variety of newspapers and magazines, including *Parents.com, Good Housekeeping, Ladies' Home Journal, Family Circle, USA Weekend, Better Homes and Gardens,* the *New York Post, Family Travel Newsletter,* and *Diversion.*

Other books by Stapen are *Great Family Vacations: Northeast, Great Family Vacations: South, Great Family Vacations: West,* and *Fun with the Family in Virginia* (Globe Pequot); and *Cruise Vacations with Kids* and *Ski Vacations with Kids* (Prima).

Stapen lives in Washington, D.C., and travels whenever she can with her husband and two children.

Introduction

There is a Chinese proverb that says the wise parent gives a child roots and wings. By traveling with your children, you can bestow many gifts upon them: a strong sense of family bonds, memories that last a lifetime, and a joyful vision of the world.

Traveling with your children offers many bonuses for you and your family. These days no parent or child has an excessive amount of free time. Whether you work in the home or outside it, your days are filled with meetings, deadlines, household errands, and carpool commitments. Your child most likely keeps equally busy with scouts, soccer, music lessons, computer clinics, basketball, and/or ballet. When your family stays home, your time together is likely to be limited to sharing quick dinners and overseeing homework. If there's a teen in your house, an age known for endless hours spent with friends, your encounters often shrink to swapping phone messages and car keys.

But take your child on the road with you, and both of you have plenty of time to talk and be together. Traveling together gives your family the luxury of becoming as expansive as the scenery. Over doughnuts in an airport lounge or dinner in a new hotel, you suddenly hear about that special science project or how it really felt to come in third in the swim meet. By sharing a drive along a country road or a visit to a city museum, your children get the space to view you as a person and not just as a parent.

Additionally, both you and your kids gain new perspectives on life. Children who spend time in a different locale, whether it's a national forest or a city new to them, expand their awareness. For you as a parent, traveling with your kids brings the added bonus of enabling you to see again with a child's eye. When you show a six-year-old a reconstructed Colonial village or share the stars in a Tennessee mountain night sky with a thirteen-year-old, you feel the world twinkle with as much possibility as when you first encountered these sights long ago.

Part of this excitement is a result of the exuberance kids bring, and part is from the instant friendships kids establish. Street vendors save their best deals for preschoolers, and, even on a crowded rush hour bus, a child by your side turns a fellow commuter from a stranger into a friend. Before your stop comes you'll often be advised of the best toy shop in town and directed to a local cafe with a kid-pleasing menu at prices guaranteed to put a smile on your face.

New perspectives also come from the activities you participate in with your children. Most of these activities you would probably pass up when shuttling solo. Whether it's finding all the dogs in the paintings at an art museum, playing miniature golf at a resort, or trying horseback riding in a park, you always learn more when you take your kids.

Surprisingly, traveling with your kids can also be cost-effective and practical. By combining or by extending a work-related trip into a vacation, you save money since your company picks up a good part of your expenses. Because tag-along-tots on business trips are an increasing trend, several hotel chains have responded with a range of family-friendly amenities including children's programs, child-safe rooms, and milk and cookies at bedtime.

For all these reasons traveling with your children presents many wonderful opportunities. It is a great adventure to be a parent, and it is made more wondrous when you travel with your children. You will not only take pleasure in each other's company, but you will return home with memories to savor for a lifetime.

Family Travel Tips

Great family vacations require careful planning and the cooperation of all family members. Before you go you need to think about such essentials as how to keep sibling fights to a minimum and how to be prepared for medical emergencies. While en route you want to be sure to make road trips and plane rides fun, even with a toddler. You want to be certain that the room that is awaiting your family is safe and that your family makes the most of being together. When visiting relatives, you want to eliminate friction by following the house rules. These tips, gathered from a host of families, go a long way toward making your trips good ones.

General Rules

1. Meet the needs of the youngest family member. Your raft trip won't be fun if you're constantly worried about your three-year-old being bumped overboard by the white water the tour operator failed to mention or if your first-grader gets bored with the day's itinerary of art museums.
2. Underplan. Your city adventure will dissolve in tears—yours and your toddler's—if you've scheduled too many sites and not enough time for the serendipitous. If your child delights in playing with the robots at the science museum, linger there and skip the afternoon's proposed visit to the history center.
3. Go for the green spaces. Seek out an area's parks. Pack a picnic lunch and take time to throw a Frisbee, play catch, or simply enjoy relaxing in the sun and people watching.
4. Enlist the cooperation of your kids by including them in the decision making. While family vacation voting is not quite a democracy, consider

your kids' needs. Is there a way to combine your teen's desire to be near "the action" with your spouse's request for seclusion? Perhaps book a self-contained resort on a quiet beach that also features a nightspot.

5. Understand your rhythms of the road. Some families like traveling at night so that the kids sleep in the car or on the plane. Others avoid traveling during the evening cranky hours and prefer to leave early in the morning.
6. Plan to spend time alone with each of your children as well as with your spouse. Take a walk, write in a journal together, play ball, share ice cream in the snack shop, etc. Even the simplest things done together create valuable family memories.
7. Have a sense of humor. Attractions get crowded, cars break down, and kids spit up. Remember why you came on vacation in the first place—to have fun with your kids.

Don't Leave Home Without

1. *Emergency medical kit.* The first thing we always pack is the emergency medical kit, a bag I keep ready to go with all those things that suddenly become important at 3:00 A.M. This is no hour to be searching the streets for baby aspirin or Band-Aids. Make sure your kit includes items suitable for adults as well as children. Be sure to bring:
   - aspirin or an aspirin substitute
   - a thermometer
   - cough syrup
   - a decongestant
   - medication to relieve diarrhea
   - bandages and Band-Aids
   - gauze pads
   - antibiotic ointment and a physician-approved antibiotic, just in case
   - a motion-sickness remedy
   - sunscreen
   - insect repellent
   - ointments or spray to soothe sunburn, rashes, and poison ivy
   - something to soothe insect stings
   - any medications needed on a regular basis
   - tweezers and a sterile needle to remove splinters

   Keep this kit with you in your carry-on luggage or on the front seat of your car.
2. *Snack food.* As soon as we land somewhere or pull up to a museum for a visit, my daughter usually wants food. Instead of arguing or wasting time and money on snacks, I carry granola bars with me. She munches on these reasonably nutritious snacks while we continue on schedule.
3. *Inflatable pillow and travel products.* Whether on the road or in a plane,

these inflatable wonders help me and the kids sleep. For travel pillows plus an excellent variety of light yet durable travel products including hair dryers, luggage straps, alarms, adaptor plugs for electrical outlets, and clothing organizers, call Magellan's (800-962-4943). TravelSmith (800-950-1600) carries these items as well as clothing, mostly for teens and adults.

4. *Travel toys.* Kids don't have to be bored en route to your destination. Pack books, coloring games, and quiet toys. Some kids love story tapes on their personal cassette players. For innovative, custom-tailored travel kits full of magic pencil games, puzzles, and crafts for children three and a half or older, call Sealed With A Kiss (800-888-SWAK). The packages cost about $35. Surprise your kids with this once you are on the road. They'll be happy and so will you.

Flying with Tots

1. Book early for the seat you like. Whether you prefer the aisle, window, or bulkhead for extra legroom, reserve your seat well in advance of your departure date.
2. Call the airlines at least forty-eight hours ahead to order meals that you know your kids will eat: children's dinners, hamburger platters, salads, etc.
3. Bring food on board that you know your kids like even if you've ordered a special meal. If your kids won't eat what's served at mealtime, at least they won't be hungry if they munch on nutritious snacks.
4. Be sure to explain each step of the plane ride to little kids so that they will understand that the airplane's noises and shaking do not mean that a crash is imminent.
5. Stuff your carry-on with everything you might need (including medications, extra kids' clothes, diapers, baby food, formula, and bottles) to get you through a long flight and a delay of several hours . . . just in case.
6. Bring a child safety seat (a car seat) on board. Although presently the law allows children under two to fly free if they sit on a parent's lap, the Federal Aviation Administration and the Air Transport Association support legislation that would require all kids to be in child safety seats. In order to get a seat on board, the seat must have a visible label stating approval for air travel, and you must purchase a ticket for that seat. Without a ticket you are not guaranteed a place to put this child safety seat in case the plane is full.
7. With a toddler or young child, wrap little surprises to give as "presents" throughout the flight. These work wonderfully well to keep a wee one's interest.
8. Before boarding let your kids work off energy by walking around the

airport lounge. Never let your child nap just before takeoff—save the sleepy moments for the plane.

9. If you're traveling with a lot of luggage, check it curbside before parking your car. This eliminates the awkward trip from long-term parking loaded down with kids, luggage, car seats, and strollers.

Road Rules

1. Use this time together to talk with your children. Tell them anecdotes about your childhood or create stories for the road together.
2. Put toys for each child in his or her own mesh bag. This way the toys are easily located and visible instead of being strewn all over the car.
3. Avoid long rides. Break the trip up by stopping every two or three hours for a snack or to find a rest room. This lets kids stretch their legs.
4. When driving for several days, plan to arrive at your destination each day by 4:00 or 5:00 P.M. so that the kids can enjoy a swim at the hotel/motel. This turns long hauls into easily realized goals that are fun.

At the Destination

1. When traveling with young children, do a safety check of the hotel room and the premises as soon as you arrive. Put matches, glasses, ashtrays, and small items out of reach. Note if stair and balcony railings are widely spaced or easily climbed by eager tots and if windows lack screens or locks. Find out where the possible dangers are, and always keep track of your kids.
2. Schedule sight-seeing for the morning, but plan to be back at the resort or hotel by early afternoon so that your child can enjoy the pool, the beach, miniature golf, or other kid-friendly facilities.
3. Plan to spend some time alone with each of your children every day. With preteens and teens, keep active by playing tennis or basketball, jogging, or doing something else to burn energy.
4. Establish an amount of money that your child can spend on souvenirs. Stick to this limit, but let your child decide what he or she wants to buy.

With Relatives

1. Find out the rules of your relatives' house before you arrive, and inform your kids of them. Let them know, for example, that food is allowed only in the kitchen or dining room so that they won't bring sandwiches into the guest bedroom or den.
2. Tell your relatives about your kids' eating preferences. Let the person doing the cooking know that fried chicken is fine, but that your kids won't touch liver even if it is prepared with the famous family recipe.

3. To lessen the extra work and expense for relatives and to help eliminate friction, bring along or offer to shop and pay for those special items that only your kids eat—a favorite brand of cereal, juice, frozen pizza, or microwave kids' meal.
4. Discuss meal hours. If you know, for example, that grandma and grandpa always dine at 7:00 P.M. but that your preschooler and first-grader can't wait that long, feed your kids earlier at their usual time, and enjoy an adult dinner with your relatives later.
5. Find something suitable for each generation that your kids and relatives will enjoy doing together. Look over old family albums, have teens tape-record oral family histories, and have grade-schoolers take instant snapshots of the clan.
6. Find some way that your kids can help with the work of visiting. Even a nursery-school-age child feels good about helping to clear a table or sweep the kitchen floor.

Family Travel Planners

These specialists can help you assess your family's needs and find the vacation that's best for you.

- ***Family Travel Network.*** (FTN) on AOL has lots of information and advice about family vacations and destinations as well as bulletin boards. Find out what other parents think of various places. Once on AOL, click "Keyword" and type in "Family Travel Network."
- ***Family Travel Times.*** This on-line newsletter offers the latest information on hotels, resorts, city attractions, cruises, airlines, tours, and destinations. For information call (212) 447-5524; www.familytraveltimes.com.
- ***Family Travel Forum.*** This newsletter has information about family trips. You can contact them at 891 Amsterdam Avenue, New York, NY 10025; (212) 665-6124; www.familytravelforum.com.
- ***Rascals in Paradise.*** Specializing in family and small-group tours to the Caribbean, Mexico, and the South Pacific, some Rascals' tours include nannies for each family and an escort to organize activities for the kids. Call (800) U-RASCAL for more information.
- ***Grandtravel.*** This company offers a variety of domestic and international trips for grandparents and grandchildren seven through seventeen. (800) 247-7651.
- ***Grandvistas.*** Grandparents can take their grandkids on a few trips, too. Destinations typically include South Dakota, Nevada, and Wyoming. Call (800) 647-0800.
- ***Families Welcome!*** This agency offers travel packages for families in European cities and New York. With rental of a hotel room or apart-

ment, you receive a "Welcome Kit" of tips on sight-seeing, restaurants, and museums. (800) 326-0724.

- ***Family Explorations.*** Trip destinations include Ireland, Costa Rica, and Honduras, plus service-oriented trips overseas and stateside getaways such as Pennsylvania and Maine. (800) WE-GO-TOO.

The prices and rates listed in this guidebook were confirmed at press time. We recommend, however, that you call establishments before traveling to obtain current information.

Help Us Keep This Guide Up to Date

Every effort has been made by the author and editors to make this guide as accurate and useful as possible. However, many things can change after a guide is published—establishments close, phone numbers change, facilities come under new management, housing costs fluctuate, and so on.

We would love to hear from you concerning your experiences with this guide and how you feel it could be made better and be kept up to date. While we may not be able to respond to all comments and suggestions, we'll take them to heart and we'll make certain to share them with the author. Please send your comments and suggestions to the following address:

The Globe Pequot Press
Reader Response/Editorial Department
P.O. Box 480
Guilford, CT 06437

Or you may e-mail us at:

editorial@globe-pequot.com

or the author at:

stapenc@aol.com

Thanks for your input, and happy travels!

1 Alberta

Banff

Banff, Canada's first National Park, is a breathtaking four-season resort in the heart of Alberta's Canadian Rockies. The town of Banff and the tiny village of Lake Louise, forty minutes west, are the park's civilized centers. Banff (the town) is surrounded by a ring of majestic mountains and exudes the atmosphere of a European resort—but don't be surprised to see an elk walking Banff Avenue. Beyond "civilization" is truly spectacular scenery: 2,564 square miles of varied terrain where wildlife roam free among towering peaks, lush forests, alpine valleys, rivers, glaciers, hot springs, and lakes, including Lake Louise, one of the region's most popular destinations. This splendid setting provides countless recreational opportunities for families, from winter skiing to fair-weather pursuits: boating, hiking, horseback riding, cycling, and more.

Getting There

The nearest airport is **Calgary International** (403-292-8400). You can rent a car here or take a bus to the town of Banff, ninety minutes to the west. Lake Louise is forty minutes farther west.

Via Rail no longer serves Banff. **Rocky Mountaineer Railtours** (800-665-7245) runs two-day east- and/or westbound rail tours between Vancouver, Banff, and Calgary from May to early October, with an overnight stay in Kamloops, British Columbia. Add-on hotel and sightseeing packages and car rentals in Banff can also be arranged.

Bus service is provided by the following companies. **Greyhound of Canada** (800-661-8747, Canada or 800-332-1016, Alberta) serves Banff from various points in Canada, including Calgary. **Laidlaw Transportation** (403-762-9102), on the arrivals level of Calgary Airport, transports passengers anywhere in the park. **Brewster Transportation** (800-661-1152) also offers scheduled bus service from the airport to Banff and Lake Louise. **Banff Airporter** (403-762-3330 or 888-449-2901; www.banff.net/airporter) provides door-to-door luxury van service between Banff and the Calgary Airport.

Banff

AT A GLANCE

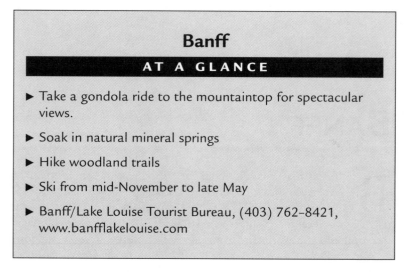

- Take a gondola ride to the mountaintop for spectacular views.
- Soak in natural mineral springs
- Hike woodland trails
- Ski from mid-November to late May
- Banff/Lake Louise Tourist Bureau, (403) 762-8421, www.banfflakelouise.com

TransCanada Highway 1 from Calgary leads to Banff and Lake Louise. From Banff, Lake Louise also can be accessed by a slower but more scenic route, the Bow Valley Parkway, which runs parallel to Highway 1 on the other side of the river and has interpretive signs, scenic viewpoints, and picnic sites.

Getting Around

If you're driving, a map is helpful within the park, since few of the drives connect directly to the TransCanada Highway. The town of Banff is located 10 miles inside the park's entrance. The Banff Information Centre, 224 Banff Avenue (403-762-1550), shared by the Tourism Bureau and the Canadian Parks Department, is open daily year-round. A brochure titled *Banff and Vicinity Drives and Walks* lists drives and attractions, with maps indicating their locations. The Centre also has information on hiking, biking, and trails. For information on attractions, accommodations, and activities, call the Banff/Lake Louise Tourism Bureau (403-762-8421).

Access for persons with disabilities is provided for those visiting Banff National Park. Services include rest rooms, showers, reserved parking spaces, elevators, ramps, campsites, and some trails. There is also a TDD number available (403-762-4256). To find out which restaurants, hotels, shops, and attractions also offer special services, contact the Banff Visitor Centre (403-762-1550) for a copy of the *Free Wheelin'* access guide.

What to See and Do

How you spend your days will depend on whether you visit in summer or in winter, when the area becomes a skier's dream. Spring and fall (when the foliage is outstanding) offer some of the activities available to winter and summer visitors, at lower prices and with fewer crowds.

Here are some sensational sights your family shouldn't miss.

Banff on the Internet

Before heading for Banff, a great way to introduce your kids to the area is to go on-line at www.worldweb.com/parkscanada-banff/kids.html. Banff National Park has a Web page call "Kid's Stuff" that has information about the animals in the area, what it was like 12,000 years ago, what an osprey is, and other nature-oriented tidbits. Kids will also enjoy hearing a bulgling elk and a howling wolf. And for the adults, the page links to other Banff and Lake Louise sites.

Banff Area

Sulphur Mountain Gondola, open daily from December 26 to mid-November, south on Banff Avenue to Mountain Avenue, then 1½ miles to the gondola's lower terminal (403-762-2523, www.banffgondola.com; upper terminal, 403-762-5438). This is an eight-minute journey aboard four-passenger glass-enclosed gondolas to the mountaintop, where observation decks offer spectacular views of Banff and the Bow Valley. (The Summit Complex at the top and the observation decks are completely handicapped accessible.) For more scenic views, try the short, easy hiking trails along the mountain ridges. One of the most popular of the trails is the walkway to Sanson's Peak, following the footsteps of meteorologist Norman Sanson (his restored 1903 weather observatory is here), who walked to the top of the mountain every day for thirty years to check the weather.

The Summit Complex houses two restaurants, a gift shop, a snack bar, and rest rooms. The Summit Restaurant, with seating in the round that provides a great view for everyone, is cafeteria style; the Panorama Room is buffet style. Both serve breakfast, lunch, and dinner. The gift shops stock both film and single-use cameras.

Cave and Basin National Historic Site, 311 Cave Street (403-762-1566; www.worldweb.com/parkscanada-banff). The discovery of natural hot springs here in 1883 led to the creation of Canada's first National Park two years later to preserve the springs and encourage visitors. You step through a tunnel to see the cave's hot springs. There are also a bathhouse and Basin springs on view. (The sulfur smell of the springs, reminiscent of rotten eggs, may be too strong for some kids.)

Interpretive exhibits, videos, and self-guiding tours tell the story of the discovery. Take a free guided walk along the boardwalk on the hillside above the site.

Another boardwalk follows a marsh trail, which shows how the heated mineral water from the hillside has resulted in lush vegetation. Telescopes, benches, and interpretive signs are provided along the way.

Up the hill, less than a mile west on Mountain Avenue (next to Sulphur Mountain Gondola), **Upper Hot Springs,** 101 Mountain Avenue (403-762-1515), offers an outdoor soaking pool of hot water that bubbles up from Sulphur Mountain. Once considered therapeutic, the waters are now appreciated for their relaxing effect. Children ages three and older are allowed, but the temperature (about 104° F) and the strong sulfur smell may bother some kids (and adults). You can use towels for a small fee. Massages are also offered at the spa, by appointment only; call (403) 762-1515 for information. The pool is open all year (though closed periodically for maintenance); skiers find the waters soothing for their sore limbs, and the view of Mount Rundle is spectacular.

Lake Louise

This turquoise lake edged by Mount Victoria is truly stunning. Stop by the Lake Louise Information Centre, Samson Mall (403-522-3833), for tourist information. The architecturally striking building shows a multimedia presentation, *The Building of the Canadian Rockies,* and has exhibits on the area's natural and human history.

Château Lake Louise, the only resort on the lake, hugs the lake's eastern shore. Canoes can be rented at the boathouse on the left side of the resort; call (403) 522-3511. A popular stroll (best for kids because it's level) starts in front of the château and follows the lake's northwest shore for about 1½ miles. You walk below the high cliffs at the far end of the lake, where rock climbers can often be observed. At the muddy delta, just beyond the cliffs, the paved walk ends—and this is where families with young children will want to stop. Hardy, fit families accustomed to hiking may turn this stroll into a day trip by continuing on the somewhat strenuous trail (now called the Plain of the Six Glaciers), which climbs about 2½ miles over a rocky creek, gravel fields, and, ultimately, to icy glaciers. Mountain goats can often be seen on the slopes of the glaciated peaks surrounding the area. You'll end up at the rustic **Plain of the Six Glaciers** teahouse, where beverages, light lunches, and snacks are served during the summer. Prices are a bit steep because food is brought in via helicopter or packhorses.

If all this hiking sounds like too much work, consider taking the **Lake Louise Summer Mountain Lift,** a twenty-minute ride atop Whitehorn Mountain. The lift is located across the valley from the Château Lake

Animal Alert

Even in the middle of town, you may come within arm's length of an elk. If you go camping bears may invite themselves to your campsite. Never feed the animals or get too close to them, no matter how tame they may appear. Here are some tips on how to deal with our fellow mammals:

- **Elk** have become more numerous around Banff in the last decade. These harmless-looking animals can attack without warning. During the mating (August and September) and calving (May and June) seasons, elk can become quite territorial and aggressive. Do not, under any circumstances, get any closer than 50 meters (150 feet). Watch for signs of agression, such as raised ears or stamping feet.
- **Bears**—all of them, no matter what color or size, including cuddly-looking cubs—are dangerous. Never approach or feed a bear. Check on bear sightings in any area you are planning on camping in or hiking/biking through. If you see bear signs (tracks, droppings), leave the area immediately. Never leave food or garbage unsecured. Report all sightings of bears or bear activity to park officials. If you encounter a bear, don't run or cry out. Stay calm, rereat slowly, and avoid eye contact. Ask for a copy of the brochure *You Are in Bear Country* from any information center or any of the warden offices.
- **Deer** may be aggressive when seeking food. When frightened, they can lash out with their hooves. Dogs are especially vulneralbe and should be left at home or in vehicles. Do not feed deer or approach them in any way.
- **Bison** are dangerous and unpredictable, and may charge without warning. Don't get out of your vehicle to look at them, even if the bison seem very far away. Bison can run three times faster than you can. Never come between a female and her calf.
- **Cougar** attacks are very rare, but you should still be aware of their possible presence. Never go hiking alone or leave children unattended. If confronted on the trail by a cougar, do not stare into its eyes or run or crouch down. Instead, back away slowly.
- **Vehicle and wildlife collisions** occur, but please remember to slow down for wildlife. Animals move unpredictably—be alert, especially at dusk or dawn.

Report any bear sightings, any animal agression, and, of course, any collisions immediately to Banff Park Dispatch at (403) 762-4506.

Louise resort. Although there are open-air chairs, families can take an enclosed gondola car or a covered "bubble" chair. Bring a picnic lunch to eat on the mountain slopes. Call (403) 522-3555 for information; open June to September.

Museums

The following museums, all in the town of Banff, are worth a visit.

Banff Park Museum National Historic Site, 92 Banff Avenue (403-762-1558; www.worldweb.com/parkscanada-banff/museum.html), houses a taxidermy collection of animals, from birds to grizzly bears, indigenous to the park. Built in 1903, this is the oldest natural history museum in western Canada, and the building, an unusual type of architecture known as "railroad pagoda," is a Canadian Historic Site. Kids will especially enjoy the hands-on Discovery Room. Admission is $2.25; open year-round.

Banff Natural History Museum, Clock Tower Mall (403-762-4652). The museum displays the geological evolution of the Rockies via dioramas, models, fossils, and a twenty-minute audiovisual show on the eruption of Mt. St. Helens. It's open year-round; admission is free.

Whyte Museum of the Canadian Rockies, 111 Bear Street (403-762-2291; www.whyte.org). Everything in the museum portrays the cultural heritage of the Canadian Rockies. The museum's four galleries feature changing exhibits of contemporary and historic art and a heritage collection of artifacts and photos. Tours of the six heritage homes on the museum grounds are given in the summer. Open daily in summer, with abbreviated winter hours.

Buffalo Nations Luxton Museum, 1 Birch Avenue (403-762-2388; www.buffalonations.org). Kids enjoy the exhibits here, honoring the heritage of the Indians of the Northern Plains and Canadian Rockies. Displays include regalia, hunting equipment, and dioramas of native and pioneer life. The building that houses the museum is an old fortlike structure overlooking the Bow River. The museum is operated by the Buffalo Nations Cultural Society, representing Stoney, Blackfoot, Blood, Sarcee, and Peigan tribes. Open daily year-round.

Programs are usually held nightly in the theater at the **Banff Visitors Centre,** and on weekends at some of the campgrounds, including Lake Louise, Tunnel Mountain, and Johnston Canyon. Although there are no programs especially for children, topics are chosen to appeal to the widest variety of ages, and, if there are many children in the audience, the program will be aimed at them. Check the posted program schedules at campground kiosks, or at the Canadian Parks Service Visitors Centre, 224 Banff Avenue (403-762-1550), and at the Lake Louise Visitor Reception Centre, Samson Mall (403-522-3833).

Adventures

Here are some ways for active families to enjoy the best that Banff has to offer.

Boating. **Lake Minnewanka,** about 15 miles northeast of the town of Banff, off the TransCanada Highway, is the park's largest lake and the only one on which powerboats are allowed. You can rent 16-foot boats with outboard motors from mid-May to Labor Day from **Lake Minnewanka Boat Tours** (their office is on the dock) or take one of their guided tours to the end of the lake (403-762-3473). They also provide fishing licenses, which are required in the park, and fishing equipment rentals. The lake, noted for its trout, splake, and Rocky Mountain whitefish, is one of the park's most popular fishing spots.

Cycling. The Banff Visitors Centre has a list of rental shops and a trail-bike pamphlet. Beware of traffic and wildlife while you ride. Because of the bike's speed and relatively quiet approach (compared with hikers), trail cyclists are vulnerable to sudden bear encounters. So make noise; put bear bells on your pedaling shoes. (See "Animal Alert!" p. 5.)

Dogsled Racing. The season runs from about November 1 to April 1. Experienced mushers pick you up at the Banff Springs Hotel (403-762-2211); afterward, you're welcome to take photos and visit with the friendly Siberian huskies. Two adults fit comfortably in the sleds, plus a child or two, depending on size (babies are welcome). Reserve at least several days in advance from **Mountain Mushers Dog Sled Tours,** P.O. Box 1721, Banff T0L 0C0, (403-762-3647).

Fishing. **Mountain Fly-Fishers** offers year-round fishing, from a four-hour trip to multiday camping, with a fly-fishing instruction service for beginners, (403-678-9522 or 800-450-9664).

Horseback Riding. There are several stables and outfitters in the area: **Warner Guiding and Outfitting Ltd.,** 132 Banff Avenue (office in the Trail Rider store), has trail rides that run from one hour to a full day, generally from mid-April to mid-November (403-762-4551). While no strict age limits apply, nine years is the recommended age for the backcountry trips that operate from July 1 to the end of September. These range up to six days; but a good ride with children is the 10-mile route along Bow River to Sundance Lodge on Brewster Creek for a two-day stay.

Brewster Lake Louise Stables (403-762-5454; www.brewsteradventure.com), located to the right of the Château Lake Louise, specializes in guided half-day trail rides around the lake and up to the **Plain of the Six Glaciers** or all-day trips farther afield. There is no strict age limit; a small child may be allowed to ride with a parent. During the winter horse-drawn sleigh rides follow the lakeside trail.

The opulent Banff Springs Hotel is one of many first-class accommodations in this exciting area.

River Rafting. **Rocky Mountain Raft Tours** offers float trips along the Bow River (follow Wolf Street to the river). Trips are either one or three hours in length; children's rates are available; no age minimum, but use common sense. Inquire about whether the trip is a float or white-water journey. Call (403) 762–3632.

Canadian Rockies Rafting Company (403–678–6535) offers interpretive float trips on the Bow River outside Banff or half-day white-water rafting trips on the Kananaskis River.

Skiing

Ski season generally operate from mid-November to late May. There are three resorts within the park, linked with one interchangeable ski/shuttle bus pass, available from **Ski Banff/Lake Louise,** Box 1085, Banff (403–762–4561 or 800–661–1431—western Canada). The company also offers vacation packages and other ski services. For extreme skiers, heli-skiing trips are coordinated by **R.K. Heli-Ski Panorama** (250–342–3889 or 800–661–6060; www.rkheliski.com), specalizing in novice heli-skiers, minimum age 19; intermediates also welcome; day and week packages available. A note of caution: This type of excursion can be dangerous and is not appropriate for young children or pre-teens.

Banff Mount Norquay (403–762–4421; www.skibanfflakelouise.

Camping

Banff National Park has ten campgrounds. All are on a first-come, first-served basis. Check out time is 11:00 A.M., so arriving by then gives you a good chance of securing a site.

- **Tunnel Mountain Campground** is within walking distance of downtown Banff, 321 full-service sites, 188 power only, 618 nonservice sites.
- **Two Jack Main Campground** is located on the scenic Minnewanka Lake loop drive and has 381 campsites in a secluded, wooded area; flush toilets, no showers. Across the road is **Two Jack Lakeside Campground** (74 sites), which does have showers.
- **Castle Mountain Campground** is close to a small store, gas station, and restaurant, but its 43 sites are still in a wooded area; flush toilets, no showers, kitchen shelters.
- **Protection Mountain Campground,** with 89 sites, is located in a great area for hiking; flush toilets, no showers.
- **Johnston's Canyon Campground,** located across from Johnston's Canyon, has 132 sites surrounded by awesome scenery, like the canyon's two waterfalls; showers.
- **Lake Louise Campground** has RV sites with electric hookup and 216 unserviced sites and is near Lake Louise village; no showers.
- **Mosquito Creek Campground**'s 32 sites have a terrific view of the sandstone cliffs of Bow Peak and Mount Hector; pit toilets, no showers.
- **Waterfowl Lake Campground** is a great place for those interested in fishing, with its 116 sites so near Mistaya River, Waterfowl Lake, and the Cirque and Chephren Lakes; flush toilets, no showers.
- **Rampart Creek** is a small campground (50 sites) but a great area for viewing wildlife; pit toilets, no showers.

For information on when individual campgrounds are open, call the Canadian Parks Service at (403) 762-1500 or go on-line at www.worldweb.com/parkscanadabanff/campgrou.html.

com), ten minutes northwest of downtown Banff, is the closest major ski resort to town. It is also the region's oldest. Famous for its beginner and expert terrain, the resort has expanded its intermediate skiing area by seventy acres. Twenty-five groomed trails are currently offered. Norquay also features night skiing and a snowboard park. The visitor's service complex has a restaurant/lounge, cafeteria, day-care services for ages nineteen months to six years (ski lessons available, if desired), ski rentals, and retail shops. Ski and Play, for three- to six-year-olds, offers hourly lessons. Ages six to twelve can take two-hour lessons (lunch not included) with Club Adventure. Snowboarding group camps are also offered.

Lake Louise; (403) 256-8473 or (800) 258-SNOW—Alberta, September to April or (800) 567-6262—Western Canada/Pacific Northwest, October to April; www.skibanfflakelouise.com. This ski area is 35 miles west of Banff and 115 miles west of Calgary. Situated in Banff National Park, it offers four distinct mountain faces and a variety of runs that range from gentle novice—green runs are accessible from every lift—to challenging expert terrain. There are 1,500-foot black-diamond descents. Destination skiers are also drawn to Lake Louise for its small-town hospitality and big-city elegance. Day care for infants eighteen days to eighteen months and toddlers nineteen months to six years is available, either hourly (minimum three hours) or daily. Kinderski, for three- and four-year-olds, offers one- and two-hour lessons. Ages three to six have supervised indoor and outdoor play. Ages five to twelve can take a Kids Ski program.

Sunshine Village (403-762-6500; www.skibanflakelouise.com). Sunshine Village has the only ski-in/ski-out accommodations in the Banff National Park. Good choices are the Sunshine Inn; (800) 372-9583—Alberta/(800) 372-9583—Canada/(800) 661-1363—U.S. Sunshine receives more than 30 feet of snow per year, enough to keep the runs going with 100 percent natural snow. More than half the terrain of Sunshine's three mountains is for intermediates. A three-million-dollar expansion has opened up new terrain with unlimited glade skiing and long, challenging double-black-diamond runs. For beginners there are treeless trails. The Tiny Tigers day care center is offered for ages nineteen months to five years. For three- to five-year-olds, there is the Tiny Tigers Ski & Play, with private lessons. Young Devils features six levels of classes for kids six to twelve.

Theater, Music, and the Arts

The **Banff Centre for Fine Arts,** St. Julien Road (403-762-6301), is the site of year-round cultural events, including ballet, opera, jazz, dance, theater, and free recitals and concerts. It's also headquarters for the annual **Banff Festival of the Arts,** running from the end of May through the third week of August, with plays, dance, opera, concerts, visual-arts exhibitions, and more. For ticket information call the box office at (403) 762-6300.

Shopping

Cascade Plaza, 317 Banff Avenue, offers upscale shops (Polo Ralph Lauren, Esprit, Boardwalk, Robin K) as well as those that sell Canadian art and artifacts. There's a food court on the concourse level. The shops along **Banff Avenue** sell Canadian-made goods and souvenirs, British woolens, and Irish linens. For authentic Indian crafts, be sure to see the **Banff Indian Trading Post** (403-762-2456) where, for nearly a century, the Stoney Indians of Morely have sold their handicrafts. There are also selections of native artworks from other Canadian tribes.

Side Trips

If you have older kids who don't mind a slow, winding car trip, venture out along the **Icefields Parkway** (Highway 93 North), 78 miles north of Lake Louise to the **Athabasca Glacier.** You'll see the highest, most rugged mountains in the Canadian Rockies, and you can spot moose, bears, elk, goats, and sheep along the way. Twenty miles north of Lake Louise, stop at **Bow Summit,** the highest point on the parkway. A short access road leads to the **Bow Summit–Peyto Lake viewpoint area.** Peyto Lake, shaped like a grizzly bear, has a distinctive color, ranging from pale green to deep turquoise.

The Columbia Icefield, one of the largest accumulations of ice and snow south of the Arctic Circle, is on the boundary of Banff and Jasper National Parks. Continuous snow accumulations feed eight major glaciers, including the **Athabasca,** 4 miles long and located directly across from the **Columbia Icefield Visitors Center** (403-852-7030). The center has maps, brochures, and schedules for interpretive events, such as guided hikes and evening programs, given by park naturalists, as well as a scale model of the entire ice fields (interactive displays) and audiovisual presentations on the area. Cafeteria, rest rooms, and accommodations on site.

Kids like the narrated tour of the icy slopes of the glacier aboard a specially designed Brewster "Snowcoach" bus. (Brewster also has round-trip sightseeing tours on luxury motor coaches from Banff or Lake Louise.) Passengers are allowed to step out onto the slippery glacier. Contact **Columbia Icefield Snowmobile Tours,** P.O. Box 1140, Banff T0L 0C0 (403-762-6735). Tours are available May 1 to mid-October. Children's rates apply for ages six to fifteen; under age six free when sharing a seat with an adult. Reservations aren't required; the busiest time at the ice field is from 11:00 A.M. to 3:00 P.M.

Special Events

Annual events, fairs, and festivals include the following.

January. Banff/Lake Louise Winter Festival, ten days of ski races, skating parties, barn dances, and wine tastings; Ice Magic International Sculpture Competition and Exhibition, magnificent creations designed by ice sculpting teams, displayed through February.

March. Canadian Powder 8 Championships.

April. Banff/Lake Louise Western Heritage Jubilee, a tribute to Canada's western heritage.

May. Banff/Calgary Road Race.

June. Banff Television Festival, a conference of TV producers, writers, and actors who meet to sell TV shows, which are shown to the public for free.

July. Banff Festival of the Arts; Canada Day Celebration.

August. Buffalo Nation Days, with a parade and native dancing.

September. The Masters at Spruce Meadows, Calgary, the richest show-jumping tournament in the world; Melissa's Mini-marathon.

October. Taste of Banff/Lake Louise.

November. Banff Festival of Mountain Films and Books, a weekend of lectures, demonstrations, and adventure shows surrounding a festival of mountaineering films and books.

December. Women's World Cup Downhill & Super G Races at Lake Louise.

Where to Stay

An accommodations guide and a bed-and-breakfast directory are available from the **Banff/Lake Louise Tourism Bureau** (403–762–8421). The bureau can also give you information on the fifteen campgrounds within the park; three have electricity, and four have showers.

The bureau advises summer visitors, particularly those arriving on weekends, to make reservations in advance. Summer months are very popular and there have been days, particularly in August, when every park lodging was filled by noon; visitors were sent to Calgary and Lake Louise.

Banff/Lake Louise Central Reservations owns and operates the computerized central reservations for hotels in Banff, Lake Louise, and Jasper

National Park (800-661-1676). Despite the splendid winter skiing, summer (early June to early October) is the high season in Banff, with higher prices.

Banff

Families have excellent lodging options in Banff. Here are a few that are family-friendly.

Banff Springs, Spray Avenue (403-762-2211 or 800-441-1414; www.cphotels.ca). This majestic Canadian Pacific hotel is an historic landmark styled after the baronial castles of Scotland. Even if you aren't staying here, tour the hotel and its grounds. On property are a twenty-seven-hole golf course, fifty shops, tennis courts, a bowling alley, indoor and outdoor pools, and fourteen restaurants. Solace, a European-style spa, offers steam rooms, spa treatments, and a juice bar (403-762-1772). An enchanting Festival of Christmas starts in November and runs through January 1, with organized activities such as hayrides, skating parties, scavenger hunts, evening stories by the fire, and a nightly Lighting Ceremony.

Douglas Fir Resort, 525 Tunnel Mountain Road (403-762-5591 or 800-661-9267; www.douglasfir.com). The resort has one- and two-bedroom condos with full kitchens, perfect for families. The convenience store, coin laundry, and barbecues come in handy too. So does the complex, with two indoor water slides, a children's pool, and a video games room (open to nonguests for a fee and free to guests). Ski packages are available in winter.

Lake Louise

Château Lake Louise is 2½ miles southeast off TransCanada Highway 1 (403-522-3511 or 800-441-1414; www.cphotels.ca). This large lakeside resort offers a pool, six restaurants, and a shopping arcade on site. Some suites are available. During ski season a supervised playroom is open for ages two and older.

Others are the **Rimrock Resort Hotel** in Banff (403-762-3356 or 800-661-1587; www.rimrock.com) and the **Post Hotel** (800-661-1586). Rimrock features good cuisine, including a children's menu, a pool, an exercise facility, and good mountain views. It is also located next to the sulfur hot springs and the Sulphur Mountain Gondola. Don't be fooled by the Post Hotel's age. Despite its fifty years, it offers whirlpool tubs, fireplaces, and lodge furnishings. Family-oriented movies are shown on weekends in its conference center.

Where to Eat

A helpful restaurant guide is available from the Banff/Lake Louise Visitor Centre. You'll find a wide selection of restaurants in the town of Banff, including the ubiquitous **McDonald's,** 116 Banff Avenue (403-762-5232), which also serves pizza. **Hard Rock Cafe,** 137 Banff Avenue (403-760-2347), is a perpetual favorite. It is located downtown in Banff, and its menu lists the chain's typical meals of burgers, wings, and rock 'n' roll. **The Station Restaurant at Lake Louise,** 200 Sentinel Road (403-522-2386) displays vintage railcars in a historic log station. **The Caboose** (403-762-3622), CP Rail Station, Elk and Lynx Streets, offers beef, seafood, and a self-service salad bar amid railway memorabilia and a rustic decor. A children's menu is available. **Timberwolf Pizza & Pasta Café** in Lake Louise Inn (403-522-3791) offers pizza and homemade pasta in a casual setting.

Grizzly House, 207 Banff Avenue (403-762-4055), specializes in steak and fondue, though there's also buffalo and rattlesnake on the menu. The kids love the atmosphere, complete with totem poles and Indian crafts. Dine outdoors, if you prefer.

For More Information

Banff/Lake Louise Tourism Bureau: 224 Banff Avenue, Banff; (403) 762-8421; www.banfflakelouise.com; www.worldweb.com/parkscanada-banff/parks.htm.

Canadian Parks Service: (403) 762-1550

Visitor Reception Centre: Samson Mall; (403) 522-3833

Each center is open daily, year-round.

The park trails and other facilities are constantly being upgraded to be accessible to the physically challenged. Contact the Tourism Bureau or Parks Canada for more information.

Emergency Numbers

Ambulance, fire: (403) 762-2000

Lake Louise fire: (403) 522-2000

Police: Royal Canadian Mounted Police; (403) 762-2226

Warden: To report an aggressive animal, call the Banff Wardens Office (403-762-4506) or the Lake Louise Warden Office, closed Wednesday and Thursday (403-522-2000).

Hospitals: Banff's Mineral Springs Hospital, 301 Lynx Street (403-762-2222); Lake Louise Medical Clinic, 200 Hector (403-522-2184)

Pharmacy: There are no twenty-four-hour pharmacies. Cascade Plaza Drug, Cascade Plaza, Banff Avenue at Wolf (403-762-2245). Gourlay's Pharmacy, 229 Bear Street (403-762-2516); Harmony Drugs, 111 Banff Avenue (403-762-5711).

CALGARY

Set in the lovely rolling foothills of the magnificent Canadian Rockies, Calgary achieved international attention when it hosted the 1988 Winter Olympics. Originally an outpost of the North West Mounted Police, the city became a mecca for "Cattle Kings" who built mansions and sprawling ranches when the transcontinental railway reached town in 1883. Later, Calgary thrived as an oil boomtown. Although still one of Canada's major oil centers with a population of 810,000 and a downtown sparkling with shiny skyscrapers, the city has managed to retain a small-town feeling. That friendly, Old West atmosphere comes alive during Stampede Week in July, when everyone dons western gear for a "rip roarin'" good time.

The feeling also extends to kids. In mid-1993, Calgary proclaimed itself "child-friendly" and is encouraging businesses to create places for children to play while parents shop, to provide adequate rest rooms, and, in restaurants, to offer more toddler seating and to provide crayons and paper. An advisory committee of kids ages seven to seventeen meets regularly with city administrators to discuss issues concerning the younger set.

GETTING THERE

Calgary International Airport (403-292-8477) is about 3 miles (twenty-minute drive) from the city center. Children keep busy at Kidsport on the departure level by piloting a jet, watching movies, building with Legos, and playing with other toys. Parents must stay with children. The **Airporter Bus** (403-531-3907) is the most efficient way to get to town. Car rentals and taxi service are available.

VIA Rail no longer serves Calgary. **Greyhound,** 850 Sixteenth Street S.W. (403-265-9111), provides frequent service throughout Canada.

By car, Calgary is on TransCanada Highway 1, which runs from coast to coast, and on Highway 2 from the border. **Rocky Mountaineer Railtours** (800-665-7245) offers a two-day rail trip through the Rockies from Calgary to Vancouver.

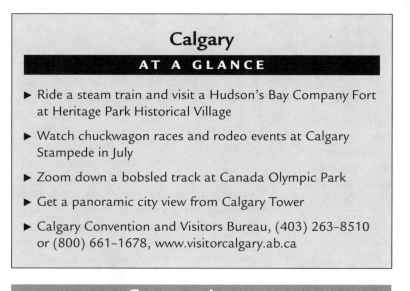

Calgary
AT A GLANCE

- Ride a steam train and visit a Hudson's Bay Company Fort at Heritage Park Historical Village
- Watch chuckwagon races and rodeo events at Calgary Stampede in July
- Zoom down a bobsled track at Canada Olympic Park
- Get a panoramic city view from Calgary Tower
- Calgary Convention and Visitors Bureau, (403) 263-8510 or (800) 661-1678, www.visitorcalgary.ab.ca

Getting Around

Calgary is divided into quadrants, with Centre Street providing the east-west dividing line, and the Bow River and adjacent Memorial Drive dividing north from south.

Calgary Transit (403-262-1000) operates an excellent public bus and light rail transit (LRT) system known as C-train. Travel within the downtown core (between City Hall and Tenth Street S.W.) is free. Maps and information are available at the Calgary Transit information center, 270 Seventh Avenue S.W. The C-train and most buses are wheelchair accessible.

What to See and Do

Historic and Cultural Attractions

The **Calgary Science Centre,** 701 Eleventh Street S.W. (403-221-3700; www.calgaryscience.ca), has interactive exhibits in the large Discovery Hall. Activities there usually complement a current, traveling exhibit. Watch movies on the 70mm large-format screen in the Discovery Dome. A series of mystery plays (such as Agatha Christie's *Murder in the Vicarage)* are held in the facility's Pleiades Mystery Theatre throughout the year.

The **Calgary Chinese Cultural Centre,** 197 First Street S.W. (403-262-5071). This facility, by the Bow River in the heart of downtown, is quite an eyeful. The impressive six-story Great Cultural Hall was modeled after the Temple of Heaven in Beijing, which took more than 100,000 man-hours to build. Twenty-two artists from mainland China con-

Heritage Park Historical Village

This sixty-six-acre park, western Canada's largest living history park, presents life in western Canada prior to 1914. The original buildings were moved here from various locations throughout Alberta. Hop aboard the old steam train that travels throughout the village. Visit a Hudson's Bay Company Fort, a one-room schoolhouse, an oil rig, a bakery, an ice-cream parlor, and a working grain mill. Try your luck at the antique midway. The village is on the edge of the Glenmore Reservoir, and for an extra fee you can take a stern-wheeler cruise aboard the S.S. *Moyie.* Inquire about the variety of family programs throughout the year. Free breakfast with admission during summer.

Heritage Park Historical Village, 1900 Heritage Drive S.W. at Fourteenth Street; (403) 259-1900; www.heritagepark.ab.ca.

tributed the hand-painted, gold-foiled paintings on the dome. Supported by four columns representing the four seasons, the dome boasts 561 dragons and forty phoenixes. The museum contains a number of paintings and artifacts from various dynasties, including a full-scale replica of terra-cotta soldiers from the First Dynasty and a pot filled with water that, when rubbed with two hands, gives the illusion that the water is dancing. Special concerts and events are frequently held in the auditorium. In addition to the arts-and-crafts shop with goods from mainland China, there is a restaurant, an herb shop, and a snack shop.

Energeum, 640 Fifth Avenue S.W. (403-297-4293; www.eub.gov.ab.ca). Operated by the Energy Resources Conservation Board, this free museum devoted to fossil fuel is small but surprisingly interesting. Watch the big-screen video on Alberta's first oil discovery, then try some computer games and interactive displays—including a chance to put your gloved hand into some "black gold." Be sure to see the pink 1958 limited edition Buick in the memorabilia display; it's a beauty.

The largest museum in western Canada, the **Glenbow Museum,** 130 Ninth Avenue S.E. (403-268-4100; www.glenbow.org), focuses on the area's settlement and its native peoples. There's lots of colorful "stuff" that should appeal to kids: Inuit art and artifacts, a Blackfoot teepee, a mineral exhibit, modern art and sculpture, military artifacts that include armor, a large gun collection considered one of the country's best, stamps, coins, and a collection of carriages. Some exhibits incorporate interactive displays. This museum also hosts major traveling exhibits, so check to see what's currently on display.

The **Calgary Aero Space Museum,** 64 McTavish Place N.E. (403-250-3752; www.asmac.ab.ca). View vintage aircraft such as the 1913 *West Wind,* Calgary's first airplane, as well as 1960s jets.

More Attractions

Calaway Park, 6 miles west of Calgary on the Trans-Canada Highway and Springbank Road; (403) 240-3824. This is western Canada's largest amusement park. Enjoy the rides, a petting farm, mazes, miniature

Fort Calgary Historic Park

At **Fort Calgary Historic Park,** 750 Ninth Avenue S.E. (403-290-1875), experience Calgary's history firsthand. Located at the confluence of the Bow and Elbow Rivers, at the site of the 1875 North West Mounted Police post, the forty-acre park is within walking distance of downtown. First stop: the **interpretive center** to see a fifteen-minute video on the area's history that emphasizes the Mounted Police. Next: the **Discovery Room** where kids (and adults) can, among other things, try on Mounted Police uniforms and have their picture taken next to a stuffed bison. The permanent exhibit room features life-size recreations of important figures from Calgary's past. Step outdoors to enjoy the beautiful surroundings. A short, paved trail leads to the site of the fort, which is being reconstructed. The adjacent **1906 Deane House,** 806 Ninth Avenue S.E. (403-269-7747), serves as a restaurant, offering lunch, afternoon tea, and Murder Mystery dinner theater. The house was built in 1906 for the Mounties' Commanding Officer, Captain R. B. Deane, and is operated as part of the park. The building beside the Deane House is the oldest (1876) in Calgary that is still on its original site. Open May to mid-October.

golf, fishing, a driving range, live entertainment, cinema, shopping, and special events. Family passports are available. The park is open daily in July and August and on weekends only in May, June, September, and October. An RV park and campground are on property; for reservations call (403) 249-7372.

Calgary Tower Inc., 101 Ninth Avenue S.W. (403-266-7171; www.calgarytower.com). Take an elevator ride to the top of the 626-foot tower for spectacular views of prairies and the Rockies from the observation deck or revolving restaurant. On special occasions, the Calgary Olympic Flame that tops the tower is lit.

Parks, Gardens, and Zoos

Calgary Zoo, Botanical Gardens and Prehistoric Park, 1300 Zoo Road N.E., St. George's Island (403-232-9300; www.calgaryzoo.ab.ca). Accessible via a river walkway over the Bow River, this world-renowned facility houses some 1,500 animals who live in indoor and outdoor natural habitats. Popular attractions include the underwater viewing area for sea lions and seals, and the children's petting zoo.

The Canadian Wilds exhibit debuted in 1993 with the Aspen Wood-

Canada Olympic Park

This impressive place is where the bobsled, luge, and ski-jumping competitions took place during the 1988 Olympics. Tour on your own or take a guided bus tour that goes to the top of the 990-meter ski jump tower, the highest point in the city, and to the twisting bobsled/luge track. Get some thrills by careening down the bobsled track at 95 miles per hour on the **Bobsleigh Bullet.** In summer, take the chairlift for scenic views and pedal along the paths of the mountain bike park. In winter, check out the ski programs.

At the **Olympic Hall of Fame** (403-247-5452) feel what it's like to speed down a twisting track on the bobsled simulator and find out just how high the ski tower is on the ski jump simulator. Exhibits present highlights of all the winter Olympic games since 1924.

Canada Olympic Park, 88 Canada Olympic Road S.W.; (403) 247-5452.

lands, the first phase of a ten-year project to create five unique ecosystems of the Canadian wilds. The Canadian Rockies section is a simulation of high mountain habitats and their inhabitants. The Aspen Woodlands, a transitional habitat where the prairie meets mountains, is the most endangered in Canada. The zoo feels that by highlighting habitats close to home, visitors will become aware of the fragility of these areas. Using only plants and animals native to the area, the zoo has created four acres of rolling hills and valleys filled with wildflowers and aspen. White-tail deer, mule deer, and (in the coming months) elk graze in the meadows. Native birds fly freely in the aviary.

Explore a human-size magpie nest, travel through a tunnel to view elk from a special blind, and walk through a fox's den to get a peek at these creatures. The colorful graphics appeal to kids. Docents are available to answer questions. The zoo is planning a $12 million Africa habitat, the TransAlta Tropical Africa Pavilion. It will provide a 10,000-square-foot new home for the gorillas and feature a rain forest. The exhibit should be complete in 2002.

Dinosaur fans delight at the twenty-seven life-size models in Prehistoric Park, an eight-acre area with lakes, badlands, and swamps. The Botanical Gardens, with thousands of plant species, provide a fragrant, relaxing refuge.

Devonian Gardens, Toronto Dominion Square, Seventh Avenue between Second and Third Streets S.W. (403-268-3830). If the weather's bad, this 2.5-acre indoor park provides a welcome oasis with 16,000 tropical plants and 4,000 local plants, plus waterfalls, fountains, ponds, playgrounds, a reflecting pool, and occasional lunchtime entertainment. Stores and restaurants, located below the gardens, offer another fun refuge.

Olympic Plaza, corner of Macleod Trail and Seventh Avenue S.W. (403-268-5203), was created for the medal presentations during the 1988 Winter Olympics. Now this plaza is an outdoor activity center, with skating in the winter and special events year-round. Note: You must bring your own skates; there are no rental facilities here.

Prince's Island Park, Third Street S.W. at the Bow River, is accessible by footbridges from either side of the river. Stop here and enjoy the surroundings, including a playground, fitness trails, and a snack bar.

Village Square Leisure Centre, 2623 Fifty-sixth Street N.E. (403-280-9714), Calgary's indoor water-park attraction. There are five water slides, a diving tank, kiddies' pool, concessions, and ice skating.

Western Heritage Center

Cowboys are the heroes at the **Western Heritage Center,** Box 1477, Cochrane (403-932-3514; www.whcs.ab.ca), and ranching is the theme. Interactive exhibits show you riding a horse, teach you how to lasso a bronc, and let you brand a model calf. Picnic tables available.

Theater, Music, and the Arts

The *Calgary Herald* and the *Calgary Sun* are good sources of information on local entertainment. There are also a number of free publications at newsstands, hotels, and other locations around town that list entertainment, including *Where Calgary, Downtown Calgary, CityScope, Vox* (a publication of the University of Calgary), and *Impact* (a health/fitness/lifestyle magazine).

Theater is alive and well in Calgary, and chances are you will find a play to appeal to the whole family. The Convention and Visitors Bureau can help arrange tickets (check out the events on-line at www.visitor.calgary.ab.ca), or call Ticket Master Alberta at (403) 270-6700. For the little ones, **StoryBook Theatre** (403-291-2247) offers matinees at the Pumphouse Theatre, 2140 Pumphouse Avenue S.W.

Sports

The **Calgary Flames Hockey Club** (403-261-0475) skates from October to April at the Canadian Airlines Saddledome (403-261-0455). The **Calgary Cannons Baseball Club** (403-284-1111), number one minor league affiliate of the National League Pittsburgh Pirates plays at Burns Baseball Stadium from April to October (403-284-1111; www.cannons.fanlink.com). **Calgary Stampeders Football Club** (403-289-0205 or

Royal Tyrrell Museum of Palaeontology

Dinosaurs rule at this museum just as they did sixty-five million years ago in Alberta. Walk through a re-created dinosaur habitat populated by the world's largest display of complete dinosaur skeletons. Learn about dinosaurs at the computer exhibits and watch scientists restoring dinosaur fossils. Stroll through a prehistoric garden called a "paleoconservatory"; it houses more than one hundred species of plants that once grew in this area. You can even go on a dinosaur dig; sign up for these tours in advance.

Royal Tyrrell Museum of Palaeontology, P.O. Box 7500, Drumheller, about 80 miles northeast via Highway 9; (403) 823-7707; www.tyrrell.magtech.ab.ca.

800-667-FANS—Canada), a member of the professional Canadian Football League, kicks off at McMahon Stadium, 1817 Crowchild Trail, from July to November 30.

Race City Motorsport Park, 700, 323 Eleventh Avenue S.W. (403-264-6515), hosts stock and sports car, truck, motorcycle, and drag racing.

Shopping

The **Eau Claire Market,** Second Avenue and Second Street S.W. (403-264-6450), downtown on the Bow River, adjacent to Prince's Island Park, is a shopping and entertainment complex. It combines a fresh-food market, specialty retail shops, restaurants, and an **IMAX Theater** (403-263-IMAX) plus a cinema.

The downtown shopping core runs from First Avenue S.W. on the east to Eighth Street S.W. on the west. Shoppers are protected from the elements by an enclosed-walkway system of bridges at least 15 feet above grade level, known as "Plus 15s."

There are several shopping centers downtown; the largest is the **Toronto Dominion Square 1000,** 333 Seventh Avenue S.W. (403-221-0600 or 403-221-1368), which includes the Devonian Gardens (described earlier) and two anchor department stores—Eaton's and The Bay—plus about one hundred specialty shops.

Side Trips

Once in Drumheller, you're not far from **Reptile World,** 1222 Highway 9 South, Drumheller (403-823-8623), where among the 150 reptiles are some of the rarest in North America. Hands-on exhibits (do you dare hold a boa?).

Banff and **Banff National Park** are 80 miles west of Calgary on TransCanada Highway 1. Though it's possible to do in a day, we advise setting aside several days for a visit (see Banff chapter).

Special Events

Contact the Calgary Convention & Visitors Bureau for more information on the following events.

January. PlayRites Annual Festival of New Canadian Plays.

January–February. Calgary Winter Festival.

March. Rodeo Royal, Stampede Park.

May. International Children's Festival; Lilac Festival.

June. The National equestrian event, Spruce Meadows; CariFest, a Caribbean festival.

July. Calgary Stampede; Calgary Folk Festival; Shakespeare in the Park (evenings); North American Invitational equestrian event, Spruce Meadows.

August. International Native Arts Festival; Alberta Dragon Boat Races; Afrikadey!, a festival of African arts and culture.

September. The Masters equestrian event, Spruce Meadows; Artwalk at various locations throughout town; Old-Time Fall Fair (CQ), Heritage Park: horse-pull competitions, entertainment, displays.

Mid-November–Mid-December weekends: Twelve Days of Christmas, Heritage Park.

December–January. Lions Club Christmas Lights Display, Confederation Park.

Calgary Stampede

This is the big one: Ten days in July of Westen-themed fun kicks off with a parade and features rodeo events, chuck-wagon races, concerts, shows, an amusement park, agricultural exhibitions, and more. Everybody dresses western style. Plan ahead for a visit: Attendance is more than one million.

Calgary Stampede, 1410 Olympic Way S.E.; (403) 261-0101 or (800) 661-1260; www.calgary-stampede.com.

Where to Stay

The Calgary Convention & Visitors Bureau offers an accommodations directory and a booking service (800-661-1678). If you're coming for the Stampede, reserve well in advance. The **Bed and Breakfast Associates of Calgary,** Box 1462, Station M, Calgary T2P 2L6 (403-543-3900), handles forty rooms in Calgary and the surrounding area.

One of the largest hotels in Calgary, the luxurious **Westin Hotel,** 320 Fourth Avenue S.W. (403-266-1611 or 800-228-3000), offers the Westin

Buffalo Jump

The **Head-Smashed-In Buffalo Jump Interpretive Centre** (403-553-2731), 11 miles west of Highway 2 on Highway 85, Fort Macleod, ninety minutes south of Calgary, sounds gruesome, but it is quite an interesting attraction. Several levels of displays built into a cliff re-create the hunting techniques used by Native American tribes. For more than 6,000 years, Plains Indians hunted buffalo by driving them over this cliff to their death. Highly valued, the buffalo provided fresh meat, warmth, tools, and shelter. A film simulates the jump, and guided tours led by members of the Blackfoot Confederation are available. Browse the displays and Indian artifacts, and walk the trails located above and below the cliff. This site is considered the best-preserved buffalo jump site anywhere; it's a visit your family won't soon forget.

Kids Club amenities. These include child-friendly rooms, children's sport bottle or tippy cup upon check-in, as well as a safety kit with a nightlight, Band-Aids, and emergency phone numbers. Rooms feature bath toys and bath products for kids, and parents can request—at no charge—jogging strollers, potty seats, bicycle seats, and step stools. Restaurants and room service also feature children's menus.

Sheraton Suites Calgary Eau Claire, 117 Kearney Lake Road (403-266-1611 or 800-937-8461), is a relatively new all-suite property and it has an indoor pool.

Another new property with an indoor pool is the **Four Points Sheraton,** 8220 Bowridge N.W. (403-288-4441), situated across from Olympic Park.

Some moderately priced options are in the northeast part of the city. The **Hampton Inn & Suites,** 2420 Thirty-seventh Avenue N.E. (403-250-4667 or 800-HAMPTON), has an indoor pool and offers a complimentary continental breakfast. The **Ambassador Motor Inn,** 802 Sixteenth Avenue N.E. (403-276-2271 or 800-661-1447), features family suites with kitchenettes, a restaurant, and an outdoor pool.

Where to Eat

Contact the Calgary Convention & Visitors Bureau for dining information. There's no distinct local cuisine, but plenty of diversity.

Buzzards Cowboy Cuisine, 140 Tenth Avenue S.W. (403-264-6959; www.cowboycuisine.com) serves chuck-wagon fare amid ranching mem-

Calgary's Winter Festival draws people from all over the world.

orabilia. Bottlescrew Bill's pub serves 200 types of beer. **Mescalero,** 1315 First Street S.W. (403-266-3339), is a mix of Southwestern and South American. **Teatro,** 200 Eighth Avenue S.E. (403-290-1012), has good Italian dishes and wood-fired pizza. **Boston Pizza** has fifteen locations around town. The chain eatery the **Old Spaghetti Factory,** 222 Third Street S.W. (403-263-7223), located in the Eau Claire Market, serves moderately priced pastas that please kids.

Mother Tucker's Food Experience, 345 Tenth Avenue S.W. (403-262-5541), features prime rib, a salad bar, and homemade desserts. There's a children's menu. Teens and preteens like the **Hard Rock Cafe,** 101 Barclay Parade S.W. (403-263-ROCK), with its rock 'n' roll memorabilia, pastas, and burgers. Take your teens who want to try some Canadian regional fare, including Alberta beef, to the **River Cafe,** 200 Eighth Avenue S.E. (403-261-7670).

For More Information

The **Calgary Convention & Visitors Bureau,** 237 Eighth Avenue S.E., Alberta T2G 0K8 (403-263-8510 or 800-661-1678; www.visitor.calgary.ab.ca), supplies helpful information. Year-round visitors centers are at Calgary Tower, 120 Ninth Avenue S.W. at Centre Street, and at Calgary International Airport, arrivals level. Calgary **Handi-Bus Association** (403-276-1212) provides service to the disabled.

Emergency Numbers

Ambulance, fire, police: 911

Poison Centre: (403) 670-1414

Hospital: Alberta Children's Hospital, 1820 Richmond Road S.W.; (403) 229-7211

Twenty-four-hour pharmacy: Shoppers Drug Mart Chinook Centre, 1323 North 6455 Macleod Trail South; (403) 253-2424

3 Alberta

EDMONTON

Alberta's cosmopolitan capital has its share of appealing attractions for vacationing families. For starters, there's the West Edmonton Mall, the world's largest, with everything from a wave pool to a roller coaster. But there's more to Edmonton than mall heaven. In summer, add bountiful festivals. All year long enjoy the museums, concerts, cultural and sporting events, and the superb natural beauty that includes 8,500 acres of parkland stretching along the lush North Saskatchewan River Valley that curves through the city. Don't forget the clean subway system, friendly people, and a fascinating heritage that started with the fur trade and includes a lively past as a Klondike boomtown.

GETTING THERE

All passenger-airline service originates from one airport, **Edmonton International Airport,** 18 miles south of the city; (780) 890-8382 or (800) 268-7134. For shuttle information, contact Sky Shuttle at (780) 465-8515.

Via Rail offers transportation between Edmonton and other major Canadian cities. The station is downtown at 12360 121 Avenue; (780) 422-6032 or (800) 561-8630—Canada.

Greyhound Bus Lines has service from Edmonton to all points in Canada and the United States. The station is downtown at 10324 103 Street (780) 421-4211. **Red Arrow Express,** 10014 104 Street (780-424-3339), provides motorcoach service between Edmonton, Red Deer, Calgary, and Fort McMurray.

The two major highways that run through Edmonton are the Yellowhead TransCanada Highway (#16), running east and west, and Highway 2, running north and south.

GETTING AROUND

The city street system is on a grid, with streets running north and south, and avenues running east and west. A series of downtown pedestrian walkways (pedways) offers easy access to shopping, hotels, and cultural

Edmonton

AT A GLANCE

- Go on a space mission at the Edmonton Space and Science Center
- Shop the West Edmonton Mall, the world's largest
- Step back in time at Fort Edmonton Park, a living history museum
- Stroll through areas of flowers and along nature trails at the Devonian Botanic Gardens
- Visitor Information Centre, (780) 496-8400 or (800) 463-4667; www.cdc.org

facilities. Downtown parking information and maps are available at the **Edmonton Visitor Information Centres;** (780) 496-8400 or (800) 463-4667.

The city has both bus and light rail transit (LRT). The **Edmonton Transit Downtown Information Centre** is open weekdays at 100 A Street and Jasper Avenue, or call (780) 496-4611 daily for route and schedule information.

What to See and Do

Museums and Historical Attractions

Alberta Legislature, 10800 97 Avenue (780-427-7362; www.assembly.ab.ca), is the seat of the province's government. Older kids may enjoy the free guided tours given every hour of this grand, ornate building, on which construction began in 1907. (When you get to the fifth floor, listen to what seems to be a torrential downpour: actually, it's the echo of the fountain five stories below.) The beautiful grounds—with fifty-seven acres of flowers, fountains, pools in summer, and a skating rink in winter—make this an extremely pleasant place to linger.

Fort Edmonton Park, Whitemud and Fox Drives, (780-496-8787; www.gov.edmonton.ab.ca/parkrec/fort). Step back in time at this low-key historical theme park located on 158 acres on the south bank of the North Saskatchewan River and home to more than sixty period buildings. The fort is a replica of the 1846 home base of the Hudson's Bay Company fur trading industry. Costumed interpreters grade furs, repair

Edmonton Space and Science Center

From the outside, this facility resembles a sleek, modernistic flying saucer; inside are fascinating exhibits. Most kids head straight to the **Challenger Centre,** a simulator composed of a mission control and the space station Alpha 7. With the use of computers, television cameras, small robots, and simulated isolation chambers, kids transform themselves into astronauts. Call ahead to schedule a visit.

Discovery Land, located in the Discovery Gallery, features Lego blocks (to build an igloo), a walk-on piano, a jungle gym, a beehive (to see bees making honey), a potter's corner (with puppet shows and the inner workings of a clock), and lots of hands-on activities for kids ages two through eight. In the **Universe Gallery,** kids can hop on a scale that measures what they'd weigh on other planets, see a moon rock, and pilot a lunar excursion module to a safe landing. In the **Rotunda,** visitors participate in science demonstrations called Brain Teasers (how can you balance seven nails on the head of one nail?) and see the inner workings of an amateur radio station.

The **IMAX Theater** has a four-story high screen and 4,200-watt Digital Surround Sound, and the **Margaret Zeidler Theatre** boasts the largest planetarium dome in Canada. More than 200 computer-controlled projectors, special effects, and a laser system combine with a powerful audio system to offer visitors unforgettable laser-light music concerts, live plays, and planetarium shows. New in 1999, in the **North Gallery,** is "Forensics . . . the Science of Whodunit!," an interactive crime simulation the entire family will enjoy. (Come early for this one; the lines are long.) Visitors explore the hallways of a rooming house where a body has been found, and help solve the crime in the crime lab, working at the fingerprint, ballistics, blood, and witness/suspect stations.

If the weather is clear, stop by the **public observatory,** where attendants show you how their four astronomical telescopes work. For snacks, stop by the Café Borealis.

Edmonton Space and Science Center, 11211 142 Street; (780) 452-9100 or (780) 451-3344 for recorded information; www.edmontonscience.com.

a boat, and bake bread in an outdoor oven. Kid volunteers may get to assist. Three long streets transport visitors to different periods in the city's history. On 1885 Street, a small frontier town, take a horse-drawn wagon ride (small additional charge), browse in quaint shops, visit homesteaders on their farms, and see the blacksmith in action at his forge. On

You can bodysurf, swim, suntan, or spin down a water slide at the world's largest indoor water park, located at the West Edmonton Mall.

1905 Street, the city appears as it did in the year it became the provincial capital. Step into the penny arcade to have your palm read and hop aboard the streetcar for a ride. On 1920 Street, explore the brickyard and greenhouses, stop by the Ukranian bookstore, then have a soda at the old-time soda fountain. Daily special events and programs include visitor participation, and there are seasonal events such as the Spring Carnival, Harvest Festival, Storytelling Festival, and Spooktacular. (In the fall and winter, the park is open for special events only.) A steam engine travels the length of the park (no additional charge). Pony rides are available for an extra fee. This pleasant park, without a lot of glitz, appeals to younger school-age kids. It's especially charming at Christmas when the park can be toured by horse-drawn sleigh or wagon (depending on the snow), and you can see the different street windows elaborately decorated for the Christmas Reflections program.

Combine a visit to Fort Edmonton Park with a stop at the **John Janzen Nature Centre,** at the southwest corner of Quesnell Bridge, adjacent to the park (780–496–2939; www.gov.edmonton.ab.ca/parkrec/RVC). The place is noted for the displays of the small creatures that inhabit the river valley, such as salamanders, frogs, and snakes. A new exhibit hall features thirty-two interactive displays featuring animals as architects. Visitors can pull out a work area and learn how beavers make dams and birds build nests. Surrounding the center are 2.2 miles of marked nature trails. Free admission.

A Day in the Park

The **North Saskatchewan River Valley** runs through the center of town, providing acres of parkland—the longest stretch of urban parkland in North America. There are 33 miles of hiking, biking, jogging, and groomed ski trails, plus golf courses, boat launching sites, picnic areas, nature walks, and skating areas located in a series of linked parks called Edmonton's Ribbon of Green. At **Hawrelak Park,** beside Groat Road on the south side of the river, enjoy a lake stocked with trout, pedal boats, a playground, barbecue grills, and lots of room for kids to romp. Call the **Edmonton Parks and Recreation River Valley Outdoor Centre** (780-496-7275) for information on specific facilities and events within the park system. In summer take tots to the wading pools and older kids to the indoor and outdoor pools. Particularly popular: the Wave Pool at **Mill Woods Recreation Centre,** 7207 28 Avenue; (780) 496-2929.

For people with mobility limitations, Edmonton's River Valley Trails can be accessed using specially designed motorized carts. These carts are available for rent ($5.00 an hour) at the **Rundle Park Family Centre** (Rundle Park is at 2909 113 Avenue) and can be booked in advance by calling (780) 496-2966.

Telephone Historical Centre, 10437 83 Avenue (780-441-2077). Kids tend to like this hands-on facility, where they walk through a telephone cable and see an audiovisual show presented by a robot who interacts with the audience. There are also an old-fashioned operator's desk and a very new-fashioned video phone. Closed Sunday and Monday.

Provincial Museum of Alberta, 12845 102 Avenue (780-453-9100; www.pma.edmonton.ab.ca). Devoted to Alberta's human and natural history, this museum focuses on the Ice Age and boasts a gigantic mammoth skeleton. The Bug Room, which has live inhabitants, proved so popular that the temporary exhibit is now a permanent fixture. (Kids enjoy looking at their bug friends through magnifying glasses.) The Syncrude Gallery of Aboriginal Culture brings 11,000 years and 500 generations of history to life through recorded voices, film, lights, the latest computer technology and more than 3,000 artifacts. Some of these artifacts are more than 9,000 years old and on display for the first time.

John Walter Museum, located in Kingsmen Park at 10627 93 Avenue (780-496-7275; www.gov.edmonton.ab.ca/parkrec/rvc), is a quiet reminder of Edmonton's earliest days. John Walter was one of Edmonton's first entrepreneurs, and there are four historic dwellings on this site, including his first home. Every Sunday there are interactive programs for families, with pioneer activities such as candle dipping, available free of charge.

Also located in Kingsmen Park is the **Kingsmen Sports Centre,** a complete fitness and aquatic facility.

Parks and Zoos

Muttart Conservatory, 9626 96A Street (780-496-8755; www.gov.edmonton.ab.ca/parkrec/muttart). The four pyramid-shaped glass pavilions set along the river valley house more than 700 species of flowers, plants, and trees from tropical, arid, and temperate zones. In the show pavilion, displays change frequently. The Conservatory is open year-round—where else would you find bananas growing in January, especially in Canada? For a lovely view of downtown, stand by the reflecting pools at the base of the pyramids.

Valley Zoo, 133 Street and Buena Vista Road (780-496-6911; www.gov.edmonton.ab.ca/parkrec/zoo). Spend several fun-filled hours at this seventy-acre zoological garden featuring more than 350 animals, including an African veldt and a bird of prey exhibit plus daily elephant and sea lion training demonstrations. The kid's section has a storybook theme. Other attractions include camel, paddleboat, and pony rides; a train; and merry-go-round.

More Attractions

After a full day at the mall, treat yourself to the peace and tranquility of **Devonian Botanic Gardens,** 6 miles west of Edmonton on Highway 16A, then 9 miles south on Highway 60 (780-987-3054; www.discoveredmonton.com/devonian). The botanic gardens are located within 190 acres of rolling sand dunes and large ponds. Nature trails and boardwalks make it possible to explore protected ecological areas and to bird-watch. Bring a picnic: Benches are located along the trails. View collections of flowers such as peonies and irises, visit a 2,000-square-foot orchid display house, the Kurimoto Japanese Garden, a tropical butterfly house featuring more than thirty species of exotic butterflies, and see aspen and jack-pine forests, as well as the Native People's Garden. This is the perfect place to find your center again.

Cruise or enjoy dinner on the North Saskatchewan River aboard the ***Edmonton Queen Riverboat,*** located at Rafter's Landing, across from the Convention Center (780-424-2628; www.edmonton.queen.com). The cruise lasts an hour and may be better suited to older children.

Theater, Music, and the Arts

For information on the arts, check the city's two daily newspapers, the *Edmonton Journal* and *Edmonton Sun,* or the weekly entertainment publications, *Where* and *Billy's Guide.* TicketMaster outlets (780-451-8000) located throughout the city handle tickets for most events. There are sixteen professional theater companies in town, including **Fringe Theatre Adventures,** 10330 84 Avenue (780-448-9000), in the heart of historic Old Strathcona, with a variety of story theater, puppetry, music, adapted classics, and modern theater for young people. **The Citadel Theatre,** 9828 101 A Avenue (780-426-4811), offers world-class plays from September to May. The Northern Alberta International Children's Festival (see Special Events) takes place every May in suburban St. Albert. More family entertainment can be found at **The Stage Polaris,** 7114 98 Street (780-432-9483), where shows for the very young are performed. **Heritage Amphitheatre,** the largest outdoor amphitheater in western Canada, is the summer home of the Edmonton Symphony Orchestra and the Festival City Pops Orchestra. Set in William Hawrelak Park (south of Goat Road Bridge), this amphitheater is a lovely place to spend a summer's evening. Call (780-496-7275) for a calendar of events.

The **Edmonton Opera** (780-429-1000), **Edmonton Symphony Orchestra** (403-428-1414), and **Alberta Ballet Company** (780-447-6812) performs in the Northern Alberta Jubilee Auditorium, on the campus of the University of Alberta, 87 Avenue and 114 Street (403-433-7741).

Sports

Golf. There are more than fifty golf courses in and around Edmonton. The city operates three public golf courses: **Victoria Golf Course** in Victoria Park, River Road, and 116 Street, is Canada's oldest municipal golf course. It is typically suited to mid-handicap players and features wide fairways. **Riverside Golf Course,** 8630 Roland Road (780-496-8702), is for more experienced golfers, with its 6,423-yard course heavily treed with gently rolling hills. **Rundle Golf Club,** in Rundle Park, 2909 113 Avenue, is an executive par-three 2,858-yard course suited for the senior, practicing player, or beginner. Club rentals and golf lessons are available at each course.

After a full day of golfing on the greens, take the kids to **Planet Golf,** West Edmonton Mall, Entrance 8 (780-483-7888), for a game of miniature golf in the dark with balls and putters that glow.

Professional Sports: Edmonton is home to four professional sports teams. The **Edmonton Oilers** (780-451-8000), who have won the NHL's Stanley Cup Championship several times, play from October to April in the Skyreach Centre, 11230 110 Street; tickets are available from TicketMaster. The **Edmonton Eskimos** are members of the Canadian Football League and play from June to November at Commonwealth Stadium; 111 Avenue and Stadium Road; (780) 448-3757. The **Edmonton Trap-**

The West Edmonton Mall

The **West Edmonton Mall** (780-444-5200) is more than just a mall, it's an attraction in itself, even for those who run from malls. With 5,200,000 square feet—the equivalent of forty-eight city blocks—this is the world's largest mall. There's just about everything for everybody: more than 800 stores and services, including seven major department stores, more than 130 women's clothing stores and one hundred menswear stores, in excess of forty-five shoe stores, and many toy, souvenir, sports, book, and record shops. Highlights:

- **Galaxyland** (780-444-5300) is the world's largest indoor amusement park, featuring the world's largest indoor triple-loop roller coaster and a special children's area called **Galaxy Kids Playpark.**
- **Dolphin Lagoon** and **Sea Life Caverns** have bottle-nosed dolphin shows, giant sea turtles, and sharks.
- The **Ice Palace** is a mammoth-size skating rink under a glass dome.
- **Deep Sea Adventure** gives you the feeling of exploring the ocean depths from inside a submarine.
- **World Waterpark,** a five-acre indoor water park, has more than twenty different water activities, including miles of water slides, many hot tubs, and an interactive play area for toddlers and parents called The Little Caribbean.
- **Planet Golf,** a miniature golf center, has a new swing on things: play in the dark with balls and putters that glow.

pers, members of the Pacific Coast League, play baseball from April to September at Telus Field, 96 Avenue and 102 Street. Tickets are available at the gate (780-429-2934), or through TicketMaster. The **Edmonton Drillers,** members of the National Professional Soccer League, play from November to March at the Skyreach Centre. Tickets are available at the gate (780-471-5425) or through TicketMaster.

Shopping

If you find West Edmonton Mall (described earlier) too daunting, there are several more reasonably sized malls downtown (100 to 103 Streets). The **Old Strathcona Historic Area,** extending around 82 Avenue (Whyte Avenue) and 104 Street, is a pleasant place to stroll and shop. Restored buildings in the area date back to 1891, the year the Calgary/ Edmonton railroad arrived. Browse at the trendy boutiques and year-round farmer's market (780-439-1844) that sells crafts and fresh vegetables.

Side Trips

Reynolds-Alberta Museum, 4705 50 Avenue, about 6/10 mile west on Highway 13, Wetaskiwin (800-661-4726; www.gov.ab.ca/~mcd/mhslram/ram.htm). Located about forty minutes south of Edmonton, this sprawling, sparkling museum is devoted to transportation, agriculture, and industry, and is also the home of **Canada's Aircraft Hall of Fame.** The museum evolved from the private collection of the Reynolds family, who had started a small local automobile service center in 1910. The exhibits and audiovisual displays of vintage bicycles, cars, aircraft, and agricultural and industrial machinery—and their impact on life throughout the province—delight adults and kids alike, especially presented against such nostalgic backdrops as a 1920s grain elevator, a 1940s service station, and a 1950s drive-in theater. This is not a place where stationary artifacts from the past are revered in hushed silence. Instead, you can get behind the wheel of a Model T racer, take a place on a miniature moving assembly line in the car factory, or operate a "Gerber spout," a device that controls the distribution of grain into various bins in a grain elevator. Outdoors on the 156-acre grounds, the vintage machines come to life. Cars and bicycles cruise, farm equipment chugs, and aircraft fly overhead on a regular basis. Other items not to miss: **Canada's Aviation Hall of Fame** shares space with the **Reynolds Aviation Museum.** Besides biographical panels of the 145 current inductees, there are also seventeen fully restored vintage aircraft on display, including a rare 1942 Hawker Hurricane, a 1946 Bellanca Senior Skyrocket, and a 1940 North American Yale. The Transportation Collection includes a 1905 Oldsmobile curved-dash Runabout, a 1912 Harley-Davidson Silent Grey Fellow, and a 1927 LaSalle convertible coupe. For snacks as well as lunch and dinner, the Galaxy Cafe offers meals and panoramic views. Be sure to ask about special events, live entertainment, and traveling displays.

Elk Island National Park is a nature preserve of unspoiled parkland located 30 miles east of Edmonton, just outside the town of Fort Saskatchewan, on

Edmonton Adventures

- Climb the walls at the **Vertically Inclined Rock Gym,** 8523 Argyll Road (780-496-9390), which welcomes families and climbers from five to eighty-five years old. The facility contains 6,000 square feet of climbing terrain. Try bouldering, top roping, and lead climbing.
- Watch the **Canadian Finals Rodeo** (888-800-7275), the largest indoor sporting event held in western Canada, with prize money of close to half a million dollars. Canada's top ten champions compete in professional rodeo's six premier events—saddle bronc, bareback, bull riding, calf roping, steer wrestling, and barrel racing. Held every November.
- Jet boat on the North Saskatchewan River for a view of Edmonton with **Klondike Jet Boats** (780-486-0896).

Highway 16 (780-992-2950). The park was created to save the area's elk from extinction. Today, within the park's fences, herds of elk, moose, and bison live undisturbed (along with hundreds of birds) and can be seen roaming free as you drive through the park. Yes, bison can be dangerous, but they should leave you alone unless provoked. Pick up a copy of *You Are in Bison Country* at the Park Information Centre, just off Highway 16, for safety tips. The center of "people activity" within the park is Lake Asotin, which has hiking trails, picnic areas, a nine-hole golf course, and cross-country skiing in the winter. Check the Asotin Interpretive Center (780-922-5790) for films and a schedule of daily activities.

About a half mile east on Highway 16 is the **Ukrainian Cultural Heritage Village,** Highway 16 (780-662-3640; www.gov.ab.ca/~mcd/mhs/uchv/uchv.htm). It tells the story of the Ukrainian immigrants and the development of their settlement in east central Alberta from 1892 to 1930. Costumed interpreters re-create a variety of historical characters. Tour farmsteads and the town site, whose historical buildings include a hardware store, and relax with a ride in a horsedrawn grain tank.

Very young children love **Alberta Fairytale Grounds** (780-963-8161), 15 miles west on Highway 16, just west of the town of Stony Plain. The owner of this private park uses handcrafted puppets and fairytale scenes to delight the younger set as they follow a path through the woods.

Special Events

Contact Edmonton Tourism for more information on the following annual festivals.

March. Northlands Farm and Ranch Show; Local Heroes International Screen Festival features films and workshops.

May. International Children's Festival, St. Albert Theatre, a five-day event with music, mime, puppetry, dance, and theater from around the world; Dream Speakers Festival, an international celebration of First Nations art and culture.

June–July. The Works: A Visual Arts Celebration covers the entire spectrum of visual, environmental, wearable, and even edible art; International Jazz City Festival.

July. International Street Performers Festival includes clowns, acrobats, mimes, magicians, and jugglers performing for ten days in more than 900 free shows downtown; Klondike Days, ten days of food, fun, music, costumes, an old-time fair, international trade and cultural exhibits, the largest traveling midway.

August. Heritage Festival features music, dance, costumes, arts, and food from around the world; The Fringe, a nine-day theatrical event featuring seventeen theaters, three outdoor stages, and more than 1,200 performers; Folk Music Festival has more than sixty acts, eight stages, workshops, food, handicrafts, and music.

December 31. First Night Festival, more than seventy-five live performances of music, theater, visual arts, and a rooftop fireworks spectacular.

Where to Stay

Fantasyland Hotel, West Edmonton Mall, 17700 87 Avenue (780-444-3000 or 800-737-3783). Altogether, there are 355 guest rooms, with 118 theme rooms, including Igloo, Victorian Coach, Hollywood, Polynesian, and Arabian themes. Some, such as the Canadian Rail room, have particular appeal to families: The berths of the train cars are perfect for kids. With the giant mall/recreation center right at your doorstep, this could be a family fantasy come true.

The Crowne Plaza-Château Lacombe, converted to the **Holiday Inn Crowne Plaza,** 101 Street at Bellamy Hill (780-428-6611 or 800-2CROWNE), features La Ronde, the city's only revolving restaurant. The **Westin Hotel Edmonton,** 10135 100 Street, Edmonton, Alberta T5J 0N7 (780-426-3636 or 800-WESTIN-1), offers the Westin Kids Club amenities. These include child-friendly rooms, children's sports bottle or tippy cup upon check-in, as well as a safety kit with a night-light, Band-Aids, and emergency phone numbers. Rooms feature bath toys and bath products for kids, and parents can request—at no charge—jogging strollers, potty seats, bicycle seats, and step stools. Restaurants and room service also feature children's menu.

Where to Eat

Edmonton Visitors Guide has a short listing of restaurants, but with more than 2,000 eateries to choose from, it's hard to select a mere handful. Contact Edmonton Tourism; they often have free publications, such as *Where* and *Billy's Guide,* which list restaurants. Ethnic food, particularly Italian, is always a good bet with kids. Two to recommend: **The Old Spaghetti Factory,** 10220 103 Street (780-422-6088), and **Packrat Louie Kitchen and Bar,** 10335 83 Avenue (780-433-0123), has a varied menu, including pizza, roasted chicken, and jumbo shrimp with bourbon cream sauce and garlic linguine. For moderately priced breakfast, lunch, or dinner, search out a **Smitty's Family Restaurant,** where steaks, chicken, burgers, pancakes, and waffles are among the specialties. There's one at the Edmonton Centre (780-425-6526) and ten other locations citywide. Any **Boston Pizza** location, such as 9308 34 Avenue (780-436-9086), is also a good bet. The eatery serves more than pizza, and Edmonton is where the chain began. Teens like the rock memorabilia and the burgers and pasta served at **Hard Rock Cafe,** Bourbon Street, West Edmonton Mall (780-444-1905).

For More Information

Edmonton Tourism has a **Visitor Information Centre,** open daily at Gateway Park (Highway 2), 2404 Calgary Trail Northbound S.W. (780-496-8400 or 800-463-4667 to have a visitor's guide sent to you). An information center is located at City Hall and at the International Airport arrivals level (780-890-8382; www.ede.org).

DATS (Disabled Adult Transportation System) gives disabled visitors a temporary registration number. For further information or to register, call (780) 496-4570. To book transportation, call (780) 496-4567.

Emergency Numbers

Ambulance, fire, police: 911

Poison Center: (800) 332-1414

Children's hospital: Alberta Children's Hospital, 1820 Richmond Road S.W. , offers emergency services for children eighteen and younger; (780)-229-7211

Twenty-four-hour emergency room: Royal Alexandra Hospital, 10240 Kingsway Avenue; (780) 477-4111

Twenty-four-hour pharmacy: Shoppers Drug Mart, 8210 109th Street; (780) 433-2424

Denver

The Mile High City is a green, tree-lined metropolis that, you may be surprised to know, is not in the mountains, but rather on high, rolling plains (flatter than Manhattan) *near* the mountains. With the edge of the Rocky Mountains just 30 miles west, Denver is a year-round recreational mecca—and with a rich selection of museums, plus the largest performing arts complex outside of New York's Lincoln Center, Denver is a cultural mecca as well. Add to that more than 300 days of bright sunshine a year, a summer that's comfortably dry, a winter during which the snow comes and goes (the heavy snows usually fall in the mountains and you can frequently golf in January), and you have the makings for a family vacation paradise.

Getting There

Denver International Airport, the world's largest airport, covering 53 square miles (twice the size of Manhattan Island), is 35 miles from downtown Denver. Public buses (see Getting Around) transport passengers into town, and private shuttle service, taxis, and car rentals are available.

Amtrak, Union Station, Seventeenth and Wynkoop (800-USA-RAIL), is a hub on the major east-west routes, with three arrivals and three departures daily. (The basement of the station contains one of the largest model railroads, which can be viewed the last Friday of every month.)

Greyhound (800-231-2222) is at Denver Bus Terminal, Nineteenth and Arapahoe.

Denver is at the crossroads of several major highways: I-70 from the west and east, I-25 from the north and south, and I-76 from the northeast.

Getting Around

Beyond downtown, you will need a car or public transportation.

Regional Transportation District (RTD) (303-299-6700) provides public transit for metropolitan Denver/Boulder. The **RTD Cultural**

Denver

AT A GLANCE

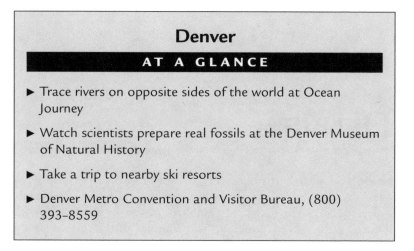

- Trace rivers on opposite sides of the world at Ocean Journey
- Watch scientists prepare real fossils at the Denver Museum of Natural History
- Take a trip to nearby ski resorts
- Denver Metro Convention and Visitor Bureau, (800) 393-8559

Connection Trolley (303-299-6000; www.rtd-denver.com), which operates from Memorial Day to Labor Day, goes to Denver's top cultural attractions (leaving every thirty minutes) for an all-day nominal fare. The shuttle buses on the Sixteenth Street Mall are free and take visitors for 1 mile through the heart of downtown on the pedestrian promenade.

The Ski Train, 555 Seventeenth Street (303-296-1-SKI), makes a two-hour journey through the Rockies, through twenty-six tunnels, stopping at the foot of Winter Park's major lifts. The train operates Saturday and Sunday throughout the ski season.

What to See and Do

Museums and Historical Sites

The **Children's Museum of Denver,** 2121 Children's Museum Drive, I-25 and Twenty-third Avenue (303-433-7444; www.cmdenver.org). Be prepared to have fun at this top-notch facility geared toward toddlers to eight-year-olds. Kids explore, create, and discover the worlds of art, nature, and science. Older kids are invariably drawn to the miniature TV studio, where they read the news or work the camera. Bank on It is a superb way for kids to learn that money doesn't grow on trees. At KidSport, families can learn to Rollerblade, ski, snowboard, or guide a sled dog on an outdoor ski hill that is operable year-round. (In fact, every fifth grader in Denver must take a ski lesson here.) Two new areas planned for 1999 openings are Maze-eum and the Center for the Young Child. Ask about special workshops and programs.

The **Colorado History Museum,** Thirteenth and Broadway (303-866-3682), is a wonderful place to learn about this state's colorful past. Dioramas, photos, artifacts, and exhibits portray the rich western her-

Denver Museum of Natural History

Known for its "enviroramas," dioramas with sound effects, the **Denver Museum of Natural History** has much to interest families. Highlights:

- **Explore Colorado: From Plains to Peaks** has eleven scenes depicting the state's plants and wildlife. Discovery boxes reveal a quail nest with eggs, and other items. Interactive videos explain animal families and Colorado weather patterns.
- **Hall of Life** features more than thirty exhibits on nutrition, fitness, and related subjects. Use a "life card" to store information on your height, weight, blood pressure, and pulse rate and get a printout at the end of the tour.
- **Prehistoric Journey** starts with an underwater view of ancient seas where the first life forms appeared. Then a land trail leads you through a Cretaceous creek bed as you hear dinosaurs roar, water flow, and crickets chirp. You also visit a Nebraska woodland and a Kansas coast (yes, Kansas was shoreline property 295 million years ago). Real fossils are displayed as well as "Lucy" (Australopithecus afarensis), a full reconstruction of a 3.6-million-year-old transitional form between humans and apes. Watch scientists prepare specimens at the fossil lab.
- **Coors Mineral Hall** has gems, minerals, and meteorites. Walk into a re-created mine to see the Sweet Home rhodochrosite pocket, a wall of deep red translucent crystals, and view 102.41-troy-ounce "Tom's Baby," the largest gold mass ever discovered in the state.
- **Edge of the Wild** presents Colorado critters. Listen to elk bugle and bison grunt; track a mountain lion with radio-telemetry.
- **Botswana Africa Hall**'s enviroramas depict zebras, water hogs, baboons, and greater kudu around a watering hole.
- **Egyptian Mummies** reveals mummification secrets through computed axial tomography (CAT) scans. See a real mummy skeleton.
- **Phipps IMAX theater** shows films on a screen four-and-a-half stories tall and six-and-a-half stories wide.
- **Crane North American Hall** features exhibits on the Cheyenne, a reconstructed Navajo hogan, and a Hopi pueblo.
- **Gates Planetarium** has shows on the solar system.
- **Special Activities.** Reserve well in advance for family camp-ins. These overnights in the museum focus on different topics.

Denver Museum of Natural History, 2001 Colorado Boulevard; (303) 322-3704 or (800) 925-2250; www.dmnh.org.

Black American West Museum

Many black cowboys helped settle the West, as Paul Stewart, founder and curator of the **Black American West Museum and Heritage Center, the Dr. Justina Ford House,** 3091 California Street (303-292-2566; www.coax.net/people/lwf/bawmus.htm) discovered. At this museum, which contains one of the best collections of western black memorabilia, listen to the oral histories of wranglers, miners, and entrepreneurs. Learn how rodeo star Bill Pickett came to invent the art of "bulldogging" (steer wrestling). Find out about freed slave Clara Brown, who traveled to California on a wagon train, became a laundress of miners' shirts, and saved and invested wisely to amass a small fortune, which she used to buy freedom for her friends and relatives in Kentucky. Ask about the hands-on programs scheduled throughout the year for children.

itage of covered wagons, Indian dances, buffalo hunts, miners, pioneers, fur trappers, and cowboys—stuff that most kids love.

Stop by the museum store for a unique selection of Native American and Colorado crafts. There's also a leading Western research library here.

At the **Colorado Railroad Museum,** 17155 West Forty-fourth Avenue, Golden (303-279-4591 or 800-365-6263), train lovers enjoy viewing the more than sixty historic locomotives and cars exhibited on fourteen acres. Inside are model railroads and other train memorabilia.

Colorado State Capitol, Broadway and Colfax (303-866-2604). While younger kids may be bored stiff at the Colorado State Capitol, older kids should appreciate a visit to this building, modeled after the U.S. Capitol in Washington, D.C. Free tours are offered weekdays from 9:00 A.M. to 2:30 P.M. The fifteenth step on the west side is exactly 1 mile high. The dome is covered with 200 ounces of 14K gold, but the building's really valuable material is the rare Colorado rose onyx. The entire world's supply was used as wainscoting in the building. The Rotunda offers a splendid panoramic view of the entire Front Range, from Pikes Peak north to the Wyoming border.

The **Denver Art Museum,** Fourteenth Avenue and Bannock Street (303-640-2793; www.denverartmuseum.org). The largest in a fourteen-state radius, this museum is a work of art itself, resembling a medieval fortress, with twenty-eight sides and ten stories covered with more than a million Corning gray glass tiles, each of which reflects light in a different way. Interactive learning tools throughout the galleries make the museum especially appealing to younger visitors. Kids like the Western and American Indian galleries, complete with dugout canoes, totem poles (housed in a two-story atrium), toys and games, and what many consider to be the world's finest example of Native American art. The museum also has an outstanding collection of pre-Columbian and Spanish Colonial art. Family workshops are offered the first Saturday of the month and Family Backpacks, full of hands-on games and activities, are available every Saturday; both are

Ocean Journey

Flash floods and Sumatran tigers are two of the surprises at **Ocean Journey,** Denver's new $93 million aquarium tracing rivers on opposite sides of the world. The raging waters depict the Colorado River crossing the Sonoran Desert en route to Mexico's Sea of Cortez, and the fierce beasts live in an Indonesian rain forest, source of Sumatra's Kampar River. Kids can walk through an acrylic tunnel and be surrounded by moray eels and rainbow-colored fish, see sharks swim in a 320,000-gallon tank, and handle sea stars, hermit crabs, and sea urchins at a touch table. Family overnights are scheduled to start in January 2000.

Ocean Journey will be linked to Denver's Children's Museum by an historic light rail trolley along the banks of the Platte River. The open-air trolley, similar to those that operated in Denver at the turn of the century, will also connect with Mile High Stadium.

Ocean Journey, US West Park, 700 Water Street; (303) 561-4450; www.oceanjourney.org.

free of charge. Art Stops—tables with touchable art objects manned by trained interpreters—are also featured. A major collection of nineteenth-century Western-themed work by Remington, Russell and others will be on display in 2000.

The Denver Museum of Miniatures, Dolls and Toys, 1880 North Gaylord Street (303-322-3704). There's a delightful assortment of tiny treasures housed in the historic Pearce-McAllister Cottage, an 1899 Colonial Revival house. Although the building itself and the period furnishings may bore kids, the upstairs rooms filled with period toys and dollhouses won't. Pick up a "treasure hunt" sheet so that your kids can answer the questions and receive a small token from the gift shop. Saturday Art Workshops are held on the first Saturday of each month.

United States Mint, West Colfax at Cherokee Street (303-844-3582). Don't miss a chance to show your kids how coins are made: More than five billion coins are produced here each year, and 40 million coins are stamped each day. This is the second largest storehouse of gold bullion in the nation, after Fort Knox. The free tours, weekdays from 8:00 A.M. to 2:45 P.M., reveal the fascinating process, from stamping to counting and bagging. Your chances of gaining admission are better if you line up in the morning; if possible, try to be in line before 1:30 P.M. Chances are you won't leave without buying a unique coin souvenir (not sold elsewhere) from the gift shop.

Amusement Centers and Parks

Six Flags Elitch Gardens, 2000 Elitch Circle, (303-595-4FUN; www.elitchgardens.com). This fifty-eight-acre amusement park, with its 105-year-old history, was updated in 1999, with a new spine-tingling Boomerang megacoaster that sends riders face first down a 125-foot drop before rocketing them through three pulse-pounding looping inversions and then repeating the process backward at speeds of more than 50 miles per hour. If you're still able to walk after that one, there are twenty-eight other thrill rides, among them Twister II, the longer and taller version of the famed wooden coaster, and Disaster Canyon, a simulated white-water raft ride. There are scenic Rocky Mountain views from Total Tower and of the sweeping downtown vista from atop the Ferris wheel. Kiddieland features ten tot-pleasing rides, not the least of which is the handcrafted carousel. Formal flower gardens, waterfalls, and evening concerts, musical revues, and circus acts add to the festive atmosphere. Open May through October.

Lakeside Amusement Park, I-70 and Sheridan Boulevard (303-477-1621), has forty big rides, including the Cyclone Roller Coaster, and fifteen rides in its Kiddies Playland, plus a Coal Burning Miniature Steam Train to whisk visitors around the park and its beautiful lake. Open May through October.

Tiny Town and Railroad, 6249 South Turkey Creek Road (303-697-6829). This teeny, tiny town will tickle tykes, with a steam train ride around one hundred handcrafted miniature structures, including Old West buildings in rural and mountain settings. The facility is open May through October and decorated with Christmas lights during the holiday season.

Water World, Eighty-eighth Avenue at Pecos Street (303-427-SURE). Water World, which claims to be America's largest water park, features forty attractions on sixty-five acres. It has everything from twisting water slides and oceanlike wave pools to the Fun H_2Ouse for the older crew and Wally World for tots. Open Memorial Day through Labor Day.

Parks and Zoos

Denver has the largest city park system in the nation, with 205 parks in the city and 20,000 acres of mountain parks. The most prominent is **City Park,** Seventeenth Avenue and Colorado Boulevard. Here you'll find the Museum of Natural History as well as two lakes, picnic sites, play grounds, playing fields, tennis courts—and the beautifully landscaped **Denver Zoo** (see page 45).

More than 1,200 vibrantly colored butterflies surround visitors at the **Butterfly Pavilion and Insect Center,** 6252 West 104th Avenue off U.S.

Denver Zoo

Located on seventy-five acres, the **Denver Zoo** has a collection of 3,500 animals representing 685 species. Highlights:

- **Primate Panorama,** a 7.15-acre naturalistic habitat, has waterfalls and thick vegetation. Encounter a Sumatran orangutan, a Celebes black ape, and Kondu, a 550-pound silverback, as well as white-haired gibbons, silvered-leaf langurs, two-toed sloths, pygmy marmosets, and golden lion tamarinds.
- **Penguin Habitat** replicates the rocky cliffs of the Chilean coast and is home to ten Humboldt penguins.
- **Tropical Islands: Komodo Dragons** is the new habitat for the rare Komodo dragons, the world's largest lizards. The Denver Zoo is one of only twenty-one zoos in the United States to have these lizards, some of which reach 300 pounds.
- **Tropical Discovery** features exotic venomous snakes, alligators, crocodiles, piranhas, and anacondas.
- **Northern Shores** has glass-walled underwater viewing areas. See polar bears and California sea lions swim in the exhibit's pools.
- **Children's Kraal** is a children's zoo open in warm weather. Pet pygmy goats, primates, and other animals and watch performances by musicians, artists, and storytellers.

Denver Zoo, 2300 Steele Street; (303) 376–4800; www.denverzoo.org.

Highway 36, Westminster (303–469–5441). Flitting from leaves to flowers, the butterflies sometimes alight on the shoulders or heads of surprised children and adults. This simulated tropical forest is humid (take your coats off before you enter) with 80-degree temperatures and 70-percent humidity—a great place to warm up in winter. Besides ducking the winged beauties, children like learning about these real "morphing" heroes of the rain forests and observing their dry, leaflike chrysalis, the cocoon from which the butterflies emerge. More things that fly, creep, and crawl on display include Madagascar hissing cockroaches, a hive of bees, and a rose-colored tarantula.

Another Denver park: **Buffalo Bill's Memorial Museum and Grave,** Top of Lookout Mountain, I–70 exit 256 (303–526–0747). This famous frontier scout and showman wanted to be buried in Wyoming, but because he died in Denver, he is buried on this site, some twenty minutes west of town. Along with the gravesite are guns, outfits, and posters from his Wild West Show and exhibits on the Pony Express and frontier life. If everyone has taken his or her Dramamine, hold on as you leave the museum for a drive on the curving Lariat Loop Trail to Golden.

Stop and smell the roses at **Denver Botanic Gardens,** 1005 York Street (303-331-4000 or 4010 for recorded information), and its newly opened Romantic Gardens. Also newly renovated is the Tropical Conservatory, which in January of 2000 will add a dinosaur model to its rain forest. Also here are Japanese and Rock Alpine plant gardens and other exotic species, located both indoors and outdoors on twenty-one lovely acres. Kids will enjoy the Children's Storybook Gardens, held throughout the summer, that uses children's books (*The Wizard of Oz, Charlotte's Web*) to teach kids about plants.

Shopping

Downtown at the **Sixteenth Street Mall,** with its pedestrian promenade, you find dozens of shops, outdoor cafes, and plenty of restaurants. The mall got even merrier with the addiion of **Denver Pavilions,** which opened in November 1998 adjacent to the Adam's Mark Hotel. This complex is anchored by **Niketown,** a megastore complete with its own basketball court. Other stores include **Virgin Records,** a **Hard Rock Cafe,** and a fifteen-screen movie complex.

Lower downtown (also called LoDo) is the old section where Victorian warehouses have been converted into art galleries, discos, pubs, restaurants, and condo lofts. The new **Stadium Walk** has shops, movie theaters, and a Planet Hollywood.

The 140 upscale stores of **Cherry Creek Shopping Center,** 3000 East First Avenue (303-388-3900 or 800-424-6360), include Saks, Neiman Marcus, and—hold on to your wallets—F.A.O. Schwarz. Also here are thirty-one art galleries and some of the city's most beautiful displays of outdoor sculptures, gardens, fountains, and parks. A number of shops around town sell Native American and southwestern art, jewelry, and furnishings.

Built to be suggestive of a Rocky Mountain Ski Lodge, the **Park Meadows Shopping Center,** junction of C-470 and I-25, about 12 miles south of Denver in Douglas County, houses Colorado's first Nordstrom department store. The ski ambience comes from the wood-beam ceiling (the largest in Colorado), two massive stone fireplaces, and a red rock "mountain" with trees, waterfalls, and wildflowers. If you like to hunt for bargains, head to the outdoor **Mile High Flea Market** (303-289-4656), held weekends and Wednesdays on eighty paved acres at I-76 and Eighty-eighth Avenue. Along with the hundreds of vendors, there are food stalls and amusement and pony rides for the kids at Colorado's largest flea market.

Theater, Music, and the Arts

There's always something entertaining going on in Denver—from evening concerts at the Botanic Gardens and the Zoo to big-name tours at the city's two large amphitheaters (Red Rocks and Fiddlers Green). Tickets for many events can be purchased at the Ticket Bus on the Sixteenth Street Mall at Curtis Street.

Cultural events abound at the **Denver Performing Arts Complex** (The PLEX), 1245 and Champa Street. Call (303) 893-4100 or (800) 641-1222 for tickets and show schedules. Second only to New York's Lincoln Center in capacity, this complex, with 9,000 seats in ten theaters, offers symphony, opera, theater, and dance performances year-round. Event listings can be found on the Internet at www.denver.org.

Sports

Denver's National League baseball team, the **Colorado Rockies** plays in Coors Field. Purchase tickets by calling (303) ROCKIES (762-5437).

The NFL Super Bowl champs, the **Denver Broncos,** play at Mile High Stadium, 1700 Federal Boulevard (303-433-7466), until their new football stadium is ready in 2001. Beginning in October 1999, hockey fans can watch Stanley Cup winners (they won their first year in Denver) **Colorado Avalanche** play in the Pepsi Center, a new $160 million, 19,000-seat arena on the edge of LoDo. (The **Denver Nuggets** will also play their 1999 season there.) The American Professional Soccer League Team, the **Colorado Foxes,** play at Englewood High School Stadium, 3800 South Logan, from May to August. Call (303) 840-1111 for information. And don't forget Denver's WNBA women's basketball team, the **Colorado Xplosion** (303-893-3865).

Side Trips

Colorado is ski country, and Denver is a fairly short drive from a variety of top-notch areas. Winter Park, about 70 miles northwest of Denver, is a popular ski destination. (The Ski Train, detailed in Getting Around, delivers skiers right to the base of the mountain.) **Winter Park** (303-726-5514 or 800-453-2525) features more than 130 trails of diverse terrain.

For parents who want to catch up with their kids' ski skills, and for kids who want to learn, Winter Park offers an excellent kids' ski school and special workshops. Discovery Park, with 20 acres of trails, terrain gardens, gentle slopes, and three chairlifts, gives even the most skittish beginner enough space to learn. In addition, Winter Park has a nursery for infants two months and up and a nonski program for ages through five. Most kids ages three and four enjoy the ski-and-play programs on their own little "mountain." Older kids and teens perfect skills in daylong kids' classes.

In Summit County, ninety minutes west of downtown Denver, there are several ski areas, all with good kids' ski programs: **Keystone Resort/Arapahoe Basin** (303-468-2316 or 800-222-0188), **Copper Mountain** (303-968-2882 or 800-458-8386), and **Breckenridge** (303-453-5000 or 800-800-BREC). (For summer vacationers, golf, tennis, horseback riding, mountain biking, and sailing on nearby Lake Dillon are the main attractions.)

Vail/Beaver Creek (303-949-5750 or 800-622-3131) is 100 miles west of town. For details on area ski resorts, contact Colorado Ski Country at its airport booth or in town at 1560 Broadway, Suite 1440, Denver 80202 (303-837-0793).

Special Events

Check with the Convention and Visitors Bureau for details on these events:

January. National Western Stock Show and Rodeo includes Children's Ranchland, junior show and sale, buffalo, goats, and lots more.

March. Powwow brings seventy Native American tribes to the Denver Coliseum (303-455-4575).

May. Cinco de Mayo, one of the largest cultural events in Colorado, featuring food, entertainment, and activities for the kids (303-534-8342).

June. Cherry Blossom Festival, Sakura Square; Juneteeth, celebration commemorating the end of slavery with food and events, parade, open stage, Gospel Extravaganza.

July. Buffalo Bill Days, with parade, crafts fair, and Wild West Show, Golden; Denver Black Arts Festival features African-American artists and entertainers in City Park, (303-329-3976); Cherry Creek Festival, Fourth of July weekend (303-355-2787).

Late August–Early September. Colorado State Fair, the state's largest single event (800-444-FAIR).

September. Octoberfest, Larimer Square (303-447-0816).

Where to Stay

A listing of accommodations, ranging from bed-and-breakfast inns to all-suite hotels, can be found in the *Official Visitor's Guide;* call (800) 489-4888. **Bed and Breakfast—Rocky Mountain,** 639 Grant Street, 80203 (303-860-8415), is a free reservation service for inns and home stays throughout the state.

Downtown hotels include a number of well-known chains. The all-suite **Residence Inn by Marriott,** 2777 Zuni (303-458-5318 or 800-331-3131), offers free breakfast daily and free light dinner and cocktails on weekdays.

The **Courtyard by Marriott,** 934 Sixteenth Street (303-571-1114 or 800-331-3131), is located at the Sixteenth Street Mall. Another relatively new property, the **Teatro Wyndham Great Heritage Hotel,** 1100 Fourteenth Street (303-228-1100), is adjacent to the Performing Arts Complex. The **Oxford Hotel,** 1600 Seventeenth Street (303-628-5400), is a smaller, restored hotel near Union Station.

Embassy Suites Hotel and Athletic Club at Denver Place, 1881 Curtis (303-297-8888 or 800-733-3366), also offers complimentary breakfast and cocktails. **The Hyatt Regency Denver,** 1750 Welton Street (303-295-1234 or 800-233-1234), has an outdoor pool, a jogging track, and tennis courts. A bargain downtown, **Comfort Inn-Downtown,** Seventeenth Street and Tremont (303-296-0400 or 800-4-CHOICE), was once part of **Brown Palace,** the city's Victorian landmark, and shares the hotel's distinctive atrium lobby. Complimentary breakfast is included. The **Westin's Tabor Center,** 1672 Lawrence Street, 80202 (303-572-9100 or 800-228-3000), offers the Westin Kids Club amenities. These include child-friendly rooms, children's sports bottle or tippy cup upon check-in, as well as a safety kit with a night-light, Band-Aids, and emergency phone numbers. Rooms feature bath toys and bath products for kids, and parents can request—at no charge—jogging strollers, potty seats, bicycle seats, and step stools. Restaurants and room service also feature children's menus.

Where to Eat

Denver's *Official Visitor's Guide* offers a descriptive listing of restaurants. Don't be surprised if you find buffalo steaks on the menu: The city, considered the buffalo capital of the United States, serves more of the meat (said to be lower in fat, calories, and cholesterol than beef) than any other city. A restaurant, **Denver Buffalo Company,** 1109 Lincoln Street (303-832-0880), three blocks from the State Capitol, serves its own ranch-raised buffalo along with seafood, poultry, pasta, and other dishes. The complex also has a trading post and art gallery.

The **Buckhorn Exchange,** 1000 Osage Street (303-534-9505), founded in 1893 by one of Buffalo Bill's scouts, serves prime rib, buffalo steaks, and elk as well as the more mundane chicken. Warn your kids about the mounted animal heads. The **Cadillac Ranch,** 1400 Larimar Street (303-820-2288), serves western fare with a southwestern flare. Try the Buffalo green chili and the Rocky Mountain trout. The pizza at

Brewpubs for Parents

Denver is the brewing capital of the world, home to Coors Brewery, the largest single brewery in the world. Center Denver (LoDo) has fifteen brewpubs and microbreweries, restaurants that brew and serve fresh beer that's not bottled and can't be purchased anywhere else. On any given day, you'll be able to taste between forty and fifty different beers in LoDo. Just be sure you have a designated driver to get you home.

- **Coors Brewery,** Twelfth and Ford Streets, Golden (303-279-6565), just 12 miles from Denver, produces more than seventeen million barrels of beer a year. Free tours Monday through Saturday cover every aspect of the brewing process, from germinating barley to bottling the finished product. And you get a free sample at the end of the tour.
- **Wynkoop Brewing Company,** 1634 Eighteenth Street (303-297-2700), is the first of the brewpubs and the largest. The company's comedy club, upscale pool hall (thirty tables), and excellent restaurant complement its collection of award-winning beers that include Elvis Brau, Pattie's Chili Beer, and Splatz Porter, named after the pub cat.
- **Sandlot Brewing Company,** 2161 Blake Street (303-298-1587), is the only brewpub in the world located in a baseball stadium—Coors Field. Beer names, natch, include Squeeze Play Wheat and Slugger's Stout.
- **Rock Bottom Brewery,** 1001 Sixteenth Street (303-534-7616), located in the Sixteenth Street Mall, has one of the city's largest outdoor cafes and frequently features jazz groups on an elevated stage above the brewing kettles. Home of Molly's Titanic Brown Ale, a dark ale honoring Denver's *Titanic* survivor, "Unsinkable" Molly Brown.
- In October, Denver hosts America's largest beer festival, the **Great American Beer Festival.** More than 325 brewers participate, serving more than 1,300 different beers, ales, stouts, porters, and lagers. In June, the locals hold the **LoDo BrewFest,** where forty handcrafted Colorado beers are served along with music, food, and other festivities.

Beau Jo's, 2700 South Colorado Boulevard, University Hills shopping center (303-758-1519), has been voted the best by readers of the city's newspapers.

The **Rocky Mountain Diner,** 800 Eighteenth Street (303-293-8383), has won praise as "the best home cookin' in Denver." Specialties are the roast duck enchiladas and the panfried catfish, but for less adventursome eaters the place serves the typical comfort foods: burgers, mashed potatoes, and turkey sandwiches.

For something completely different, take the kids to **Casa Bonita,** 6715 West Colfax at Pierce (303-232-5115). This huge facility seats 1,200 and serves Mexican and American food in a Mexican village setting, complete with strolling mariachis, high divers, gunfights—and a volcano.

For More Information

The Denver Visitor Information Center, 1668 Larimer, in the Tabor Shopping Center (303-892-1112), or the Metro Convention and Visitors Bureau, 1555 California Street (800-393-8559) offers more than 500 free brochures and maps. **Wheelchair Getaways of Colorado** (303-674-1498 or 800-238-6920), rents accessible full-size luxury vans by the day, week, or month.

Emergency Numbers

Ambulance, fire, police: 911

Poison Control: (800) 882-2073

Pharmacy: Clay Drug, 9297 Federal Boulevard; open until midnight, (303) 426-8901

Hospital: Saint Joseph Hospital, 1835 Franklin Street (303) 837-7240

5 Idaho

Boise and the Surrounding Rocky Mountain Region

Families feel welcome in Boise, Idaho, a small, friendly metropolis in the foothills of the Rocky Mountains. Boise, the state's capital and largest city, appears like a green oasis in the middle of the surrounding brown hills, earning it the nickname the City of Trees. The Boise River cuts through the center of town, and the Greenbelt bicycle and pedestrian path that follows the river offers year-round recreation. Boise also is a convenient gateway to fun and adventure: An abundance of white-water rivers, mountain slopes and lakes, forest trails, and dramatic desert landscapes offer families a variety of ways to enjoy the great outdoors.

Getting There

Boise Air Terminal (208-383-3110), 8 miles southwest of downtown off I-84, is served by several airlines, including Delta, Northwest, Horizon, Sky West, Southwest, and United. Car rentals are available at the terminal.

For bus transportation, **Greyhound**'s station is at 1212 West Bannock Street (208-343-3681 or 800 231-2222). By car, Boise is reached by I-84.

Getting Around

A car is really a necessity to explore Boise and the surrounding area. **Boise Urban Stages** (208-336-1010) offers public bus transportation around town, with schedules available at City Hall or by calling the company.

Spring through fall, the **Boise Tour Train,** a narrated tour aboard a replica of an 1890s locomotive, departs from Tour Train depot in Julia Davis Park between Myrtle Street and the Boise River (208-342-4796) and travels to the city's historical sights.

Boise Area

AT A GLANCE

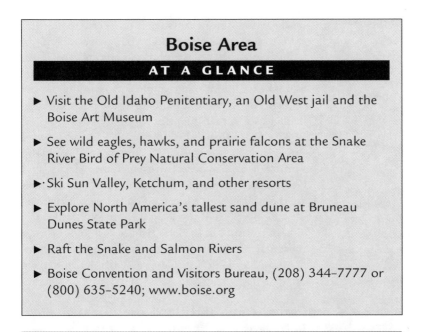

- Visit the Old Idaho Penitentiary, an Old West jail and the Boise Art Museum
- See wild eagles, hawks, and prairie falcons at the Snake River Bird of Prey Natural Conservation Area
- Ski Sun Valley, Ketchum, and other resorts
- Explore North America's tallest sand dune at Bruneau Dunes State Park
- Raft the Snake and Salmon Rivers
- Boise Convention and Visitors Bureau, (208) 344-7777 or (800) 635-5240; www.boise.org

WHAT TO SEE AND DO

Museums

Julia Davis Park (208-384-4240), in the heart of town between Myrtle Street and the Boise River, contains museums, the zoo, botanical gardens, and more (see Parks, Zoos, and Gardens).

Idaho Historical Museum, 610 Julia Davis Drive (208-334-2120). Two floors of exhibits reveal the colorful history of Idaho and the Pacific Northwest. Among the reconstructed interiors are a Chinese apothecary shop, an Old West saloon, a blacksmith forge, and a vintage kitchen. Among the period pieces on display are beaded moccasins and Native American clothing.

Visit the **Discovery Center,** 131 Myrtle Street (208-343-9895), at the end of the park. Here you can play with magnetic sand, see your shadow on the wall, and create giant bubbles. These are some of the more than one hundred hands-on exhibits that teach kids about science. An echo tube and afterimage, for example, explain about delayed perception. A sun tracker brings a beam of sunlight into the museum for solar experiments.

Elsewhere in town is **The Basque Museum,** 611 Grove Street (208-343-2671). The only Basque museum in the United States, the museum includes the Cyrus Jacobs-Uberuaga House (the oldest brick house in Boise, built in 1864). During the 1900s, it served as a boardinghouse for newly arrived immigrants from northern Spain, who came to central Idaho's rocky terrain to work as sheepherders. Black-and-white photographs collected from local families and original furniture re-create the era, as do the traditional dance nights held throughout the year and upon request. Exhibits in the main building detail aspects of Basque culture.

The State Capitol, Jefferson Street and Capitol Boulevard (208-334-2470), constructed of Idaho sandstone and marble from Vermont, Alaska, and Georgia, offers free self-guided tours and exhibits on gems and timber products. Several statues may interest kids: a replica of the *Winged Victory of Samothrace,* a gift from Paris; *The Patriot,* a tribute to a 1972 disaster in which many miners died; and a dignified commemorative depicting George Washington atop a horse.

Boise Art Museum

Founded in 1937, the **Boise Art Museum,** 670 Julia Davis Drive (208-334-2120), is Idaho's premier visual arts institution. Located in Julia Davis Park, the museum features a sculpture court and outdoor sculpture garden plus eighteen galleries. Permanent exhibits revolve around an extensive collection of American realist art. Kids should have no trouble picking out things they like from the watercolors, drawings, and other media portraying animals, urban scenes, flowers, and portraits by such artists as Red Grooms, Georgia O'Keefe, and Edward Hopper. The museum presents more than twenty-five special exhibitions yearly, featuring works by locally, regionally, and nationally known artists.

Check the schedule for Kids' Day! and family Art Saturdays. The museum store sells books, toys, jewelry, and crafts for children of all ages.

Parks, Zoos, and Gardens

Julia Davis Park, spanning more than ninety acres, features playgrounds, tennis courts, boat rentals, picnic facilities, a rose garden, free summer entertainment at the band shell, and kid-pleasing attractions.

Ever expanding, the **Idaho Botanical Garden,** 2355 Penitentiary Road (208-343-8649), is a living museum of plants. Among the twelve specialty gardens are children's, Alpine, contemporary English, meditation, and Idaho native plant gardens.

Boise's **Greenbelt** links a network of five parks along the Boise River. **Ann Morrison Park,** between Americana Boulevard and the river, is the city's largest, with 4 miles of trails. The park's 153 acres include playgrounds, picnic areas, and tennis courts. You can rent skates and bicycles at Wheels R Fun, on the west end. For further information on the city's parks, call the Park System (208-384-4240).

Morrison-Knudsen Nature Center (208-368-6060), a four-and-a-half-acre habitat between Warm Springs Avenue and the river, has outdoor viewing windows where visitors observe different facets of the underwater life of a mountain stream. An interpretive center features hands-on exhibits revolving around wildlife and the flow of the river. The facility has an indoor

Go to Jail

The **Old Idaho Penitentiary,** 2445 Old Penitentiary Road (1½ miles east on Warm Springs Avenue, then left), grew from a single-cell building in 1870 into an Old West complex that served as a regional prison until 1973. A tour of the museum reveals portraits of famous inmates and lawmen, as well as captured contraband weapons and artifacts. An eighteen-minute slide show tells about this penitentiary's colorful past. Inside the compound, view the effects of a riot, see several cell houses, a punishment area nicknamed Siberia, the Women's Ward, Death Row, and the Gallows. A former dormitory houses several hands-on exhibits detailing the history of electricity. A former prison shirt factory now sports a transportation display of a 1903 steam fire pumper, buggies, and other vehicles. Call (208) 334-2844 for information.

aquarium, an outdoor lagoon with sturgeon, bass, and rainbow trout, an outdoor nesting ground for ducks and geese, and a beaver pond.

The **World Center for Birds of Prey** is off I-84 on South Cole Road, on the outskirts of town; (208) 362-8687. This endangered species facility has an interpretive area with a number of hands-on activities. At the Tropical Raptor Building, see such birds as the giant harpy eagle, whose wingspan nears 7 feet. In spring, watch via one-way mirrors as incubated eggs hatch into young peregrine falcons. Enraptured and want more? Visit the **Snake River Birds of Prey National Conservation Area** (208-384-3300). It's one hour from Boise near San Falls Dam off Highway 69, south of Kuna. This area boasts the world's largest concentration of nesting eagles, hawks, and prairie falcons. Access to the area is gained by way of some fairly rough gravel roads. Although you can see the area on your own, the best way to tour is via guided boat trips (see Outfitters).

Skiing

Beyond Boise, there's the great outdoors: snow-packed mountains, raging rivers, lush forests, and rugged canyons. Some of the following make perfect day trips, while others, farther afield, are suitable for a weekend (or longer) trip.

Bogus Basin Ski Resort, 16 miles north of the office on 2405 Bogus Basin Road (208-332-5100 or 800-367-4397), is the closest ski resort to Boise. Sister mountains Deer Point and Shafer Butte offer 2,600 skiable acres, seven chairlifts, and extensive night skiing. Day care is available for ages six months and older. At ski classes, ages three to twelve learn and perfect techniques. Snowboarding is available for ages eight and older. Nordic skiers can glide along the region's scenic trails.

Sun Valley Resort (800-786-8259; www.sunvalley.com). Sun Valley is about a two-and-a-half-hour drive from Boise. Situated in the rugged Sawtooth range, Sun Valley was the nation's first destination ski resort, built in 1936. Sun Valley is typically ranked among the top ski resorts for terrain, lifts, lines, challenge, food, and lodging. Sun Valley's uniqueness lies in its near-perfect pitch, which creates exceptionally long runs with no dead spots on the way down. Another plus—practically nonexistent lift lines. With nearly eighty runs on 2,054 acres, Sun Valley sports variety, and it welcomes snowboarders. Cross-country skiers have 40 kilometers of groomed trails on which to glide. Families can sign up for family lessons geared for all ages.

Sun Valley is the place to go to to get young kids enthusiastic about cross-country skiing. An innovator in making Nordic skiing accessible for children, Sun Valley pioneered child-size tracks in 1987. While adult tracks are set 9½ inches apart, the kids' tracks are about 5 inches apart, enabling little feet to get a lot more glide. Kids also love Sun Valley's Children's Terrain Garden, an obstacle course with strategically placed colorful cut-out figures.

The Sun Valley Playschool cares for nonskiing tots from six months to six years. Three- and four-year-olds can sign up for cross-country and downhill lessons; ages five to twelve have full-day ski programs.

For lodging and reservations, contact the Sun Valley-Ketchum Chamber of Commerce at (208) 726-3423, (800) 634-3347, or at their Web site, www.visitketchum.com.

Zoo Boise

Visit **Zoo Boise,** 355 North Julia Davis Drive (208-384-4260). Noted for its large display of birds of prey, the zoo exhibits fifteen different species of hawks, owls, vultures, and eagles, including bald eagles. Idaho's native elk, deer, and bighorn sheep delight kids, as does the petting zoo. The zoo is only one of five in North America to feature a moose habitat.

Rafting

In a class by itself, **Hell's Canyon National Recreation Area** encompasses more than 650,000 acres. Straddling the Snake River in Idaho and Oregon (two to three hours north of Boise), Hell's Canyon features rugged outdoor river country. The gorge is more than a mile deep in some locations, making it the deepest river gorge on the continent. This is an area of desert slopes, rugged mountain peaks, cool lakes, and clean streams. Cougars, bobcats, elk, deer, mountain goats, and bighorn sheep live within the forests and ridges. The more than 1,000 miles of hiking trails range from easy to difficult, though access roads to trailheads are often narrow, steep, and rocky.

Most people concur that **Heavens Gates Overlook** offers the best view into the canyon from Idaho. To reach this spot, drive a half day from the south end of Riggins via an extremely steep and winding gravel road, Forest Road 517. A strenuous ½-mile trail, open from July to September, provides an access to the overlook. A better and easier way to explore the canyon is via an aluminum jet boat or a float trip.

Salmon River Canyon raft trips take you down the last 53 miles of the Salmon River, known for its class II–III waves and sandy beaches. Three outfitters offer trips geared for families: **River Odysseys West** (ROW) (800-451-6034 or 208-765-0841; www.rowinc.com), **Outdoor Adventure River Specialists** (OARS) (209-736-4677 or 800-346-6277; www.oars.com); and **Rocky Mountain River Tours** (208-345-2400 or 208-756-4808). For more information, contact **Hells Canyon National Recreation Area** (208-628-3915) or the **Outfitters and Guides Association** (208-342-1438).

Desert Dunes

At **Bruneau Dunes State Park,** one hour south of Boise on Highway 51 (208-366-7919), you'll find North America's tallest dune, 470 feet. A 5-mile, self-guided nature trail explains the desert habitat. Stroll in the early morning or late evening, the best times for observing the desert wildlife, and you might see a rabbit dart by or an eagle soar. Get your camera ready; sunrises and sunsets are spectacular. The park has a campground, an environmental education center with area wildlife and natural history displays, and an observatory complex with a 25-foot telescope.

More Outdoor Adventures

Summer visitors to Sun Valley often head 7 miles north to the **Sawtooth National Recreation Area** in the state's Central Rockies, for the alpine lakes, dense forests, and nearly 600 campsites. If you come from Boise, access the area via the Ponderosa Scenic Byway, State Highway 21. At mile #125, stop to see the spectacular views of Stanley Lake Overlook. You'll soon come to the point where this scenic highway converges with State Highway 75 (Sawtooth Scenic Byway) at the town of **Stanley,** headquarters for several Salmon River outfitters. If you stop at the **Stanley Ranger Station** (208-774-3681), pick up a cassette and player that tells you about the sites as you travel south. The tape and recorder may be returned at the **Sawtooth Visitor Information Centre** (208-726-8291), just north of Ketchum and Sun Valley on Highway 75 (or pick up the tape at Sawtooth and drop it off at Stanley if you're coming from Sun Valley). The visitor center has year-round information on camping, hiking, biking, and campfire programs.

Closer to Boise, the verdant forests surrounding the city of **Cascade** and the **Payette River,** one-and-a-half hours north of Boise via Highway 55 (Payette River Scenic Route), offer more recreation. Outfitters take you down three forks of the Payette River, a popular white-water destination on half-, full-, or three-day outings.

National Oldtime Fiddlers' Contest

Toe-tapping tunes take over Weiser, Idaho, about ninety minutes west of Boise, when some of the world's best fiddle players compete at the **National Oldtime Fiddler's Contest and Festival** in June. Musicians, who come from as far away as Japan and Australia, perform ballads, waltzes, hoedowns, jigs, and other mountain music at the official programs in the high school auditorium.

But half the fun is outside. Impromptu groups jam on the sidewalks, playing rounds of stomp-your-feet and clap-your-hands ditties such as "Wrassled with a Wildcat" or "Maggots in the Sheep Hides" (feel free to sing along). On the park stage, cloggers kick up their heels and choirs belt out country tunes. The down-home Americana continues with a parade, barbecue, and a bikers' rodeo, where big boys on Harleys roar around and race barrels.

Tickets for the competition range from $3.00 to $12.00. The park events are free. Most of Weiser's limited accommodations book up a year in adance, but the town turns its parks, soccer fields, and football fields into campgrounds. More accommodations are available in Ontario, Oregon, 16 miles away.

For information: The National Oldtime Fiddlers' Contest; (800) 437-1280; www.fiddlecontest.com.

Theater, Music, and the Arts

In season, **Ballet Idaho** (208-343-0556) performs at the Morrison Center of Boise State University (BSU), 1901 University Drive. Look for classic holiday performances such as *The Nutcracker.* **The Boise Philharmonic** (208-344-7849) also plays at the Morrison Center, sometimes accompanied by **Boise Master Chorale** (208-344-7901), which also presents a series of their own concerts. The **Oinkari Basque Dancers,** an internationally known troupe, perform several times during the year in celebration of their culture.

Sports

Boise Hawks semiprofessional baseball team plays mid-June through early September at Memorial Stadium, 5600 Glenwood, at the edge of the Fairgrounds (208-322-5020). The **Idaho Steelheads,** a WCHL team, play at the Bank of America Center, Capitol Boulevard and Front Street, October through March (208-331-8497).

Shopping

Boise Towne Square Mall, on the west edge of the city, I-84 at Franklin and Cole Roads (208-378-4400), has more than 185 specialty shops, larger stores such as J.C. Penney, Sears, the Bon Marché, and Dillards, plus a fast-food court. At **Made in Idaho USA** (208-378-1188), at the mall, browse a majority of products made or grown in Idaho. Downtown shops include **Toycrafters World,** 276 North Eighth Street (208-345-2971), featuring handcrafted toys from around the world, with an emphasis on those made of wood.

Shakespeare

The **Idaho Shakespeare Festival** performs a full summer season, including one contemporary play, in an open-air amphitheater along the Boise River. Call (208) 336-9221.

Side Trips

In addition to the skiing, rafting, and other adventurous possibilities listed above, there are some shorter, tamer side trips, many of them accessible via the state-designated Scenic Byways. A popular swimming area with Boise residents is **Lucky Peak Reservoir,** 8 miles northeast on Highway 21 (208-344-0240). It has Sandy Point, a swimming beach with lifeguards, located below the dam, and a picnicking and marina area.

Continue on Highway 21 northeast to **Idaho City** (about 45 miles from Boise), a well-preserved gold rush town with many structures from the 1860s. Walk along the planked boardwalks that lead past the old jail where criminals carved their names on the wooden walls; Boise Basin Museum, with a collection of gold rush artifacts; an old schoolhouse; the Idaho World building; **The Boise Basin Mercantile,** the state's oldest general store; and other landmarks. Visit the Greater Idaho City Chamber of Commerce, 215 Montgomery Street (208-392-4148) or call the Visitor Information Center (208-392-6040).

The entire Boise Basin is surrounded by **Boise National Forest** (208-373-4007), encompassing more than two-and-a-half million acres, including 900 miles of hiking trails, the headwaters of the Boise and Payette Rivers, ghost towns, and abandoned mines. Big game roam through large areas of the forest in the summer. Cross-country skiing and snowmobiling are popular winter activities.

Special Events

Contact the Boise Convention and Visitors Bureau (800-635-5240) for information on the following.

January. Winter Carnival Week, Sun Valley.

February. Winter Carnival, nationally acclaimed week-long event with giant ice sculptures and races, McCall (about 100 miles north of Boise) .

March–October. Drag racing season at Boise's Firebird Raceway.

May–September. Wednesday entertainment, food, and music at Alive After Five, The Grove, downtown pedestrian mall.

June–August. Idaho Shakespeare Festival, Boise; Boise River Festival.

July. Fourth celebrations throughout the city parks; Liberty Parade downtown in the evening and fireworks at the Fairgrounds at dusk.

August. Western Idaho Fair, ten-day event, Boise.

September. Art in the Park displays arts and crafts, Julia Davis Park.

November. Festival of the Trees, four- or five-day event; volunteers decorate then auction trees and sell crafts, Boise Convention Center.

December. Fantasy of Lights; Holiday Lights Tour.

Where to Stay

The Boise Visitors Guide has a lodging listing, including several bed-and-breakfast inns. Here are a few choices for families.

The Owyhee Plaza Hotel, 1109 Main Street (208-343-4611, 800-821-7500—ID, or 800-233-4611). The hotel has a convenient downtown location, one hundred guest rooms, plus a courtyard swimming pool. Airport shuttle is free.

Residence Inn Marriott, 1401 Lusk Avenue (208-344-1200 or 800-331-3131). It has penthouses with a bedroom and bath on the second floor, a full kitchen, and complimentary breakfast buffet.

Doubletree Hotel Boise Downtown, 1800 Fairview Avenue, and **Doubletree Hotel Boise Riverside,** 2900 Chinden Boulevard (800-547-8010). Both have outdoor pools, coffee shops, and laundry service.

Idaho Heritage Inn, 109 West Idaho (208-342-8066). This six-room bed and breakfast close to downtown offers complimentary newspapers, full breakfast, plus bicycles.

Where to Eat

The *Boise Visitors Guide* features a dining guide.

The **Brick Oven Beanery,** Eighth and Main Street on the Grove (208-342-3456), serves regional American fare. **Red Robin Burger and Spirits Emporium,** 267 North Milwaukee (208-323-0023), gets Boise's vote for the best burgers. There's also one on the lake at Park Center, east on Beacon off Broadway (208-344-7471). Parents appreciate the children's menu and outdoor patio. For deep-dish pizza, pasta, sandwiches, and salads—all kid pleasers—try **Chicago Connection Pizza,** at two locations: 7070 Fairview (208-377-5551) and 3931 Overland (208-344-6838). Sample the Basque cuisine at **Onati,** 3544 Chinden Boulevard (208-343-6464), where specialties include lamb and seafood dishes. For tasty lunches and yummy desserts, try **Cristina's Bakery & Coffee Bar,** corner of Fifth and Main Streets (208-385-0133). Pastries, breads, and gourmet coffees are among the treats offered by this local favorite.

For More Information

For Boise travel information: **Boise Convention & Visitors Bureau/ Southwest Idaho Travel Association,** 168 North Ninth Street, Suite 200 (208-344-7777 or 800-635-5240; www.boise.org).

Emergency Numbers

Ambulance, fire, police: 911

Hospital: St. Luke's Regional Medical Center, 190 East Bannock, (208) 381-2222, twenty-four-hour emergency service

Pharmacy: The pharmacy in the twenty-four-hour Albertson's Grocery Store (208-344-8660), 1650 West State, has the latest hours in town (open until 10:00 p.m.)

Poison Control Hotline: (800) 860-0620

Northern Idaho's Panhandle

Northern Idaho, or Idaho's "panhandle," is a region of dense forests, lakes, meadows, and mountains covered with huge cedar and fir trees—a green, pristine slice of "God's country." Coeur d'Alene, in the southern part of the panhandle about 16 miles from the Washington state border, is a major resort area. For thousands of years Schee-Chu-Umsh Indians called the territory in what became Idaho's northern panhandle their home. During the early nineteenth century, as French explorers and fur traders moved through the region, the tribe came to be known as Coeur d'Alêne, French for "heart of an awl." Some speculate the Indians acquired this new name on account of their shrewd and tough trading practices. Later in the century prospectors found gold in the Coeur d'Alene Mountains. But the region earned its mark on the map with silver, a discovery that made Coeur d'Alene the hub of one of the richest mining districts in the world.

Coeur d'Alene at present names a lake, a river, a mountain range, a mining district, a forest, and a city, and the area is regarded as the "Playground of the Northwest." Sixty lakes can be found within a 60-mile radius of the city, making the region a popular summer destination. Winter brings snowmobiling, and Alpine and Nordic skiing.

Getting There

Coeur d'Alene is 35 miles east of Spokane, Washington, on I-90. Although **Coeur d'Alene Airport** at Hayden Lake provides service for small private jets, most people find access more convenient through **Spokane International,** which is located approximately forty-five minutes west of Coeur d'Alene. Vans, taxis, rental cars, and shuttles are available from both airports. **Brooks Sea Plane Service** (208-664-2842 or 208-772-9059) offers seaplane service to Coeur d'Alene.

Northern Idaho's Panhandle

AT A GLANCE

- Fish and boat on 25-mile long Lake Coeur d'Alene
- Hike and moutain bike along scenic trails
- Go underground on the Sierra Silvermine Tour in Wallace
- Coeur d'Alene-Post Falls Convention and Visitors Bureau, (800) 292-2553
- Silver County: Idaho, Montana, Washington, (888) 326-4611, www.silver-country.com

Getting Around

Unless you plan on staying in one place, a car is a necessity, as there is no public transportation. Rent a car in Spokane or in Coeur d'Alene. **OmniBus,** 2315 Monte Visa Drive, Coeur d'Alene (208-667-6664), runs group tour buses to northern Idaho attractions and provides shuttles to and from the airports.

What to See and Do

Coeur d'Alene

The major attraction is **Lake Coeur d'Alene,** a big, blue expanse stretching for 25 miles, covering 25,100 acres, and featuring 135 miles of shoreline. The **Coeur d'Alene Resort,** Second and Front (208-765-4000 or 800-826-2390), is the town's premier resort property. (See Where to Stay.) Kids like walking on the resort's 3,300-foot floating boardwalk, reputedly the world's longest. The path leads by the dock, restaurants, and boat, canoe, and kayak rental shops. A summer kid-pleaser is a tour of the lake. **Lake Coeur d'Alene Cruises,** Independence Point Dock (208-765-4000), offers narrated one-hour tours of the lake.

In the winter, boats with heated, enclosed viewing areas cruise into Beauty Bay, where migrating bald eagles stop for a salmon feast.

Canoes, kayaks, paddleboats, and Jet Skis can be rented from the **City Dock** on Independence Point. **Coeur d'Alene City Park,** Lakeside Drive

Outdoor Adventures

- **Mountain Biking, Fishing, Horseback Riding, and Swimming. Farragut State Park,** 13400 East Ranger Road, Athol (208-683-2425), is popular for its lake and outdoor activities. During World War II this area served as the second largest naval training station in the world. The 43-mile long, 1,255-foot deep Lake Pond Oreille was used for submarine testing. The grounds have a model airplane flying field and a small museum detailing the area's history.
- **Horseback Riding. Rider Ranch** (208-667-3373), a real working ranch just east of Coeur d'Alene, offers guided horseback rides on scenic trails.
- **Hiking. Q'emlin Riverside Park,** Post Falls, situated on 4 miles of the Spokane River Gorge, is a great place for easy hiking. Along some of its fourteen marked trails, you'll pass waterfalls, streams, scenic overlooks, and sheer rock outcroppings. The park has benches, picnic areas, a playground, and a lifeguarded swimming area.

  Another popular trail is the Route of the Hiawatha, a 13-mile stretch along the abandoned route of the Milwaukee Railroad between St. Regis, Montana, and the north fork of the Coeur d'Alene river near Avery, Idaho. You'll pass through eleven tunnels and cross nine trestles with great views.
- **Snowmobiling.** Wallace has been called one of the top snowmobiling locales in the west. Silver Country, 50,000 square miles of Idaho, Montana, and Washington, takes in Wallace, which is the hub of the Silver Country 1,000 Mile Trail System. Guided trips and hourly rentals are available from **Silver Country** (888-326-4611).

and First Street, has a public beach. This sandy area stretches west, joining the **North Idaho College Beach,** which offers views of the lake and the Spokane River. Along these sandy shores the Coeur d'Alene Native Americans used to camp and enjoy salmon bakes.

Tubbs Hill, Third Street and the Lake, adjacent to the Third Street City Dock, provides a scenic lookout. A 136-acre city park on land homesteaded in 1882 by German immigrant Tony Tubbs, this undeveloped bit of shoreline in Coeur d'Alene has the **Tubbs Hill Historical Nature Walk,** a 2-mile loop that affords scenic views of the lake. A trail guide is available from the Coeur d'Alene Parks Department, 221 South Fifth Street (208-769-2252).

Museums and Historic Sites

Although they are not major attractions, **Fort Sherman** and the **Museum of North Idaho** offer places to visit when your kids want something to do off the lake. Fort Sherman, North Idaho College Campus (208-664-3448), has two of Idaho's oldest structures. Construction on this frontier fort began in 1878. Built to maintain peace in this once remote, yet rapidly growing region, Fort Sherman's mission was to help establish settlements, to watch the nearby Canadian border, and to protect railroad and telegraph crews. Only three of the fort's original fifty-two buildings remain intact. Walking tours lead through an ammunition depot, officer's quarters, and a chapel.

The Museum of North Idaho, 115 Northwest Boulevard (208-664-3448), open April 1 to October 31, exhibits items and life-styles from frontier life. A blacksmith shop, an old-time kitchen, logging equipment, mineral samples, photographs of steamships, and mining and Indian culture are displayed.

Silverwood Theme Park

Set up to suggest a Victorian-era mining town, **Silverwood Theme Park** delights kids with train rides, carnival attractions, and two roller coasters. **Timber Terror,** a wooden roller coaster, travels at 55 miles per hour. **Tremors,** Silverwood's newest roller coaster, drops riders into underground tunnels and through the gift shop. At **Tinywood,** preschoolers can sample a tot-size coaster, climb on a tree house, and get into friendly water fights.

Silverwood Theme Park, North 26225 Highway 95 (208-772-0515), is 14 miles north of Coeur d'Alene.

More Attractions

Idaho's oldest public building is the **Cataldo Museum** at **Old Mission State Park** (208-682-3814). Located 35 miles east of Coeur d'Alene at exit 39 off I-90, this structure was assembled without any nails. Craftspeople used only woven straw, adobe mud, and pegs to secure the foot-thick walls and ceiling. Check the schedule for the living-history demonstrations.

Go Kart Family Fun, West 3585 Seltice (208-667-3919), keeps your kids on the fast track. Near I-90, this amusement park offers go-carts, laser tag, miniature golf, bumper boats, an ice skating rink, and an arcade. For a more serene afternoon, take a hike on some of the area's trails.

Shopping

Twenty-eight miles east of Spokane, **Prime Outlets at Post,** exit 2 off I-90 (208-773-4555), is worth a stop. Merchants include Levi's, OshKosh, London Fog, Fieldcrest, and Farberware. The malls are open daily.

Downtown Coeur d'Alene encompasses more than 350 businesses. **Harvey's Coeur d'Alene Pendleton,** Sherman and Third, sells men's and women's apparel as well as Pendleton wool blankets. **Wiggett Mall**

and Marketplace comprises 21,000 square feet of shops spread across four stories. Antiques, collectibles, artisan work, and jewelry are sold here. Even if you aren't buying, the ambience of creaking wood floors and the aromas of popcorn and coffee make window-shopping an experience. **Journey's,** Fourth and Front, features a selection of Native American goods from forty cultures. Beads, baskets, pottery, moccasins, and jewelry are sold. **The Penny Candy Store,** Sherman Avenue (208-667-0992) sells penny candy and inexpensive items of interest to kids. **One of a Kind,** Sherman Avenue (208-664-5145) sells crafts made by local artists.

Coeur d'Alene also offers the **Plaza Shops,** 210 Sherman Avenue (208-664-1111). The prices at these jewelry and clothing shops reflect their association with the Coeur d'Alene Resort.

Going Underground

If you've never been underground in a mine, don a hard hat for the **Sierra Silver Mine Tour,** 420 Fifth Street; (208-752-5151). During this one-hour guided walking tour through a mine tunnel, the guide points out such early twentieth-century equipment as the Diamond Drill machine, which drills for a core sample, and the "slusher," which brings the rock out and dumps it. The best part is the blasting board demonstration. The guide explains how the five-hole burn method was employed to ignite the dynamite that blasted through these rock walls. Special effects create the flash and boom of the blast. Buy your tickets in town and take the trolley to and from the mine. A taped narration during the ride to the mine highlights the history and the historic sites in town.

Kellogg and Wallace

East of Coeur d'Alene on I-90 are Kellogg and Wallace. **Kellogg** is best known for the **Silver Mountain** ski area (208-783-1111). With a 3.1-mile gondola trip, Silver Mountain bills itself as "the world's longest single cable ride." The area's two peaks, Kellogg and Wardner, reach 6,300 and 6,200 feet, respectively. In summer and fall the gondola ride offers scenic vistas, or you can hike and mountain bike on the trails at the summit; and on a clear day you can see Montana to the east and Canada to the north.

In winter Silver Mountain offers SKIwee classes for ages five to twelve. MINIrider is a program for seven- to twelve-year-olds who want to learn how to snowboard. Ages two through six can either play in day care or receive lessons, or combine both in the Minor's Camp.

About 50 miles from Coeur d'Alene, **Wallace,** the "Silver Capital of the World," is listed on the National Historic Register because some of its buildings are more than one hundred years old. Many feature their original cast-iron cornices, pilasters, and decorative glass. Just such features, as well as its mountain background, made Wallace the place where the movie *Dante's Peak* was shot. Remember the main street that is blasted apart by the volcano's force? That scene was shot in downtown Wallace and the scene in which the bridge collapses was shot on the Coeur d'Alene River just north of town.

During the nineteenth century, Wallace served as a Panhandle hub of mining and railroading. **The Wallace District Mining Museum,** 509 Bank Street (208-753-7151), is housed in an old bakery. Displayed are mine lighting devices ranging from stearic candles and oil lamps to more modern electric lamps as well as other tools and artifacts. A twenty-minute video, *North Idaho's Silver Legacy,* screened in the forty-person theater, shows the toil of mining.

The **Northern Pacific Railroad Museum,** Sixth and Pine Street, Old Wallace depot, Wallace (208-752-0111), focuses on the importance of railroads to this region. Most kids will find the static displays boring. The first floor re-creates the interior of a train station, complete with ticket window, a telegrapher's desk, and heavy oak waiting benches. Upstairs exhibits depict the route of the North Coast Limited. The museum has a rare, 13-foot glass map of the Northern Pacific Railroad. Kids giggle at the early 1900s high tank flush toilet.

July Powwow

The **July-amsh Powwow,** Post Falls at the Greyhound Park (800-523-2464), is one of the largest powwows in the United States. Hundreds of dancing and drumming Native Americans compete wearing full regalia. Storytellers relate Indian legends and craftspeople sell traditional jewelry, clothing, and other items. The venue is air conditioned.

Avoid the **Oasis Rooms Bordello Museum,** 605 Cedar Street, Wallace (208-753-0801). The twenty- to thirty-minute guided tour through one of Wallace's most famous brothels simply features peeks at several 1950s tacky bedrooms. The gift shop downstairs, along with some revealing lingerie, has a collection of interesting books about strong women pioneers and trail-blazers in the West.

Side Trips

Spokane, 35 miles west of Coeur d'Alene, offers several family-friendly attractions. Many consider **Waterfront Park** to be the city's centerpiece. This one-hundred-acre tract of paths, cut through by the river, features amusement rides, mini-golf, an ice rink, and an IMAX theater. But the best known attraction in the park is the still operational **Looff Carousel,** a 1909 antique carousel with fifty-four hand-carved horses. The **Centennial Trail** follows the Spokane River from Riverside Park to Coeur d'Alene, Idaho.

Cheney Cowles Museum and Historic Campbell House, 2316 West First Avenue (509-456-3931), has exhibits concerning the development of the Northwest region and local Indian cultures. Changing shows include traditional and contemporary arts and historical and current issues exhibitions.

Hidden Creek Ranch

If you like dude ranches but you want more than just riding, then hightail it to **Hidden Creek Ranch,** where the rodeos mix with Native American lore and the riding instruction is innovative.

At Hidden Creek you can trot, walk, and canter through a pristine Idaho wilderness of Rocky Mountains cut with clear running streams. The head wrangler's mantra—"the horse is the mirror of the rider"—pins the trail problems squarely on your doing. By the third time you head out, you learn not to blame Pokey Joe's staccato steps on a bad hay day, but on your stiff body language and short reins. Such new sensitivity about the horse/rider partnership makes you better at everything from riding the range to racing barrels.

But even the best cowboy needs some time out of the saddle. Along with trapshooting and fishing, you can sample the Indian part of the West. Try a sweat lodge, take a medicine trail hike, and learn a sacred circle dance.

And did we mention such cushy vacation accoutrements as massages, maid service, comfortable rooms in modern log cabins, waiters, and an evening cocktail hour? With a capacity of forty to fifty guests, including children, Hidden Creek is large enough to hire experienced wranglers and small enough to pay particular attention to its guests. The caveat: putting up with a somewhat rigid schedule of meals, meetings, and rides. Nevertheless, you will have fun, on and off the horse, and you'll come away a better rider. From mid-June through August there's a kids' program for age three through teens. The typical package is six days. From Coeur d'Alene, Hidden Creek Ranch is 30 miles south of I-90 along I-95.

Information: **Hidden Creek Ranch,** (800) 446-DUDE, or call **American Wilderness Experience,** (800) 444-DUDE.

Don't miss **Cat Tales Endangered Species Conservation Park,** North 17020 Newport Highway, Mead (509-238-4126; www.spokane.net/cattales). On this four-acre preserve north of Spokane, paths weave through natural habitats dedicated to big cats. Residents include bobcats, Bengal tigers, leopards, panthers, and mountain lions. Arrive late in the afternoon to catch the educational demonstration and feeding time, when the cats are most active.

Spokane's Manito Park & Gardens, 4 West Twenty-first Avenue (509-625-6622), is an urban landscape of five gardens. Duncan Garden is a formal garden, with roots dating back to ancient Egypt, Persia, and

Rome. Annual plantings begin in May and peak from mid-July through early October. Rose Hill blooms with 1,500 roses. There are also beds of antique and miniature roses. Joel E. Ferris Perennial Garden displays perennials native to the Northwest. Spokane/Nishinomiya Japanese Garden is a serene place, whose design is meant to soothe. Gaiser Conservatory couples tropical foliage with floral displays.

North of Spokane Highway 20, **Gardner Cave,** part of Crawford State Park (509-446-4065 or 800-562-0990), is the second largest limestone cave in Washington. The chambers were created about 70 million years ago, when rock collapsed as mountains were forming. Walks through the stalagmites and stalactites are guided by park staff.

For more information contact the Spokane Convention and Visitors Bureau, 926 West Sprague Street 180, Spokane (509-624-1341; www.spokane-areacvb.org).

Special Events

May. American Heritage Days; Huck Finn River Fest.

July. Bayview Daze lighted boat show; Historic Skills Fair.

August. International Water Fight Competition; Festival of the Falls; Northern Idaho Fair and Rodeo.

September. Paul Bunyan Days.

Where to Stay

Coeur d'Alene Resort, Second and Front (208-765-4000 or 800-826-2390), is the area's most well-known property. Built in 1986, this 338-room hotel added upscale accommodations to a resort area previously dominated by quaint, yet charming, bed and breakfasts and the ubiquitous chain motels. The resort's facilities include two swimming pools, a fitness center, a spa, tennis courts, and a watersports center. An eighteen-hole golf course—with the world's only floating green—is shared with its adjacent sister resort. Both welcome families.

While there are more than a dozen cozy B&Bs in the area, few will permit children younger than twelve. **O'Neils Bed and Breakfast,** 1221 Coeur d'Alene Avenue (208-664-5356), has only a handful of rooms, but it is one of the few that welcomes children. Rooms are wallpapered with sheet music, and each comes with vinyl records and record players. The suite has a separate kitchen and sitting area with cable TV. There is a dog kennel beyond the house for pets.

In Hayden a family-friendly bed-and-breakfast inn is the **Clark House on Hayden Lake,** East 4550 South Hayden Lake Road (208-772-3470 or

800-765-4593). Among the more than a dozen campgrounds is **Coeur d'Alene KOA Kampgrounds,** East 10700 Wolf Lodge Bay Road (208-664-4471). Facilities include Kamping Kabins and Teepee, terraced sites, and separate tenting areas. There is a heated pool, a hot tub for adults, miniature golf, a playground, a game room, and bike rentals.

Where to Eat

Visitors Plus+, the Coeur d'Alene Chamber of Commerce, provides a restaurant guide. Some suggestions include **Heathcliff,** 301 East Lakeside (208-667-0269), a deli making soups, salads, hot and cold sandwiches, and desserts. Try the Grubsteak Chili, a one-hundred-year-old recipe passed down from Aunt Tillie, who moved into the region with her husband, Gus, in the 1800s. Another good sandwich shop is **Java,** 324 Sherman Avenue (208-667-0010). It serves cereal, eggs, and baked goods for breakfast. Hot and cold sandwiches, soup, and pizza top its lunch menu. **Applebee's,** 280 West Appleway (208-762-1000), is open brunch through dinner. Signature items include Bourbon Street steak, low-fat veggie quesadilla, and blackened chicken salad. Hamburgers, sandwiches, and fajitas are also on the menu. **IHOP,** 2301 North Fourth Street (208-765-5032); **Pizza Hut,** 212 West Appleway (208-765-5032); and **Kentucky Fried Chicken,** 218 Appleway (208-664-3838), are among the fast-food standbys.

In Wallace you can rustle up some cheap, kid-pleasing fare at the **Pizza Factory,** Bank Street (208-753-9003). Along with pizzas you can get pasta, sandwiches, calzone, and kids' plates. Adjacent is **Mrs. Dean's Old-Fashioned Ice Cream Parlor.** Not only do children like the sundaes, they also like sitting on the high stools. The **Historic Jameson Saloon,** Pine and Sixth Streets (208-556-1554), looks like a turn-of-the-century Western saloon, with its ceiling fans and brass-trimmed wooden banquettes. The moderately priced burgers, salads, chicken fingers, and pasta make this a good family pick.

For More Information

Visitors Plus+, P.O. Box 850, Coeur d'Alene 83816; (208) 664-3194

Kellogg Chamber of Commerce, 608 Bunker Avenue, Kellogg 83837; (208) 784-0821

Coeur d'Alene–Post Falls Convention and Visitor Bureau, 510 East Sixth, Post Falls 83854; (800) 292-2553

Wallace Chamber of Commerce, P.O. Box 1167, Wallace 83873; (208) 753-7151

Silver Country (888) 326-4611; www.silver-country.com

Idaho's Internet site: www.doc.state.id.us.

Emergency Numbers

Police, fire, and medical emergencies: 911

Coeur d'Alene Police Department: (208) 769-2320

Coeur d'Alene Fire Department: (208) 765-1112

Kootenai Medical Center: 2003 Lincoln Way, Coeur d'Alene; (208) 666-2000 or (208) 664-3000

7 Illinois

CHICAGO

Chicago, one of the Midwest's most popular destinations, offers great architecture and art, world-class museums, a top-notch aquarium, and miles of lakefront and bicycle paths. Stroll through the parks and the zoo, pedal by the lake, take a boat ride, and play ball on the beach. In this exciting city you and your kids won't be bored. Take your family on weekends when hotels are discounted, or be sure to bring the kids along on a business trip so that all of you can savor this dynamic city.

GETTING THERE

O'Hare International Airport (773-686-2200), 17 miles from the Loop, is served by most major airlines. The **Chicago Transit Authority** (CTA; 312-836-7000) offers train transportation between Chicago and O'Hare. Train service originates beneath O'Hare Terminals 1, 2, and 3, and in Chicago at the Dearborn Subway station. **Midway Airport** (773-838-0600), 15 minutes from the Loop at 5700 South Cicero Avenue, is the second most traveled airport in Chicago. A one-hundred-year-old plan will come to completion with the Northerly Island Park, on which construction has just begun. Formerly the site of Meigs Field, a landing strip for private planes, the park will feature a botanic garden, ball fields, marinas, and a wildlife refuge.

Amtrak (800-USA-RAIL) stops at Chicago's Union Station, 210 South Canal Street (312-558-1075). **Continental Bus Airport Service** (312-454-7800) shuttles to and from Chicago's main airports. **Greyhound/Trailways** buses (312-781-2900) stop at Chicago station, 630 West Harrison Street.

The main highways to Chicago are I-90, which cuts across Chicago's northwest axis and becomes the Chicago Skyway south of the Loop; I-94 (the Dan Ryan Expressway), which runs north-south. From the south, take I-55 (Stevenson Expressway) and I-57. From the west, take I-294 west of Chicago and I-88.

Chicago

AT A GLANCE

- See sharks, whales, dolphins, sea otters, and thousands of fish at the John H. Shedd Aquarium and Oceanarium
- Stroll the lakefront parks and the zoo
- Explore Egyptian tombs, Pacific cultures, and the world of bugs at the Field Museum of Natural History
- Go on an animated fly-through of the Milky Way at the Adler Planetarium and Astronomy Museum
- Chicago Office of Tourism, (312) 744-2400, www.ci.chi.ilus/tourism

GETTING AROUND

The key to Chicago's streets is to know where you are in relation to Lake Michigan, due east of the city, which looms like an inland ocean. Chicago's north-south axis is Madison Avenue, and its east-west axis is State Street. As you move away from these streets, addresses increase 100 for each block. The city is in a grid pattern, so it's easy to find your way around.

Chicago's elevated train system, fondly called the "El," operates six routes throughout the city and suburbs. For information contact RTA Travel Information Center at (312) 322-6777 or (800) 972-7000, or the CTA office (312-836-7000) on the seventh floor of the Merchandise Mart. Fares can be paid in cash or in tokens, which are offered at, among other places, Jewel and Dominick's grocery stores.

CTA buses (312-836-7000) travel along Chicago's major streets. For both the bus and the El, senior citizens, the physically challenged, and children seven to eleven receive discounted fares and transfers. Kids six and younger ride for free. For a **PACE** bus (312-836-7000), which provides additional service, wait at the blue-and-white PACE signs. PACE transfer tickets are valid for El trains. The hearing impaired can get transportation information by dialing TDD (312) 836-4949.

METRA offers train service from the suburbs into the city, with eleven commuter routes transporting riders from 225 outlying stations to four

Chicago stations. Call (312) 322-6777 weekdays from 8:00 A.M. to 5:00 P.M., (312) 836-7000 evenings and weekends.

In inclement weather, one of the best ways to get around Chicago is using a series of underground walkways called **Pedways.** Under the Illinois Center at Michigan Avenue and the Michigan Avenue Bridge can be found a network of walkways that lead to stores in the Loop area as well as the major train stations. There are also entrance elevators in Loop buildings and subway stations. Maps of the Pedways are available in hotels at the Illinois Center.

Sometimes the easiest and quickest way to get somewhere is by boat. **Wendella Commuter Boats,** Michigan Avenue Bridge at the Wrigley Building (312-337-1446), offers boat taxi service on the Chicago River at prices competitive with CTA transit. Boats leave every ten minutes from a commuter dock at Madison Avenue, or from the Wendella dock at the Michigan Avenue Bridge below the Wrigley Building during rush hour. Besides its seven-minute Madison-Wrigley Building route, the company offers extended trips into Lake Michigan, as well as two-hour, ninety-minute, and one-hour guided tours. Senior citizens and kids under eleven receive discounted tickets.

What to See and Do

Must-See Museums

At the **Museum of Science and Industry,** Fifty-seventh Street and Lake Shore Drive (773-684-1414; TDD 773-986-2302; www.mschicago.org), the diverse exhibits take you on a fun tour of fact and fantasy. A walk through a U-505 German submarine captured in 1944 makes the hard-to-envision world of undersea gauges, gizmos, and cramped quarters real. Browse silent-screen-star Colleen Moore's elaborate Fantasy Castle. With its tapestries, and more than 1,000 miniature pieces, this dollhouse delights the child within and the one by your side. Explore the human body by walking through a 20-foot pulsating heart and by looking at fetuses floating in bottles.

Train buffs won't want to leave the model train exhibit, with its eight railroads that run through reconstructed sets of the Midwest, the Great Plains, the Grand Canyon, and California. Find your way to the model of the 1930s Pioneer Zephyr (located in the lowest level of the parking garage), America's first diesel-electric, stainless steel passenger train.

Two more picks are the OMNIMAX theater, with its five-story-high dome screen, and, for kids ages seven to twelve, the Kids Stairway, a Path to Self Discovery. This interactive exhibit is designed to build children's self-esteem, help them discover feelings, and teach them about alcohol and substance abuse. A visit here serves as a start to important discus-

John G. Shedd Aquarium and Oceanarium

John G. Shedd Aquarium and Oceanarium is one of the world's largest indoor marine mammal habitats. Kids really enjoy this undersea world of brightly colored fish, coral reefs, turtles, sea otters, dolphins, and whales. More than 2,000 aquatic animals representing 650 species from North America, the Caribbean, Asia, Africa, and Australia are on exhibit.

- **Coral Reef Tank.** Green moray eels slither out of crevices, hawksbill turtles float lazily, silver barracudas and sharks zigzag through the water, and schools of rainbow-colored tropical fish swim in this 90,000-gallon tank. At 11:00 A.M. and 2:00 P.M., watch the action as divers feed the fish.
- **Indo-Pacific Gallery.** Admire such brightly colored wrigglers as the yellow longsnout butterfly fish and the white-and-brown spotted clown fish.
- **Oceanarium.** With its sweeping view of Lake Michigan, the Oceanarium dazzles. The facility re-creates a Pacific Northwest coastal environment. Walk through a mini rain forest, accompanied by the sounds of chirping birds, crickets, and waterfalls. Sea otters swim in tidal pools. There are beluga whales and a colony of penguins. Five times daily at the dolphin shows in the amphitheater, learn why dolphins lobtail (slap their tails on the water), breach, porpoise (leap out of the water and enter again), and tail walk (move backward on their tails).
- **Family overnights.** On special family overnights (register in advance) you get close to the animals without the crowds, learn about marine life at naturalist-led workshops, and fall asleep to the soothing sight of hundreds of tropical fishing gliding by.

John G. Shedd Aquarium and Oceanarium, 1200 South Lake Shore Drive; (312) 939–2438; www.sheddnet.org.

sions you and your children continue later.

For another, less intense take-home "item," visit the gift shop, where your kids can bring home a bit of science fun with a physics game, a rocket model kit, an anatomical coloring book, stickers, and puzzles.

The **Adler Planetarium and Astronomy Museum,** 1300 South Lake Shore Drive (312–322–0304 or TDD 312–322–0995; www.astro.uchicago.edu/adler), as of January 1999, has an entire new look and a new way to explore the stars and planets, with the opening of its Sky Pavilion, a 60,000-square-foot addition to the existing museum. Four galleries and the StarRider Theater take visitors through a 3-D computer-animated fly-through of the Milky Way Galaxy, into the Solar Observatory and its live images of sunspots and solar flares, and through a 4,500-square-foot exhibit of our own solar system. In the StarRider Theater, kids also enjoy viewing computer-generated animations that allow them to react to what they're seeing and to use controls on the armrests of their chairs to change the outcome.

Sky Shows shuttle visitors through fifteen million years of galactic history to revisit the origins of the universe. As part of the Evening Sky Shows, which occur each Friday night, the planetarium gives close-up looks at the moon, planets, and galaxies via the planetarium's 20-inch telescope, which is hooked up to a large-screen closed-circuit monitor.

Heavenly is what you're likely to call the art at the **Art Institute of Chicago,** Michigan Avenue at Adams Street (312-443-3600 or TDD 312-443-3890; www.artic.edu). Spanning more than forty centuries from Mayan to modern, this place is a visual treat. Among the highlights are the prized collection of French impressionist and post impressionist paintings by Degas, Monet, and Renoir, the extensive collections of classical, American and Asian art, Marc Chagall's stained-glass work *American Windows,* and the Thorne Miniature Rooms, which are replicas in miniature of European (late sixteen to twentieth centuries) and American (seventeenth century to the 1930s) decorative arts and architectural interiors.

The Institute's **Kraft Education Center,** a just-for-kids-and-families place that has changing exhibitions, a computer, storytelling, and often hands-on workshops, also features an exhibit explaining the paintings of artists such as van Gogh and Monet in terms children can understand. Tuesdays are free admission days at the Art Institute.

If the Art Institute piqued your interest in the arts, then head to the **Museum of Contemporary Art,** 220 East Chicago Avenue (312-280-2660; www.mcachicago.org). The facility boasts one of the nation's largest collections of art created since 1945, with works by Francis Bacon, Ann Hamilton, Jasper Johns, Jeff Koons, Andy Warhol, and Alexander Calder. A 1996 addition gave MCA seven times the exhibit space and includes a gift shop, bookstore, restaurant, 300-seat theater (where kids can enjoy viewing older movies and comparing them to present-day films), and a terraced sculpture garden with a great view of Lake Michigan. Classes for children and family workshops are regularly held; ask for a schedule.

The city's history comes alive at the **Chicago Historical Society,** Clark Street at North Avenue (312-642-4600; www.chicagohistory.org). Learn about pioneer life in the Illinois Pioneer Life Gallery, where the daily activities of early settlers are brought to life through demonstrations of household and farmyard chores. Or climb aboard the *Pioneer,* the first twelve-ton

Field Museum of Natural History

Across the street from the Shedd Aquarium, the **Field Museum of Natural History** is an amazing place. Housed in a 1921 building that museum officials claim to be the largest marble structure in the United States, the museum's exhibits are interesting and interactive. There's too much here for one visit, so let your kids hit the highlights, pausing at what intrigues them.

- **Inside Ancient Egypt** demystifies and explains the ancient burial rites. Walk into a re-created Egyptian tomb and learn about mummies, hieroglyphic, and embalming. See your face transformed with "Egyptian" features and find out the symbolism of the pyramid.
- **Traveling the Pacific** brings you to the world of outrigger canoes, intricately carved masks, and a re-created Tahitian market.
- **Into the Wild** takes you through habitats as diverse as prairies, wetlands, lakes, and cliffs to learn about birds and other critters.
- **Living Together** focuses on how people of different cultures deal with the issues of home, self-image, and community using videos, dioramas, and interactive displays throughout the exhibit.
- **Underground Adventure** gives visitors a chance to explore the fascinating world of soil from a "bug's-eye" perspective, with a Micro Soil Lab (a soil environment re-created at one hundred times life-size). You can see an earwig mother guarding her babies and come eye to eye with a crayfish burrowing to the water table. In the exhibit's Mud Room area, kids can examine real soil creatures.
- The **McDonald's Fossil Preparation Laboratory** is a new state-of-the-art facility. Through windows, watch museum preparators at work on *Sue,* the largest and most complex Tyrannosaurus rex ever found. (Sue's completely prepared skeleton is scheduled to be mounted for display in the year 2000.) A reading rail below the lab's windows helps explain the tools and techniques used in the preparation process.
- **Family Overnights** enable you to roam through the museum after-hours as part of a workshop. Select from such diverse themes as how to read Egyptian hieroglyphic, recognize dinosaur footprints, or identify owl calls. After a snack, listen to a storyteller recount Eskimo or African legends or go on a treasure hunt. When the lights go out, you might join a group for a flashlight tour of the

(continued)

Field Museum of Natural History *(continued)*

Egyptian tombs or walk into the prairies, oceans, and forests of "Into the Wild." Then cuddle up in your sleeping bag, maybe next to a bushman or the gorilla, or among the thousands of mounted birds. Family overnights generally occur each month. Fees are charged and you must book well in advance (312-322-8854).

Field Museum of Natural History, Roosevelt Road, Lake Shore Drive; (312) 922-9410; www.fmnh.org.

locomotive to steam through this railroad town, and find out what Mrs. O'Leary's cow did or didn't do in the Great Chicago Fire of 1871.

In the Hands-On-History Gallery, children can trade animal pelts for tin utensils, shop from one of the first Sears catalogs, and bang shoes or tap on a typewriter to create sound effects for a radio show. In the exhibit Go West, interactive displays simulate boarding a train and heading west. America in the Age of Lincoln offers a chance to learn about slavery and the destructive power of the Civil War, plus see the bed upon which Lincoln died.

More Attractions and Views

A Chicago institution of another sort is Frank Lloyd Wright. At the **Frank Lloyd Wright Historic District Visitors Center,** 158 North Forest Avenue, Oak Park 60301 (708-848-1500), take a guided tour of this architect's home and studio, and see the birthplace of the Prairie School of architecture. Wright's vision and others made this midwest city famous for its buildings.

From the **Sears Tower Skydeck,** Jackson Boulevard between Franklin Street and Wacker Drive (312-875-9696), or from 1,000 feet up in the **John Hancock Center Observatory,** 875 North Michigan Avenue (312-751-3681), enjoy a panoramic view of Chicago, which on a clear day can include a glimpse of Michigan, Indiana, and maybe even Wisconsin.

For some great skyline views, visit the **Navy Pier,** 600 East Grand Avenue (312-595-1000). The Pier also features a 150-foot-high **Ferris wheel,** a musical carousel, a large-screen **IMAX theater,** the 1,500-seat **Skyline Stage** (312-595-PIER) for music and entertainment, and **Crystal Gardens.** From the Navy Pier you can board a Lake Michigan boat cruise for a spectacular view of Chicago's world-famous skyline.

The **Chicago Children's Museum** at Navy Pier, 600 East Grand Avenue (312-527-1000; www.chichildrensmuseum.org), offers a playful

The exhibits at Chicago's Field Museum of Natural History will intrigue adults and kids alike.

place where kids can try their hands at inventing (the Inventing Lab), construct a dam on a river (WaterWays), role-play in a Chicago Fire Department ambulance (Safe & Sound), climb a rope ladder from the deck to the crow's nest of a lake-faring vessel (the Kovler Family Schooner) and much, much more. Of special interest is Dinosaur Dis-

Make a Deal

Watch the art of the deal at Chicago's big three exchanges. From visitor's galleries look at the bustling floor frenzy at the **Chicago Board of Trade,** 141 West Jackson Boulevard (312-435-3590), open 8:00 A.M. to 2:00 P.M. It's the oldest and largest futures exchange. The **Chicago Mercantile Exchange,** 30 South Wacker Drive (312-930-8249), is open 7:30 A.M. to 3:15 P.M.; and you can visit the **Chicago Board Options Exchange** at 400 South LaSalle Street (312-786-5600), from 8:30 A.M. to 3:15 P.M.

covery, an exhibit featuring a 100-million-year-old dinosaur in the Great Hall. Visitors can play the role of paleontologist by piecing together the claw and bones of the creature's forelimb, comparing the cast skeleton to a small flesh model, and learning how the expedition team unearthed twenty-five tons of bone and rock to find the remains. Also check the schedule for crafts workshops so your kids can create their own special Chicago souvenir.

Opening in the fall of 1999 is the **Nature Museum** at the **Chicago Academy of Sciences,** Fullerton Parkway and Cannon Drive (773-549-0606; www.chias.org), an environmental museum where people can explore nature in exhibits such as the Butterfly Haven (a 28-foot-tall greenhouse with live butterflies and moths), City Science (a two-story house whose infrastructure has been peeled away so you can meet the creatures that live in city homes), and Wilderness Walk (where you can walk through a variety of different ecosystems). In the Children's Gallery, a kid-friendly area designed specially for ages three to eight, kids can dig under the prairie or swim into a beaver lodge (and not get soaked) with underground and aboveground displays where your family can talk, read, think, and wonder.

A museum of a very different kind is found at the **Chicago Car Exchange,** 14085 West Rockland Road, Libertyville (847-680-1950; www.specialcar.com/cce), 35 miles north of downtown Chicago. A must for any car lover, the Exchange has more than 200 collectible cars to see and/or buy, such as a 1965 Thunderbird convertible, a 1932 Chrysler coupe, a 1952 Mercedes-Benz cabriolet, and a 1916 Ford Roadster.

If you happen to be stuck with kids at O'Hare International Airport, the world's busiest airport, then drop by the **Kids on the Fly Children's Museum**. There is an air-traffic-control tower that has an actual air-traffic-control recording, as well as an exhibit where kids can pass layover time by building skyscrapers with Duplo blocks. Kids can pretend to be pilots in a cargo plane that has a special treasure in it. While your kids play, you can check on the status of your flight at the museum's information center. The interactive museum is located in Terminal 2.

Parks, Gardens, and Zoos

Parks along the lakefront were part of Chicago's design. These include **Lincoln Park, Grant Park, Burnham Park, Jackson Park,** and **Washington Park.** All have playing fields and usually host a festival or two

Outdoor Art

Some of Chicago's most interesting and expressive art is found in its outdoor sculpture. Take a walk around the Loop and pleasure in the following works.

- The **Picasso sculpture,** Richard J. Daley Center, 50 West Washington Street, was a gift to the people of Chicago from the artist. The 50-foot-tall, 162-ton rust-colored steel work is of cubist design and completely unexplained. Some say it's a woman's head; others say it's Picasso's pet Afghan hound. On summer weekdays at noon, there's a free performing arts presentation in front of the sculpture.
- On the Clark Street side of Daley Plaza, in front of the James R. Thompson Center, 100 West Randolph Street, is a black-and-white 29-foot-tall round fiberglass piece, ***Monument with Standing Beast*** by Jean Dubuffet.
- Looking across Daley Plaza to Washington Street you'll see ***Miro's Chicago,*** Joan Miro's forklike interpretation of the Windy City.
- ***Flamingo*** by Alexander Calder, in front of the Dirksen Building at the Federal Plaza on Dearborn, between Adams and Jackson Streets, is 53 feet tall, constructed of ¾-inch-thick steel plates, and is one piece of art that can be walked through. Calder chose the name "Flamingo" because, he said, the work was "sort of pink and has a long neck."
- Mark Chagall's mosaic ***The Four Seasons,*** at One North Dearborn in front of the First National Bank, is made of hand-chipped stone and glass fragments and was restored in 1990 at a cost of $1 million.

throughout the year. Grant Park hosts the Taste of Chicago Festival in July, the Blues Fest in June, and a Jazz Fest in September. An 18-mile bike path cuts through these parks and offers scenic views of both the lake and Chicago's skyline; for more information on the park's bike path, call (312) 744-8092.

From November through March, take the family ice skating on the **State Ice Rink** at State and Randolph Streets (312-744-3370). You can rent skates and enjoy hot chocolate at downtown Chicago's free-admission ice rink.

Brookfield Zoo, First Avenue and Thirty-first Street, Brookfield (708-485-0263; www.brookfieldzoo.org), 14 miles west of downtown Chicago, is known for its innovative naturalistic exhibits and its international role in animal breeding and conservation. Covering 216 acres,

Brookfield features more than 2,200 animals, including 150 species of mammals and 120 species of reptiles and amphibians. Visit Tropic World and the Fragile Kingdom for Brookfield's most ambitious attempts at re-creating nature. Tropic World portrays life in the three great rain forests: Africa, Asia, and South America. The exhibit features a mixture of fauna, free-roaming small animals, exotic birds, and three daily thunderstorms. The Fragile Kingdom highlights desert, rain forest, and mountainous regions. The Seven Seas Planetarium features a 2,000-seat indoor dolphinarium, with bottle-nosed dolphins on display. Outside the dolphinarium, visitors can wander rocky shores that replicate the Pacific Northwest and watch walrus, seals, and sea lions. The Children's Zoo offers tame animals to pet and hands-on activities, like Be a Bird, where kids can test their ability to fly using a flying strength machine. And don't miss the zoo's newest exhibit, Habitat Africa! During the winter, there are heated tours of the zoo aboard the Snowball Express. Brookfield Zoo can be accessed by I-55 and I-290 (Stevenson and Eisenhower Expressways), as well as I-294 (Tri-State Tollway).

Chicago Botanic Garden, Lake Cook Road, ½ mile east of I-90-94 (Edens Expressway), Glencor; (847) 835-5440. This blooming, 300-acre wonder contains a sensory garden for the visually impaired, a nine-acre prairie and nature trail, and a three-island authentic Japanese Garden. Be sure to visit the greenhouses, gift shop, and the Museum of Floral Arts. Ask about scheduled hands-on activities for children and the garden's seasonal festivals.

Minutes north of downtown, the **Lincoln Park Zoo,** 2200 North Cannon Drive (312-742-2000; www.lpzoo.com), is the place to bring your kids for a city safari. Take a close look at a swimming polar bear, elephants, rhinos, giraffes, gorillas, orangtuns, and chimpanzees. With more than 1,000 animals from around the world and scheduled feedings throughout the day, this is a great place for kids to get to know about the animal kingdom. For the wee ones, head for the Pritzker Children's Zoo, where they can pet tame animals and learn about wildlife.

Tours

For **Architecture/Walking** tours of the city contact the following: **Chicago Architecture Foundation,** 224 South Michigan Avenue (312-922-3432; www.architecture.org); **Charnley-Persky House Tours,** 1354 North Astor Street (312-573-1365); **Chicago Cultural Center Architectural Tours,** Chicago Cultural Center, 78 East Washington Street (312-346-3278); **Oak Park Tour Center/Frank Lloyd Wright Tour,** 951 Chicago Avenue, Oak Park (708-848-1500 or 708-848-1976); and **Pullman Historic District,** 11111 South Forrestville Avenue (773-785-8181).

Boat Tours. Chicago's First Lady, southwest corner and lower level of the Michigan Avenue Bridge and Wacker Drive (708-358-1330), offers lunch, brunch, and dinner tours of Chicago sailing aboard the ***Chicago's First Lady*** 1920s-style luxury cruiser. **Mercury, Chicago's Skyline Cruiseline,** southwest corner and lower level of the Michigan Avenue Bridge (312-332-1353), offers daily one-hour, ninety-minute, or two-hour cruises and skyline tours during the morning, afternoon, and evening from May 1 through October 1 (ask about the Pirate Cruise for Kids). **Chicago from the Lake,** North Pier Terminal, 455 East Illinois Street (312-527-1977 or 527-2002), offers a ninety-minute tour of the Chicago River or the Chicago skyline; both tours are led by a member of the Chicago Architecture Foundation. Available May 1 to October 1.

Gangsters

Untouchable Tour's **Chicago's Original Gangster Tour** takes you back to Chicago's gangster days. Visit Al Capone's, John Dillinger's, and Bugs Moran's notorious hangouts and hit spots. For reservations call (773) 881-1195.

Bus Tours. **Gray Line Sightseeing Tours** (312-251-3107) offers daily comprehensive tours, as does Chicago Motor Coach (312-666-1000). Chicago Motor Coach also offers a ninety-minute double-decker bus tour of the city, with eight stops along the way where you can get off or on throughout the day. Stops include the Sears Tower, the Art Institute, the Field Museum, the Navy Pier, the Water Tower, Michael Jordan's restaurant, State and Washington (shopping area), and Wacker and Michigan (hotel area).

For a slow-paced, sweet, horse-drawn tour in a buggy, see the **Chicago Horse and Carriage Company,** southeast corner of Pearson Street and Michigan Avenue (312-94-HORSE); or try the **Noble Horse,** available at the southwest corner of Pearson and Michigan (312-266-7878).

Shopping

Hit the Magnificent Mile's shops along Michigan Avenue, from the Chicago River north to Oak Street. If you have time for just one stop, you might visit **Water Tower Place,** 835 North Michigan Avenue (312-440-3165), which has department stores such as Marshall Field's and Lord & Taylor, as well as specialty shops such as Benetton, Laura Ashley, a Disney Store, Beauty and the Beast, F.A.O. Schwarz, and, for snacks, Aunt Diana's Old Fashioned Fudge, Mrs. Field's Cookies, and California Pizza Kitchen.

For the budget-minded State Street also includes TJ Maxx and Filene's Basement. Kids can play in Toys "R" Us and the Sharper Image. Restaurants in the area offer everything from famous Chicago-style pizza to Chinese and Thai food.

Chicago Talk Shows

If being a member of a talk show audience sounds like fun, Chicago offers three of the largest shows to choose from:

- **Oprah Winfrey Show**, Harpo Studios, 1058 West Washburn Street; (312) 591-9222
- **Jenny Jones Show,** NBC Tower, 454 North Columbus Drive; (312) 836-9485
- **Jerry Springer Show,** NBC Tower, 454 North Columbus Drive; (312) 321-5365.

Call at least two weeks in advance for tickets.

Performing Arts

Chicago offers cutting-edge theater, good comedy, and well-done plays. Home to some of the best are the **Steppenwolf Theatre,** 2851 North Halstead (312-472-4141); **Second City,** 1616 North Wells (312-337-3992); and **Second City Children's Theater.** Around Christmas, the **Goodman Theater,** 125 East Monroe Avenue (312-855-1524), puts on *A Christmas Carol;* and the **Arie Crown Theater,** McCornick Place (312-791-6000), hosts *The Nutcracker* ballet.

Some children's theaters include the **Animart Puppet Theater,** 3901 North Kedzie Avenue (312-267-1209); **The Children's Theatre Fantasy Orchard** (Chicago Historical Society), 1629 North Clark Street (312-539-4211); and **DePaul Merle Reskin Theatre,** 60 East Balbo Drive (312-362-8455). **Hystopolis Puppet Theater,** 441 West North Avenue (312-787-7387), offers sophisticated puppet plays, and the **Stage Left Theater,** 3244 North Clark Street (312-883-8830), offers plays about social issues aimed at kids. Check local listings or call the **Theater Information Line** at (312) 977-1755.

The **Chicago Symphony Orchestra,** as well as other orchestras and singers, perform at the **Civic Opera House** (312-346-0270) and the **Lyric Opera House** (312-332-2244), both located at 20 North Wacker Drive.

Looking for art galleries? Head to Chicago's "Su-Hu" district, located aptly enough at the intersection of Superior and Huron Streets.

What child wouldn't enjoy a performance of *The Nutcracker* or *Swan Lake?* Now you can see the famous Joffrey Ballet of New York, which moved to Chicago in the spring of 1996.

More Useful Numbers. **Hot Tix** booths are at 24 South State Street, Chicago; 1020 Lake, Oak Park; and 1616 Sherman Avenue, Evanston. They offer half-price day-of-performance and full-price advance tickets for theater, music, dance, and all TicketMaster events. Call (312) 977-1755 for hours and additional booth locations. **TicketMaster** (312-559-8989 or 559-1212) offers full-price tickets for theater, dance, and musical events.

Lake Geneva

Lake Geneva (www.wistravel.com/lakegnva.html), a Wisconsin lakeside community, is an easy ninety-minute drive northwest of the city with much to offer families:

- **Lake Geneva Cruise Line** (800-558-5911 or 414-248-6206) offers daily tours of the lake, including a brunch cruise aboard *Belle of the Lake,* a replica of a turn-of-the-century lake steamer that leaves from Rieviera Docks for a three-hour tour past Victorian boathouses and lakeside estates. A walk-and-cruise option allows you to walk part of the 26-mile walking trail that encircles the lake and then hop on board for brunch and the remainder of the cruise.
- **Uncle John's Fun Park,** 1275 Townline Road (414-248-6200), has a go-kart track, miniature golf, and multispeed batting cages.
- At the **Grand Geneva Resort Hotel** (800-558-3417; www.grandgeneva.com) you can enjoy a spa, golfing, horseback riding, fitness classes, tennis, and the Grand Adventure Kids Club, a supervised children's program.
- Lake Geneva's **Main Street** is lined with shops, boutiques, and restaurants. Or you can grab a map at the Chamber of Commerce (800-345-1020) and take a walking tour of the town.

Sports

Chicago is the ultimate destination for sports enthusiasts. Check out these local teams: **Chicago Bears football,** Soldiers Field Stadium, 425 East Mcfetridge Drive; (312) 663-5100.**Chicago Blackhawks hockey,** United Center, 1901 West Madison Street; (312) 455-7000. **Chicago Bulls basketball,** United Center, 1901 West Madison Street; (312) 559-1212.**Chicago Cubs baseball,** Wrigley Field, 1060 West Addison; (773) 404-CUBS. **Chicago White Sox baseball,** Comiskey Park, 333 West Thirty-fifth Street; (773) 924-1000.

Side Trips

More amusements are not too far away at **Six Flags Great America,** in Gurnee, I-94 at Route 132 (847-249-1776). This amusement park has rides for kids and adults as well as an IMAX theater.

If shopping for bargains is your forte, don't miss **Gurnee Mills Outlet,** Gurnee, I-94 at Route 132 (800-YES-SHOP). Browse the bargains at this mall's more than 200 manufacturers' and retail outlets.

Head to Indiana for the **Indiana Dunes National Lakeshore** (219-926-7561) and **Indiana Dunes State Park** (219-926-1952). Only a ninety-minute drive south of the city lies Mount Baldy, the park's tallest dune, along with miles of hiking trails and actual sand beaches.

Make a trip south into Illinois to **Starved Rock National Park** for beautiful woods, trails, rivers, waterfalls, and the famed Starved Rock cliff. The **Wisconsin Dells** also attract lots of Chicagoans.

Special Events

January. Magnificent Mile Crystal Carnival, (312) 642-3570.

February. WinterBreak Chicago Festival, with giant ice sculptures, concerts, and sporting events, (312) 744-3315.

March. South Side St. Patrick's Day Parade, (708) 239-7755. Yes, the river's green for one day.

April. Del Corazon Mexican Performing Arts Festival, (312) 738-1503; Chicago Cubs and Chicago White Sox Baseball seasons start; Chicago Latino Film Festival, (312) 663-1600; State Street Bridge House Gallery, located under lower Wacker Drive at State Street. If you're in the gallery at the right moment, you can watch the counterweights of the State Street Bridge drop away as the bridge is lifted; through October 1999.

June. Chicago Blues Festival, (312) 744-3315; Chicago Gospel Festival, (312) 744-3315; Chicago Country Music Festival, (312) 744-3315; the first ever Cows on Parade, life-size bovine works of art paraded along Michigan Avenue to the State Street Bridge House Moo-seum, (312) 744-6630.

July. Independence Day Concert and Fireworks, (312) 294-2420; Venetian Night, (312) 744-3315.

August. Chicago Air and Water Show, with civilian and military aircraft and watercraft, (312) 744-3370; "Viva! Chicago" Latin Music Festival, (312) 744-3315.

September. Chicago Jazz Festival, (312) 744-3370; Celtic Festival, (312) 744-3315; World Music Festival, with music from around the world, (312) 744-3315.

October. Chicago International Film Festival, (312) 332-FILM.

November. Christmas Around the World Holiday of Lights, (773) 684-1414; The Magnificent Mile Lights Festival, lighting ceremony and spectacular fireworks, (312) 642-3570; City of Chicago Holiday Tree Lighting Ceremony at Daley Plaza, (312) 744-3370; Holiday Parade, (773) 935-8747.

December. New Year's Eve celebration include S.A.F.E. Night with clowns and magicians, no alcohol, (312) 747-2606; celebrations at the Navy Pier, (312) 747-3370; and a 2000 Minute Party, "Dance 'til the Dawn of the New Millennium, held throughout the city in 1999, (312) 744-4405.

WHERE TO STAY

Embassy Suites Hotel, 600 North State Street (312-943-3800), offers suites and a hot breakfast, as does the **Doubletree Guest Suites,** 198 East Delaware Place (312-664-1100 or 800-424-2900). **The Hyatt Regency Chicago,** 151 East Wacker Drive (312-565-1234 or 800-233-1234), offers big-hotel amenities, plus the Camp Hyatt kids' menus, and a 50-percent discount on a second room for the kids. They do not usually offer children's activities.

The Four Seasons Hotel, 120 East Delaware Place (312-280-8800), comes with large rooms and special turndown of milk and cookies for the kids (ask). The **Holiday Inn-Mart Plaza,** 350 North Orleans Street (312-836-5000), the **Radisson,** 160 East Huron Street (312-787-2900 or 800-325-3535), and the **Days Inn-Lake Shore Drive,** Lake Michigan and the Navy Pier (312-943-9200), are less costly options.

Marriott's Lincolnshire Resort, 10 Marriott Drive (800-228-9290 or 847-634-0100), is located forty-five minutes from downtown. The Children's Activity House has plenty of activities that will amuse kids, including swimming, relay races, crafts, movies, and outdoor games. The resort sponsors supervised activities in one-hour blocks on weekends. Different age groups participate at different times; call to confirm times. There is a theater on the premises that features occasional children's productions as well as standard movie fare.

WHERE TO EAT

The Berghoff, 17 West Adams Street (312-427-3170), is famous for its bratwurst, sausage, schnitzel, and strawberry shortcake. **Carson's For Ribs,** 612 North Wells Street (312-280-9200), offers barbecued ribs, chicken, and children's menus. **Claim Company,** 900 North Michigan Avenue (847-247-0033), serves chicken, ribs, burgers, and has kids' menus and crayons for paper-covered tabletops. **Ed Debevic's Short Orders Deluxe,** 640 North Wells Street (312-664-1707), open for lunch and dinner, is a 1950s-style diner with a nostalgic atmosphere and inexpensive diner fare , including five-way chili, roast turkey, chicken fried steak, burgers and fries, meatloaf, and cherry cokes.

You can't visit Chicago without sampling the deep-dish pizza. **Giordano's,** 747 North Rush (312-951-0747), serves up the traditional thick, Chicago-style pizza. **Pizzeria Uno,** 29 East Ohio (312-321-1000), is the birthplace of Chicago-style deep-dish pizza. Uno also serves generous portions of soup, sandwiches, and salads. **Pizzeria Due,** 619 North Wabash (312-943-2400), Uno's sister restaurant, serves the same tasty, Chicago-style deep-dish pizza.

If your kids are basketball fans, they might like dining at **Michael Jordan's Restaurant,** 500 North La Salle (312-644-DUNK). This midpriced place offers Jordan's pregame meal of steak and potatoes and other Jordan favorites such as pasta, macaroni and cheese, filet of sole, and peach pie. The **Navy Pier,** in the heart of Chicago, 600 East Grand Avenue (312-595-PIER), features fifty acres of parks, gardens, shops, and eateries. **House of Blues** (312-527-2583), a music-themed restaurant and blues club, is located in Marina City.

For More Information

Contact the **Chicago Office of Tourism,** Chicago Cultural Center, 78 East Washington Street (312-744-2400). Also, travel counselors are available at (800) 2-CONNECT or at www.ci.chi.il.US/Tourism.

Emergency Numbers

Ambulance, fire, police: 911

Children's Memorial Hospital: Children's Plaza at Fullerton and Lincoln Avenues; (773) 880-4000

Poison Control: Northwestern Memorial Hospital emergency room; (312) 908-2000

Twenty-four-hour pharmacy: Walgreen's, 757 North Michigan Avenue; (312) 664-8686

INDIANAPOLIS

The movers and shakers of this heartland USA town made a concerted effort to establish Indianapolis as a sports center. After they built the arenas and stadiums, numerous athletic organizations came, bringing with them top sporting events. The results are great facilities—many of which are available for public use—and a city known as the Amateur Sports Capital of the United States.

Besides watching world-class competitions, visitors to Indianapolis enjoy two surprises: the world's largest children's museum and, nearby, Conner Prairie, a re-created pioneer town.

GETTING THERE

Indianapolis International Airport (317-487-9594) is 8 miles (about fifteen minutes) from downtown. The airport services America West, America West Express, American, American Eagle, American Trans Air, Chicago Express, Comair, Continental, Continental Express, Delta, Northwest, Pro Air, Skyway, TWA, United, United Express, USAirways, and USAirways Express. Call the individual airlines for flight information and reservations. **Indy Connection** (317-241-2522) offers limousine, minibus, and van service to downtown.

Amtrak pulls into Union Station, 350 South Illinois Street (800-USA-RAIL). For bus information, call (800) 231-2222. The local terminal is located at 350 South Illinois (317-267-3071).

Three major U.S. highways—I-69, I-70, and I-65—lead directly to Indianapolis, and I-74 leads traffic into the bypass route, I-465.

GETTING AROUND

The public bus system, the **METRO** (317-632-1900), is equipped to serve physically challenged riders; call (317) 635-3344 for schedules. There are several cab companies, including Yellow Cab (317-637-5421).

Indianapolis

AT A GLANCE

- Explore the world's largest children's museum
- Time travel to 1836 at Conner Prairie, a living history site
- Learn about Native American culture and Western art at the Eiteljorg Museum
- Watch car races at the Indianapolis Motor Speedway
- Indianapolis City Center visitor's center, (317) 237-5206 or (800) 468-INDY; www.indy.org

What to See and Do

Museums

Eiteljorg Museum of American Indian and Western Art, 500 West Washington Street (317-636-WEST, www.eiteljorg.org). The Eiteljorg holds one of the most extensive collections of American Western art and Native American art and artifacts in the country. Situated next to an old grain elevator, the Eiteljorg looks both incongruous and intriguing. Cleverly designed to resemble the adobe architecture of the Taos (New Mexico) Pueblo, the museum houses a first-rate collection of paintings and bronzes by such artists as Charles Russell, Frederic Remington, Georgia O'Keeffe, and members of the original Taos artists' colony. Spirited Hands: Continuing Traditions in Native American Art displays art from ten regions of North America and features pottery, basketry, and clothing, with an eye-catching array of everyday artifacts decorated with beadwork. Ask your kids to compare the varying cradle boards (carriers used to transport infants) fashioned by the different tribes.

The Eiteljorg Museum is currently undergoing a major expansion that will eventually increase its exhibit space by more than half. The new space will include a new contemporary gallery, an education center with hands-on activities for kids, a new restaurant, a 250-seat theater, and an expansion of the gift shop, where kids love spending their allowances on drums, posters, cards, charms, and some great T-shirts. The museum will also have a new terrace and sculpture garden.

Every June the museum hosts the largest Indian Market in the Midwest; a Western Festival/Chili Cookoff is held in September.

The World's Largest Children's Museum

The Children's Museum of Indianapolis, 300 North Meridian Street (317–924–5431; www.childrensmuseum.org), with 356,000 square feet of space on five levels, is the world's largest museum for children and certainly one of its best. Calling itself "America's largest builder of small discoveries," this museum appeals to kids to interact. The **What If** gallery targets ages six to ten by presenting three exhibits requested by more than 1,000 children: a dinosaur dig where kids can dig for fossils, an underwater coral reef, and an Egyptian mummy. **Playscape** lets toddlers to six-year-olds experiment with water, shapes, and sand, and includes a giant birdhouse and a tree house. Kids can contribute to the *Children's Express,* a working children's newspaper published once a week in the *Indianapolis Sentinel.* The newly renovated gallery **All Aboard!** offers kids a chance to see toy trains and operate some of the switches and signals on the track, as well as the steam locomotive *Reuben Wells* that operated between 1868 and 1898.

In the **CFAX (Center for Arts Exploration)** gallery, pre-teens and teens can paint and dance, and its Tech Corner features opportunities to synthesize music and create graphic designs on a computer. Erupting volcanos, tropical rain forests, and more are larger than life in the **IWERKS CineDome** theater, with its 76-foot domed screen. And if your kids are feeling antsy after the film, they can climb the walls—literally—in the 12,000-foot **Science Works** exhibit. The gallery has a 22-foot limestone climbing wall with three different degrees of difficulty (safety harnesses are provided). Kids can also dig for fossils, use a pedal-operated dump truck at the construction site exhibit, and build and "sail" a boat.

Be sure to ride the Victorian carousel, browse the antique doll collection, and explore the French fur-trading post. For special kids' events, call the **Kidsline** at (317) 924–KIDS. The museum's restaurant, Reflections, has family-friendly menus from McDonalds and Pizza Hut, as well as a variety of other options, and the museum store features science and art-and-crafts items.

Indianapolis Museum of Art, 1200 West Thirty-eighth Street (317–923–1331; www.ima-art.org), is not only an art museum with European, American, contemporary, Asian, and African art on permanent display, the facility also features a 152-acre park, a botanical garden, a theater, a concert terrace, and a restaurant. In this museum, the seventh largest art

African-American Heritage

Indianapolis' African-American community, the sixteenth largest in the country, has always possessed a rich heritage, as reflected in activities around town.

- **Crispus Attucks Museum,** 1140 Dr. Martin Luther King Jr. Street (317–226–4613), celebrates the contributions and achievements of African-Americans in its four galleries.
- **Eiteljorg Gallery of African Art at the Indianapolis Museum of Art,** 1200 West Thirty-eighth Street (317–923–1331), is considered one of the most comprehensive collections of its kind in the United States, with more than 1,400 pieces representing all major art-producing regions of sub-Saharan Africa, particularly from the Yoruba people and the Benin Kingdom of Nigeria.
- **Freetown Village,** 617 Indiana Avenue (317–631–1870), uses a first-person living history format to depict the lifestyles of African-Americans living in Indiana following the Civil War. Storytellers give craft demonstrations and talk about their lives using dialects, costumes, and crafts that are historically correct.
- **Conner Prairie's Historic Village,** 13400 Allisonville Road, Noblesville (317–776–6000), a living-history museum depicting Indiana life in the nineteenth century, features four characters of African-American heritage who tell their stories.
- **Asante Children's Theatre,** 617 Indiana Avenue (317–638–6684), explores African culture and history through theater from September through June at the Madame Walker Theatre Center. Call for schedule.

museum in the United States, be sure to see the Eiteljorg Collection of African Art. The masks, carvings, and jewelry appeal to kids. A special touch: The videos near the displays show the masks in motion being worn in ceremonial dances. Other highlights include the largest collection of J.W.M. Turner works outside the United Kingdom, a comprehensive collection of Oriental art, and the famous *Love* sculpture by Robert Indiana (remember the Love stamp?) out on the lawn. Allow time to stroll the botanical gardens and browse the gift shop.

In 1999, the museum acquired a collection of works by nineteenth-century French painter Paul Gaugin. The museum is working with the city to develop an **Art and Nature Park** on the one hundred acres of land surrounding the museum, which would feature a lake and hiking and biking trails, along with the sculpture exhibits. Regularly scheduled children's progams are available throughout the year; call for information. Each summer, the museum hosts a one-day family festival celebrating African and African-American art and culture called AfricaFest, featuring music and dance, children's activities, crafts demonstrations, and traditional African and Caribbean dishes.

Sports Museums

Serious about sports, Indianapolis boasts several museums dedicated to the subject.

Indianapolis Motor Speedway Hall of Fame Museum, 4790 West Sixteenth Street (317-481-8500; www.indyracingleague.com). If your kids collect model racing cars and root for their favorite speed demon, they will love it here. Crammed into the two large galleries of this hall are the sleek, shiny, and select cars—more than thirty of them—from the world of racing. Admire the 1914 Duesenberg driven by Eddie Rickenbacker (the first car to reach the amazing speed of 79 miles per hour), A.J. Foyt's four winning cars, and recent Indy champions. The walls feature photographs of racing's Hall of Fame.

Do your kids want to brag they rode the Indy? Then board the bus for a narrated trip around the track and a close-up view of the stands, work pits, and famous finish line. End the day at the Official Trackside Gift Shop, where exclusive collector's items are sold along with fun racing mementos.

National Art Museum of Sport, University Place Conference Center and Hotel (317-274-3627). Although small, consisting of several galleries and a second-floor office hallway, this museum is the largest in the United States devoted exclusively to sporting art. The general collections and special exhibitions rotate. You might see oils, prints, and sculpture on boxing, baseball, basketball, horse racing, or hockey. A visit here could be a good way to interest your sports enthusiast in art.

Several other sports museums are worth a browse. **The Indiana Convention Center & RCA Dome,** One RCA Dome (317-262-3410; www.iccrd.com). Go inside the stadium and look at the VIP suites and the locker rooms as part of a tour of the 60,500-seat slice of history. The site has hosted the NCAA Final Four basketball games, and, of course, it is the home of the Indianapolis Colts. The tour includes an eight-minute multimedia show. Guests on the tour can also inspect the Astroturf and tour the owner's suite. For more information, call (317) 237-DOME.

Victory Field Baseball Park opened in July 1996. The open-air, 13,500-seat stadium is home to the Indianapolis Indians, a Triple-A farm team for the Cincinnati Reds.

More Museums and Attractions

- **Indiana Transportation Museum,** State Road 19 North in Forest Park, Noblesville (317-773-6000; www.itm.org). Besides featuring such classic trains as a 1926 C&O caboose, an 1898 private railroad coach, and a 1918 Like Micado engine, the museum also offers scenic rides on the *Atlanta Express* on weekends.
- **Indiana Medical History Museum,** 3045 West Vermont Street (317-635-7329; www.imhm.org), is great fun for kids. There are brains in jars, plus old-fashioned stethoscopes, X-ray machines, pathology lab equipment, and more than 15,000 artifacts in twelve historic rooms and a changing exhibits gallery.
- **Indiana State Museum,** 202 North Alabama Street (317-232-1637), contains artifacts of Indiana's history and culture from fossils to contemporary art. The museum will be moving to a new facility in the new White River State Park complex in 2001.
- **The Crown Hill Cemetery,** 700 West Thirty-eighth Street (317-925-8231), the nation's third largest. If your kids aren't spooked by graves you can see the final resting place of Civil War veterans, as well as the burial sites of President Benjamin Harrison, Hoosier poet James Whitcomb Riley, and legendary "Public Enemy" John Dillinger.

Located in New Castle, the **Indiana Basketball Hall of Fame,** One Hall of Fame Court, New Castle (765-529-1891; www.hoopshall.com), pays homage to Indiana's love of hoops. Interactive exhibits take you onto the playing floor and into the locker rooms.

More Attractions

President Benjamin Harrison Home, 1230 North Delaware Street (317-631-1898; www.surf-ici.com/harrison). This sixteen-room Italianate mansion, designated a National Historic Landmark, has been restored to its late-1880s appearance and features many original family pieces, plus rotating exhibits about the twenty-third President of the United States. On the first Wednesday of every month (except January, July, and August), the museum presents Life from Delaware Street, with costumed actors performing the roles of President and Mrs. Harrison, their cook, and visitors to the house. Throughout the year, hour-long tours are given on the hour and half-hour.

Hook's Historic 1890 Drug Store and Pharmacy Museum, 1180

The Children's Museum of Indianapolis is, as its motto professes, "a place where children grow up and adults don't have to."

East Thirty-eighth Street (317–924–1503), is outfitted like a Victorian soda parlor; grab an ice-cream cone along with turn-of-the-century ambience and then wander through the museum, with its antique dental, medical, and pharmaceutical equipment. In late 1999, the museum will relocate into two renovated downtown buildings at 201 and 207 South Meridian Street.

Indianapolis War Memorials

- **Soldiers and Sailors Monument,** located downtown in the center of Monument Circle, is dedicated to the valor of Indiana's soldiers and sailors who served in the Civil War. An observation tower (there's an elevator) provides a panoramic view of the city skyline. In September 1999, a new Civil War Museum is scheduled to open. The museum will present the experiences of native Hoosiers during the war, using photographs, letters, and diaries.
- **The USS *Indianapolis* Memorial,** east bank of downtown canal, Walnut Street footbridge (317-924-1484 or 800-482-5242), honors those men who lost their lives when the *Indianapolis* was torpedoed and sunk by the Japanese just two weeks before the end of World War II. Of the estimated 800 survivors (out of a crew of 1,197), only 318 survived the five days in the water before rescue, primarily because of shark attacks.
- The **Indiana World War Memorial,** 431 North Meridian Street (317-232-7615), is dedicated to Indiana soldiers killed in the two world wars, the Korean conflict, and the Vietnam War. It displays military weapons, uniforms, jeeps, a Navy Terrier missile, and a helicopter. The Shrine Room, with twenty-four stained glass windows, also features a 17- by 30-foot American flag suspended from the center of the room. On the ground floor of the memorial is a reconstructed log cabin, depicting the living conditions during the wars in the nineteenth century. Coming in 2000 will be a reconstructed World War I bunker that visitors can walk through and exhibits on the Spanish-American War.
- North of the memorial are the **American Legion Mall,** that includes the American Legion State and National Headquarters, and the **Veterans' Memorial Plaza,** where the flags of all fifty states are flown.

The **Murat Temple,** 510 North New Jersey Street (317-635-2433), modeled after an Islamic mosque, is the largest shrine temple in the world. Make an appointment for a tour and check out the temple's stained glass windows, theater, mosaic mural, and the Egyptian room constructed like Tutankhamen's burial chamber. Adjacent is the **Murat Centre,** 502 North New Jersey (312-231-0000), a performing arts center and concert hall that hosts Broadway shows and touring entertainment.

If your kids are older than eighteen (or if you're still a bit of a child yourself), then go to the **Stephen Johansson Karting Center,** 3549

Lafayette Road (317-297-KART). You can zoom around a track for fifteen minutes at about 30 miles per hour at the first indoor cart-racing center in the home of America's most famous car race. Younger kids aren't allowed to drive nor to be passengers.

Little ones are welcome at **Holcomb Observatory and Planetarium** at Butler University, 4600 Sunset Avenue, at the south edge of Holcomb Gardens (317-940-9333), where Friday and Saturday evenings can be spent looking at the stars through the 38-inch Cassegrain reflector telescope. If your family's more interested in virtual reality, try **United Artist Entertainment Complex,** Circle Centre, 49 West Maryland Street (317-237-6356). This nine-screen movie entertainment complex includes a virtual theme park with the latest in virtual reality computer-simulated experiences, such as gliding over the Grand Canyon, among other excitements.

Amateur Sports Facilities Open to the Public

As the Sports Capital of the United States, the city offers visitors world-class facilities not just for watching, but for doing. Simply show your hotel-room key to take advantage of the inexpensive entry fees and the top-rated facilities, which are open to the public when not hosting major events. Always call first to check availability and to find out about any age restrictions.

Indiana University Natatorium, 901 West New York Street (317-274-3518). Bring your own towel and a lock for the lockers, and swim, swim, swim in this first-class pool. Doing laps here, your teens will feel like Matt Biondi, Summer Sanders, or Rowdy Gains. Work out at the aerobics classes and in the weight room.

Indiana University Track & Field Stadium, 901 West New York Street (317-274-3518). Located in the same complex as the natatorium, the check-in for the track-and-field facility is at the east entrance of the natatorium. Jog on the 400-meter outdoor rubber lanes.

Indianapolis Tennis Center, 755 University Boulevard (317-278-2100), has indoor and outdoor courts. While it's better to bring your own racket, a limited number are available for use at no charge. Lessons are available too.

National Institute for Fitness and Sport, 250 North University Boulevard (317-274-3432). Parents and teens especially appreciate working out on the Olympic-quality training equipment and running on the 200-meter indoor track.

Indiana World Skating Academy, Pan American Plaza, 201 South Capitol Avenue (317-237-5565), is an indoor rink. For more skating September through April, try the **Perry Ice Rink,** 451 East Stop 11 Road (317-888-0070).

Major Taylor Velodrome & BMX Tracks, 3649 Cold Spring Road (317-327-VELO), is the site of many national cycling competitions. Riders must be at least eight years old and wear helmets. Next door the BMX

> **EnterCitement**
>
> A major $200 million theme park and entertainment and business center is in the works for Indianapolis, scheduled to open in the spring of 2000. The 510-acre EnterCitement, located 20 miles west of downtown will feature:
>
> - **Schitterbahn Indiana,** the nation's largest indoor/outdoor waterpark;
> - a 300-room **Ramada Resort and Conference Center;** and
> - **Garfield's Adventure America,** named for America's favorite "fat cat." It will include Crossroads, an early twentieth-century Indiana main street; Indiana Adventure, rustic America with a log flume ride and two roller coasters; Fat Cat Kingdom, with another coaster; and Midway, a modern state fair with a carnival atmosphere and two more coasters.

Track offers more training possibilities. Enjoy rowing and paddling at the **Regatta Course at Eagle Creek,** 7840 West Fifty-sixth Street (317-298-9456).

Parks and Zoos

White River State Park, 801 West Washington Street (317-634-4567 or 800-665-9056), is located on 250 acres downtown and encompasses, among other attractions, the Indianapolis Zoo, the National Institute for Fitness and Sport, and the Eiteljorg Museum of American Indian and Western Art. Also here is Indiana's only IMAX theater, a 416-seat theater that shows 3-D, 2-D, and Hollywood movies on a six-story screen. Several major projects include the new NCAA Headquarters and Hall of Champions, an interactive museum celebrating intercollegiate athletics; a Medal of Honor Memorial dedicated to recipients of this country's highest honor; a new home for the Indiana State Museum; and White River Gardens, a 3.3-acre showpiece of indoor and outdoor gardens, with a 5,000-square-foot glass conservatory and hedge mazes.

The Indianapolis Zoo, 1200 West Washington Street (317-630-2001; www.indyzoo.com) is well worth a visit. Known for its large dolphin pavilions (check the time for daily shows), this sixty-four-acre "cageless" zoo exhibits animals in waters, deserts, forest, and plains. The Waters building, always a favorite, features penguins, reef fish, tortoises, and seals. The Deserts Biome, an enclosed conservatory filled with cacti and other desert plants, takes you by free-roaming lizards, tortoises, and hummingbirds.

In addition, young kids covet the pony and elephant rides, as well as time on the trolley, the train, and the carousel. A stroll through this beautiful zoo is a delight, especially in spring, when beds of black-eyed Susans, daylilies, and lilacs bloom.

The Zoo also features a maze and a Bumping Bullfrog ride (on inner tubes), a playground, and hosts special events every month of the year. In May, attend the Zoopolis 500, a humorous take-off on the famed Indy race. In this race, two tortoises—A.J. and Lyn St. James—vie for the championship. On Thursday nights in July and August, stay after-hours for Animals and All That Jazz performances by local groups. In October there's Halloween

ZooBoo, a zoo-wide event with safe activities that include trick-or-treat locations throughout the zoo, costume contests in the Dolphin gallery, plus a special dolphin show, and a Not-So-Scary animal show featuring bats and snakes.

Eagle Creek Park, 7840 West Fifty-sixth Street (317-327-7110), is run by the Indianapolis Department of Parks and Recreation and stretches for more than 3,000 acres. One of the largest municipal parks in the country, the fun here includes swimming, sailing, and canoeing in the 1,300-acre reservoir.

Shopping

For shopping and even some entertainment, head to **Circle Centre,** 49 West Maryland Street (317-681-8000). This entertainment and retail complex features more than one hundred specialty shops, department stores such as Nordstrom and Parisian, restaurants and nightclubs, a nine-screen movie theater, and a virtual-reality theme park, United Artists Entertainment Complex. Circle Centre also contains the Indianapolis Artsgarden, a space for the local arts community's performances and exhibitions.

City Market, 222 East Market Street (317-634-9266), is an eclectic mix of more than thirty shops and stalls; June through October there's also an outdoor farmers' market every Wednesday. The **Indianapolis Downtown Antique Mall,** 1044 Virginia Avenue (317-635-5336), has forty shops on two levels offering a wide-variety of antiques and collectibles, including glassware, art pottery, and country items.

Special Tours

If young children get cranky during the early evening hours, take a soothing horse-drawn carriage ride around the city. Stately Percherons pull the carriages of **Colonial Carriages,** 435 South Senate Avenue (317-637-2002), and **Yellow Rose Carriages,** 1327 North Capitol Avenue (317-634-3400), which pick people up in front of the Crowne Plaza, Union Station. On this half-hour tour, you can sit back and enjoy Indianapolis lit up at night. The horses take you around the landmark **Soldiers and Sailors Monument,** in the center of Monument Circle past the **State Capitol Building,** Capitol Avenue and Washington Street (317-232-8687), by the famed **RCA Dome,** 100 South Capitol (317-262-3452), and to **Union Station,** Georgia Street between Meridian Street and Capitol Avenue. Besides falling in love with the horses, your kids will enjoy the leisurely pace and the Cinderella ambience.

Carriage tours are available year-round, weather permitting, Monday through Friday from 6:30 P.M. to midnight, and Saturday and Sunday from 3:30 P.M. to 1:00 A.M. While you can hail a coach most evenings, reservations are strongly suggested for Saturday night.

Performing Arts

Deer Creek Music Center, 12880 East 146th Street (box office, 317-776-3337; main office, 317-841-8900). This outdoor covered amphitheater seats 18,000 and hosts musical performances in summer. The **Indiana Repertory Theatre,** 140 West Washington Street (317-635-5277), has three stages in a restored 1927 movie palace and presents both classical and contemporary plays. **Ballet Internationale–Indianapolis,** 502-B North Capitol Avenue (317-637-8979), performs full-length and contemporary ballets at the Murat Centre. **Indianapolis Civic Theatre,** 1200 West Thirty-eighth Street, Indianapolis Museum of Art (box office, 317-923-4597; main office, 317-924-6770), uses volunteers and professionals. This is the home of the Kid Connection, an adult acting group that tours Midwestern elementary schools. **Indianapolis Opera,** 250 East Thirty-eighth Street (box office, 317-940-6444; main office, 317-283-3531), performs at Clowes Memorial Hall, Butler University. **Indianapolis Symphony Orchestra,** 45 Monument Circle (box office, 317-639-4300 or 800-366-8457; main office, 317-262-1100), performs classical and popular music each season at the historic Hibert Circle Theatre. In summer there are performances under the stars at Conner Prairie (see Day Trips). **The Phoenix Theater,** 749 North Park Avenue (317-635-7529), performs off-Broadway and contemporary plays. Nationally known stars lead this resident professional company as they perform musicals in the summer at Hilton University's Brown Theatre. **Beef and Boards Dinner Theatre,** 9301 North Michigan Road (317-872-9664), is an Equity troupe that serves up Broadway shows in dinner-theater format.

For performing arts schedules at local universities, contact **Clowes Memorial Hall,** Butler University, 4600 Sunset Avenue (317-940-6444).

For tickets, call the individual box offices listed above, or try these agencies: **TicketMaster** (317-239-5151) and **Tickets and Travel,** 1099 North Meridian Street, Suite 100 (317-633-6400).

Sports

The **Indiana Pacers,** a National Basketball Association team, play at the Market Square Arena, 300 East Market Street (main office, 317-263-2100; tickets, 317-239-5151). Catch the **Indianapolis Colts,** a National Football League team, at the RCA Dome, 100 South Capitol Avenue, P.O. Box 535000 (317-297-7000). The **Indianapolis Indians,** the farm-league team of the Cincinnati Reds baseball team, plays from April to November at Victory Field, 501 West Maryland Street (317-269-3545). The **Indianapolis Ice,** 1202 East Thirty-eighth Street (317-239-5151), affiliate of the Chicago Blackhawk hockey team and member of the IHL league, play their games at the Indiana State Fairgrounds and at Market Square Arena.

The **Little League Baseball Central Region Headquarters,** 4360

North Mitthoeffer Road (317-897-6127), hosts the Central Region Little League Baseball Championship each August, the winner goes on to the World Series. Find out about the summer camps held at this thirty-acre facility.

SIDE TRIPS

Zionsville, a northern suburb of Indianapolis, features nineteenth-century architecture and houses a varied selection of shops and restaurants along brick-lined streets. Lincoln stopped here in 1861 to speak while en route to Washington, D.C., for his inauguration. A monument dedicated to the speech stands near the train station. Guided walking tours are available. Annual events include Country Market Arts Fair in May and a Fall Festival in September. For a brochure, write to Zionsville Chamber of Commerce, 125 South Elm Street, or call (317) 873-3836 from Tuesday to Friday, 10:00 A.M. to 4:30 P.M.

Indiana Dunes National Lakeshore. The lakeshore, in Indiana's northwestern corner, covers 13,000 acres along the southern shores of Lake Michigan. In season enjoy swimming, fishing, hiking, and cross-country skiing. Dunes, of course, are big here. See the view from the top of Mount Baldy, the lakeshore's tallest dune. As the area is located on a north-south migratory route, seasonal bird watching is great here. There are also horseback riding trails, and camping sites are available for rent from April through October. The visitor's center at Kemil Road and U.S. 12 has information, pamphlets, and maps. Call or write to Indiana Dunes National Lakeshore, 1100 North Mineral Springs Road, Porter 46304; (219) 926-7561; www.nps.gov.

The **French Lick Springs Resort,** 8670 State Road 56, French Lick 46432 (800-457-4040 or 812-936-9300), caters to children by offering summertime family programs, such as the Kids Klub, for ages five through twelve, and Chuckwagon Cookouts every night of the week. There's also swimming, tennis, horseback riding, surrey rides, and bicycling, plus two golf courses, one designed by Donald Ross. Ask about reduced rates for children.

SPECIAL EVENTS

Festivals and Sporting Events

Additional information about all events is available by calling the Visitors Center at the Indianapolis City Center; (317) 237-5206 or (800) 468-INDY.

January. Indianapolis Auto Show, Convention Center.

It's Always 1836

Conner Prairie is a 250-acre living-history museum with about forty buildings. Just fifty minutes from Indianapolis, the facility transports you to 1836. History is anything but boring here. Kids will be intrigued by the costumed interpreters who make the frontier come alive. In **Prairietown,** the doctor's wife tells you how her piano had an easier trip from the East than she did, and the carpenter shows you how to fashion a chair leg. At the **Golden Eagle Tavern,** Martha Zimmermann bakes cookies and warns you about the dangers of women traveling alone. It's hands-on fun at the **Pioneer Adventure area,** where kids try their skill at weaving, grinding corn, and walking on stilts, a popular pioneer pastime.

The seasonal events are fun as well. On July 4th kick up your heels at a traditional village celebration. During August the Indianapolis Symphony Orchestra performs evening concerts in the museum's outdoor amphitheater. Bring a picnic supper and blanket for the lawn. Special fall events include demonstrations of hog butchering—the real thing—and smoking meats pioneer style.

Conner Prairie is planning major expansions over the next five years. In 1999, the **Museum Center** will be renovated to include a multimedia theater and a 5,000-square-foot orientation exhibit. In 2000, several additions will be made, including an 1815 **fur-trading outpost** along the White River, and a **Delaware Indian encampment,** where visitors will learn about the culture and lifestyle of the Indians in a riverfront settlement. In 2001, plans are for the addition of a **Quaker meetinghouse,** and in the next two years a working farm will be added, along with a water-powered mill, metal trestle bridge, and nature center.

Conner Prairie, 13400 Allisonville Road, Noblesville (317–776–6000; www.connerprairie.org).

February. Big Ten Women's Basketball Tournament, RCA Dome.

March. NCAA Men's and Women's Division I and II Indoor Track and Field Championships, RCA Dome; NCAA Division I Men's Basketball Tournament; Indiana High School Athletic Association (IHSAA) Boys' Basketball Finals; St. Patrick's Day parade, downtown.

April. Hossier Horse Fair and Expo, Indiana State Fairgrounds.

May. The Indianapolis 500 is held Memorial Day weekend each year. The city celebrates with a month of events that include a minimarathon, a parade, and the 500 Festival Kids' Day—the largest festival for children in the city. The fun includes splashing paint on old cars, racing Big Wheel bikes, and creating arts and crafts. The fair is generally held around Monument Circle. Although overshadowed by the Indianapolis 500, the A.J. Foyt's Hulman Hundred may be more fun to watch with kids. More than thirty cars compete on the dirt track of the Indiana State Fairgrounds.

June. Savor more than six tons of Indiana strawberries at the Strawberry Festival, Monument Circle, downtown; Indy Jazz Fest, various sites downtown; Midsummer Fest, Monument Circle; Indian Market, Eiteljorg Museum.

July–August. FourthFest at World War Memorial Plaza; Indiana Black Expo, Convention Center; Kroger Circlefest, a family-oriented celebration at Monument Circle.

August. Indiana State Fair at the fairgrounds; Africafest, Indianapolis Museum of Art.

September. National Hot Rod Association (NHRA) U.S. Nationals, Indiana Raceway Park; the Hossier Storytelling Festival at the Indianapolis Arts Center hosts storytellers from around the country who share their personal stories, fairy tales, folk tales, and literature with an audience of roughly 3,000; Western festival and Chili cookoff, Eiteljorg Museum.

October. ZooBoo and Art Fair and Fall Festival, Indianapolis Zoo; Oktoberfest, various locations around town.

November. Harvest Festival of Foods, Eiteljorg Museum.

December. Conner Prairie by Candlelight, a holiday candlelight tour; Christmas at the Zoo; Celebration of Lights.

Where to Stay

Embassy Suites Hotel—Downtown, 110 West Washington Street (317-236-1800 or 800-EMBASSY). Situated just blocks from the Indiana Convention Center and RCA Dome, this all-suite hotel offers families extra space and the conveniences of a microwave, refrigerator, coffeemaker, and fold-out sofa bed. The property also has an indoor pool.

Crowne Plaza at Union Station, 123 West Louisiana Street (317-631-2221 or 800 2-CROWNE). Located across from the RCA Dome, this hotel has 276 rooms, twenty-six of which are authentic Pullman-car suites permanently parked on tracks off the hotel's main floors. Named for famous personalities of the twenties and thirties such as Diamond Jim Brady and Greta Garbo, these cars are furnished with period pieces and reproductions; many have pull-out sofas, and all add fun to an overnight stay. Lurking near the trains are white fiberglass statues of soldiers, sailors, and people of the era. Called the "ghosts" of Union Station, they add charm. The hotel also has an indoor pool and fitness center. Be sure when requesting rooms you are not near the pool or central atrium, which can be noisy.

Hyatt Regency Indianapolis, One South Capitol Avenue (317-632-1234 or 800 233-1234). Located directly across from the Indiana Convention Center and RCA Dome and connected by a skyway to the City Centre Mall, this hotel features a twenty-story atrium with a 20-foot waterfall in the lobby, and an indoor pool.

The **Westin Indianapolis,** 50 South Capitol Avenue (317-262-8100 or 800-228-3000). Located in downtown's business district, the hotel has a restaurant and lounge, indoor pool, and exercise facilities. **Comfort Inn West,** 5855 Rockville Road (317-487-9800 or 800-323-2086), is just 2 miles from the airport and has a playground for kids.

Where to Eat

Capitol Food Court, 25 Market Street (317-634-4148), houses Ed and Marge's Cafeteria and a variety of fast-food restaurants: Long John Silver's, Wendy's, Arby's. **Charlie & Barney's Bar & Grill,** National City Center (317-636-3101), serves award-winning chili, gourmet burgers, fresh soups and salads, and specialty sandwiches. **India Garden Restaurant,** 143 North Illinois Street (317-634-6060), offers casual dining at reasonable prices. At the **Old Spaghetti Factory,** 210 South Meridian Street (317-635-6325), you'll get family dining at family prices and get to sit in a trolley car or a canopy bed while enjoying the restaurant's antique decor.

The Indianapolis Convention and Visitors Association offers a visitor's guide that lists many family-friendly restaurants throughout the city.

For More Information

Begin your visit with a stop at the visitor's center in the **Indianapolis City Center,** 201 South Capitol Avenue (800-468-INDY or 317-237-5206; www.indy.org). Browse the more than 300 brochures, examine the model of the city, and watch the eight-minute slide show, a fast-paced pastiche of city images. The hours are Monday through Friday 10:00 A.M. to 5:30 P.M., Saturday 10:00 A.M. to 5:00 P.M., and Sunday noon to 5:00 P.M. Call for information about weekend packages and special events.

Emergency Numbers

Ambulance, fire, and police: 911

Poison Control: (317) 929-2323

Hospital: Riley Hospital for Children, at Indiana University Medical Center, 702 Barnhill Drive; (317) 274-5000

Twenty-four-hour pharmacy: CVS, 1744 North Illinois; (317) 923-1491

9 Kansas

WICHITA

Wichita, the largest city in Kansas and a major aviation and agriculture center, is cosmopolitan without being too slick; residents sport a friendly, open manner and are happy to help tourists. There are plenty of attractions in town, and Wichita also makes an excellent base from which to explore such exciting sites as a Cosmosphere and Space Center just a day trip away.

GETTING THERE

Wichita Mid-Continent Airport (316-946-4700), 5 miles west of downtown on Highway 54, is served by a number of major airlines. Car rentals, taxis, and shuttles (many hotels run their own) are available at the airport.

Amtrak (800-USA-RAIL) doesn't stop in Wichita (the closest stop is in Newton, 30 miles north).

Greyhound/Trailways provides transportation nationally from the depot at 312 South Broadway (316-755-4000 or 800 800-2814).

GETTING AROUND

Metropolitan Transit Authority buses (316-265-7221) run regular daytime routes in Wichita, except for Sunday. Three nineteenth-century-style trolleylike buses serve downtown and major tourist destinations.

WHAT TO SEE AND DO

Museums and Historical Attractions

Omnisphere and Science Center, 220 South Main (316-337-9174). There is a nominal admission to this museum of hands-on exhibits that teach kids the basics of physics, chemistry, and astronomy. There's an extra fee for the changing planetarium shows and live science demonstrations with audience participation. In the summer, the museum's magician and illusionist performs, and other kids' programs are offered.

Wichita

AT A GLANCE

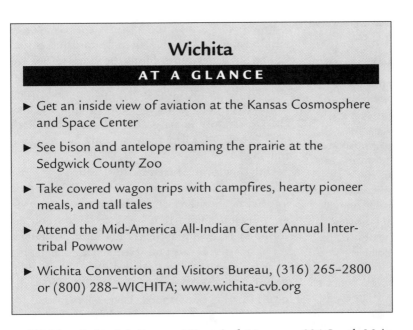

- Get an inside view of aviation at the Kansas Cosmosphere and Space Center
- See bison and antelope roaming the prairie at the Sedgwick County Zoo
- Take covered wagon trips with campfires, hearty pioneer meals, and tall tales
- Attend the Mid-America All-Indian Center Annual Inter-tribal Powwow
- Wichita Convention and Visitors Bureau, (316) 265-2800 or (800) 288-WICHITA; www.wichita-cvb.org

Wichita-Sedgwick County Historical Museum, 204 South Main (316-265-9314). Inside this imposing 1892 City Hall building (a National Historic Site) are some delightful exhibits that kids enjoy, including the Child's World area with doll and toy collections, a 1910 drugstore, a Victorian home, and a Wichita-built Jones Six automobile. A renovated Magic City exhibit, featuring artifacts and historic photos from Wichita's buffalo-hunting days, recently reopened.

Five minutes west of downtown are three riverside museums that, along with the botanical gardens listed below, comprise the **Museums on the River:**

The Indian Center Museum, 650 North Seneca (316-262-5221; www2.southwind.net/~icm/museum). The museum is inside the arrow-shaped Mid-American All Indian Center, a Bicentennial gift to all Native Americans from the people of Wichita. The location: at the confluence of the Big and Little Arkansas (pronounced "arKANSAS" in these parts) Rivers, where the Wichita tribe camped more that one hundred years ago. At this meeting point stands a striking 44-foot-tall sculpture, *The Keeper of the Plains,* that kids find quite impressive. The center displays changing exhibits of traditional and contemporary Native American works by artists such as Paul Goodbear and Blackbear Bosin. Try to come on Tuesday when volunteers prepare American Indian cuisine, including Indian tacos, meatpies, and fry bread.

Lake Afton Public Observatory, 247th Street West and MacArthur Road (316-978-7827; www.twsu.edu/~obswww). Located 15 miles southwest of Wichita, this place is a lovely spot to spend an evening (open Friday and Saturday after sunset, and Sunday evenings during the summer). See Saturn's rings, the moon, star clusters, and galaxies through the 16-inch telescope. Kids can make their own telescope and play astronomy computer games. The Observatory is across from **Lake Afton Park** (316-794-2774), where there's fishing, boating, and camping.

Old Cowtown Museum, 1871 Sim Park Drive (316-264-0671 or 316-264-6398; www.old-cowtown.org). Relive Wichita's frontier days at this historic village museum, a circa 1865-1880 cattle town on the Chisholm Trail with authentically furnished homes and businesses. Located on seventeen acres along the Arkansas River, Old Cowtown includes original buildings, such as the Munger House, built in 1869, the town's first log house/hotel. There's lots for kids to like, including a main street straight out of a Western movie, a fully stocked general store, the town's first jail, a one-room schoolhouse, a blacksmith at work, and a livestock area with Texas longhorn cattle. Costumed interpreters answer questions, and on selected days in July and August, Girl Scouts in period clothing reenact childhood activities, from attending school to helping with washboard laundry. The newest addition to the museum is the five-acre 1880 DeVore Farm, with an authentic farmhouse, barn, smokehouse, hog pen, and machinery shed. Kids enjoy watching the cow milking demonstration, as well as seeing how butter is churned and corn is harvested.

Summer weekends at the museum, which is open weekends year-round and daily March through October, include reenactments, nineteenth-century music, theatrical performances, or cooking demonstrations. Other events include the Independence Day celebration in July; a county fair in October; Hooves, Hay and Halloween; and an old-fashioned Christmas.

The Wichita Art Museum, 619 Stackman Drive (316-268-4921; www.feist.com/~wam). This museum is worth a stop if you have time—it's free except during selected traveling shows. The beautiful mother-and-child paintings by Mary Cassatt invariably appeal to youngsters. Other American works by such artists as Charles Russell, Winslow

Attend a Powwow

Each summer on the last weekend in July, 10,000 people from across the nation gather in the open area behind the Indian Center Museum for the **Mid-America All-Indian Center Annual Intertribal Powwow.** Featured are Native American dancers and singers in traditional dress, Native American foods (fry bread, tacos, meat pies), and handmade crafts (silver and turquoise jewelry, beaded bags, dream catchers).

Smaller events held at the Indian Center throughout the year include the **Wichita Indian Art Market and Exhibition** in the spring, the **River Festival Rendezvous** in May, and the **"Keeper of the Plains" Art Auction,** fair, and powwow in October.

Kansas Cosmosphere and Space Center

About 45 miles northwest of Wichita is the **Kansas Cosmosphere and Space Center,** 1100 North Plum, Hutchinson (316-662-2305 or 800-397-0330; www.cosmo.org). The **Hall of Space Museum** holds the world's largest collection of space suits, a full-scale replica of the space shuttle, an SR 71 Blackbird spy plane, the largest number of Russian space items outside of Moscow, and a collection of space artifacts second only to the Smithsonian Institution. (The Center was recently named an affiliate of the Smithsonian.) There are also a multimedia **planetarium,** an **IMAX dome theater,** which envelops visitors with its dome screen and digital sound, and **laser light shows.** (The larger-than-life IMAX films can sometimes be too realistic for very young children.)

Two new attractions include the **Cold War Gallery,** with displays of Sputnik I and II satellites and German VI and V2 rockets, and the **Apollo Gallery**, with artifacts from Apollo I through XI, including the actual Apollo XIII command module *Odyssey.*

Your kids may want to return someday for the five-day **Future Astronaut Training Program** for students entering the seventh, eighth, or ninth grade.

Homer, Thomas Eakins, and Edward Hopper are also on display. A changing interactive gallery of art experiences is intriguing for both kids and adults.

Parks, Gardens, and Zoos

Botanica, 701 Amidon (316-264-0448; www.botanica.org). At this "living museum of plants," your senses will be delighted by nine and a half acres of colorful tulips, irises, daylilies, mums, wildflowers, and other flowers. From spring to fall, more than 350 varieties of roses bloom in the Rose Garden. Reflecting pools, streams, and a pond of goldfish and Japanese koi add kid appeal to this fragrant facility. Kids also enjoy watching butterflies emerge from their cocoons during the summer months in the Butterfly House, where more than 5,000 butterflies fly freely. In the Aquatic Collection, kids can wonder at the Giant Water Platter, whose leaves grow to 8 feet in diameter. The Woodland Walk, a ¼-mile wood-chip trail laid out by Boy Scouts, is full of native plants, birds, and small wild animals. A natural area with poisonous plants is a good place to show kids how to identify poison ivy, poison hemlock, and other no-nos. New in 1999 is the Sensory Garden, designed especially for the physically challenged, with plants at a convenient level for those in wheel-

Children's Museum of Wichita

The **Tot Tug** for toddlers has preschool toys and a model train. Younger kids love the colorful three-story maze that looks like a small village from the outside; inside are challenging crawling and climbing spaces. Playacting is encouraged: kids can be judges, doctors, or firefighters, thanks to true-to-life costumes and props. Kids can travel through time in the **Prairie House** with its miniature furniture, tepee, and chuck wagon. Older kids like the challenging science-related activities in the **Young Explorers** exhibit. Weekends are lively, with original puppet shows on Saturday and a Sunday Concert series. Frequent traveling exhibits add spark to this already dynamic facility.

The Museum will close at the end of 1999 and reopen in the spring of 2000 as **Exploration Place,** located on twenty acres on the west bank of the Arkansas River, reaching north from Second Street and west toward Handley. There will be four pavilions, each focusing on a different aspect of our world: **Exploring Human Life** (learning about people and our health), **Kids Explore** (kids can have fun while learning about their world), **Exploring Our Only Home** (learning about the land, water, and air), and **Exploring Flight and Design** (how do birds fly? how do we?). Almost all the exhibits will be hands-on. Exploration Place will also have two theaters and a **Simulation Center,** where visitors will be placed in the middle of explorations of the ocean depths or flying over the mountains.

Children's Museum of Wichita, 435 South Water; (316–267–2281).

chairs, and flowers with particularly strong aromas for the visually impaired. Special events, including festivals, parties, concerts, plus seasonal flower shows, are held throughout the year. Catered lunches are sold on Wednesdays, and guided tours are offered April through October; both require reservations.

More Attractions

Barnacle Bill's FantaSea Water Park, 3330 North Woodlawn (316–682–7031 for taped information, or 682–8656). The only water-oriented theme park in the state, Barnacle Bill's runs the gamut from small wading pools with slides for tiny tots to large (six-story high) water slides and a giant wave pool. Captain Kidd's Cove provides adventure for the littlest ones. Grab a bite at the concession stand, or bring your own cooler (no

Sedgwick County Zoo

This fine 247-acre zoo, open 364 days a year, allows compatible groups of animals to roam within natural barriers in habitats resembling different geographic areas of the world. The number one tourist attraction in Kansas, the Sedgwick County Zoo has more than 2,000 animals of 436 species. Its largest exhibit, the **North American Prairie,** features a skywalk over a habitat where bison and antelope roam, as well as grizzly bears, cougars, and Mexican grey wolves. Elsewhere, birds fly free in a **Tropical Rain Forest,** reptiles and amphibians slither and crawl through a dark **Herpetarium,** and rhinos, zebras, elephants, lions, and monkeys roam in various enclosures.

Three different **Children's Farms** are here: At the American farm, visitors can pet sheep and see cows being milked. At the Asian farm, children will see water buffalo and yaks. The African farm features camels and Nigerian dwarf goats for kids to pet. New in 1999 is the **Pride of the Plains** exhibit, featuring lions (in a nativelike kopje rock home), warthogs, and meerkats, surrounded and separated by large moats. Have lunch or a snack at the restaurant on the premises.

Sedgwick County Zoo, 5555 Zoo Boulevard (northwest edge of town, just off I-235); (316) 942-2213; www.scz.org.

glass or alcohol allowed). The park is open May through Labor Day; call for specific days.

The **Joyland Amusement Park,** 2801 South Hillside (316-684-0179). This typical amusement arena has adult and kids' rides, including a 100-foot Sky Coaster, an arcade, bumper cars, and a miniature train tour. The park is open April through September.

The 21st Century Pyradomes, 3055 North Hillside (316-682-3100). Drive by to see the eight distinctive geodesic domes designed by H. Buckminster Fuller, and a 60-foot pyramid inspired by (what else?) the pyramids of Egypt. Should you desire, tours are offered Monday through Friday at 1:30 P.M.

Tree Trunk Art, as it's known, can be found at numerous spots throughout town. Artist Gino Salerno has recycled old tree trunks into forty delightful pieces of art that kids adore, including *Wizard of Oz* characters, which can be found at **Watson Park,** 33044 South Old Lawrence Road. For other locations, call the parks department at (316) 268-4361.

Wichita Boat House and Arkansas River Foundation Museum, 335 West Lewis (316-264-3174). Situated on the east bank of the

Self-Guided Tours

Wichita Convention and Visitors Bureau has information on two self-guided tours that contrast the area's cowboy past with its aviation future.

- The **Wichita Western Heritage Tour,** a trail through the Old West that touches on Wichita's western heritage, highlights ten Old West sites around the city. Among the stops are the **Chisholm Trail Historical Marker,** northeast corner of Douglas Avenue at McLean Boulevard. This limestone monument marks the spot where, between 1867 and 1874, more than three million Texas Longhorns crossed the Arkansas River on their way to Abilene, the final stop on the legendary cattle trail. **Highland Cemetery,** 1001 North Hillside, is the final resting place of the original Buffalo Bill, William Mathewson, whose monument and gravesite are on the high ground of this pioneer cemetery. Mathewson—not to be confused with William Cody, the Buffalo Bill of the Wild West Show—was a sharpshooter, buffalo hunter, and Indian fighter in the 1860s and '70s. Wichita's **Eaton Hotel,** 523 East Douglas, considered in its Chisholm Trail days to be the finest hotel between Kansas City and Denver, is famous for having its bar smashed to smithereens by prohibition crusader Carrie Nation in 1900. A twenty-page Heritage Tour brochure is available from the bureau in English, Spanish, French, German, and Japanese.
- **Come Fly With Us** takes you on a tour of "Wichita, the Air Capital of the World," with stops at Boeing, Raytheon Aircraft, Bombardier Learjet, McConnell Air Force Base, the National Institute for Aviation Research, the Kansas Aviation Museum, and the Kansas Cosmosphere and Space Center.

Information for both tours is available at the Wichita Convention and Visitors Bureau, 100 South Main, Suite 100; (316) 265–2800 or (800) 288–WICHITA.

Arkansas River, the Boat House offers boat rides, rentals, and relaxation on the water. Displays include the *Jayhawk,* one of three racing yachts used by Wichita native Bill Koch to win the 1992 America's Cup.

Sportsworld, 1010 North Webb Road (316–682–3700), is the area's largest family sports complex. It features two miniature golf courses, batting cages, go-cart tracks, kiddie-car tracks, and a one-hundred-game video arcade.

Of Special Interest

- **Kansas African-American Museum,** 601 North Water Street (316-262-7651), chronicles Wichita's black heritage from its earliest days to present, with thousands of artifacts in its Heritage Collection.
- **Frank Lloyd Wright Allen-Lambe House,** 255 North Roosevelt Street (316-687-1027; www2.southwind.net/~allenlam), is the last of the Prairie Style homes, designed by Wright in 1915. One-hour tours are available by appointment.
- **Great Plains Transportation Museum,** 700 East Douglas Street (316-263-0944; www.gptm.org), the railroad museum of Kansas, features a Sante Fe steam engine, a Burlington caboose, diesel locomotives, and much more.
- **Kansas Aviation Museum,** 3350 South George Washington Boulevard (316-683-9242), houses the Kansas Aviation Hall of Fame in the original Wichita Municipal Airport, plus artifacts and planes such as the Cessna 310 and a 1928 Swallow in the midst of restoration.

Theater, Music, and the Arts

The Convention Bureau's Fun Fone (316-262-7474 or 888-272-9424; www.wichita-cvb.org) offers daily updates of entertainment and special events. The downtown Century II complex is where most cultural activities take place, including **Metropolitan Ballet** (316-687-5880), which performs the *Nutcracker* each Christmas season; **Music Theatre of Wichita** (316-265-3107), staging five different productions each summer; **Wichita Symphony Orchestra** (316-267-7658 or 316-267-7658; www.wso.org), whose performances include Young People's Concerts; and **Wichita Pops** (316-263-4717), featuring the grand old Wurlitzer organ from New York's Paramount Theater in several concerts throughout the year. **Wichita Children's Theatre,** 201 Lulu (316-262-2282), performs both here and at their own theater.

Shopping

Dorothy and Toto hailed from Kansas, so it's only natural that *Wizard of Oz* artifacts are sold at shops throughout the town and state. At **The Best of Kansas** at the Hay Market, 5426 East Central (316-685-0611), you'll find Oz memorabilia as well as native arts, crafts, and food products.

Get yourself and your pardners outfitted with boots, jeans, and cowboy hats at **Sheplers Western Wear,** the world's largest western store, 6501 West Kellogg (316-946-3600). Wichita is also the home of Coleman prod-

Wagon Train Trips

The town of El Dorado is the home of the **Flint Hills Overland Wagon Trips,** 120 South Gordy (316-321-6300 for reservations; 316-283-2636 for information). Trips leave on selected spring, summer, and fall weekends for picturesque overnight rides on horses, covered wagons, and stagecoaches. Meals, campfires with singing and tall tales, plus hearty pioneer meals and snacks are included. All ages are welcome, but we wouldn't advise it for those with very young or fussy kids, who might find the trip bumpy and boring once the novelty wears off.

ucts, an extensive line of camping items. The **Coleman Factory Outlet Store and Museum,** 239 North St. Francis (316-264-0836), offers a wide assortment of discounted products as well as a display of vintage Coleman items. **Bradley Fair at Wilson Estates,** Rock Road at Twenty-first Street (316-262-6400), has more than one hundred stores and restaurants, as do **Towne East Square** (316-686-3341) and **Towne West Square** (316-945-1236), Wichita's main shopping malls. And in the **Old Town District** (316-262-3555; www.oldtownwichita.com), turn-of-the-century buildings have been turned into the largest shopping, dining, and entertainment area in Kansas.

Sports

The **Wichita Wings,** a Major Soccer League team, play at the Kansas Coliseum, I-135 at Eighty-fifth Street North (316-262-3545). **Wichita Wranglers,** an AA minor league baseball farm team for the Kansas City Royals, go to bat at Lawrence-Dumont Stadium, 300 South Sycamore (316-267-3372). The **Wichita Thunder** hockey team (316-264-GOAL; www.wichitathunder.com) also plays at the Kansas Coliseum.

Side Trips

The Kansas Travel and Tourism Division's *Attractions Guide* has a helpful listing divided by geographical areas, as well as other tourist literature.

For swimming and other watersports, head thirty minutes northeast of town to **El Dorado Reservoir and State Park,** Highway 177 (316-321-7180), which sports the state's largest recreational lake (8,000 acres of water, 640 campsites). Enjoy fishing and swimming at two beaches (no lifeguards) as well as a marina (no boat rentals), hiking trails, and picnicking.

Hutchinson, 45 miles northwest of Wichita, is home to the **Dillon Nature Center,** 3002 East Thirtieth (316-663-7411). This thirty-acre site has woods, prairie, marshes, and ponds that attract hundreds of different wildlife species. Two miles of trails, picnic areas, a fishing pond, and a garden make this a pleasant stop. Admission is free, although there are sometimes fees for special programs.

Just west of Hutchinson on Highway 96 is another treat for kids: the

Hedrick Exotic Animal Farm (316-422-3296). Joe and Sondra Hedrick raise and train animals for petting zoos and for camel, ostrich, and pig races throughout the country. The assortment of animals on this working farm also includes zebras, llamas, goats, kangaroos, and exotic birds. Open daily, the farm offers tours for a fee.

There's lots more in the Hutchinson area, including two state parks, a small zoo, and the nearby **Yoder Amish Community,** with shops selling handicrafts, furniture, and baked goods. Call the Greater Hutchinson Convention/Visitors Bureau for more information; (316) 662-3391 or (800) 658-1777.

Just ten minutes to the east of Wichita is the quaint town of Kechi, an antique lover's paradise. Officially recorded as the "Antique Capital of Kansas," Kechi offers an incredible variety of crafts and heirlooms at its twenty-four shops. There are no convenience stores here, no movie theaters, not even a gas station. But it attrcts antiques dealers from all over the country. After spending time along **The Boardwalk** and in **Kechi Alley,** stop by **Geno's Bar B-Q** (316-744-1497) for a sandwich, or **Creek House Kitchen** (316-744-1732) for a home-cooked meal.

Country Critters Puppet Factory, 217 Neosho in Burlington, 95 miles northeast of Wichita (316-364-8623), provides an interesting tour for kids. See how the puppets are created, sewn together, decorated, and packaged for shipment. The tours are offered twice daily on weekdays; call first to reserve.

Special Events

Contact the Wichita Convention and Visitors Bureau for details on the following annual events.

January. Darryl Starbird Rod & Custom Car Show, (918) 257-8073; Wichita Boat Show, (316) 264-9121.

April. Kansas Newman Renaissance Faire, with arts and crafts, dramatic and musical performances, authentic games and activities, (800) 736-7585.

May. Wichita River Festival, ten days of parades, bike and bathtub races, old-fashioned socials, hot air balloons, and the grand finale—Wichita Symphony's *1812 Overture* (young kids might not like the cannons, but they will like the fireworks that follow), (316) 267-2817; Kansas Polkatennial, with three days of nonstop polka music and dance, (316) 283-1488.

July. Inter-Tribal Mid-America All-Indian Powwow is an opportunity to learn cultural heritage, such as traditional dances, (316) 262-5221; an 1876 Fourth of July, Old Cowtown Museum, (316) 264-0671.

September. Wichita Black Arts Festival, Wichita State University, (316) 691-1499; Fall Festival Arts & Crafts Show, (316) 265-2020.

October. Wichita Asian Festival, with traditional costume fashion shows, dances, skits, karate demonstrations, and Asian food, (316) 689-8729; Old Sedgwick County Fair, first weekend, at Old Cowtown Museum, re-creates an 1870s fair with music, craft demonstrations and sales, antique buggies, wagon rides, steam-operated carousel, traditional foods, costumed reenactments, and theatrical performances, (316) 264-0671.

Late November–December. Old-Fashioned Christmas, Cowtown, Monday through Saturday evenings after Thanksgiving, with music, programs, and refreshments, (316) 264-0671.

December. Wichita Winterfest, a weekend of strolling carolers, roasted chestnuts, cider, activities, and entertainment, (316) 943-4221.

Where to Stay

The Wichita Convention and Visitors Bureau has a Lodging Guide that lists a few bed-and breakfast inns, although there is no B&B reservation service. A wide assortment of reasonably priced accommodations range from budget motels, including **Super 8 Motel,** 527 South Webb Road (316-686-3888 or 800-800-8000), to full-service hotels. Be sure to ask about weekend packages. Some choices: **Guild Plaza Hotel,** 125 North Market (316-263-2101 or 800-445-9097). This hotel has a cafe, free cribs, an indoor pool, and an airport van. **Wichita Suites,** 5211 East Kellogg, U.S. 54 (316-685-2233 or 800-243-5953). Choose from studio or one- and two-bedroom suites, all with refrigerators. There's also a heated pool, exercise equipment, and free cribs (but no rollaways). The **Wichita Marriott,** 9100 Corporate Hills Drive (316-685-2233 or 800-228-9290), has good-sized rooms and an indoor and outdoor pool. The **Residence Inn by Marriott Downtown,** 411 South Webb Road (316-686-7331 or 800-331-3131). This all-suite hotel offers lots of space with equipped kitchens and complimentary breakfasts.

Where to Eat

The Wichita Convention and Visitors Bureau has a helpful restaurant listing. An interesting note: Wichita is the birthplace of **Pizza Hut,** and the chain sometimes opens up prototypes in town to test new architecture or new menu items. Check locations with the Convention and Visitors Bureau.

A few family friendly selections: **Spaghetti Warehouse Italian Grill,** 619 East William Street (316-264-7479), serves Italian and American lunch and dinner, with a kid's menu available. Youngsters like the tableside hibachi cooking at **Kobe Steak House,** 650 North Carriage Parkway (316-686-5915), open for dinner seven days a week and offering a kid's menu. Reservations are suggested.

Other popular spots are **Black Canyon Grill,** 3731 North Rock Road (316-636-2121); **Yia Yia's Eurobistro,** 8115 East Twenty-first Street (316-634-1000); and the four-star **Olive Tree Restaurant,** 2949 North Rock Road (316-636-1100).

For more information

Wichita Convention and Visitors Bureau: 100 South Main, Suite 100 (316-265-2800 or 800-288-WICHITA; www.wichita-cvb.org). Two satellite offices on I-35 are open summers only, both inside Hardee's Restaurants: Towanda Service Area, 20 miles north of town, and Belle Plaine Service Area, 20 miles south of town.

The Kansas Travel and Tourism Division, 700 Southwest Harrison, Suite 1300, Topeka 66603-3712 (800-2-KANSAS).

Emergency Numbers

Ambulance, fire, police: 911

Twenty-four-hour Poison Control Information Center: (316) 688-2277

Hospital: Medical Center, 550 North Hillside; (316) 688-2468

Pharmacy: Cumming's Pharmacy, 501 North Hillside, near Wesley Medical, is open every day of the year from 8:00 A.M. to midnight; (316) 682-4565.

DEARBORN AREA

Dearborn, Michigan, about 12 miles west of Detroit, was founded by auto pioneer Henry Ford and welcomes two million tourists a year. They invariably head straight to the Henry Ford Museum and Greenfield Village, the most visited indoor/outdoor historical complex in North America. The museum alone is worth the trip, but you'll find other interesting and fun things to do with your family in this city of 90,000 and the surrounding area. Downtown Detroit, which can be hot in summer, has some interesting African-American heritage attractions.

GETTING THERE

Detroit Metropolitan Airport, about fifteen minutes west of the museum and village, is served by major commercial airlines (call individual carriers for information). Car rentals are available at the airport. **Commuter Transportation Company** (313-946-1000 or 800-351-5466) provides hourly coach service from the airport to major hotels in Dearborn from 6:45 A.M. to midnight. Taxis are plentiful. Detroit's **City Airport** (313-267-6400) is 30 miles east and serves commuter airlines.

Amtrak (800-USA-RAIL) runs trains to Dearborn's station, near Michigan Avenue and Greenfield. **Greyhound/Trailways** bus line serves Detroit's downtown terminal at 1000 West Lafayette Street. Call (313) 963-9840 or (800) 231-2222 for information about fares and schedules. Interstate highway systems provide easy access to Dearborn; take I-94 from the northeast and west, I-75 from the south.

GETTING AROUND

Taxis are available at hotels and on call. **SMART Bus** (Southeast Michigan Area Rapid Transit) buses (313-962-5515) serve Dearborn's major arteries and also operate between Detroit and the Henry Ford Museum and Greenfield Village. The **Classic Trolley** is available for charter trips (313-945-6100).

Dearborn and Detroit

AT A GLANCE

- Explore the Henry Ford Museum and Greenfield Village
- Visit the Nature Center and the Zoological Park in Detroit
- Tour the Charles W. Wright Museum of African-American History—the largest African-American history museum in the United States
- Dearborn Chamber of Commerce, (313) 584-6100

What to See and Do

Museums

Henry Ford Museum and Greenfield Village, 20900 Oakwood (313-271-1620 or 800 343-1929). Visitors arriving at the museum expecting to see endless displays of cars are pleasantly surprised to find there's so much more. One thing is for sure: You'll never hear the word "boring" uttered by your kids while you're on the premises.

Be sure everyone wears very comfortable shoes; you will cover a lot of ground. (Although strollers are rented in Greenfield Village for a nominal fee, they aren't allowed in all the buildings.) The museum has twelve acres of exhibits; the adjacent outdoor Greenfield Village spreads out over eighty-one acres. Ideally, you should spend two days here, allowing one day per attraction. Admission is separate, but combination and two-day tickets are available.

At the entrance, there's a replica of Philadelphia's Independence Hall. Inside, fascinating exhibits show how technology changed life in America. Both kids and parents will enjoy the Automobile in American Life exhibit, which includes original landmarks such as an entire 1946 diner, a 1940s Texaco service station, a 1950s drive-in movie theater, and a 1960s Holiday Inn room, along with one hundred historically significant cars. All kids love trains, and yours will revel in the museum's enormous 600-ton Allegheny locomotive, used to haul huge coal trains. It's part of a transportation exhibit that also includes aircraft, horse-drawn vehicles, streetcars, and firefighting apparatus. Other museum highlights include the limousine in which President John F. Kennedy was shot and Robert Byrd's 1925 plane, the first to fly over the North Pole.

African-American Heritage

Explore Arican-American history in the Detroit metro region. In addition to the slave houses at the Henry Ford Museum & Greenfield Village, highlights of an African-American history tour are:

- **Charles W. Wright Museum of African American History,** 315 East Warren Avenue; Detroit (313-494-5800; www.detnews.com/maah). At 120,000 square feet, this is the largest African-American museum in the United States. Walk through a reconstructed slave ship, see a reproduction of Martin Luther King Jr.'s jailhouse door, and read the letters of Frederick Douglass and Booker T. Washington.
- **National Museum of the Tuskegee Airmen,** housed at Historic Fort Wayne. Exhibits tell the story of this all-black group of pilots who fought in WW II.
- **Detroit Institute of the Arts,** 5200 Woodward Avenue, Detroit (313-833-7900). The collection, which traces art from ancient to modern times, presents works from ancient Egypt and contemporary art from Africa.
- **Motown Historical Museum at Hitsville USA,** 2648 West Grand Boulevard,Detroit (313-875-2264). Tour Motown founder Barry Gordy's apartment and the original recording Studio A. See rock 'n' roll memorabilia of such Motown legends as the Jackson Five, Smokey Robinson, and the Supremes.

A must-see (and must-do) is the **Innovation Station,** a 3,200-square-foot interactive learning game on the main concourse that offers all ages a chance to find creative new ways to solve problems. About thirty players team up at various activity stations to provide the manpower (pedaling bicycles and turning hand cranks, for example) and brainpower (sorting balls by color for example) to propel thousands of brightly colored balls through a network of tubes and sorting devices into bins. If a problem develops, everyone "brainstorms" to provide a solution. The game takes from twenty to thirty minutes.

The colorful **Made in America** multimedia exhibit uses hands-on activities, video and film presentations—even a troupe of cartoon characters—to show visitors of all ages how industry affects their lives. Kids will be fascinated by the overhead conveyer that carries a continuous flow of American-made products—including a kitchen sink. Also on view are a giant light-bulb-making machine, a step-inside hydroelectric generator, and a touch-screen computer that lets visitors feel what it's like to run an electrical power plant.

The adjacent **Greenfield Village** features more than eighty homes, workplaces, and community buildings from different periods and locations, each displaying the day-to-day processes that helped build this nation. Some are homes of famous people: the Wright Brothers' model Ohio home (their Cycle Shop is elsewhere in the Village); the city home of Noah Webster, author of America's first dictionary; the farm where Henry Ford was born and raised; and tire magnate Harvey S. Firestone's 1880s farm, where costumed interpreters perform daily tasks. Other residences reveal the struggles and adversities faced by less famous people: the 1850 slave homes from a Georgia plantation, for instance, and the wilderness home of an eighteenth-century Connecticut family.

Other highlights: **Thomas Edison's Menlo Park Laboratory** is restored to its 1880 state and includes more than 400 inventions created here, including the phonograph and incandescent light. (Who knows how many future inventors will be inspired by what they see?) Nearby, the Sarah Jordan Boarding House, one of the first residences wired for electric light, housed several of Edison's assistants.

Your kids can take part in the day's lessons at **Scotch Settlement School,** which Henry Ford attended, or enjoy hands-on activities and old-fashioned games on The Green. Demonstrations in glassblowing, pottery, and other crafts are also fascinating for kids, and you can buy many of the products created in the museum gift shop.

Samantha at Greenfield Village

If you have a daughter enamored of Samantha, the doll in the American Girls Collection, see Greenfield Village from Samantha's point of view. The tour, available on weekends and also during the week in summer, is charming. Girls, dressed identically to the dolls they clutch (bring your own) and their accompanying grownups meet Samantha's aunt and uncle, ride in a "newfangled" automobile, and march in a suffrage parade. Call (800) 343-1929 for information and reservations.

Learn about the innovators of the automotive industry at the **Automotive Hall of Fame.** Located conveniently next to the Henry Ford Museum, you can learn about speed demons like Wilbur Shaw, the first driver to win consecutive Indy 500 titles. There are also exhibits about business leaders, like former Chrysler chairman Lee Iacocca.

Suwanee Park will delight the entire family with 1913 carousel rides. Stop for a soda at the old-fashioned 1870 ice-cream parlor. For an extra fee you can ride a paddle-wheel boat or steam-powered locomotive around the village perimeter. Narrated carriage tours (sleigh tours in the winter, weather permitting) and 1931 bus rides are also available for an additional charge.

Henry Ford Estate

If your museum visit whets your family's interest in Henry Ford, stop by his mansion, 1 mile away. Tour the house with its self-contained power plant, which is connected to the mansion by a tunnel, or stroll along the gardens and trails on the grounds. In the summer, follow a self-guided forty-five-minute walking tour that passes a tree house, bathhouse, boathouse, and scenic views. Christmastime brings Santa's Workshop, breakfast with Santa, a floral tour of the estate, and special holiday events. **Henry Ford Estate,** Fair Lane, the campus of University of Michigan Dearborn, off Evergreen and U.S. 12 (313-593-5590).

From early January to mid-March, there is a single admission fee to both museums, although visitors to Greenfield Village may view building exteriors only.

Parks and Zoos

The Detroit area has another zoo: the **Detroit Zoological Park,** Woodward Avenue and Ten Mile Road (I-696), Royal Oak (a northern suburb of Detroit, about 12 miles from Dearborn); (313) 398-0900. This zoo is one of the country's largest and most modern. It has 125 acres of landscaped grounds with cageless exhibits grouped according to continent, simulating the animals' natural habitats. Don't miss the four-acre chimpanzee exhibit. There's also a miniature railroad ride around the park. You can buy food, or bring your own and picnic. Allow about four hours for a visit here.

Performing Arts

The Greenfield Village Theatre Company (313-271-1620) performs time-honored plays suitable for family viewing at the Henry Ford Museum Theater throughout the year. Although season subscriptions are sold, individual tickets and dinner/theater tickets also are available.

Shopping

Fairlane Town Center, between Hubbard Drive, Evergreen Road, Southfield Expressway (M-39), and Michigan Avenue (U.S. 12), is one of the state's largest indoor malls, with The Disney Store and two toy stores of special interest to kids. The information center on the lower level is the place to stop for bus schedules, tips on lodging, and the answers to other questions. The mall is open every day; call (313) 593-3330 for more information.

Sports

Sporting enthusiasts may want to take in a **Detroit Tigers** baseball game at Tiger Stadium; a new stadium will be ready in 2001. **The Lions** play football at the Pontiac Silverdome, but a new domed stadium next to the open-air baseball stadium is planned. The **Detroit Pistons** play basketball at the Palace of Auburn Hills, while **Red Wings** hockey games are played in the Joe Louis Arena, part of the city's downtown riverfront Civic

Learning about cars is just one of the many activities kids can participate in at the Henry Ford Museum and Greenfield Village complex.

Center. Games are frequently sold out; you can order tickets in advance of your visit from TicketMaster (313-645-6666) or call the Detroit Visitor's Hotline (see For More Information) for specifics.

SIDE TRIPS

If your kids have never been to Canada, you can take a quick trip some 15 miles south of the border to the pleasant town of **Windsor, Ontario.** That's right—south. Look at a map, and you'll see that Dearborn and Detroit are actually north of Windsor, Ontario, where you can grab a bite to eat and stroll around town. Access is via bridge or tunnel. If you're in town during the **International Freedom Festival** (see Special Events), you'll find plenty to do during the weeklong celebration of Canada Day and Independence Day.

Cranbrook is the former estate of George Booth, publisher of *The Detroit News.* It's now a well-known cultural and educational center 18 miles away from Dearborn, in Bloomfield Hills. Surrounding Booth's home are forty acres of public gardens, woods, pine walks, and two lakes. Also on the property: an art museum, which exhibits both contemporary

Belle Isle

Belle Isle is reached via a toll-free bridge at East Jefferson Avenue and East Grand Boulevard, Detroit (313-267-7115). About 15 miles from Dearborn, it's the nation's largest urban island park, with 1,000 acres of wooded paths and drives, including one that goes along the shore. Recreational possibilities abound here: golf, tennis, and swimming (at a sandy beach with lifeguards). Signs point the way to the various attractions.

- Younger kids will love the terrific **playground,** where they can climb up and down nets and over wooden structures, crawl through tunnels, and slide down poles.
- **The Nature Center** (313-267-7157) has wooded trails where you can view plants, animals, and changing exhibits (donations requested). Allow about an hour for the thirteen-acre zoo where, for a fee, you can stroll the winding elevated walkway and view uncaged animals in natural settings.
- **Dossin Great Lakes Museum** (313-267-6440) is worth a visit with older kids who may appreciate the restored smoking lounge taken from the 1912 steamer *City of Detroit III,* complete with walls of hand-carved oak work. There's also a 40-foot hydroplane (*The Miss Pepsi*), observation deck, periscope, and ship-to-shore radio messages (donations).
- **Whitcomb Conservatory** (313-267-7134) blooms with six seasonal flower shows. There are permanent displays of palms, ferns, and cacti, as well as one of the country's largest orchid collections, and it's all free.
- **The Aquarium,** one of the country's oldest, exhibits various freshwater fish from the Great Lakes and beyond.

art and artwork by students at Cranbrook schools; a science history museum with a large mineral collection; a planetarium with weekend shows; and a nature center. Call (313) 645-3000 for information.

Special Events

Call the Detroit Visitor's Hotline for more information on area goings-on. The Dearborn Chamber of Commerce also publishes a calendar of events. There are three notable area fairs and festivals.

March. Maple Syrup Festival, Cranbrook Institute of Science, Bloomfield Hills, first three weekends.

Late June–early July. International Freedom Festival, a celebration shared by Detroit and Windsor, Ontario, with fireworks, parades, craft shows, and entertainment. Ford Senior Players Championship Tournament, Players Club, Dearborn (313–441–0300), which is kicked off by the Dearborn Ford Festival.

Late August–early September. Ten-day Michigan State Fair, Michigan Exposition and State Fairgrounds, Detroit.

Where to Stay

Some Dearborn hotels offer packages that include tickets to the Henry Ford Museum and Greenfield Village. Request a list from the Dearborn Chamber of Commerce (see For More Information). Three of these are also on the Classic Trolley circuit, making them especially convenient.

The Dearborn Inn, 20301 Oakwood Boulevard (313–271–2700 or 800–228–9290), a Marriott hotel, is a renovated landmark building with three separate wings: Main Inn, Colonial Lodge, and Famous Americans Colonial Homes suites. It's a good choice for families. Call (313) 593–1234 or (800) 233–1234.

Hyatt Regency Dearborn, Fairlane Town Center (313–593–1234 or 800–233–1234) offers a shopping mall at your doorstep, plus an indoor pool, restaurants, a fitness center, and more.

Quality Inn–Fairlane, 21430 Michigan Avenue (313–565–0800), is ½-half mile from the Henry Ford Museum and Greenfield Village and features an outdoor pool, on-site picnic grounds, complimentary breakfast, VCRs, movie rentals, and refrigerators. Also on the site is the Dearborn Historical Museum (313–565–3000), which you might not bother visiting unless you're a guest at the inn or an avid history buff. Exhibits show the development of Dearborn in two historical buildings: one, part of an original arsenal; the other, the original powder magazine, which stored ammunition as early as 1839.

Another family-friendly choice is the **Hampton Inn of Dearborn,** 20061 Michigan Avenue, Dearborn (313–436–9600 or 800–HAMPTON). Rooms come with free movies and continental breakfast.

Also worthy of note: For the big splurge, there's the **Ritz-Carlton Dearborn,** Fairlane Plaza (313–441–2000 or 800–241–3333).

Where to Eat

The Dearborn Chamber of Commerce offers a helpful restaurant guide that includes maps and general price ranges. East Dearborn is home to the largest Middle Eastern population in the United States, and if you like that style of cooking, locals say you can't go wrong at any of their restaurants. **LaShish,** 12918 Michigan (313-584-4477), is a casual family restaurant serving authentic Middle Eastern dishes and fresh juices. Some other styles of cooking: **Bill Knapp's of Dearborn,** 3500 Greenfield (313-271-7166), serves affordable American food and has a children's menu. No matter when your family's appetite kicks in, **Andoni's Family Dining,** 1620 North Telegraph (313-582-2024), open twenty-four hours, can whip up a satisfying meal. **Dimitri's,** 2424 South Telegraph, Dearborn (313-565-7066), offers a wide selection at moderate prices.

For More Information

Dearborn Chamber of Commerce, 15544 Michigan Avenue, has helpful pamphlets and brochures (313-584-6100). **Metro Detroit Convention & Visitor's Bureau** (313-202-1800 or 800-338-7648; www.visitdetroit.com.)

Emergency Numbers

Police and fire: 911

Henry Ford Hospital at Fairlane Center: (313) 593-8100

Hospital: Oakwood Hospital, 18101 Oakwood Boulevard; (313) 593-7000

Poison Control: (313) 745-5711

Twenty-four-hour pharmacy: Rite Aid, Shaefer at Ford Road; (313) 581-3280

11 Michigan

TRAVERSE CITY AREA

Along with being the "Cherry Capital of the World," the Traverse City, Michigan, area is known as a "Great Lakes Paradise." This city of 17,000—the largest in Northwest Lower Michigan—is blessed by a superb location at the head of Grand Traverse Bay on Lake Michigan's northern shore. Grand Traverse County has a population of 70,000. (The bay is separated into east and west sections by the scenic Old Mission Peninsula.) Situated on the 45th parallel, halfway between the equator and the North Pole, the area has four distinct seasons. Summers offer miles of beaches, fabulous freshwater fishing, and countless recreational possibilities. Winter's bountiful snows bring cross-country and downhill skiing, snowmobiling, sledding, and skating. Add fall's spectacular foliage and abundant fruit harvests and spring's white and pink cherry blossoms, and you'll see why families come back season after season, year after year.

GETTING THERE

The area is easily accessible by car via state highways. Traverse City's **Cherry Capital Airport** (616-947-2250) is serviced by several national and regional carriers. Hertz and Avis car rental agencies are at the airport; others are in town.

Taxis and **BATA (Bay Area Transportation Authority)** bus service (616-941-2324) are also available. **Greyhound** buses (616-946-5180) link Traverse City to the Upper Peninsula and southern Michigan. There's no train service to this area.

GETTING AROUND

Although there are buses, taxicabs, and limousine services, it is quickest and easiest to have a car.

Traverse City Area

AT A GLANCE

- Enjoy 250 miles of Lake Michigan Shoreline
- Climb dunes, canoe, fish, and hike at Sleeping Bear Dunes National Lakeshore
- Sail the bay aboard a tall ship
- Golf at more than a dozen courses
- Traverse City Convention and Visitors Bureau, (616) 947-1120 or (800) TRAVERS

WHAT TO SEE AND DO

Museums and Zoos

Dennos Museum Center, 1701 East Front Street, Traverse City (616-922-1055 or 800-748-0566; dmc.nmc.edu). Located at the campus entrance of Northwestern Michigan College, this spacious museum's motto is "Come Alive Inside." **The Discovery Gallery**'s hands-on exhibits are fun. Among them: an antigravity mirror that gives you the illusion of floating, and Recollections II, a video experience that transforms a child's movements into multicolored delayed-motion images.

Unique to the museum is **Weiss I** (named after its creator, Detroit area artist and musician Ed Weiss), a sound wall with multicolored wood panels that produce different sounds when touched: percussion, synthesizer, and even "rap." Older kids also like the **Arctic Spirit gallery,** a collection of Inuit art considered one of the most complete in the country. The graceful *Dancing Bear* sculpture at the entrance is a charmer, and the *Enchanged Owl* print by a master artisan appeared on a Canadian postage stamp. There are also three galleries with changing exhibits and a spacious sculpture garden. Open daily until 5:00 P.M.

The **Music House Museum,** 7377 U.S. 31 North, Acme, about 6 miles east of Traverse City; (619-938-9300; www.musichouse.org). Automated instruments, including music boxes (like an Orchestral Corona music box made in 1899), nickelodeons, player pianos (a 1919 Hamburg, a 1925 Weber Duo-Art Steinway-Welte), and a vintage hand-carved Belgian dance organ are diaplayed in a nineteenth-century farm complex. Guided tours last ninety minutes.

Clinch Park Zoo, Grandview Parkway at Cass, Traverse City (616-922-4906). Northern Michigan wildlife such as bear, otters, bison, and beavers; an aquarium with native game fish, including trout and perch; a beach; and a miniature steam-train ride make this stop a hit with kids.

Grand Traverse Lighthouse Museum, Leelanau State Park, CR-629, Northport (616-386-9145). This lighthouse, on the tip of the Leelanau Peninsula, is one of the oldest on the Great Lakes and has recently been turned into a living-history museum. Relive nautical history by touring the tower that looks to Lake Michigan, and the museum where a Fourth Order Fresnel lens is displayed.

City Opera House, 112½ East Front Street, Traverse City (616-922-2050). If you're downtown and want to break from shopping, this 1891 Victorian opera house is quite impressive. Tours are available, if arranged in advance, but even without a tour visitors will still be able to appreciate the vaulted ceiling, gilded molding around the stage, and elaborate murals.

Tall Ship Cruises

Listed on the National and State Registers of Historic Sites is the tall ship ***Malabar,*** 13390 West Bay Shore Drive; (616) 941-2000 or (800) 678-0383. Become an "old salt" for the day aboard this replica of an eighteenth-century topsail, gaft-rigged sailing vessel. Three cruises lap the bay daily: noon to 2:00 P.M. (lunch served), 3:00 to 5:00 P.M., and 7:00 to 9:30 P.M. (dinner served). Also available: three- to six-day Windjammer cruises on the tall ship ***Manitou.***

More Attractions

Amon Orchards and Farm Market, U.S. 31 North, Acme (616-938-9160 or 800-937-1644). You can buy cherry mustard and pick your own fruit. Young children like the petting zoo, and there are cider-making demonstrations in the fall. Kids love it here! Closed November through April.

Candle Factory, Grandview Parkway, Traverse City (616-946-2280). This leading retailer features candle-making demonstrations at various times daily, by appointment.

Pirates Cove Adventure Park, U.S. 31 North, Traverse City (616-938-9599). Sunken treasure and challenging minigolf.

River Country Funland, U.S. 31 North, Traverse City (616-691-7887). A kids' paradise, with miniature golf, go-carts, bumper boats, a water slide, and more.

Beaches and Parks

With 250 miles of Lake Michigan shoreline, beaches are the big summer attraction here. All have free public access, and the following particularly appeal to families. Take the kids beachcombing for Petroskey stones—

Canoeing and Kayaking

Salamander's, Traverse City (616-946-9446), offers kayak demonstrations every Thursday night and will supply maps and tips about which rivers are best for your skill level. **Alvina's Canoe & Boat Livery,** Interlochen (616-276-9514), can put you on the Betsie River. For the Crystal River, try **Crystal River Canoe Livery,** Glen Arbor (616-334-3090). For the Platte River, use **Riverside Canoe Trips,** Honor, near the Platte River Bridge (616-325-5622).

gray hexagonal-patterned petrified coral. (If you don't find any, they're sold in local gift shops.)

East Bay: Many hotels and motels are located here, on a strip of beach called the **Miracle Mile,** or across the street.

West Bay: **Bryant Park,** at the foot of Garfield, is the area's best for families with young children; kids can safely wade in the shallow water. There are also picnic areas, a large playground, and rest rooms. **Clinch Park,** on Grandview Parkway at Cass, (see previous zoo listing) is also popular, with more than 1,500 feet of sandy beach plus rest rooms and concessions. Because of the boats in the area, however, this is best for families with teens. **Elmwood Township Park,** off M-22, a mile north of the M-72 junction, is another family favorite, with playground and rest rooms.

Kids Kove, on the grounds of the Grand Traverse County Civic Center, is a guaranteed good time for younger kids. It's a 15,000-square-foot play structure designed by area schoolkids and includes mazes, a play lighthouse, swings, slides, and other traditional playground equipment. There's also a jogging track that loops around the Civic Center.

Ski Areas and Resorts

These destination resorts close to Traverse City entice families with a variety of children's programs, affordable packages, and après-ski fun. Since most are open year-round, these resorts also make great warm-weather destinations, offering mountain biking, golf, tennis, and other summer recreation. Always inquire about packages when you call. In addition, the Traverse City Convention and Visitors Bureau lists public downhill and cross-country trails.

Shanty Creek/Schuss Mountain Resort, Bellaire (616-533-8621 or 800-678-4111; www.shantycreek.com). Located 38 miles from Traverse City, this resort offers two ski areas 3½ miles apart but connected by a free shuttle. Summit Village is primarily for beginners and intermediates; Schuss Village, with a greater vertical drop, has more demanding terrain. Snow Stars (ages three to five) and Kids Academy (ages six to eleven) teach youngsters the joy of skiing. There's also snowboarding instruction. Lodging at this all-season resort is in 600 rooms, suites, and condos. Ice skating, horse-drawn sleigh rides, indoor/outdoor pools, tennis, and a beach club round out the fun.

Sleeping Bear Dunes National Lakeshore

Sleeping Bear Dunes National Lakeshore, about 30 miles west, includes 33 miles of Lake Michigan shoreline dotted with beaches. The one at **North Bear Lake,** central park area, reportedly has the warmest water. According to the Chippewa Indian legend that gave the park its name, a mother bear and her cubs swam across Lake Michigan to escape a forest fire. The mother waited on shore for her cubs, who lagged behind. It's said she still keeps watch in the form of a large, dark hill of sand, while her cubs became the North and South Manitou Islands.

- **Sand Dunes.** The park boasts large dunes, deposits left by melting glaciers some 11,000 years ago, that rise more than 400 feet above Lake Michigan. If your kids are old—and adventurous—enough, you can try the **Dune Climb,** 5 miles north of Empire on M-109.
- **Canoeing and Fishing.** The Platte River, on the southern end, and Crystal River, on the north, with adjacent lakes, provide ideal fishing and canoeing. Rentals are available from **True North General Store** (formerly Crystal River Canoes) where you can also buy sandwiches, groceries, gifts, and gasoline (616-334-3090).
- **Hiking and Skiing.** Thirty-five miles of marked trails are set aside for hiking and cross-country skiing. At the **Coast Guard's Historic Maritime Museum,** 1 mile west of Glen Haven, displays relate the area's maritime history. The 7.4-mile Pierce Stocking Scenic Drive (open mid-May through early November) offers scenic views of the dunes, Lake Michigan, and the offshore Manitou Islands. (See Side Trips.)
- **Campgrounds.** There are two campgrounds: one in Glen Arbor (616-334-4634), without showers; the other in Honor (616-325-5881), with hot showers available.

The park is open in winter for cross-country skiing and snowshoeing. Stop at **Philip Hart Visitors Center** in Empire, at the center of the park, for brochures and slide shows (616-326-5134).

For those interested in cross-country skiing, Summit Village and Schuss Village are linked via two routes and 30 kilometers of trails groomed for both classical and skating, with some sections laid out along the Cedar River and a shuttle pickup at the midway point. In the summer, golf takes over. The three eighteen-hole golf courses were designed by

Horseback Riding

This area's many scenic riding trails are particularly lovely in spring and fall. **Ranch Rudolf** (616-947-9529), offers rides as well as fishing and canoeing outings. The specialty at **Mountain View Riding Stables** (616-228-4639) are rides through the woods for children and inexperienced riders. If you want more formal riding lessons, call **Casalae Farms** (616-946-8490), where instruction is given in both Western and English styles.

Arnold Palmer, Warner Bowen, and William Diddle.

Sugar Loaf, Cedar Loaf; (616) 228-5461 or (800) 952-6390; www.theloaf.com. This resort, 18 miles northwest of Traverse City, has slopes ranging from gentle ones for beginners to one of Michigan's steepest ski verticals at 500 feet. There are a Sugar Bear Center for preschoolers and a Kid's Club for five- to twelve-year-olds. There is slopeside lodging in hotel rooms, town houses, or condos. Look for midweek packages and special weeks when kids sleep, ski, and eat free. Also available are instruction in telemark and back-country skiing. The resort opens in the summer when golf is the big attraction at the two courses fashioned by Arnold Palmer's design company.

For intermediate and advanced skiers, night skiing offers a serene alternative experience on the slopes. Available at all Traverse City area resorts, night skiing is not only a bargain because of lower lift ticket rates, but it's also a chance to ski favorite slopes when they're less crowded.

Golf

Traverse City is called "Michigan's Golf Coast," with dozens of courses throughout the area. The natural landscape of the area–the roll of the land, the dunes, the brooks, and water views–makes this an ideal area for golf courses. It has certainly brought pros–Jack Nicklaus, Arnold Palmer, Tom Doak, and Jerry Matthews–to Traverse City to design courses. Most of the architects have allowed the natural terrain to dictate the shape of the course.

Most of the courses are at resorts, but it is not necessary to be a guest to use their facilities. And for those just starting out, most of the following are some of the best courses in the area.

The Bear, 6300 U.S. 31 North, Grand Traverse Resort, Acme; (616) 938-2100 or (800) 748-0303. Jack Nicklaus designed this eighteen-hole championshiop course–site of the Michigan Open–with its elevated fairways and hummocks that recall golf's Scottish heritage. The Bear is the centerpiece of the Grand Traverse Resort and is consistently rated in the top one hundred resort courses in the United States. The course winds through summer fruit orchards and is suited for the more advanced golfer. A more forgiving course is opening here in 1999–The Wolverine designed by Gary Player. Also available at Grand Traverse is Jim McLean's Golf School, which offers lessons to junior golfers.

Shanty Creek Golf Course, One Shanty Creek Road, Bellaire (616-553-8621 or 800-678-4111). One of three at the Shanty Creek Resort, this course was *Golf* magazine's Silver Medal winner in 1996 and is one of the more open-style courses in the area. Unlike the Bear, this course can accommodate all skill levels. The Schuss Mountain Golf Course, also part of the same resort, is one of the more popular public golf courses. The Legend, the third course, was designed by Arnold Palmer. Cedar River Golf Club, designed by Tom Weiskopf, debuted in 1999. Shanty Creek offers packages for children and parents and has clinics for children under seventeen years of age.

Sugar Loaf Resort Course, 4500 Sugar Loaf Mountain Road, Cedar (616-228-5461 or 800-968-0574). For kids interested in joining their parents on the fairways, Sugar Loaf Resort Course offers a five-day instructional course for juniors held the first week in July. Sugar Loaf's newest course, King's Challenge, was designed by Arnold Palmer and is near the Leelanau Peninsula, offering views of Lake Michigan and Manitou Islands.

High Point Golf Club, 555 Arnold Road, Williamsburg (616-267-9900 or 800-753-PUTT). Rated as one of the Hundred Best Courses in the United States by *Golf* magazine in 1997, this course offers an open-style front nine and a forested back nine, resulting in dramatic contrast. Average golfers manage very well here. Juniors, up to age fourteen, get special rates.

Fly Away

- **Parasailing.** Special parachutes pulled by powerboats provide an exciting way to see East and West Bays. Call Traverse Bay Parasail; (616) 929-7272.
- **Ballooning.** One-hour flights at sunrise or sunset allow you to see the four seasons from on high. Call Grand Traverse Balloons; (616) 947-7433.
- **Gliding.** Take off from sand dunes near Lake Michigan and enjoy a scenic flight. Call Traverse City Hang Gliders/Paragliders; (616) 922-2844.

Performing Arts

The Traverse City Players perform year-round at the **Old Town Playhouse** (616-947-2210), including kids-only productions, while the refurbished **State Theatre** on Front Street, downtown, hosts professional touring productions, such as *Forever Plaid.* The **Dennos Museum Center**'s winter series includes performances by the local jazz society, folk singers, and musicians. Classical music lovers can attend concerts by **The Traverse City Symphony** (616-947-2210) between October and April. The internationally known **Interlochen Center for the Arts,** 17 miles south of Traverse City on Route 137 (616-276-6230; www.michiweb.com/interlochen), presents free or nominally priced year-round concerts by the faculty, students, and renowned international performers. **Old Town Playhouse,** 148 East Eighth Street, Traverse City (616-

Something Different

- **Storytelling.** Oral poetry, music, and storytelling around a campfire are offered every Friday and Saturday night, June through Labor Day, in Stone Circle, about twenty-five miles north of Traverse City (616-264-9467). This is a fun and interesting way for families to end the day and to get to know more about the local culture. The Leelanau School also offers poetry and storytelling on an adjacent beach on Friday from June through Labor Day (616-322-4062).
- **Train rides through the valley.** Revisit the elegance of rail dining on the Grand Traverse Dinner Train as it meanders through the Boardman River Valley and Pere Marquette Forest (616-93-DEPOT).

947-2210). Instead of the movies, take your kids to a play. It's more cultural and less expensive. Children's plays are performed here throughout the summer, and kids get in for $10.00. Call for a schedule.

Shopping

Shopping in the area is notable for its diversity, from shopping in quaint port towns such as Leland, Northort, and Suttons Bay to the hustle of downtown Traverse City.

Several shops in Old Town Traverse City cater to kids. **Children's World** offers toys, games, and dolls; **Horizon Books** stocks books, educational supplies, toys, and more; **Dandelion** has clothing and other items; **Hocus Pocus** is a magic and novelty shop; and there's **Grand Bay Kite.** The Cobblestone area has been voted the premier shopping district in Michigan for the past few consecutive years. Colorful awnings canopy the entrances to many of the coffee bars, specialty boutiques, restaurants, and bistros.

Popular malls include **Cherryland Mall,** South Airport Road (across the street from **Skateworld** roller rink), where there's a hobby shop, and a video-game arcade, plus **Grand Traverse Mall,** U.S. 31 and South Airport Road, with a carousel, food court, multiplex theater, and game arcade.

Bargains abound at **Horizon Outlet Center,** 3639 Marketplace Circle, an outdoor outlet mall with more than thirty stores, including Levi/Dockers and Eddie Bauer. There's also a ten-screen cinema.

Side Trips

Wineries

There are ten wineries in the area; some open seasonally, others year-round. Winery tours and tasting times change, so call ahead to check.

Those located along the Leelanau Peninsula include **Boskydel Vineyards** (616-256-7272), specializing in dry to semi-dry table wines; **Good Harbor Vineyards** (616-276-7165), maker of chardonnay and Riesling; **Leelanau Wine Cellars** (616-386-5201 or 800-782-8128), offering a full line of vinefera, hybrid, and fruit wines; **L. Mawby** (616-271-3522), featuring award-winning table wines; **Shady Lane Cellars** (616-947-8865), specializing in chardonnay and Riesling; and **Willow Vineyards** (616-271-4810), offering chardonnay, pinot noir, and pinot gris wines.

Along the Old Mission Peninsula are **Bowers Harbor Vineyards** (616-223-7615), maker of chardonnay, Johannesburg Riesling, and pinot gris; **Chateau Chantal** (616-223-4110), producing chardonnay, Riesling, pinot noir, gewürztraminer, merlot, and pinot menier; **Chateau Grand Traverse** (616-223-7355), offering chardonnays, Rieslings, and ice wines; and **Peninsula Cellars** (616-223-4310), a family-operated winery producing regionally expressive wines.

South Manitou Island

The 8-square-mile **South Manitou Island** is worth a trip. It's part of the Sleeping Bear Dunes National Lakeshore (see above) and several miles offshore. Drive along the coast on scenic M-22 to the picturesque fishing village of Leland, where ferries (no cars allowed) leave daily (616-256-9061). Sights include the Valley of the Giants, consisting of 500-year-old light cedar trees, scenic dunes, historic lighthouse, and a late-1800s cemetery. There are also dozens of shipwrecks. Kids can stand on the shoreline and see the shipwrecked Liberian freighter *Francisco Morazon*. There are guided jeep tours and overnight camping—no food for sale and no visible bathrooms. Even if you're only planning a day's excursion, it's a good idea to bring food and canteens or water bottles. The "wilder" North Manitou Island isn't recommended for families.

Special Events

These calendar highlights include a sampling of area events.

January. Discover Michigan Skiing, special rates for beginners, Shanty Creek Resort.

February. Michigan Special Olympics at Sugar Loaf Resort, winter sports competitions for handicapped children and adults.

March. Slush Cup Weekend, a winter carnival at Shanty Creek Resort featuring skiers in costume crossing a 40-foot pond, and a Kids Day (ages five through fourteen) with a Seal Slide, a Silly Slalom, and a NASTAR-style race.

May. Mesick Mushroom Festival, carnival, rodeo, flea market, music, and parade, (616) 885-1144; Cherry Blossom Days, wine tasting in area wineries, art exhibits, (616) 223-4110.

Summer. Interlochen Arts Festival, featuring concerts by nationally known artists throughout the summer, (616) 276-6030.

June. Ribs, Bibs, Tall Ships & Kids, tall ship rally, rib cook-off, music, games for kids, (616) 946-2723.

July. National Cherry Festival, eight days of fireworks, parades, concerts, competitions, Ferris wheels, and lots of cherries! (616) 947-4230; Suttons Bay Jazz Festival, the best of classic jazz by the water, (616) 271-4444.

August. Sleeping Bear Dunegrass & Blues Festival, outdoor music fest from early morning until sunset featuring bluegrass and rock, arts and crafts, (616) 326-5287; Buckley Old Engine Show, free steam train rides, large steam engines, antique cars, old tractors, (616) 269-3750.

Late September–early October. Fall color season and winery tours.

Thanksgiving–Christmas. Hometown Holiday features a host of special gala activities and events, plus affordable packages.

Where to Stay

The area offers more than 4,700 hotel rooms in every price range. The Traverse City Convention and Visitors Bureau publishes lodging brochures. Always inquire about special packages. The bureau also operates a central reservations service; call (800) TRAVERS. In addition to the ski and summer resorts already mentioned, the following places in Traverse City have special family appeal.

In the East Bay Area

These lodgings are on or near the "Miracle Mile" beaches. **The Beach Condominiums,** 1995 U.S. 31 North, on East Bay, gives families a chance to stretch out in thirty units that sleep four and feature sundecks, whirlpool baths, kitchens, and cable TV. Outside there's a beach, heated pool, and hot tub. Call (616) 938-2228. **Driftwood Motel,** 1861 U.S. 31 North, on East Bay, boasts a beachfront and large indoor pool and recreation area with game room and whirlpool. Choose from poolside or economy rooms; most have refrigerators and cable TV. Free lift tickets at Mt. Holiday for each registered guest in your party. Call (616) 938-2178. **Sugar Beach Resort,** 1773 U.S. 31 North, Traverse City (616-938-0100 or 800-509-1995). Family suites are available. Continental breakfast is provided and there is an indoor pool.

Other Area Lodging

Grand Traverse Resort, 6300 U.S. 31 North, Acme, contains 750 rooms, suites, and condos, some with refrigerator, fireplace, and whirlpool; ten restaurants and lounges; shopping gallery; indoor-outdoor tennis; pools and whirlpools; weight room; aerobics studio; cross-country skiing; championship golf; and seasonal activities for

Grand Hotel

The **Grand Hotel,** located on Mackinac Island in Lake Michigan, about 102 miles from Traverse City, is an American classic. This Victorian-era grande dame was built in 1887 as a summer getaway for the midwest's wealthy. Geraniums bloom and rocking chairs rock on the 660-foot front porch—the longest in the world. The resort has a formal feel; dinner is always a five-course meal.

A nice touch for families: There are no cars on the island, 85 percent of which is a state park. Even the taxis and the rental vehicles are horse-drawn carriages. The hotel sends a liveried driver in a horse-drawn carriage to meet guests at the ferry dock.

In summer the resort offers two free, supervised children's activities daily: a bike-hike for ages four to twelve from 11:00 A.M. to 2:00 P.M. and a children's dinner from 6:00 to 9:30 P.M. A storyteller starts the evening at 5:30 P.M. in Rebecca's Room, the kids' playroom. Family activities include boccie ball, biking, croquet, and swimming in the 250-foot-long pool—the lake is too cold for swimming. Golf, tennis, and horseback riding are available on the island. Visit Fort Mackinac, a restored eighteenth- and nineteenth-century outpost where costumed interpreters reenact military life.

Grand Hotel, Mackinac Island; (800) 334-7263; www.grandhotel.com.

kids. Call (616) 938-2100 or (800) 748-0303; www.gtresort.com.

Hampton Inn, 1000 U.S. 31 North, is across from State Park Beach, 3 miles from downtown, and adjacent to River Country Funland. The 127 units include complimentary continental breakfast, local phone calls, and airport transportation. There's also an indoor pool, whirlpool, and exercise room. Call (616) 946-8900 or (800) HAMPTON.

Ranch Rudolf, 6841 Brown Bridge Road, a four-season resort, comprises sixteen motel units and twenty-five campsites in Pere Marquette State Forest. Located on the Boardman River, 12 miles southeast of Traverse City, the ranch features horseback riding, canoeing, and cross-country skiing. Call (616) 947-9529.

Where to Eat

The Traverse City guide includes restaurant listings that feature everything from burgers to fresh seafood, such as Lake Michigan whitefish and rainbow trout. Morel mushrooms are a popular delicacy hunted in the local woods each spring. (Only do this if you know exactly what to look for.)

For in-between nibbles, try the famous cherry pecan muffins at **The Muffin Tin,** 115 Wellington at Front (616-929-7915), a country-style store that also sells other regional products; and the Traverse City Cherry Vanilla Fudge at **Kilwin's Chocolates,** 129 East Front Street (616-946-2403 or 800-544-0596). (Fudge is very big in this area.)

On Friday and Saturday nights at **Dills Olde Town Saloon,** 423 South Union Street (616-947-7534), kids (and adults) can sing family-style karaoke on stage to favorite tunes—including "Twinkle, Twinkle Little Star" for tots. Souvenir videos are available; ribs, steaks, seafood, and salads are on the menu (616-947-7534). At **Geppettos On the Bay,** 13641 West Bayshore Drive, dine on pasta specialties while enjoying the magnificent view (616-947-7079). **Cousin Jenny's Cornish Pasties,** 129 South Union Street, serves seven varieties, including the Breakfast Bobby (616-941-7821). **Mabel's,** 472 Munson Avenue, U.S. 31 North (two doors down from Days Inn), serves breakfast, lunch, or dinner anytime. Specialties include seven pastas, fresh steamed vegetables, Mabel's Original Vegetarian Nutburger, and "Just Enough Menus." Call (616) 947-0252. Don't be fooled by the name; the **Grand Traverse Dinner Train** serves lunch, too. Excursions wind through the north country on this restored 1950s railcar. It may not be appropriate for younger children. The menu lists such sophisticated dishes as smoked salmon and prime rib, and the prices reflect the menu selection. Call (616) 93-DEPOT.

For More Information

Brochures and guides to the area are available from **Traverse City Convention and Visitors Bureau,** 101 West Grandview Parkway, Traverse City (800-872-8377 or 800-TRAVERS). Ask for their excellent *Traverse City Area Guide* published annually.

Emergency Numbers

In Grand Traverse, Kalkaska, and Leelanau counties for ambulance, fire, police, and medical emergencies: 911

Emergency number in Antrim County: (616) 533-8627

Emergency number in Benzie County: (616) 882-4464

Munson MediCare, 550 Munson Avenue (616-359-9000), has a physician referral and health information service, 1:00 P.M. to 9:00 P.M. The hospital's Med-Care Walk-In Clinic is open twenty-four hours, seven days a week (616-935-8686). From the eastern part of town, this is most accessible in an emergency.

From the western part, head to the Munson Medical Center, 1105 Sixth Street (616-935-5000), for their Walk-In Emergency Service (616-935-6333, also the number for their physician referral service).

For the disabled, bus service within Traverse City is available from Specialized On-Call Service (SOS); (616) 947-0796.

Poison Control: (800) 632-2727

There is no twenty-four-hour pharmacy. The pharmacy at Meijer, 3955 U.S. 31 South (616-941-1793), is open 8:00 A.M.-10:00 P.M. Monday through Saturday, and 9:00 A.M.-7:00 P.M. Sunday. After closing time either of the above hospitals can provide enough medicine to last until its pharmacy opens.

12 Minnesota

MINNEAPOLIS AND ST. PAUL

The license plates—"Land of 10,000 Lakes"—are misleading. The number of lakes is actually closer to 15,000. Throw the Mississippi River into the equation, and you can see how the preponderance of water dominates life in the Twin Cities. With 949 lakes lying within the metropolitan area of Minneapolis and St. Paul, outdoor recreation is an important part of people's daily routines. There is an estimated acre of parkland for every forty-three Twin Citians, ranging from grassy city oases and the famed Minnehaha Falls in south Minneapolis to public parks that contain everything from Indian burial mounds to botanical gardens.

The abundant natural beauty that enthralls both visitors and residents of Minneapolis-St. Paul also tantalized seventeenth-century French explorer Jean Nicolet, who traveled south from Canada along the Northwest Passage seeking a route to China. Instead, Nicolet found Dakota and Ojibwe tribes, eager to exchange fur pelts for blankets, knives, tobacco, and tools. The area became a major trading post and, after being fought over during the French-Indian War, eventually became part of Minnesota.

Minneapolis-St. Paul is truly the Midwest—situated midway between the Atlantic and the Pacific. The two cities are quite different in style and design. St. Paul is the older, more traditional city, its European, East Coast feel accentuated by historic buildings, city parks, and a wide boulevard (called Summit Avenue) stocked with breathtaking mansions. Minneapolis is often called "the first city of the West," an aggressively hip place filled with contemporary architecture, a cutting-edge renovated warehouse district, and an overall atmosphere that is quicker paced and grittier than quiet St. Paul.

The winters are severe, but Minneapolis and St. Paul have Skyway systems—enclosed and climate-controlled walkways two levels above the street that connect people to downtown office buildings, restaurants, and attractions. Snow and ice removal is efficient. Summers can be quite

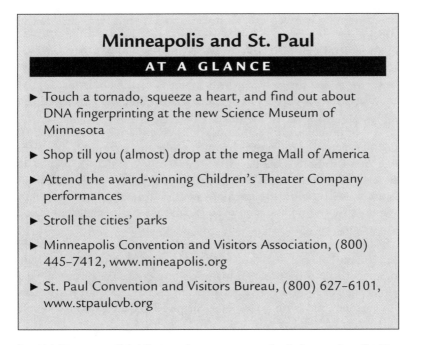

Minneapolis and St. Paul

AT A GLANCE

- Touch a tornado, squeeze a heart, and find out about DNA fingerprinting at the new Science Museum of Minnesota
- Shop till you (almost) drop at the mega Mall of America
- Attend the award-winning Children's Theater Company performances
- Stroll the cities' parks
- Minneapolis Convention and Visitors Association, (800) 445-7412, www.mineapolis.org
- St. Paul Convention and Visitors Bureau, (800) 627-6101, www.stpaulcvb.org

humid, but unpredictable summer storms can also bring cool spells. For spring and fall trips, bring jackets and other warm clothing.

Both cities welcome families, so much so that the area is often cited as one of the top ten places in America to raise children.

Getting There

Minneapolis–St. Paul International Airport (612-726-5555), located 10 miles from downtown Minneapolis and 8 miles from St. Paul, serves more than two dozen airlines. Rental cars are available at the airport.

Amtrak passengers pull into the St. Paul/Minneapolis Midway Station, 730 Transfer Road in St. Paul (800-872-7245), which is about a fifteen-minute drive from downtown St. Paul and twenty-four minutes from downtown Minneapolis. The **Greyhound/Trailways** bus terminal in Minneapolis is at 29 North Ninth Street and the St. Paul location is at Ninth and St. Peter.

Getting Around

Unless you plan to spend all your time in one downtown area or at the Mall of America in nearby Bloomington, it's advisable to rent a car. The Twin Cities operate an excellent transit system, notably with express buses running between the Twin Cities and to and from the Mall of America.

In St. Paul, call the **Capital City Trolley** (651-223-5600). Historic, rubber-wheeled trolleys circle downtown, the Cultural District, historic Lowertown, and the riverfront year-round. A half-hour circuit stops at most major attractions and retail areas. Hour-long tours of historic St. Paul are available (by reservation) on Saturdays.

In Minneapolis, call the **Minneapolis RiverCity Trolley** (612-204-0000), which runs tours of downtown Minneapolis from May through October. Two-hour or all-day passes can be purchased at three starting points: the Minneapolis Convention Center, Walker Art Center, or St. Anthony Main. (A historical narrative of this old mining town is told during the sixty-five-minute loop.) You can use the trolley as a sight-seeing bus, getting on and off at any of twenty stops around town.

There are cabs in the Twin Cities, but it's not really a taxi kind of place. Expressway I-94 connects the Twin Cities, I-35W leads you to most Minnesota sites, and cultural and historical attractions are clearly marked along the streets and highways. Both places are laid out on an easily understood grid with a few idiosyncrasies tossed in to make life interesting.

What to See and Do

Museums

The **Minnesota History Center** (operated by the Minnesota Historical Society), 345 Kellogg Boulevard West, St. Paul (651-296-6126; www.mnhs.org). An architectural masterpiece made of Minnesota materials—Rockville granite and Winona limestone—the History Center is both an innovative museum and a state-of-the-art research center. The world's largest collection of materials on the State of Minnesota is housed in the Center, including a circa 1890 fire engine, vintage Betty Crocker radio broadcasts, buffalo horns, and Native American artifacts.

The hands-on museum is organized around themes such as family, work, community, and place. The historic interpreters in period clothing bring an immediacy to the past, while special events make history anything but musty and dull. Kids especially like exploring the Minneota A to Z exhibits (baseball and below-zero weather), climbing the grain elevator, and crafting projects at the free "make and take" programs every Sunday. The Research Center features a microfilm room with forty-two self-service microfilm stations and a special collections room for fragile items. This museum has something for all ages, and the friendly staff is superbly trained to dispense boredom-free information. The gift shop has interesting items, and the on-site Cafe Minnesota is a surprisingly

Minneapolis Children's Museum

DO NOT TOUCH signs are nowhere to be found at the **Minneapolis Children's Museum,** 10 West Seventh Street, St. Paul (651-225-6000). Families are encouraged to explore their imaginations and the world through hands-on activities. Four permanent galleries are complemented by several changing exhibits, all especially created for children ages six months to ten years. In **WorldWorks,** focused on tools as a means of discovery, children operate a giant crane and create waves at the wild water table. Kids learn how to protect the environment in **EarthWorld,** highlighted by a giant anthill and four ant trails. Intercultural community is the focus of **OneWorld,** where kids can take the stage in a TV and music studio. **Habitot** lets infants and toddlers play in four Minnesota landscapes. Toddlers can climb through animal burrows and experience a forest in winter, while preschoolers can test their independence in the bluff caves. The Museum's store, **Creative Kidstuff,** sells an interesting variety of toys, books, art and science projects, and games.

good eatery specializing in regional food. In July and August, try Nine Nights of Family Fun, a series of free concerts on the History Center lawn.

Minneapolis Institute of Art, 2400 South Third Avenue (612-870-3000; www.artsmia.org). Adjacent to the Children's Theater Company, the Minneapolis Institute of Art houses more than 70,000 works spanning 25,000 years of history in a structure combining Classic Revival and contemporary steel-and-brick architecture. The complex, situated in lovely Fair Oaks Park, also contains the Minneapolis College of Art and Design, as well as the Children's Theater Company (see Theater). Twenty interactive computer learning stations for adults and older children are situated throughout the Institute, and a Family Center provides art activities and art works displayed at children's eye level, as well as a soft-sculpture play area.

The museum's diverse collection includes antiquities from around the world, a lustrous collection of Chinese jade, African masks, impressionist and postimpressionist works, photography, and a Rembrandt. Popular period rooms, which display the museum's decorative arts collection, are gaily festooned for the holidays. A major magnet for children is the 2,000-year-old mummy, as well as rooms dedicated to pre-Columbian gold objects crafted by the Incas.

The Walker Art Center, Hennepin Avenue and Vineland Place

Science Museum of Minnesota

In the fall of 1999 the **Science Museum of Minnesota,** currently located at 30 East Tenth Street, St. Paul (651-221-9488; www.smm.org), will relocate to a new building almost twice the size, at 120 West Kellogg Boulevard, St. Paul. Situated on the Mississippi River bluffs and surrounded by parkland and outdoor performance areas, the new museum features high-tech exhibits on everything from the human heart to the earliest dinosaurs. Highlights include an Omni 21 large-screen theater, five exhibit halls, and ten acres of outdoor science parks.

In the new **Hall of Human Biology,** kids learn about DNA fingerprinting at a cell lab. In the **Mississippi River Gallery,** visitors can test water samples, create mock flood conditions, and get the feel of steering a tugboat. **After the Dinosaurs** re-creates North Dakota's swamps of 58 million years ago, complete with insect sounds and mammal fossils. The skeletons of such formidable dinosaurs as stegosaurus, triceratops (one of only three complete skeletons in the world), and camptosaurus are on view. **People and Cultures** emphasizes Native Americans as well as recent immigrants such as the Hmongs. The best of the **Experiment Gallery** moves to the new museum; kids can hear secrets across a room via whisper dishes, make waves in a 30-foot tank, and "touch" a tornado. Designed as a place to play, **Kellogg Plaza,** surrounding the park, has an ice skating rink, cafe, and outdoor performance spaces.

In the meantime, the current museum is in flux, but it's still a wonderful place for your family to spend an interesting and exciting day. Probably the best place to start is at the **Science Museum Omnitheater.** Shows quickly fill up and you don't want to miss the awesome movies projected upon a dome that is 76 feet in diameter. The shows engross all ages, although some may frighten the very young. Educational entertainment is the motto of this huge museum dedicated to hands-on, interactive exhibits dealing with natural history, science, and technology. **Paleontology Hall** offers up-close and personal looks at dinosaurs, including the 82-foot-long, two-story-tall diplodocus and at a 12-foot-long fossil fish. In **Anthropology Hall,** you can learn about the food, shelter, clothing, and rituals of the world's cultures. The museum's 1.75 million natural history and science specimens include dinosaur exhibits, an Egyptian mummy, an authentic all-wood Hmong house, and other exhibits designed for science enthusiasts from preschool to high-school age.

(612-375-7622; www.walkerart.org), houses one of the nation's finest permanent collections of modern art, both American and European. There are representative works from many famous twentieth-century artists working in the media of painting, sculpture, photography, mixed media, video, and film. The Walker also boasts an enormous print collection. Children's programs are unusual and fun, with most taking place on the weekends. Past events have involved puppet making with local performance artists and a make-your-own video class.

Valleyfair Family Amusement Park

Take the ride of your life on the Wild Thing at **Valleyfair Family Amusement Park,** One Valleyfair Drive, Shakopee (800-FUN-RIDE). Towering more than 200 feet in the air, this "hyper-coaster" sends the daring up, down, and in loops at 74 miles per hour. If coasters don't thrill you, there are forty rides and a great water park where you can catch The Wave and take a 50-foot plunge. Tot Town, Bearenstain Bear Country, and an old-fashioned train delight little kids. On the IMAX theater's 60-foot screen is *Thrill Ride,* a film simulating the most thrilling rides of the world's best amusement parks. The amusement park is twenty minutes southwest of the Twin Cities on Highway 101. Open daily May through Labor Day.

Green Spaces, Zoos, and Parks

The **Minnesota Zoo,** 13000 Zoo Boulevard, Apple Valley (612-432-9000, www.mnzoo.com), twenty minutes south of the Twin Cities on Highway 77, features 450 species of mammals, birds, reptiles, and amphibians in natural habitat exhibits. The Discovery Bay: United HealthCare Marine Education Center has sharks, rays, and performing dolphins, and a Southeast Asian tropical rain forest with rare Komodo dragons. A Halloween highlight every October is Haunted Acres, which includes a hay ride through a "demon-filled" zoo and a twenty-room "phantom-filled" mansion. The **IMAX theater,** with its screen the size of a six-story building, shows films throughout the day.

Como Park, St. Paul (651-266-6400), boasts a lake, a free zoo, Japanese gardens, waterfalls, an eighteen-hole golf course, rides, and picnic areas. Concerts are held regularly throughout the summer at the Pavilion. The **Conservatory,** 1325 Aida Place (651-487-8200), complements its regular displays of exotic flora with seasonal flower shows. And the **Como Zoo,** Midway Parkway and Kaufman Drive (651-487-8201), which houses Minnesota's only gorillas and giraffes, has animal demonstrations and public feedings as well as educational programs for the public.

Mississippi Mile, Plymouth and Hennepin Avenues, Minneapolis (612-348-9300). Downtown Minneapolis is bordered by the Mississippi Mile, a riverfront parkway offering walking, jogging, and biking paths and scenic river views. Points of interest include **Nicollet Island,** home to the historic Nicollet Island Inn, the Nicollet Island Pavilion, and many examples of nineteenth-

Historic Minnesota

The **Minneapolis Historical Society** (www.mnhs.org) also sponsors twenty-three historic sites around the state, each providing a unique opportunity to experience different periods in the state's history. Among them are:

- **Historic Fort Snelling,** Highways 5 and 55 (612-726-1171). This 1827 stone fortress sits atop a hill overlooking the Mississippi River. Costumed guides re-create military drills and ceremonies from the period. Open May through October.
- **Mille Lacs Indian Museum** (320-532-3652), a one-and-a-half-hour drive from Minneapolis-St. Paul, showcases the history of the Mille Lacs band of Ojibwe. This tribe settled along the shores of the Mille Lacs Lake. The museum has videos, computer interactives, listening stations, and craft and cooking demonstrations. There's an adjacent 1930s trading post for shopping.
- **Forest History Center** (218-327-4482), a three- to four-hour drive from Minneapolis-St. Paul. Meet a lumberjack, blacksmith, saw filer, and cook in this turn-of-the-century logging camp, or board a floating "wanigan," a cook shack on the river. Climb the 100-foot fire tower and visit a restored 1930s fire service patrolman's cabin.
- **Oliver H. Kelley Farm** (612-441-6896), a forty-five-minute drive from Minneapolis-St. Paul. Step into a working 1860s farm and see a horse-drawn threshing machine, a McCormick Daisy self-raking reaper, or a plow pulled by an ox. At the farmhouse, try home crafts such as straw-hat making. Fast forward to a modern-day working farm and see how much hard work is involved even with modern technology.
- **Split Rock Lighthouse** (218-226-6372) four hours from Minneapolis-St. Paul. This lighthouse on a spectacular rocky Lake Superior bluff was completed in 1910 and has been restored to its 1920s appearance. Tour the lighthouse, the fog-signal building, and the keeper's dwelling, see a film, and explore exhibits on lighthouses and navigation.

century architecture that look small-town perfect. **Our Lady of Lourdes Church,** the oldest Minneapolis church in continuous use, and **St. Anthony Main and Riverplace** are historic structures that have been converted to a nightclub, shopping, restaurant, and movie complex. Tour the **Ard Godfrey House,** the oldest home in Minneapolis, built in 1849, and visit one of the city's liveliest spots, the **Upper St. Anthony Falls Lock and Dam** (at Portland Avenue and the Mississippi River), the uppermost of a series of twenty-nine locks connecting Minneapolis with the Gulf of Mexico. View barges and other watercraft from the lock's observation deck.

The Raptor Center, 1920 Fitch Avenue, St. Paul (651-624-4745; www.raptor.cvm.umm.edu). Located on the St. Paul campus of the University of Minnesota, the Raptor Center annually receives more than 700 injured birds of prey for treatment. A visit to this thought-provoking place starts with an audiovisual presentation introducing the medical and educational focus of the facility, followed by a live bird demonstration and a tour.

Minnesota Valley National Wildlife Refuge, 3815 East Eightieth Street, Bloomington (612-854-5900). Operated by the U.S. Fish and Wildlife Service, this center features many hands-on exhibits and computer games that allow children to explore such jobs as wildlife manager, refuge manager of a deer herd, or fire boss on a prescribed forest burn. A spectacular twelve-projector slide presentation is shown regularly in the center's auditorium, and naturalist-led programs are scheduled regularly.

Theater

More than eighty professional theater companies thrive in the area, not to mention numerous community, experimental, and dinner theater troupes.

One child-oriented choice is **The Children's Theater Company,** 2400 Third Avenue South, Minneapolis (612-874-0400). This award-winning theater, located in a mammoth white brick building attached to the Minneapolis Institute of Arts, appeals to both kids and adults.

First and foremost are the children, who are accommodated in the 746-seat auditorium with seats specially raked so that smaller theatergoers can see the stage. There's even a crying room for children to sob freely without hampering the enjoyment of other audience members. Shows are lavish and vividly staged, ranging from children's classics—*The 500 Hats of Bartholomew Cubbins* and *Babar*—to innovative renderings of new works—*Strega Nona Meets Her Match* and *Crow and Weasel.*

The Guthrie Theater, 725 Vineland Place, Minneapolis (612-377-2224; www.guthrietheater.org), was founded in 1963 by the legendary Sir Tyrone Guthrie to prove that classical repertory could exist, and indeed flourish, outside of New York and Chicago. Shakespeare, Chekhov, Ibsen, Molière, Miller, and Euripides are well represented here, and in case you fear your children are not ready for the classics, there are pretheater symposiums before selected performances. Children's guides are available at the box office. Get to the Guthrie early for a pretheater stroll through the **Walker Art Center's sculpture garden,** one of the largest public sculpture gardens in the world. It features works by Claus Oldenberg, Frank Gehry, Henry Moore, and George Segal.

Touring companies of Broadway shows land at one of three locations: **The Ordway,** 345 Washington Street, St. Paul (651-224-7661); **The State,** 805 Hennepin Avenue, Minneapolis (612-339-7007); or **The Orpheum,** 910 Hennepin Avenue, Minneapolis (612-339-7007). The Ordway, home of the Minnesota Opera Company and the St. Paul Chamber Orchestra, is a beautiful theater with impeccable acoustics, while the State and the Orpheum are historic playhouses renovated right down to the gilt trim and painted bucolic murals. Many Broadway productions have passed through the Twin Cities here.

In the summer, the **Minnesota Centennial Showboat Theatre,** Harriet Island, St. Paul (651-624-2345), presents family entertainment on a turn-of-the-century riverboat.

Visitors to the Science Museum in St. Paul may want to drop into the **Great American History Theatre, Crawford Livingston Theatre,** 30 East Tenth Street, St. Paul (651-292-4320). Past productions at this cozy, child-friendly theater include dramatizations of F. Scott Fitzgerald's *The Great Gatsby* and a countrified version of *A Christmas Carol.*

Purchase tickets for theater events at individual box offices, or call TicketMaster at (612) 989-5151.

Sports

The Twin Cities offers a variety of sports events. **The Minnesota Vikings** professional football team plays through December at the climate-controlled H.H.H. Metrodome, 501 Chicago Avenue, Minneapolis (612-989-5151). Also at the Metrodome, **The Minnesota Twins** run the bases April through October (612-375-1116). Over at the Target Center, 600 First Avenue, Minneapolis (612-673-1600), catch the court action of the **Minnesota Timberwolves,** the state's exciting NBA team. Coming in the fall of 2000 will be the National Hockey League expansion team, the **Minnesota Wild.** Games will be played in the new RiverCentre Arena at West Seventh Street and Kellogg Boulevard in St. Paul. For ticket information, call (651) 333-PUCK or (651) 222-WILD.

The Northern League **Saint Paul Saints** plays baseball to capacity crowds at the Midway Stadium in St. Paul, 117 Energy Park Drive, St. Paul (651-644-6659). A Saints game means affordable fun—tickets are reasonably priced. In addition to watching the game, patrons can get a haircut, receive a low-cost massage from a group of massage-therapist nuns, or watch the antics of the team mascot, a pig in a baseball cap.

Special Tours

- **Riverboats.** Take a scenic trip down the Mississippi River aboard an old-style riverboat. Tours from Minneapolis depart from Boom Island and travel through the upper lock for a view of St. Anthony Falls. The St. Paul cruise leaves from Harriet Island and goes to Fort Snelling. Check the schedule for baseball, Sunday brunch, and Dixieland cruises. **Padleford Packet Boat Company** (651-227-1100).
- **Gangsters. Wabasha Street Caves and Down in History Tours,** (651-224-1191) conducts the **Minnesota Mobs Tour,** exploring St. Paul's crime sites, speakeasies, and hoodlum hangouts. Stops include Ma Barker's home, John Dillinger's apartment, and locations of robberies and murders. The docents at the **Landmark Center,** 75 West Fifth Street, St. Paul (651-292-3225), the restored Old Federal Courts Building, re-create the mobster history of the famous gangster trials of the 1930s so vividly that you'll swear you see the pinstripes. Outside is Rice Park, St. Paul's oldest and prettiest city park.
- **Ghosts and Graves.** Otherworldy specters and poltergeists may or may not be spotted at Fort Snelling, the haunted City Hall, or the Guthrie Theater. Call **Wabasha Street Caves and Down in History Tours** (651-224-1191).
- **Mines and Caves. The Historical Tour of the Wabasha Street Caves** (651-224-1191) takes you through caves that were once mines, then the site of mushroom growing, and finally, in the 1930s, the home of the nightclub called "The Castle Royal."

Shopping

Mall of America, Interstate 494 and Highway 77, Bloomington (612-883-8800; www.mallofamerica.com). Think of your local mall multiplied by six, and you have the overwhelming Mall of America. Many tourists come from all over the world and never leave the mall to explore the Twin Cities. More than 40 million visitors have traipsed through the enormous complex that features 520 specialty shops, eight nightclubs (including Planet Hollywood), 12,750 parking stalls, fourteen movie theaters, a miniature golf course, an aquarium, an amusement park, and anchor stores Nordstrom, Bloomingdale's, Macy's, and Sears. Children and adults alike will be flabbergasted by the Lego Imagination Center, which features larger-than-life displays of dinosaurs, a fully operational circus, firehouse, birthday party, and spinning globe and spacecraft—all made out of Legos.

At the mall's **UnderWater World,** (888-DIVE-TIME), a 1.2-million-gallon aquarium, you walk through a 300-foot-long acrylic tunnel as if going on a deep-sea dive. Kids get a kick out of walking within inches of the 15,000 fish, including sharks, stingrays, and other exotic creatures. Exhibits detail the Mississippi River, a Minnesota lake, the Gulf of Mexico, and a Caribbean barrier reef. A thirty-five-minute taped narrative is available to complement your walk.

Plopped down in the middle of the mall is **Knott's Camp Snoopy** (612-883-8600; www.campsnoopy.com), a seven-acre indoor amusement park complete with a roller coaster and twenty-three other rides, six shops, three entertainment theaters, and nine eateries. Admission is free, and the park operates on a point pass system whereby you purchase paper tickets at booths or at automated ticket machines placed throughout the park. Be sure to set a spending limit. Parents on a budget should limit their children's rides.

Avoid the games of skill and other carnival attractions and the pricey Ford Playhouse dinner theater. Worthy attractions at Camp Snoopy include Pearson's Wilderness Theater, featuring live animals, and the Northwood Stage, which hosts live musical performances throughout the day.

Sensory overload—all the bright lights, welcoming sights, and sounds and noises—wears you down after a while, and you might be tempted to run up your credit card. Take frequent breaks for drinks or snacks at the mall's restaurants, rather than the two chaotic food courts. Taking time out for a movie or to explore the quieter (during the day) fourth level is also an option. Don't try to take in the entire structure in one day.

The crowds can also be daunting, and it's advisable to visit the mall in either early morning or late afternoon. The crowds are smaller during the week than on the often bedlamlike weekends.

If you want to shop but don't like the throngs of people at Mall of America, head to St. Paul's **World Trade Center,** Seventh and Wabasha (651-291-1715), or **Town Square,** 445 Minnesota Street (651-298-0900). These linked shopping complexes run four city blocks and include more than fifty shops and restaurants. While the World Trade Center is a mall that surrounds a three-level atrium, Town Square is tucked below the world's largest enclosed city park. An amphitheater and life-size chessboards offer shoppers a respite.

The **Grand Avenue/Selby Avenue** historic area is another of St. Paul's popular shopping and dining areas, with a collection of unique shops and galleries among its ethnic restaurants.

Bandana Square, 1021 East Bandana Boulevard (612-642-1509), is like most historic districts in cities around the country. Specialty shops and restaurants are housed in buildings listed on the National Register of Historic Places. These 1880s buildings were formerly known as the Como Shops, where Burlington Northern coaches and locomotives were painted and repaired. The Twin City Model Railroad Club is located on the square's second level. Visitors are welcome to watch the club's fantastic model railroad in operation.

SIDE TRIPS

Grand Casino Hinckley, Interstate 35 at the Hinckley exit (320-384-7101). Gambling is legal in Minnesota, and abundant, so if you want to see the state's casinos—which are less glitzy than those in Vegas or Atlantic City—this is probably the best one suited for families. A beautiful hour-and-a-half ride from the Twin Cities, this 90,000-square-foot casino features more than 1,500 loose video slots with individual progressive payouts frequently in excess of $50,000. Also featured for the avaricious types are keno, poker, and blackjack machines, fifty-two blackjack tables, bingo, and the Royal Ascot video derby, a horse-racing game. What separates this casino from others is the **Kids Quest Activity Center,** a 7,800-square-foot professionally supervised children's activity center. The casino also hosts Powwows and other Native American events on weekends. A video arcade attracts teens; restaurants are on-site.

SPECIAL EVENTS

January–February. The festival season kicks off in winter's deep freeze with the St. Paul Winter Carnival (651-223-4700). It runs for twelve days during the end of January through early February.

July. In mid-July it's Minneapolis's turn to get silly, with the Minneapolis Aquatennial (612-377-4621), an annual summer salute to water, fun, and families. Festivities include a sandcastle/sand sculpture competition, a sailing regatta, bass fishing, skateboard, and volleyball tournaments.

On Independence Day weekend, St. Paul hosts Taste of Minnesota (651-228-0018), on the grounds of the State Capitol.

August–September. The end of August through Labor Day is the Minnesota State Fair (651-642-2200), more than one hundred years old and the largest twelve-day state fair in the country.

November–December. Holidazzle Parades.

Where to Stay

The Twin Cities have myriad places to rest your travel-wearied head, from big-name chain hotels to all-suite complexes and more modest accommodations. On the high-end, there's the **Saint Paul Hotel,** 350 Market Street, St. Paul (651-292-9292). This expertly renovated hotel offers superb accommodations, one of the best restaurants in the Twin Cities—the St. Paul Grill—and a lovely view of Rice Park, the Ordway Music Theatre, and the Landmark Center.

In Minneapolis, indulge yourself at the subdued opulence of the **Marquette Hotel,** IDS Center, Seventh and Nicollet (612-332-2351). You can eat at the hotel restaurant, the same one where Mary Tyler Moore used to dine on her TV show. Two more pricey hotels, but worth it, are **The Whitney,** 150 Portland Avenue (612-339-9300), and **The Hotel Luxeford,** 1101 Lasalle (612-332-6800), luxurious suite hotels. Minneapolis also has a **Hyatt Regency Hotel,** South Thirteenth Street at Nicollet (612-370-1234 or 800-223-1234).

Moderate prices and good value can be found at the **Radisson Hotel St. Paul,** 11 East Kellogg Boulevard (651-292-1900). The hotel boasts an indoor pool with a panoramic view of the St. Paul skyline; it is connected to the Skyway system and is within walking distance of the city's most popular attractions. The **Radisson Inn Saint Paul,** 411 Minnesota Street (651-291-8800), located in the heart of downtown St. Paul, is also Skyway connected. Their counterpart in Minneapolis is the **Radisson Hotel Metrodome,** 615 Washington Avenue East (612-379-8888). **Best Inn—State Capitol,** 161 St. Anthony, St. Paul (651-227-8711), and in Minneapolis, the **Best Western Regency Plaza,** 41 North Tenth Street, Minneapolis (612-339-9311).

Suite hotels are sanity savers for families, and a terrific complex is the **Embassy Suites,** 175 East Tenth Street, St. Paul (651-224-5400). Here you will find tastefully appointed rooms with balconies offering great views of the city, complimentary breakfast and beverages, and satellite television. There are also some quite attractive weekend package deals.

If you really want to have an unusual hotel experience, check into the **Burnsville Fantasuite Hotel,** 250 North River Ridge Circle, Burnsville (612-890-9550), where you can pick out special suites decorated in futuristic, tropical, prehistoric, and other fantasy motifs.

Where to Eat

People take their food seriously in Minnesota, with an emphasis on rib-sticking fare such as steaks, wild-rice soup, humongous sticky buns, and walleye pike. Vegetarians and connoisseurs of lighter fare will like **Cafe**

Brenda, 300 North First Avenue, Minneapolis (612-342-9230). The cafe features luscious and low-fat seafood dishes, pasta, and desserts flavored with honey or maple syrup.

Hearty German cuisine can be found at **Gastof zur Gemutlichkeit,** 2300 Northeast University Avenue, Minneapolis (612-781-3860). Specialties include wienerschnitzel, sauerbraten, spaetzle, glorious apple strudels, and black forest torte. Young people love hanging out at the unspeakably hip **Loring Cafe,** 1624 Harmon Place, Minneapolis (612-332-1617), where the elite meet to drink espressos and recite poetry. Parents and children admire the Loring's funky decor and great food, including artichoke dip, designer pizzas, and filling pasta dishes; and it's so noisy in there, unruly children are just part of the scene.

A casual place in Minneapolis where you can kick back and dine is **Market Bar-B-Que,** 1414 Nicollet Avenue, Minneapolis (612-872-1111). It's home of some of the most righteous barbecued ribs in the country.

In St. Paul, families love the Old World specialties at **Cossetta's,** 211 West Seventh Street (651-222-3476). They are known for cheesy pizza, imported meats and cheeses, and monstrous calzone. The **Heartthrob Cafe,** Seventh and Wabasha (651-224-2783), is a zany place where kids are encouraged to be rambunctious. This fifties- and sixties-inspired diner sports gregarious waitpersons on roller skates who urge you to try the quesadillas, guacamole-topped hamburgers, and many-flavored malts and milk shakes.

Cafe Latte, 850 Grand Avenue, St. Paul (651-224-5687), features innovative and delicious salads, homemade soups and breads, coffee drinks, and an irresistible spread of pastries and cakes. For steaks you can't beat the **Cherokee Sirloin Room,** 886 South Smith Avenue, St. Paul (651-457-2729). The steaks are the size of Buicks, and the baked potatoes are big too.

For More Information

Visitor Information Centers

City of St. Paul Citizen Service Office, (651) 266-8989

St. Paul Convention and Visitors Bureau, (651) 265-4900 or (800) 627-6101; www.stpaulcvb.gov

Minneapolis Convention and Visitors Association, (800) 445-7412; www.minneapolis.org

Minnesota Office of Tourism, (651) 296-5029 or (800) 657-3700

Hennepin County Parks and Recreation, (612) 559-9000

Parks and recreation information, (612) 348-2141 in Minneapolis; (651) 266-6400 in St. Paul.

Other Useful Information and Numbers

Road condition information: (651) 296-3076

Traveler's Aid: (612) 726-5500

Metropolitan Transit Commission: (612) 827-7733

St. Paul area Chamber of Commerce: (651) 223-5000

Greater Minneapolis Chamber of Commerce: (612) 370-9132

The *Skyway News* and the *City Pages* feature comprehensive guides to what's happening.

Emergency Numbers

Ambulance, fire, police: 911

Poison Center: (612) 347-3141

Children's Hospital of St. Paul Children's On-Call Line: (651) 220-6868

Abbott Northwestern Hospital of Minneapolis Emergency Room: (612) 863-4233

Twenty-four-hour pharmacy: Walgreen Drug Stores, 1550 University Avenue, St. Paul; (651) 646-6165

13 Minnesota

NORTHERN MINNESOTA

Northern Minnesota has much to interest outdoor-oriented families. **The Gunflint Trail** is a 64-mile paved road in northern Minnesota near the Canadian border, which provides access to the **Boundary Waters Canoe Area Wilderness** (BWCAW), one of the largest wilderness areas in the United States. Starting in Grand Marais, Minnesota, on the north shore of Lake Superior, the world's largest freshwater lake, the Gunflint Trail winds its way through the Sawtooth Mountain Range and the BWCAW near Ely, Minnesota. Major lakes along the Gunflint Trail include Gunflint (on the Canadian border), Poplar, Saganaga, and Sea Gull, each with links or potages into more remote Boundary Waters areas. Hungry Jack, Clearwater, Flour Lake, East Bearskin, Trout, and Loon Lake are also on Gunflint Trail.

Centuries ago Native Americans fished and hunted northern Minnesota's network of lakes and streams. French-Canadian fur traders followed, plying these routes in the eighteenth and nineteenth centuries. Called *voyageurs,* these traders paddled goods, soldiers, and explorers through these scenic waters. Because the BWCAW, composed of 500 lakes interconnected by small streams and channels, is a U.S. Forest Service wilderness area, use is restricted and permits are required; obtain these in advance. Canoes provide the primary means of transportation (no motorized boats are allowed), and camping is restricted to designated areas. One mile away, use is less restricted in Voyageurs National Park. Motorboats not only are allowed, but they are the most popular means of enjoying this park.

In summer in the BWCAW and in Voyageurs National Park, families find watery adventures and classic north-country scenery. This is a back-to-basics adventure of lazy days spent paddling along chains of lakes, past islands dotted with pine trees and rimmed with pebbly shores, and of simple nights camping or staying at shoreside lodges.

In winter the region is transformed into a cross-country ski mecca. The Gunflint Trail Association maintains 175 kilometers of groomed,

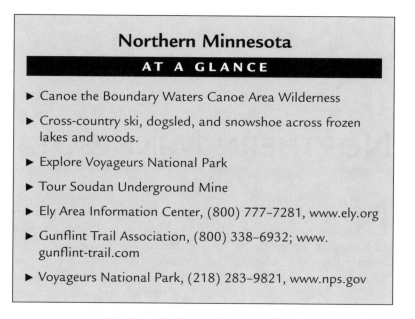

Northern Minnesota

AT A GLANCE

- Canoe the Boundary Waters Canoe Area Wilderness
- Cross-country ski, dogsled, and snowshoe across frozen lakes and woods.
- Explore Voyageurs National Park
- Tour Soudan Underground Mine
- Ely Area Information Center, (800) 777-7281, www.ely.org
- Gunflint Trail Association, (800) 338-6932; www.gunflint-trail.com
- Voyageurs National Park, (218) 283-9821, www.nps.gov

cross-country trails through these pristine woods. The Gunflint area lodges and outfitters in Ely offer additional winter fun such as dogsled trips, sleigh rides, and snowshoe tours.

Getting There

As the region is remote, most visitors drive here, some with campers in tow. Gunflint is 43 miles from Grand Marais, Minnesota, and six hours north of Minneapolis-St. Paul, which is served by the **Minneapolis-St. Paul International Airport** (612-726-5848). Many major car rental companies are represented here. International Falls also has the International Falls International Airport. By car, Voyageurs National Park is also three hours from Duluth and four hours from Winnipeg, Manitoba.

Four communities located along U.S. Highway 53 between Duluth and International Falls serve as gateways to Voyageurs National Park, providing lodging and dining options. **Crane Lake** and **Orr** provide access for persons arriving from the south. Crane Lake, the southeastern most gateway, is a good place to rent houseboats and is also a supply area for persons heading to the nearby Boundary Waters Canoe Area Wilderness, as is Ely.

The easiest way to reach Ely is to fly to Hibbing (connecting through Minneapolis-St. Paul). From Hibbing, the drive to Ely takes an hour and forty-five minutes. Arrange transportation ahead of time with **Ely Cab** (218-365-7500).

Another gateway to Voyageurs National Park is **Ash River,** 25 miles north of Orr, County Road 129 and U.S. 53. On the south shore of Lake Kabetogama, Ash River also has houseboat rental companies. **Lake Kabetogama,** about 28 miles north of Orr on County Road 122, along with a park visitor center, features about two dozen cabin and resort properties along the lake. **Island View,** about 12 miles east of International Falls on state Highway 11, is the northwesternmost gateway to Voyageurs National Park. Island View has a park visitor center, a few houseboat rental companies, and several resorts located on Rainy Lake. (See Where to Stay.)

Getting Around

Since there is no public transportation in the region, a car is necessary to reach the region's gateway communities. Dozens of outfitters guide visitors through the area by canoe, snowmobile, and dogsled and also on cross-country ski tours. Other outfitters offer advice and rent gear and equipment. Some canoe and ski outfitters provide transportation to their base lodges and outfitting centers for an additional fee.

What to See and Do

Voyageurs National Park

There is no entrance fee at **Voyageurs National Park,** 3131 Highway 53, International Falls 56649-8904 (218-283-9821; www.nps.gov). Located 15 miles east of International Falls (an entry point to Canada), the park provides a good starting point for your Minnesota lakes vacation. One of the premier water-based parks in the United States, with 39 percent of the park covered by water, Voyageurs National Park draws lots of motorboating families. Quiet isn't exactly the norm in the popular motorboating spots, but the woodland and lake views are soothing. Motorboats provide the easiest way to travel between campsites and to explore the main areas of the park.

Canoeing and Kayaking. With paddling energy and portaging stamina, you can canoe and kayak to the park's interior, marshy, and quieter regions, a trip best for families with older children.

Wildlife. Voyageurs is one of the best mainland parks for spotting bald eagles and active wolf packs. Along the water and land-based trails, keep an eye out for beavers, otters, moose, and bears, too. In May through July, rangers offer a tour boat trip to view nesting gulls and cormorants.

Fishing. The park is known as a prime fishing spot for walleye, northern pike, and smallmouth bass as well as muskie, perch, sauger, lake trout, and crappie. To fish you must obtain a Minnesota fishing license.

Black Flies and Blueberries

Mid-July through August the more than 900 islands in Voyageurs bloom with a special treat—blueberries ripe for the picking. A summer caution: Combat summer's black flies and mosquitoes by wearing light-colored, long-sleeved shirts and pants.

Boat Tours. One of the more popular boat tours is the **North Canoe Voyage,** which allows visitors to paddle along in a 26-foot replica of a North Canoe with a costumed ranger aboard. It's best to reserve ahead for these trips along Kabetogama Lake (218-875-2111) and Rainy Lake (218-286-5740). Also popular are the learn-to-paddle introductory family-oriented canoe trips and the evening two-hour star-watch cruise. Older kids may like the six-hour, round-trip cruise to historic Kettle Falls Hotel, one of the few places you can look south from the United States into Canada. Call ahead to reserve meals and at least one month ahead to reserve lodging; (800) 322-0886.

Hiking. Voyageurs has hiking trails for all ages and skill levels. Landlubbers with little kids should try the 1-mile (each way), spruce-lined **Oberholtzer Trail,** the only trail accessible by car from the Rainy Lake visitor center. The 2-mile (each way) **Blind Ash Bay Trail,** which affords scenic vistas of Kabetomaga Lake, is accessible from the Ash River Visitor Center. The heartier can tackle the 4-mile **Locator Chain of Lakes Trail,** reached by a 6-mile boat trip. You can also hike into several lakes where the National Park Service keeps canoes and boats that are free to the public. Reserve these at a park visitor center and hike in with appropriate life jackets. The park also features special **Kids Explore Voyageurs** hikes for ages seven to twelve, as well as summertime evening campfire programs on cultural and natural history.

Winter Adventures. From late December to late March, when there is sufficient snow (and there almost always is), you can cross-country ski, snowshoe, and snowmobile in the park. Ten miles of groomed cross-country ski trails are available near the Rainy Lake Visitor Center. Twice each winter rangers lead a guided, candle-ski tour along this trail. Obtain maps and information at the visitor centers.

For more information, contact the park's gateway visitor center. The **Crane Lake Information Station** (218-993-2481) is open daily from 10:00 A.M. to 4:00 P.M. late May to Labor Day. The **Kabetogama Lake Visitor Center** (218-875-2111) is open daily from 9:00 A.M. to 5:00 P.M. early May through September. The **Ash River Visitor Center** (218-374-3221) is open daily 9:00 A.M. to 5:00 P.M. late May through Labor Day, and the **Rainy Lake Visitor Center** (218-283-9821) is open daily from 9:00 A.M. to 5:00 P.M. early May through September and at selected times in winter.

Gunflint Lodge

Set on the shores of Gunflint Lake, Gunflint Lodge offers families summer and winter adventure vacations in the Boundary Waters Canoe Area Wilderness.

- **Cabins.** In summer the resort rents rustic cabins for backpackers heading to the wilderness as well as housekeeping cabins. The one- to three-bedroom units (available in winter too) can be booked with or without meals. All have a living room with fireplace and some of the more upscale cabins feature saunas, CD players, and VCRs. The chef is well known for his northwest cuisine, a nice surprise for such a remote lodge. Children under four stay free.
- **Canoeing.** Those who want to paddle and portage on their own can rent canoes and camping equipment from the Gunflint Lodge. Several times a season the resort offers guided family canoe trips. On a seven-night package, you camp for five nights and stay in rustic cabins at Gunflint Lodge on the first and last nights.
- **Horseback riding.** Horseback riding outings wind through the adjacent woods and around parts of the lake.
- **Dogsledding and Other Winter Adventures.** Winter packages combine cross-country skiing, dogsledding, snowshoeing, and ice fishing. After mushing a team with a guide for several hours, come back to your nice warm cabin and a hot meal at the lodge. Young kids can sit swaddled in blankets in the sled (an option not possible with all outfitters).
- **Snowshoeing.** Another favorite activity is snowshoeing, especially past stands of birch to Bridal Falls, a frozen waterfall swirling down a large granite outcropping.
- **Winter Package.** The lodge offers special dogsled packages and a Winter Women's Week (take your mom and your teenage daughter) for guided ski excursions, snowshoe trips, moonlight skiing and dogsledding.

Call Gunflint Lodge at (800) 362-5251, or visit their Web site at www.gunflint.com.

Boundary Waters Canoe Area Wilderness

The BWCAW lies just east of Voyageurs National Park. For information and permits for camping between May 1 and September 30, write to the Forest Supervisor, Superior National Forest, P.O. Box 338, Duluth 55801, or visit the Permit Station, located east of Ely on Highway 169, from 6:00

A.M. to 5:00 P.M. daily in summer (218-365-7681, 218-365-7600, or 800-745-3399). Reserve summer permits as far ahead as possible even as early as February 1.

Canoeing, Kayaking, and Fishing. With its more than 1,500 miles of water trails, the BWCAW affords prime waters for canoeing and fishing. Less noisy, less crowded, and accessible only to those who want to paddle a canoe or kayak and hike the islands, the BWCAW offers a more peaceful getaway than the main areas of Voyageurs National Park. Families with older children accustomed to pack-in/pack-out wilderness camping and long-distance canoeing should find this experience a get-away-from-it-all foray.

Outfitters, a few of whom offer guided summer trips, take much of the work and worry out of a wilderness camping experience. Other outfitters provide rental canoes and equipment, advice, food supplies, and specially designed lightweight equipment. Many of the canoe rental companies are in Ely. For information on outfitters contact the Forest Supervisor and call Ely's Vacation Hotline (800) 777-7281.

Cross-Country Skiing. In winter the BWCAW is a popular cross-country ski area, especially those areas located along the Gunflint Trail. Families with older children and teens who are expert cross-country skiers can ski yurt to yurt along the BWCAW's longest tracked trail, the **Banadad.** While you ski, outfitters bring your gear and food to the yurts and your car to the trail's end. Several lodges along the Gunflint Trail offer cross-country skiing. Contact **Boundary Country Trekking** (218-388-4487 or 800-322-8327; www.boreal.org/adventures). For information on skiing in and near BWCAW, contact the Gunflint Trail Association, Grand Marais 55604 (218-338-4487 or 800-338-6932; www.gunflint-trail.com) and see Where to Stay.

Ely

Ely is known for its association with the wilderness and with wolves. A jumping-off point for the BWCAW and located within the Superior National Forest, Ely is known as the "Canoe Capital of the World." Many visitors come here to rent canoes and equipment for the BWCAW experience and trips along the region's other lakes. This small town has twenty-two canoe outfitters and is within driving distance of 2,021 lakes more than ten acres in size and 1,975 miles of streams.

Ely is situated at the end of the Taconite Trail, one of the most recognized trails in the state and one that meanders through three state forests, one national forest, and numerous historical landmarks. A sweet summer treat along the Taconite Trail and paths in the BWCAW are the berries, ripe for the picking from late June through the raspberry harvest in August.

International Wolf Center

This center educates visitors about one of the world's most misunderstood creatures—the wolf. Visitors learn about the natural history of wolves by observing the resident pack (sometimes difficult to see in their enclosure) and touring the **Wolves and Humans** exhibit. Special activities include evening howling outings. Visitors imitate a wolf cry; there's a 50 percent chance the pack will howl back. Participants in the center's programs can track wolves by plane or, in winter, tie on showshoes or go dogsledding to follow the animals along trails.

In summer and in winter the International Wolf Center offers special family programs that include meals and lodging at a nearby resort. At **The Pack as Family,** a summer favorite, spend a weekend learning how the wolf family is similar to the structure of your own family.

International Wolf Center, 1396 Highway 169; (218) 365-4695 or (800) ELY-WOLF; www.wolf.org.

Like the Gunflint region, the area surrounding Ely also offers winter activities such as cross-country skiing, ice fishing, snowmobiling, and snowshoeing. In winter the Taconite Trail becomes a major snowmobiling path. Located within Ely's city limits, the 4-mile Trezona Trail circles Miner's Lake. In summer it's used by hikers and bikers and in winter by cross-country skiers.

Owned by well-known musher and adventurer Paul Schurke, **Wintergreen Lodge,** 1101 Ring Rock Road, Ely (218-365-6022; www.dogsledding.com) offers four- and five-day dogsled trips. Some departures are family oriented and some are geared more to couples, especially the upscale inn trips. Choose to camp or dogsled inn-to-inn.

Lead your own team 11 to 14 miles each day through woods and across frozen lakes and marshland. Schurke's guides are good and his Inuit dogs are large, friendly, and (mostly) hard workers. Schurke makes his own sleds; they carry gear, not people. It takes stamina to stand for six hours a day, holding onto a sled in the windy Minnesota winter so these trips are recommended for outdoor-oriented kids ages eight and older.

Since the upscale-inn package attracts romance seekers, we booked the basic inn trip. The first night's lodging at the White Pine Cabin, Timber Trail Lodge, may prove a bit too basic. The bedrooms have no heat and the bathrooms will remind you of camp. At the more comfortable Wintergreen Lodge, owned by the Schurkes, you can opt to sleep outside in a teepee or an igloo. The food is basic but plentiful, except for lunch on

Shopping in Ely

Ely has the usual small-town combination of tourist shops and staples, but a few places are noteworthy.

- **Wintergreen Northwoods Apparel,** 205 East Sheridan (218-365-6602 or 800-584-9425). Owned by Susan Schurke, Paul Schurke's wife, Wintergreen sells its own line of handmade winter outdoor clothing, including hats, gloves, anoraks, pants, and vests. For Wintergreen's dogsled trips, you can rent gear here instead of having to buy and bring your own.
- **Steger Mukluks,** 6 East Sheridan (800-MUKLUKS), sells a variety of handmade mukluks, those warm winter boots fashioned after the ones worn by Inuit Natives.
- **Piragis Northwoods Company,** 105 North Central (800-223-6565), sells winter and outdoor clothing and gear, and serves as a local clearinghouse for area outfitters.
- **Jim Brandenburg Gallery,** located on the second level of Piragis Northwoods Company store. Brandenberg's nature photography has appeared in many magazines. The gallery sells his photos of wolves, northern lights, wildflowers, and other subjects.

the trail, which consists of soup and handfuls of trail mix. Ask ahead of time for sandwiches for lunch.

Dogsledding gets you out in the wilderness without the noise of snowmobiles. Once the dogs get going, you hear just the wind, the sled runners on the snow, and the panting of the dogs. Until harnessed and running, the dogs howl in anticipation, and they can be rambunctious. For dog lovers and winter adventurers, this is a great trip.

An area kid-pleaser is the **Soudan Underground Mine State Park,** Highway 169 (218-753-2245), Minnesota's oldest, deepest, and richest iron-ore mine. On the ninety-minute tour, you descend ½ mile underground into the mine, which was in use from 1884 to 1963, and take a short spin on a mining car.

Dorothy Molter, a.k.a. the "Root Beer Lady," was a fixture of the BWCAW and known for her legendary hospitality and homemade root beer. **The Dorothy Molter Museum** (218-365-4451) comprises two log cabins that were transported out of the BWCAW to Ely. The Winter Cabin was Molter's home and is furnished just as she left it before passing away in 1986. The Point Cabin houses an interpretive center that documents Molter's and the region's history.

Side Trips

In International Falls families can visit the **Ground Mound Historic Center,** 6749 Highway 11, International Falls (218-285-3332). This state historic site is the largest American Indian burial mound in Minnesota. American Indian history and heritage can be learned at the **Bronco Nagurski Museum,** 214 Sixth Avenue, International Falls (218-283-4316). This museum houses American Indian artifacts and exhibits about gold mining and early settlers.

Special Events

February. Ely Voyager Winter Festival: Snow sculptures provide the backdrop for snow-related activities and game tastings. Arctic Blast; hundreds of snowmobiles ride through town along with sports figures. (If you dislike the sound of snowmobiles, avoid Ely on President's weekend.)

July. Voyageur Days is held around Crane Lake. Activities include fish fry, craft booth, canoe races, and powwow.

December. Snow City Festival & Parade: a welcome to winter with caroling, winter-themed floats, and candlelight walk.

Where to Stay

Voyageurs National Park

Voyageurs National Park, 3131 Highway 53, International Falls 56649-8904 (218-283-9821). The park offers 130 boat-in campsites on a first-come basis. You can rent a boat from one of the nearby resorts. **Woodenfrog State Forest Campground** (218-875-2602) offers sixty campsites on a first-come basis, and lodging is available in the four communities on the park's outskirts. For something different rent a houseboat. Among rental companies: **Rainy Lake Houseboats** (218-286-5291) and **Voyaguaire Houseboats** (800-882-6287).

The four gateway communities to Voyageurs National Park offer lodgings, mostly housekeeping cabins and motels. Some are open year-round but most are available from May through October only. For accommodations in the **Kabetogama Lake** area, contact the Kabetogama Lake Association, Box 80, Ray 56669 (218-875-2621 or 800 524-9085). For accommodations in the **Crane Lake** area, contact the Crane Lake Visitor and Convention Bureau, P.O. Box 15 VTB, Crane Lake 55725; (800) 362-7405. For accommodations in the **Ash River** area, contact the Ash River Commercial Club, Orr 55771 (800-950-2061). For accommodations in the **Rainy Lake** and **International Falls** areas, contact the International

Falls Area Visitor & Convention Bureau, 301 Second Avenue, International Falls 56649 (218-283-9400 or 800-325-5766).

Trout Lake Resort, 230 Gunflint Trail (218-387-1330 or 800-258-7688), is located 12 miles up and 4 miles east of the Gunflint Trail. This family-run lakeside resort offers seven furnished units that can accommodate between two and ten guests. Appropriate to its name, the lake is known for its trout fishing. At **Bearskin Lodge & Cross Country Ski Resort,** 275 Gunflint Trail (218-388-2292 or 800-338-4170), guests dine family style, accompanied by recorded classical music. All of the resort's fifteen units feature fireplaces; four also come with private decks. In summer the resort offers hiking trails and boats.

Northwoods hospitality is the norm at the **Golden Eagle Lodge Resort & Nordic Ski Center,** 35 Gunflint Trail (218-388-2203 or 800-346-2203). The only resort on Flour Lake, Golden Eagle has eleven cabins with private docks. All include a fireplace woodstove, and two are handicapped accessible. Five lakes are nearby for canoeing, and Flour Lake is known for its bass, walleye, and pike fishing. In summer there are intermittent nature-oriented activities for children.

On the eastern edge of Voyageurs National Park is the **Kettle Falls Hotel,** 10502 Gamma Road, Ray 56669 (218-374-4404, 218-875-2070, or 888-KF-HOTEL). A popular place for families on the Minnesota-Canadian border, this property offers housekeeping lodges with kitchenettes as well as twelve rooms (sharing three baths) in the main lodge.

Ely

Ely has a variety of accommodations. **Deer Ridge,** P.O. Box 238, Ely (218-365-4075), has ten housekeeping cabins on Garden Lake. Situated on thirty-five acres, Deer Ridge has access to the BWCAW and provides canoe outfitting trips. **River Point Resort** in Ely (800-456-5580; www.greatresorts.com), is situated on a peninsula, where the Kawishiwi River joins Birch Lake. With 2,500 feet of shoreline, the resort features a small beach, a playground, access to the BWCAW, and an assortment of vacation homes for rent.

For a traditional, family-friendly hotel, try the **Holiday Inn SunSpree Resort,** 400 North Pioneer Road (218-365-6565 or 800-365-5070). This property features an indoor swimming pool, boat rentals, and a summer children's activity program.

Trezona House Bed & Breakfast, 315 East Washington Street (218-365-4809; www.northernnet.com/trezona), has four guest rooms sharing two baths. The big white house in town is plain-looking on the outside, but comfortable inside with serviceable rooms. The Angler's room has a fishing net and pole on the wall. The hosts welcome families with kids age five and older. Rates include a full breakfast. Rollaways are extra.

A list of lodgings is available from the Ely Vacation Hotline: (800) 777-7281.

Where to Eat

Along the Gunflint Trail, the **Gunflint Lodge** is often described as having the best food between Minneapolis and the Canadian border (218-388-2294 or 800-328-3325). The **Trout Lake Resort** (218-387-1330 or 800-258-7688), the **Bearskin Lodge & Cross Country Ski Resort** (218-388-2292 or 800-338-4170), and the **Golden Eagle Lodge Resort & Nordic Ski Center** (218-388-2203 or 800-346-2203) provide family-style cooked meals daily. (See also Where to Stay.)

Ely

With a dozen or so restaurants, the Ely area is hardly a culinary mecca, but it is the place to go for the most choice in one convenient area. The **Mantel House Restaurant,** Main Street near Third Avenue (218-365-2960), is the best restaurant in Ely. Serving Continental cuisine, the Mantel House is open for dinner only on Friday, Saturday, and Sunday in winter and Wednesday through Sunday in summer. Reservations required. **Northern Grounds,** 117 North Central (218-365-2460) is open 6:30 A.M. to 10:00 P.M. This is a good choice for breakfast or lunch. The deli sandwiches, homemade soups, and desserts are good. **Cranberry's Saloon and Restaurant** (218-365-4301) specializes in American and Mexican dishes such as steaks and burgers, tacos, and a salad bar. The **Evergreen Restaurant** at Holiday Inn SunSpree Resort, 400 North Pioneer Road (218-365-6565), has lakeside dining and features regional and Continental cuisine as well as a children's menu.

For More Information

For state tourism information contact the **Minnesota Office of Tourism,** 100 Metro Square, St. Paul (612-296-5029 or 800-657-3700; www.exploreminnesota.com). The **Gunflint Trail Association** maintains 132 miles of groomed trails. For maps or lodging information, call (800) 338-6932; www.gunflint-trail.com. **International Falls Chamber of Commerce,** P.O. Box 169 International Falls 56649 (218-283-9400 or 800-325-5766). **Ely Area Information Center,** 1600 East Sheridan Street (218-365-6123 or 800-777-7281; www.ely.org).

The nonprofit **Lake States Interpretive Association,** 3131 Highway 53, International Falls 56649 (218-283-2103), offers brochures, maps, and books about Voyageurs National Park and Chippewa, Superior, and Nicolet National Forests.

Emergency Numbers

In the Ely area:

Ambulance, fire, and police: 911

Ely Police Department: 209 East Sheridan Street; (218) 365-3222

St. Louis/Lake County Sheriff: (218) 365-3222

Hospital: Ely-Bloomenson Community Hospital & Ely Area Ambulance Service, 328 West Conan Street; (218) 365-3271

Pharmacies: James Drug (open daily), 101 East Chapman Street, Ely (218-365-3130); Martinetto Drug, 40 North Second Avenue, East, Ely (218-365-6412)

ST. LOUIS

Known to pioneers as "the gateway to the West," St. Louis still welcomes visitors with a smalltown homeyness, but the city has updated its image with lots of urban attractions. Situated on the Mississippi River, the city offers paddlewheel tours, panoramic views from the top of the Gateway Arch, simple pleasures such as picnics in Forest Park, and interactive play at many excellent kids' museums, including the St. Louis Science Center, one of the country's best.

Getting There

The **Lambert–St. Louis International Airport,** 10701 Lambert International Boulevard, is 13 miles northwest on I-70 (314-426-8000). Most major airlines serve the airport, including American (800-433-7300 or 314-231-9505), Northwest (800-225-2525), United (800-241-6522 or 314-454-0088), and TWA (800-221-2000). Taxis and rental cars are available.

Greyhound/Trailways, 1450 North Thirteenth Street (800-231-2222), and the **Amtrak Station,** 550 South Sixteenth Street (314-331-3300), also offer convenient transportation to St. Louis. For train ticket reservations and information, call (800) USA-RAIL.

Getting Around

Taxis include **Yellow** (314-361-2345), **County** (314-991-5300), and **Allen** (314-241-7722). **Bi-State Transit,** 707 North First Street (314-231-2345), offers inexpensive bus transportation. St. Louis's **Metro Link** (314-231-2345), a light-rail mass transportation system, connects most major attractions within the city, including the airport, Union Station, Busch Stadium, the America's Center, and even the north St. Louis suburbs. Metro Link conveniently offers free transportation in the downtown area weekdays from 11:00 A.M. until 1:00 P.M. Rental cars, however, are still a good option for getting around.

St. Louis

AT A GLANCE

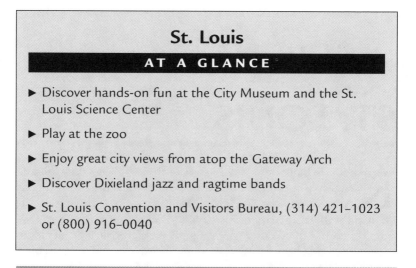

- Discover hands-on fun at the City Museum and the St. Louis Science Center
- Play at the zoo
- Enjoy great city views from atop the Gateway Arch
- Discover Dixieland jazz and ragtime bands
- St. Louis Convention and Visitors Bureau, (314) 421–1023 or (800) 916–0040

WHAT TO SEE AND DO

Museums

The **St. Louis Art Museum,** 1 Fine Arts Drive, Forest Park (314–721–0072). Originally the Palace of Fine Arts, the museum is the sole remaining building from the 1904 World's Fair. Greek columned, eagle crowned, and sited by a reflecting pool, the palace once mirrored East Coast standards of sophistication.

With 1990s renovation adding 30,000 additional feet of gallery space, more of the museum's permanent collection came out of the closet, including ancient Egyptian statues of gods and goddesses, mummies, and gold jewelry dating from 600 B.C. Other interesting features of the museum's permanent collection include dazzling works by Claude Monet and Edgar Degas. There is an exhibit on decorative arts, furniture, and household items as they evolved through history. On occasional Sunday afternoons, the museum holds special festival days for children and families. Call ahead to check.

For aviation history, and a sample of life in the American West, visit the **Missouri History Museum,** in the Jefferson Memorial Building in Forest Park (314–746–4599). The legendary exhibit of Charles Lindbergh's *Spirit of St. Louis* memorabilia is of popular interest. Backed by nine St. Louis businessmen, Charles Lindbergh bet his stamina against the tediousness of a thirty-three-and-a-half hour trans-Atlantic crossing. The museum's one-room gallery evokes Lindbergh's May 20 and 21, 1927, record-breaking flight. There's an eight-minute film and a collection of memorabilia, including flight suit, arm cup for water, hip chronometer, and diary. Logged at eighteen hours: "I've lost command of

St. Louis Science Center

Take your children to the **St. Louis Science Center,** 5050 Oakland Avenue (314-289-4444). Let your kids loose for some hands-on science fun at the Science Center's three connected buildings. Kids' eyes grow wide at the sight of the life-size ***Tyrannosaurus Rex,*** who moves and roars menacingly in the atrium. Wind your way through his world and the changing habitats to see what the land looked like when these giants roamed it and when dragonflies swooped down on the St. Louis area. At the **Human Adventure** gallery, explore perception and senses by creating patterns in a kaleidoscope, find out why "pretzels" in your ears help hearing, and how your hands can conduct an electric concert. The **Discovery Room** is a hands-on place to finger such objects of interest as skeletons, sandboxes, teepees, wheelchairs, and stethoscopes.

Space Sciences Gallery presents science fiction and fact about space travel and the planets. Create artificial gravity with the Momentum Machine, find out what telescopes tell us, and tour the planets via computer.

The tunnel between two of the buildings leads you into an underground domain of pipes and mines. Walk through a coal mine, complete with shoveling noises and canary songs, and simulated sewer where water pipes emit swishing noises. Exhibits in the **MedTech and DNA Zone galleries** look at medical equipment and advances and pose ethical questions about medical research and behavior.

Star-studded skies come alive at the **McDonnell Planetarium** (try to purchase tickets in advance, if possible). Browse the exhibits around the theater, which include an authentic Gemini space capsule, replicated space vehicles, properties of gravity, and the brilliance and power of the sun.

Outside is **Monsanto Science Park,** a hands-on educational play park. Here children image themselves in a human kaleidoscope and a giant prism, crawl through thermal tubes, switch giant gears, toss echoes down a 100-foot chamber, and roll balls across a looping track.

my eyelids . . . I've got to find some way to keep awake. There's no alternative but death or failure."

The Holocaust Museum and Learning Center, 12 Milestone Campus Drive (314-432-0020), opened in May 1995. Using text, videos, and artifacts, such as letters telling Jews in Germany that they could not vote and displays of currency that could only be used in the ghettos, the museum tells the history of the Holocaust. The museum has a special emphasis here on the Jews who immigrated to St. Louis from Europe after World War II.

After exploring Forest Park's museums, end your day with a stunning sunset stroll along the green winding lanes and expansive lawns. Forest Park also has lots of recreational activities, including golf, tennis, and ice skating (314-535-0100).

City Museum

You expect surprises from a building with a three-story-high praying mantis out front, and the **City Museum** delivers. A wacky combination of recycled mouse cages, mosaic tiles, watch bands, airplane panels, and other thrown-out stuff is resurrected as arty exhibits. Kids crawl through a sky tunnel, explore a cave, and climb into a whale's head. They can also watch glassblowers, take part in a performing dog circus, make crafts, and peruse salvaged gargoyles and other outdoor sculptures. Best for ages five and older, a trip here will energize kids' imaginations.

City Museum, 701 North Fifteenth Street; (314) 231-2489.

More Attractions

At **Six Flags St. Louis** (314-938-5300), located about thirty minutes southwest of St. Louis, you get tossed, twirled, dropped, and dunked. The themed rides take their names and attitude from DC Comics superheroes and from Warner Bros. Looney Tunes characters. Mr. Freeze is a high-tech roller coaster that blasts riders out of a 190-foot tunnel at speeds of up to 70 miles per hour. The coaster dips and dives, taking a 180-degree inverted turn. (Not for the faint of heart.) The Screamin' Eagle, a wooden coaster, drops riders 92 feet, propelling them along a track at speeds of up to 62 miles per hour. Get wet as Tidal Wave plunges you over a 50-foot waterfall in a twenty-person boat. Little kids love Looney Tunes Town, a cartoon-themed play area featuring pint-sized rides and appearances by Daffy Duck, Bugs Bunny, and other Looney Tunes characters.

At Warner Bros. Backlot guests witness the magic of movie making. Live drama, action-packed sequences, and musicals leap off the stage of five "movie sets." Guests participate in some re-creations.

What's a city without a symbol? St. Louis is synonymous with the **Gateway Arch,** at Market Street on the riverfront (314-425-4465). This 630-foot-high stainless-steel curve glinting along the riverfront marks the city's gateway position for the pioneers heading west to possibility. For a bird's-eye view, ride the tram to the Arch's top, but only if you can tolerate tight places. Make reservations when you arrive at the Arch, and be prepared for a two- to three-hour wait.

There is plenty to do while you wait. You may watch *Monument to the Dream,* a twenty-eight-minute film detailing the Arch's building trials, or meander through the nearby **Museum of Westward Expansion,** beneath the Gateway Arch (314-425-4465), and admire such pioneer

St. Louis Zoo

This ninety-acre facility is one of St. Louis's most popular attractions. At the **Emerson Electric Children's Zoo** kids learn about the animals by mimicking their behaviors through a clever combination of exhibits and play. Kids can feed lorikeets nectar, slide down a see-through chute in the otter pool, climb a spider web made of rope, and view koalas without any barriers.

At the **Living World Educational Center** kids use a combination of computers and video screens to discover the biological world. In the Animal Hall you'll be amazed at the dazzling display of four viewing levels—tanks of coral, screens that flash images of spawning salmon, a live quail, and a computer with definitions of "anthropod." In the Ecology Hall, use the computers to find out about bird feeding habits or extinct animals.

If you have limited time, pay a short but rewarding visit to the birds. They swoop and chatter in a free-flight cage, built in 1904 and claimed to be the world's largest. There are also six aviaries, which house a bald eagle, red-billed toucans, and the endangered white neck cranes. The wire that encloses the aviary is designed to fade out of view, so you get the feeling you're really walking in their natural habitat.

Stop by the **Jungle of the Apes** and see Fred, a 330-pound silverback lowland gorilla, the zoo's primate pride. The habitat of the Jungle of the Apes was developed to study great ape behavior; it offers banyan trees, black-haired chimps sunning on rocks like satisfied Buddhas. wizened-faced orangutans, and shy gorillas striking poses behind gray-limbed ersatz trees. Raja, a baby elephant born in 1992, is also quite a crowd-gatherer.

The miniature train makes it easy to get around. Your children will like riding under the waterfall and through the tunnel (warn little ones of the several minutes of darkness).

St. Louis Zoo, Forest Park; (314) 781-0900; www.stlzoo.org.

artifacts as the Native American peace medals, wooden stagecoaches, and recipes for buffalo stew. While waiting, visitors at the south leg experience Time Trams to the Top, an exhibit re-creating a mid-1800s morning on the riverfront. At the north leg, visitors relive the morning of October 28, 1965, when the last section of the arch was put in place.

The **Arch Odyssey Theater,** underground at Gateway Arch (314-425-4465), a high-tech theater, with a four-story-high screen, surrounds you with sight and sound.

Magic House

At the **Magic House,** St. Louis Children's Museum, little ones can bang pots and play peek-a-boo at Just Baby and Me. Kids can build sand sculptures, bounce balls, navigate boats, zoom down a three-story slide, explore a multilevel children's village, and produce television news shows. Dance with your shadow, tap Morse code, try computers, and crawl through tunnel mazes. This hands-on facility is geared to infants through nine-year-olds.

Magic House, St. Louis Children's Museum, 516 South Kirkwood Road; (314) 822-8900; www.magichouse.com.

Just north of the Arch, **Laclede's Landing,** between Eads and King Bridges on the Riverfront (314-241-5875), is named for Pierre Laclede, who came ashore here in 1763 to establish a fur trading post. Now, these cobbled walkways and reclaimed warehouses sport shops, bars, and restaurants.

Green Spaces and Parks

At the **Missouri Botanical Garden,** 4344 Shaw Boulevard (314-577-5100), find a still point and a vista from the meditation huts and tranquil stone paths in the Japanese Garden. With fourteen acres, this is the largest formal Japanese garden in the United States. Also, tour the Climatron, the first geodesic-dome greenhouse, and the blooming rose gardens, lily ponds, and flower-bedecked paths. Dozens of individual gardens delight the senses, particularly the Scented Garden. It features flowers noteworthy for their fragrance and texture, sculptures and fountains that fill the garden with the sounds of water and chimes, and braille markers that make this garden especially appreciated by blind visitors. End your visit with a tour of the Chinese Garden and take in the scents of lotuses, gardenias, and camellias. The pavilion and the carved marble bridge, which spans the central pool and a narrow stream, are gifts from Nanjing, St. Louis's sister city.

At the **Laumeier Sculpture Park,** 12580 Rott Road (314-821-1209), a 125-acre outdoor park, the landscape blooms with modern sculpture, some of huge proportions such as the red 100-foot-long Alexander Lieberman statue *The Way.* On these rolling hills among the pines and oaks, the angles, lines, and massive size of these innovative modern sculptures delight your eye.

Creve Couer Park, Dorsett Road (314-889-2863), has facilities for sailing, canoeing, camping, hiking, and picnicking. Winter brings ice skating and sledding; in the spring, call about fishing and boating in the park. For more outdoor activity, **Queeny County Park,** 550 Weidman Road (314-391-0900), features the Greensfelder Recreational Complex with skating rinks, outdoor pool, and tennis courts. The park also hosts the St. Louis Symphony Pops in the summer.

With young kids, head to **Faust Park** (314-532-7298) for a spin on the **St. Louis Carousel,** a 1920s beauty with sixty hand-carved animals. After a picnic lunch and playground time, walk through the **Sophia M. Sachs Butterfly House,** 40 North Kings Highway (314-361-3365), where a colorful butterfly might land on your child's shoulder.

River Cruises

Climb aboard the ***Tom Sawyer*** or the ***Becky Thatcher,*** re-created paddlewheelers, for a scenic dinner cruise on the Mississippi or a one-hour harbor cruise. Call **Gateway Riverboat Cruises,** 500 North Leonor K. Sullivan Boulevard; (314) 621-4040.

Other Attractions

Tour the **Anheuser-Busch Brewery,** I-55 and Arsenal Street (314-577-2626), the largest brewery in the world. Visitors can watch how beer is brewed in the expanded Brew House. From three stories high, check out the functioning brewery equipment. There are also some antique pieces in the Brew House, including a copper kettle and a huge hop-vine chandelier that, according to legend, belonged to the Belgian exhibit at the 1904 World's Fair. See everything from the packaging plant to the lager cellar to the Budweiser Clydesdale stables. Parents can enjoy free samples of Anheuser-Busch beers. The gift shop caters to the whole family, with items ranging from beer mugs to Budweiser T-shirts.

St. Louis has another claim to fame: offbeat museums. The **International Bowling Museum,** 111 Stadium Plaza (314-231-6340), has actual bowling alleys you can use; compare old-time alleys to modern-day lanes.

If you've ever collected toy trains, and wished for miles of track, visit the fifty-acre **Museum of Transport,** 3015 Barrett Station Road (314-965-7998). Here you'll be dwarfed by the yardful of big engines like the Union-Pacific steam locomotives, the 1890s Black Diamond, and *Big Boy,* a 600-ton steam locomotive from the forties.

Do you have a canine among your best friends? If so, you won't want to miss a visit to **American Kennel Club Museum of the Dog,** Queeny Park, 1721 South Mason Road (314-821-DOGS). Paintings, figurines, a dog-specific video theater, and a gift shop are all on the grounds of the Jarville House, a Greek Revival mansion. Bring home a souvenir for your furry pal.

Sports

Brings the kids to a **Cardinals** baseball game at Busch Stadium, 250 Stadium Plaza (314-421-3060). They can sit, if seats are available, in the special Kids Corner with the team mascot, Fredbird. Kids can test their sports skills in the Busch Stadium Family Pavilion, which has batting cages and pitching mounds along with displays of old uniforms. Periodically, there are chances to meet current and former players. Also check for hockey games and times for the sports arena. **Blues Hockey** is played at Kiel Center, 1401 Clark Avenue (314-622-5400).

Shopping

The shopping in St. Louis is as much an attraction as an activity. **Plaza Frontenac,** 97 Plaza Frontenac, Clayton and Lindbergh (314-432-5800), features ritzy apparel at Saks, Gucci, Montaldo's, and Rodier. The **St. Louis Union Station,** Market Street between Eighteenth and Twentieth Streets (314-421-6655), offers scores of shops in a century-old renovated train station. The **St. Louis Centre,** 515 North Sixth Street (314-231-5522), is a large, enclosed shopping center with four floors. Shops of interest in the **Saint Louis Galleria,** I-170 and Highway 40 (314-863-6633), include FAO Schwarz, Godiva, Crayola Kids, and Ann Taylor.

Nightlife and Performing Arts

Take a walk along **Laclede's Landing** to find some lively nighttime entertainment in St. Louis. It won't be long before you begin to hear some blues or ragtime bands playing in bars and restaurants. *The Riverfront Times,* distributed at no charge in restaurants and offices throughout the city, and the *St. Louis Magazine* both list calendars of events and nightly entertainment.

St. Louis also has a thriving performing arts scene. At **Powell Symphony Hall,** 718 North Grand (314-533-2500), listen to the **Saint Louis Symphony Orchestra,** one of the oldest symphony orchestras in the country, led by Maestro Hans Vonk. **The Muny in Forest Park** is at the **Riverport Performing Arts Center,** 14141 Riverport Drive, Maryland Heights (314-298-9944); and the **West Port Playhouse** is at 600 West Port Plaza (314-576-7100).

The **Fox Theater,** 527 North Grand Boulevard (314-534-1678), an ornate Siamese-and-Byzantine-style theater, opened in 1929 and was restored in 1981. Today it features Broadway productions such as *Phantom of the Opera,* comedians such as Jerry Seinfeld, as well as concerts and dance.

Entertain the entire family with **Bob Kramer's Marionettes**, 4143 Laclede Avenue (314-531-3313). See demonstrations of puppet making Monday through Saturday at 10:00 a.m. and 1:00 p.m. The show Puppet Follies happens every Saturday at 11:15 a.m. and 2:15 p.m. Puppets are also for sale here. There is an admission fee; call in advance for specific shows.

Gambling: Not for Kids

The riverfront sports gambling boats. Among them: The *Casino Queen,* 200 Front Street (800–777–0777), offers gambling excursions on the Illinois side of the river six times daily. Breakfast, lunch, and dinner cruises are available, but plan your child care in advance with a hotel or service because guests must be twenty-one years or older to board.

The President Casino on *The Admiral,* 802 North First Street (800–878–7411), is a large dockside casino, with slots, blackjack and craps tables, and a restaurant and delicatessen.

Side Trips

Among the 5,000 caves that gave Missouri the nickname the "Cave State," the **Meramec Caverns,** one hour west of St. Louis by way of I–44, in Stanton, are the most well known. Discovered more than 200 years ago, the caverns feature rock formations that are more than seventy million years old. You'll be amazed at the colors, the formations, the "onyx mountain," the natural pools of water, and the enormous size of the caverns. Kids marvel at the Jungle Room, named for its resemblance to a swampy jungle full of rocky "vegetation." Outside, restaurants and gift shops await.

Instead of grabbing a bite at a crowded concession, pack a picnic for **La Jolla Natural Park,** adjacent to the Meramec Caverns, along the banks of the Meramec River, and enjoy a picnic or barbecue.

Special Events

January. The Missouri Botanical Garden features the Annual Orchid Display.

February. Historic Soulard hosts a Mardi Gras Celebration.

March. St. Patrick's Day Parade.

April. St. Louis Cardinals kick off their season; the Storytelling Festival offers professional tales.

May. Riverboat races between modern-ay *Becky Thatcher* and *Tom Sawyer* commemorate National Tourism Week.

June. Sand Castle Festival, Laumeier Sculpture Park, features huge sandcastles.

July. Fair St. Louis is said to be one of the largest Independence Day celebrations in the United States, each year attracting millions to the Gateway Arch and to the St. Louis waterfront.

The busy St. Louis riverfront is a popular family attraction.

August. Artisans and craftspeople strut their stuff at the Festival of the Little Hills.

September. Early fall brings the Annual Bevo Day. A parade, plenty of food, rides, markets, and arts-and-craft shows take this festival into the night.

October. Faust Park hosts the Faust Folk Festival, with nineteenth-century-style performing arts and a crafts sale.

December. Light Up Ceremony, the Christmas Parade; keeping with tradition, the *Nutcracker* plays at Fox Theatre.

Where to Stay

For a luxury hotel stay, look into the **Hyatt Regency St. Louis Union Station,** One St. Louis Union Station (314-231-1234). Other hotels include **Courtyard by Marriott,** 2340 Market Street (314-241-9111); **Hampton Inn Union Station,** 2211 Market Street (314-241-3200); **Holiday Inn,** Ninth Street at Convention Plaza (314-621-8200); **Regal Riverfront Hotel,** 200 South Fourth Street (314-241-9500); and **Days Inn at the Arch,** 333 Washington Avenue (314-621-7900). **The Mayfair,** 806 St. Charles Street (314-421-2500), features a bar and grill, a wide variety of rooms, and easy access to all the attractions of St. Louis, making this a popular lodging choice. Families take priority at the **Summerfield Suites Hotel,** 1855 Craigshire Road (314-878-1555 or 800-833-4353). A spacious living area complete with television and VCR joins two separate bedrooms with their private baths. Fully equipped kitchens make feeding little ones easier and cheaper.

To combine a St. Louis visit with a resort stay, try the **Tan-Tar-A Resort and Golf Club,** Osage Beach (800-826-8272), about three hours from St. Louis. The resort features championship golf courses, five pools, tennis, racquetball, and dozens of other activities, plus the Lake of the Ozarks. Children's programs are offered in season.

Root Beer on Tap

Fitz's Bottling Company, 6605 Delmar (314-726-9555), is a root beer microbrewery where customers can see the root beer being brewed and watch the old bottling line. Daily specials often feature barbecue and burgers.

Where to Eat

Tony's, 410 Market Street (314-231-7007), is one of only a few Mobil four-star rated restaurants in the United States. Come early—by 6:00 P.M. if you can. No reservations are taken. Dinners come with three bread courses, attentive service, and scrumptious food. Among the specialties: veal, rigatoni, quail.

For the best burgers in St. Louis, go to **Blueberry Hill,** 6504 Delmar (314-727-0880), a St. Louis landmark decorated with pop culture items. For dinner with a view and nightly entertainment, make reservations at **Top of the Riverfront Restaurant,** 200 South Fourth Street (314-241-3191).

For relaxed dinners, try the **Old Spaghetti Factory,** 727 North First Street (314-621-0276), where pasta and special sauces dominate the menu. **Ozzie's Restaurant and Sports Bar,** 645 West Port Plaza (314-434-1000), provides a comfortable atmosphere, wood furnishings, twenty-two televisions, and many hockey, baseball, and other jerseys adorning the walls.

For Italian cuisine, try **Zia's** 5256 Wilson Avenue (314-776-0020), and taste the St. Louis specialty of toasted ravioli. For Nouvelle American cuisine, make reservations for **Faust's** in the Adam's Mark-St. Louis, Fourth and Chestnut Streets (314-342-4690). For the best bakery in town, try **Amighetti's Bakery and Cafe,** 3151 Wilson (314-776-2855). Voted one of the best in St. Louis, the breads, pizza, and ice cream are treats.

Ted Drewes Frozen Custard, Route 66 (no phone), has been drawing crowds in warm weather since 1929.

For More Information

The St. Louis Convention and Visitors Bureau: (314) 421-1023 or (800) 916-0040, for free information about lodging, restaurants, and important numbers; www.st-louis.mo.us.

Fun Phone: (314) 421-2100, for information about special events

Missouri Information Center: Interstate 270 in North St. Louis, Riverview exit; (314) 869-7100

St. Louis County Department of Parks and Recreation: 41 South Central Avenue, 63105; (314) 889-2863

Emergency Numbers

Ambulance, fire, police: 911

Highway Patrol: (314) 434-3344

Children's Hospital: The Cardinal Glennon Children's Hospital, 1465 South Grand Street; (314) 577-5600

Twenty-four-hour pharmacy: Walgreens, 4 Hampton Village Plaza Shopping Center; (314) 351-2100

Poison Control: The Cardinal Glennon Children's Hospital features a poison control center. Call the hotline at (314) 772-5200.

15 Montana

Flathead Lake and Glacier National Park

Families will never get bored in this popular corner of Big Sky Country that smiles with the openness of the West and offers some of its best scenery. Tucked in northwest Montana, the Flathead area lures golf enthusiasts with its eight courses, where the "birdies" are eagles and tundra swans. Kids love Flathead Lake, ringed by mountains, with 124 miles of shoreline, thirty-two islands, and enough fishing to last all summer. Take a boat ride to Painted Rocks to see the petroglyphs left by the Blackfoot Indians, and picnic on Wildhorse Island, a state park where deer and sheep graze.

The Flathead area also has sailing, hiking, white-water rafting, and dog sledding, as well as the scenic Waterton/Glacier International Peace Park.

Getting There

Flathead Lake and Glacier National Park are both located in the northwest section of Montana, not far from the Canadian border. The easiest way to get there is by flying into **Glacier International Airport** (406-257-5994) in Kalispell, about 25 miles southwest. Glacier International has jet service sixteen times daily, by Delta and Delta Connection (800-221-1212), Horizon Air (800-547-9308), Northwest Airlines (800-225-2525) and United Airlines (800-241-6522). **Amtrak's** *Empire Builder* (800-872-7245) follows the southern border of Glacier National Park, with stops at West Glacier, East Glacier, Essex, and Whitefish. **Intercontinental** bus lines serve Kalispell and Great Falls, where visitors can transfer to **Glacier Park, Inc. (GPI)** buses (406-226-9311, May-September; 602-207-6000, October-May). **Flathead Glacier Transportation** (800-829-7038) and **Kalispell Taxi and Airport Shuttle** (406-752-2842) offer shuttle service between the airport and Glacier.

Flathead Lake and Glacier National Park

AT A GLANCE

- Sail on and fish in Flathead Lake
- Snowmobile through Flathead National Forest
- Hike the trails of Glacier National Park
- Drive Going-to-the-Sun Road in Glacier National Park
- Kalispell Chamber of Commerce, (406) 758-2800
- Whitefish Chamber of Commerce, (406) 862-3501
- Glacier National Park, (406) 888-7800; www.nps.gov

GETTING AROUND

When traveling around Flathead Lake, you'll probably want to go by car so you can travel at your own pace, seeing as much as you'd like. U.S. 93 skirts the lake, making it one of the best routes to take. Motor cruises on the lake give another perspective, and cool off the travel-weary little ones.

Glacier National Park has **"Jammies"** (406-226-9311), vintage motor coaches built between 1936 and 1939 that travel over Going-to-the-Sun Road; they link all the hotels and lodges within the park. Drivers of the fifteen-passenger coaches, which have rollback canvas tops for better views, stop frequently for roadside explorations and picture taking.

The park is open year-round, but roads are usually only operable from mid-June to mid-October. A seven-day entrance fee is $10.00 per car. Vehicles and vehicle combinations that are longer than 21 feet and wider than 8 feet are not permitted.

WHAT TO SEE AND DO

When you arrive in the Kalispell area, you'll find yourself in the midst of acres of national parks and lake regions—a wilderness heaven. Travel south on I-93 and you'll reach **Flathead Lake,** one of the largest natural freshwater lakes in the country. Several areas of land around it comprise **Flathead Lake State Park** (406-752-5501). Northeast will take you past Kalispell, Columbia Falls, and Hungry Horse to **Glacier National Park,** on U.S. 2 and 89, near U.S. 90 and 93. Not far from Yellowstone, Grand Teton, and Shoshone, and linked with the **Waterton Lakes National**

Park (403-859-2224) in Canada, this entire area is dedicated to the preservation of wildlife and nature, and has been protected for about a century.

Flathead Lake

More than 12,000 years ago, a great glacier dredged across the land, creating a huge trough. Eventually filling with fresh, natural mountain water, this massive pool is now known as Flathead Lake (www.fcvb.org), named for the Native Americans who made the surrounding area their home hundreds of years ago. Flathead is 28 miles long and 8 to 15 miles wide. Swimming beneath the polished surface are lake trout, cutthroat trout, kokanee salmon, perch, and Lake Superior whitefish. Ice fishing has become popular during the cold months, but the regular season attracts the most sportsmen. A Montana fishing license is required at the north section of the lake; in the south, a Flathead Indian Reservation tribal permit is required. Worth a trip: Your kids will enjoy visiting **Painted Rocks** to see the petroglyphs on the rock cliffs, put there by native artists centuries ago. For further information, call the Flathead Convention & Visitor Bureau at (800) 543-3105.

Flathead Lake State Parks offer a variety of recreation, such as boating, sailing, swimming, and camping lakeside. Big Arm, 12 miles north of Polson on U.S. 93 (406-849-5255), is a popular jump-off point for boat tours of Wild Horse Island, and its pebble beach is popular with sunbathers. Finley Point, 11 miles north of Polson on Montana 35, then 4 miles west on country road (406-887-2715), has excellent lake trout and yellow perch fishing. Wayfarers, ½ mile south of Bigfork on Montana 35 (406-837-4196), is a good camp and picnic site and the best place to watch the sunset in the valley.

The glacially carved rock outcrops of West Shore, 20 miles south of Kalispell on U.S. 93 (406-844-3901), give spectacular views of the lake and the Mission and Swan mountain ranges. Wild Horse, access from Big Arm via boat (406-837-5617), one of the largest islands in the inland United States, is noted for its Rocky Mountain bighorn sheep, mule deer, bald eagles, and wild horses. Yellow Bay, 15 miles north of Polson on Montana 35 (406-752-5501), located in the heart of Montana's sweet cherry orchards, includes Yellow Bay Creek and a wide gravelly beach. In the winter, there's cross-country skiing and snowmobiling. Lake Mary Ronan, U.S. 93 at Dayton, then 7 miles northwest (406-752-5501), is a primitive 76-acre park shaded by a forest of Douglas fir and western larch.

Logan, 45 miles west of Kalispell on U.S. 2 (406-293-7190), located on the north shore of Middle Thompson Lake, has facilities for swimming, boating, camping, waterskiing, and fishing. Lone Pine, 4 miles southwest of Kalispell on Foys Lake Road, then 1 mile east on Lone Pine Road (406-755-2706), is a 200-acre park with a visitor center, hiking trails, and an archery range overlooking **The Big Mountain Ski & Summer Resort.** Whitefish Lake, 1 mile west of Whitefish on U.S. 93, then 1 mile north (406–862–3991), offers boating, swimming, and fishing.

Snowmobiling is especially popular here, with 200 miles of trails open to snowmobiling in the Flathead National Forest. The Canyon Creek Trail starts 5 miles north of Columbia Falls and leads to The Big Mountain Ski & Summer Resort, where you're welcome to relax and have lunch. Desert Mountain, a 6,400-foot peak towering over the South and Middle Fork of the Flathead River, offers one of the fastest vertical climbs on a groomed trail in Flathead, going from an elevation of about 3,000 feet to 6,400 feet at the summit. Your reward will be awesome views of the South Fork of Flathead, the Great Bear Wilderness, and Glacier National Park. Crane Mountain and Allard Trails, located near Bigfork, offer more than 40 miles of groomed trails on closed logging roads that wind up to a large ridge separating the Swan and Flathead Valleys. There are numerous play areas and a variety of terrains for all skill levels.

Glacier National Park

There are 730 miles of trails, thirteen campgrounds, and enough extraordinary scenery in **Glacier National Park** (406–888–7800; www.nps.gov) to leave you breathless. The top choice in touring the park is **Going-to-the-Sun Road,** which bisects the park across the Continental Divide. This 52-mile scenic drive is one of the nation's best, and takes you to some of the park's most interesting highlights as it spans the width of Glacier. If you begin at the west entrance, you'll be at West Glacier, just outside the park. Heading into the park, stop at the Visitor Center in Apgar, open year-round, 8:00 A.M. to 4:30 P.M.. Pick up some brochures that will tell you about the wildlife you'll encounter, short hikes off the main route, food, lodging, and other facilities located inside the park.

About 8 miles from the visitor center is **Lake McDonald and the Historic District,** where you'll see the Swiss Chalet–like lodge. Leave your car and venture into the forest at the Trail of the Cedars, a ³⁄₁₀-mile handicapped-accessible trail that takes you right through a cedar and hemlock thicket. Back in the car, about 8 more miles up the main drive is the Loop. Line up the family and take pictures with Heaven's Peak in the background. If you need a good stretch, begin the 4-mile hike to Granite Park Chalet. (Wear good shoes, the hike is rather strenuous.)

The next few miles lead to Bird Woman Falls Overlook and the Weeping Wall. Both are interesting spots and worth a peek. A few miles from the Weeping Wall is Logan Pass. This is what many visitors come to see. Step out of your car and you'll be at an elevation of 6,646 feet and steps away from the Logan Pass Visitor Center that sits atop the Continental Divide. The center features exhibits on local plants and animals and is open mid-June to mid-October.

Back in the car, continue on to the Jackson Glacier Overlook. If you've never seen a glacier, this is the best view along the entire drive to check one out. Within the next few miles, you'll pass by Sunrift Gorge, Sun Point, and Rising Sun. There are some great trails here where you can hike along streams and creeks to a water-carved gorge, an overlook of Baring Falls and St. Mary Lake. At the end of the road is the St. Mary's Visitor Center, open from late May through mid-October, at the outer limit of the park. Outside the park is the town of St. Mary, where food, restaurants, and other services are available.

Hiking and Camping.

Glacier is a hiker's paradise, evidenced by the fact that more than half of the visitors to the park report indulging in a hiking experience. With more than 700 miles of trails, there is ample opportunity for both short hikes and extended backpacking trips. A wonderful place for day hikes is the **Many Glacier Valley,** in the western region of the park. There are numerous trails to follow, some more strenuous than others (all mileage given is one-way): the Redrock Falls Trail begins at the Swiftcurrent Pass trailhead at the west end of the Swiftcurrent Motor Inn parking area. The trail leads you on a pretty easy hike for about 1.8 miles. For a little more distance, but a level trail, try the Swiftcurrent Lake Natural Trail. The trailhead is at the Many Glacier Picnic Area or the south end of the Many Glacier Hotel; the 2.4-mile trail provides great views of Mount Gould and the Grinnell Glacier. With an elevation of 1,200 feet, Iceberg Lake Trail begins behind the Swiftcurrent Motor Inn cabin area and continues on for 4.7 miles. If a more strenuous hike is in order, look for the Ptarmigan Tunnel trailhead behind the Swiftcurrent Motor Inn cabin area. This trail leads you for 5.2 miles and climbs 2,300 feet. For a real challenge, go to the Swiftcurrent Pass trailhead at the west end of the Swiftcurrent Motor Inn parking area. Hike the path for 6.6 miles while climbing 2,300 feet!

When hiking, stay on the trail and walk single-file. Minimize impact by never shortcutting switchbacks and by selecting resilient areas such as rocks or snow for rest breaks. Pit toilets are provided at backcountry campgrounds. For sanitation along the trail, dig a cathole for solid waste about 200 feet from water or trails. Cover it with soil when finished. Urinate in rocky areas that won't be damaged by animals digging for the salts and minerals found in urine. And remember that horses have the right-of-way.

Glacier Institute (406–755–1211 or 406–888–5215; www.digisys.net/glacinst) runs a variety of day workshops for families. Check out the Family Nature Hikes in the summer, which allow you and your kids to become nature detectives on a moderate 2-mile hike.

Camping is another natural at the park. Glacier National Park has

Other Hikes in the Area

Before taking any kind of extended half-day or longer hike, it's best to stop by a park visitor center to obtain needed warnings and recommendations, as well as trail guides, topographic maps, and field guides to aid you in having a rewarding and safe hiking experience.

- **Trail of the Cedars** (easy), trailhead at the Avalanche Campground; 0.4-mile loop, wheel-chair accessible, a pleasant stroll along Avalanche Creek.
- **Red Eagle Lake Trail** (easy), trailhead at St. Mary Ranger Station; an all-day hike of 15 miles round-trip in view of the St. Mary Lake mountains.
- **Cracker Lake Trail** (moderate), trailhead at Many Glacier Hotel; 12.2 miles round-trip going up 1,400 feet, through the Canyon Creek Canyon.
- **Sperry Chalet Trail** (strenuous), trailhead at Lake McDonald Lodge; 13 miles round-trip going up 4,000 feet, culminating with a sweeping view from high in a glacial hollow.

Pets are not allowed on any of the trails in Glacier National Park. For further information and a catalog of hiking in the park, call the **Glacier Natural History Association** at (406) 888-5756.

thirteen campgrounds with just under 1,000 individual sites. Fish Creek and St. Mary may be reserved up to five months in advance (800-365-CAMP; www.reservations.nps.gov), the other campgrounds are first-come first-served. Campers without reservations may inquire about site availability at kiosks located near the campground entrances. There is a camping limit of seven days in July and August, and a maximum of fourteen days in a calendar year. Pets must be kept on a 6-foot or shorter leash or in vehicles at all times.

If you venture off the main drive, you may stumble into some fascinating discoveries and beautiful sights. The park's backcountry has some great camping for the adventuresome explorer. If you do decide to go farther, make sure to get a permit at the visitor center (they're free), along with detailed maps and information about the landscape and local wildlife. Find out about tent sites, pit toilets, food storage facilities, safe cooking areas, and regulated regions. Independent travelers should be knowledgeable campers and respect the land, leaving only footprints on the trails behind them.

The only company authorized to take visitors on backcountry hiking trips is **Glacier Wilderness Guides** (800-521-7238). They provide one- to six-day trips offering everything from float trips and white-water raft-

Glacier National Park Campgrounds

- **Apgar:** May–October, $12/day; 196 sites, toilets, disposal station, hiker/biker sites
- **Avalanche:** June–September, $12/day; 87 sites, toilets, disposal station, hiker/biker sites
- **Bowman Lake:** May–September, $10/day; 48 sites, primitive campground accessible by dirt road only, large units not recommended
- **Cut Bank:** May–September, $10/day; 19 sites, primitive campground accessible by dirt road only, large units not recommended
- **Fish Creek:** June–September, $15/day; 180 sites, toilets, disposal station, hiker/biker sites available, may be reserved in advance
- **Kintla Lake:** May–September, $10/day; 13 sites, primitive campground accessible by dirt road only, large units not recommended
- **Logging Creek:** July–September, $10/day; 8 sites, primitive campground accessible by dirt road only, large units not recommended
- **Many Glacier:** May–September, $12/day; 110 sites, toilets, disposal station, hiker/biker sites available
- **Quartz Creek:** July–September, $10/day; 7 sites, primitive campground accessible by dirt road only, large units not recommended
- **Rising Sun:** May–September, $12/day; 83 sites, toilets, disposal station, hiker/biker sites available
- **Sprague Creek:** May–September, $12/day; 25 sites, toilets, primitive campground accessible by dirt road only, large units not recommended
- **St. Mary:** May–September, $15/day; 148 sites, toilets, disposal station, hiker/biker sites available, may be reserved in advance
- **Two Medicine:** May–September, $12/day; 99 sites, toilets, disposal station, hiker/biker sites available

ing to horsebacking riding and custom-designed trips for individuals and families.

Summer Activities

With such a beautiful lake, boating is a natural here, and it's another way to get into the backcountry with your kids without hiking for miles. Take a boat cruise with **Glacier Park Boat Company,** Kalispell (406-257-2426; www.montanaweb.com/gpboats). The company offers cruises from Many Glacier, Two Medicine, Lake McDonald, and St. Mary. When the boat stops across the lake, you disembark to take a ranger-led hike (you can take the next scheduled boat back to your starting point), or you

Some Camping Guidelines

For a complete set of guidelines, consult the nearest visitor center or ranger station. Your main guidelines should be (1) leave no trace of your having been there, (2) camp and travel on durable surfaces to do the least damage, (3) take out with you what you bring in, (4) minimize your use of fire. In addition:

- **Carry essentials with you,** like maps, compass, first-aid kit, food, tent, sleeping bag, appropriate footwear and clothes (layering is best), a sturdy weatherproof food and garbage bag you can hang from a tree (you'll need about 25 feet of rope for this), emergency signaling device, insect repellent. And bring what you'll need to keep the kids occupied and entertained. Involve them in gathering your gear and be sure they understand the need to be within sight of a parent at all times.
- **Be prepared for weather changes** and remember that snow covers some trails well into July. You may have to do some route finding.
- **Backcountry campgrounds** have tent sites, pit toilets, food hanging devices, and food preparation areas. There's a map at each campground telling you where everything can be found.
- **If camping on your own,** remember the rules about hanging food at least 10 feet above the ground and 4 feet out from any tree; avoid odorous foods, plan meals that have no leftovers, and never cook or eat in your tent.
- **Don't wash yourself, your dishes, or your clothes** in a lake or stream. Strain food scraps from gray water and pack them out with your garbage. Scatter the gray water at least 100 feet from lakes and streams.

Camping supplies, such as food, fuel, camping gear, and first-aid kits are sold in stores in Apgar, Lake McDonald, Two Medicine, Rising Sun, St. Mary, and East and West Glacier.

can continue on with the cruise. All fares are under $10.00; children ages four to twelve are half-price, those under four are free. The company also rents canoes, motorboats, and sea kayaks.

If fishing is your passion, that's here too. No license or permits are required to fish inside the boundaries of the park, but you do need to stop at a visitor center or ranger station to get a current copy of park fishing regulations. The general park season runs from the third Saturday in May through November 30, with some exceptions. There are daily catch and possession limits and fish that are designated catch-and-release only. There are also regulations regarding equipment, bait, and cleaning fish.

Hiking/Camping in Bear Country

Before starting out on a hiking or camping adventure, be sure to consult with a ranger about bear sightings in the area. Most people don't encounter bears (they don't want your company any more than you want theirs), but people have been seriously maimed and even killed by bears in Glacier National Park. Be sure your kids are aware of the basic rules to follow:

- **Do not approach bears.** They're very fast and you can't outrun them. This includes bear cubs, who are sure to have a parent nearby.
- **Don't surprise a bear.** Carry a whistle or speak loudly. Bears will often move away if they hear people coming.
- **If you encounter a bear,** back away slowly. Bend at the knees and turn sideways. Do not look directly into the bear's eyes, which can be interpreted as a threat. If the bear does charge you, fall to the ground and assume the fetal position to reduce the effects of the attack.
- **Never run from a bear!** It will catch you.

More Attractions

Visit the Victorian **Conrad Mansion** in Kalispell; (406) 755-2166. Built in 1895 as the home of Kalispell's city founder, C. E. Conrad, the mansion is open daily for guided tours, May 15 to October 15. The house has twenty-six originally furnished rooms and Tiffany windows.

If you're in the mood for a little shopping, stop by the **Kalispell Center Mall** (406-752-6660; www.cavanaughs.com), which has department stores, national retailers, restaurants, and boutiques.

Horseback riding can be arranged through **Mule Shoe Outfitters** at one of three corrals (Apgar, 406-888-5010; Lake McDonald, 406-888-5121; Many Glacier, 406-732-4203). Mule Shoe offers guided rides lasting from one hour to half a day around the lakes and into the valleys. For something a little faster and wetter, try white-water rafting with **Glacier Raft Company** (800-235-6781), **Great Northern Whitewater** (800-735-7897), or **Montana Raft Company** (800-521-RAFT). And if you just want to be above it all, there's **Fantasy Flight Balloon Tours** (406-755-4172).

More Summer Fun

The Big Mountain Ski and Summer Resort (406-862-1960 or 800-858-5439; www.bigmtn.com). In the summer, enjoy white-water rafting, horseback riding (a two-and-a-half-hour adventure, with a cookout at the end of the trail), chuck-wagon dinner rides, and overnight

Area Golf Courses

There are excellent golf courses from Bigfork to East Glacier, starting with **Buffalo Hill Golf Club** in Kalispell (406-756-4545). Twenty-seven holes, beautiful glacier views, mature green foliage, and Stillwater River running through the Championship 18 makes this one of the Northwest's finest golf facilities. Nearby is Montana's newest golf course, **Northern Pines Golf Club** (406-751-1950 or 800-255-5641; www.golfmt.com), designed by two-time U.S. Open Champion Andy North. **Eagle Bend Golf Course** (406-837-7300 or 800-255-5641) in Bigfork was rated among the top fifty courses in the United States by *Golf Digest* and features twenty-seven holes, including the "Nicklaus Nine." There's also **Meadow Lake Golf & Ski Resort** (406-892-7601) in Columbia Falls, **Whitefish Lake Golf Club** (406-862-4000) in Whitefish, and the **Glacier Golf Course** (406-226-9311) in East Glacier.

Most courses are open from April through October. For a free golf guide or to make reservations, call (800) 392-9795.

horse pack trips arranged through the **Montana Adventure Company** (800-321-8822). Learn fly casting from a certified Big Mountain instructor (necessary gear provided). At **The Big Mountain Bike Academy,** learn the skills necessary to pedal the mountain's 18 miles of trails (for all ability levels), or ride the gondola to the top and hike down the **5-mile Danny On Memorial Trail,** especially wonderful in mid-August when the huckleberries are ripe. (Be careful, though, because you may be competing with bears for this delicacy.) The **Alpine Adventure** program offers a half-day mountain bike ride, picnic lunch, and half-day hike for ages seven to twelve. Six times during the summer the U.S. Forest Service Environmental Education Center has an **Earth-Art-For-Kids** program for ages six to ten; local artists teach kids to create drawings and sculpture with pine cones, leaves, stones, and sticks. Stargazer talks are given by a local astronomer evenings at the Summit House, and weekly evening concerts are held on the lower slopes of the mountain. Note: There is no day care offered during the summer season.

Junior Rangers

Check with Glacier's visitor centers for information on how your kids can become **Junior Rangers.** The Heritage Center (403-859-2624) in Waterton also has kids' programs and will loan your kids backpacks filled with games and nature journals.

Winter Recreation

Cross country skiing is especially good on the eastern and western sections of Going-to-the-Sun Road. More-experienced skiiers make extended back-country trips into the park's interiors, especially around Cameron Lake and Many Glacier Valley. Flathead Valley is ideal for snowmobiling, with more

The Native American Experience

Native Americans make up about 9 percent of Montana's population. The Blackfeet Nation borders nearly all of eastern Glacier National Park; the Reservation of the Confederated Salish and Kootenai covers 1.2 million acres and surrounds half of the lake area. The Flathead Indian Reservation encompasses the southern part of Flathead Lake. Activities throughout the year provide opportunities for your family to learn more about these tribes.

- **Blackfeet, Salish, and Kootenai** tribal members give special evening campfire talks several times a week. During animated presentations, they discuss native life and culture, tell legends, and, on occasion, host a contemporary folksinger. Check the park newspaper for campground locations and times.
- **Museum of the Plains Indians** in Browning (406-338-2230) holds a world-renowned collection of ancient and modern Native American art and artifacts, and has a beautiful gift shop where replicas of these as well as original pieces of art work can be purchased.
- The **Blackfeet's North American Indian Days** are held in mid-July; Blackfeet Nation Office; (406) 338-7406.**Blackfeet Historical Tours** offers guided tours of the reservation (406-338-2058).
- There are **Salish-Kootenai festivals** throughout the year; Confederated Salish and Kootenai tribes; (406) 675-0160.
- **The People's Center** in Pablo (406-675-0160 or 800-883-5344) focuses on the Salish, Pend d'Orielle, and Kootenai tribes and includes a learning center, exhibit gallery, and gift shop.
- **Native Ed-Ventures** (406-883-5344; www.peoplescenter.org) offers a variety of tours that can be customized for families. Arrange a visit to the Flathead Reservation hosted by a Native American family. Especially popular with kids is the Traditional Encampment tour, where you live in a teepee for two days, learn the basics of setting up camp, and hear the local tribes' history and stories of the past while sitting around a campfire. Your family can also experience a traditional powwow celebration.

than 200 miles of groomed trails plus thousands of miles of national forest roads to explore. If dogsledding has always held a fascination for you, **Montana Adventure Company** (800-321-8822) organizes 12-mile treks over Stillwater State Forest trails with a ten-dog team carrying guests kept warm by elk furs.

The Big Mountain Ski and Summer Resort (406-862-1960 or 800-858-5439; www.bigmtn.com) has 3,000 acres of skiable terrain, about half of it for intermediate skiers but with plenty of advanced and beginner terrain too. Easy Street, the longest trail on the mountain (21⁄2 miles), is a great run for novices. Around the World, an easy blue run, is a confidence booster for skiers making the transition to intermediate terrain.

This resort is also known for its cruising runs and snowcat skiing. Ski packages are available, with discounted lift tickets and family fun passes. There are three-hour guided snowmobiling trips throughout the week.

Parents appreciate the fact that sleds, which can be rented from Big Mountain Sports, have seat backs and safety belts to transport toddlers (ages nine months to three years) around the village. The Big Mountain Ski and Snowboard School offers lessons to both adults and children, individuals and groups. Beginner Tot (ages three to four) gives private lessons to kids to familiarize them with skiing basics and lift-riding procedures. Little Scouts (ages five to six) have one-hour group lessons to learn skiing basics. Mountain Explorers (ages seven to twelve) is for all levels and involves kids in activities like Yahoo Trail Animal Tracks, Thursday Fun Race, and the Explorer Badge program, in which kids earn a sticker for each skill learned. The Kiddie Korner offers supervised activities—creative arts, music, cartoon time, and reading—to kids of all ages, half day, full day, or by the hour. It's open daily Thanksgiving through April 11, and three nights a week.

Side Trips

The **Waterton/Glacier International Peace Park,** U.S. 2 and 89 (403-859-2224; www.parkscanada.pch.gc.ca/waterton), made up of the Waterton Lakes National Park in Canada and the Glacier National Park in the United States, was designated to commemorate the friendship between the United States and Canada. Because the two parks share common topography, Waterton offers many of the same opportunities for adventure and recreation as Glacier: hiking, camping, swimming, boating, golfing, horseback riding, fishing, and winter sports.

At the **National Bison Range,** southwest of St. Ignatius near Dixon, your family can take a two-hour self-guided tour to watch four to five hundred bison roaming the area. The visitors center offers literature, films, pictorial displays, and exhibits pertaining to the troubled history of the bison and their amazing survival. While on your tour, look for whitetail deer, elk, and bighorn sheep.

Missoula is only two and a half hours from Glacier and worth a day trip. It has a wide range of shops and galleries, museums, historic bars, and, as home of the University of Montana, its share of laid-back coffeehouses and cozy bookstores. The North Reserve Street Shopping District is the largest indoor shopping mall in western Montana. The **Historical Museum at Fort Missoula** on South Avenue across from the Big Sky High School (406-728-3476), has an indoor area with changing exhibits pertaining to the Old West and an outdoor area with a complex of twelve historic structures, including a one-room schoolhouse and a U.S. Forest Service Lookout. Kids will be fascinated by the **Smokejumper's Center,** where they can see videos about those very brave people who fight forest fires. And the little ones will enjoy riding on the hand-carved wooden carousel in **Caras Park,** beside the Clark Fork River (406-549-8382). The **Rocky Mountain Elk Foundation Wildlife Visitor Center,** 2291 West Broadway (406-523-4545) is filled with fascinating taxidermy of elk and other North American big game animals, plus wildlife art and bronze pieces. Or catch a show at **Missoula Children's Theatre,** 425 East Broadway (406-728-PLAY), which offers a full season of entertainment for children. For information, contact the **Missoula Convention and Visitors Bureau,** 825 East Front (406-543-6623 or 800 526-3465).

Special Events

Year-round. Drum building workshops in various locations by the Drum Brothers; (800) 925-1201.

January. FIS World Cup Races, The Big Mountain.

February. Winter Carnival, Whitefish; Kandahar Cup Downhill, The Big Mountain; Northern Division Freestyle Championships, The Big Mountain.

March. Baroque Festival, Whitefish and Kalispell; Snow Rodeo, Izaak Walton Inn, Essex; Montana Special Olympics, The Big Mountain.

April. Tobacco Plains Pow Wow, Essex; Taste the Best of Bigfork.

May. Whitewater Festival, Cherry Blossom Festival, Family Forestry Expo, all in Bigfork.

May–September. Farmers Markets in Kalispell (Sunday mornings and Tuesday evenings, west end of Kalispell Center Mall) and Whitefish (Thursday afternoons, Pizza Hut parking lot)

June. Lake-to-Lake Canoe Race, Whitefish.

July. Whitefish Arts Festival; Fourth of July celebrations throughout the valley; Standing Arrow Pow Wow, Elmo; Flathead Festival of the Arts.

August. Festival of the Arts, Bigfork.

September. Wild West Day, Bigfork; Summer Games, Whitefish.

October. Glacier Jazz Stampede, Kalispell; Fiesta Days, Whitefish; Grass Drag Races, Columbia Falls.

November. Christmas Parade, Kalispell; Artists & Craftsmen Annual Christmas Show, Kalispell.

December. Holiday Stroll and Christmas Tree Lighting, Bigfork; Christmas Eve Torchlight Parade, The Big Mountain.

Where to Stay

Within **Glacier National Park,** accommodations at hotels, inns, and campgrounds can be made through Glacier Park, Inc. (602-207-6000; www.glacierparkinc.com). Accommodations in the park include **Lake McDonald Lodge,** Going-to-the-Sun Road, West Glacier (406-226-5551), which offers more than one hundred rooms from early June through late September in the main hotel and in bungalows on the lake, with beautiful views of the lake. The **Many Glacier Hotel,** on U.S. 89, East Glacier Park (406-226-5551), offers 211 rooms from early June through mid-September in a four-story wooden structure, with views of Swiftcurrent Lake. From May through October, try **St. Mary Lodge,** Junction of U.S. 89 and Going-to-the-Sun Road, St. Mary (406-732-4431), with 105 riverfront rooms.

Flathead Lake Lodge in Big Fork (406-837-4391) is a dude ranch that gives your family the opportunity to learn about the daily life of a working cowboy, while enjoying horseback rides and cookouts.

Kandahar Lodge (800-862-6098; www.vtown.com/kandahar) is a fifty-room ski-in/ski-out mountain lodge on the Big Mountain in the Valley. **Grouse Mountain Lodge** (800-321-8822; www.grmtlodge.com) has rooms (some with kitchen units) large enough for families, and is located adjacent to the thirty-six-hole Whitefish Lake Golf Course.

For information about accommodations, contact the **Montana Bed & Breakfast Association** (800-453-8870), **Montana Reservation Central** (888-224-4759; free service) or **Travel Montana** (406-444-2654 or 800-847-4868).

Where to Eat

Try breakfast in Whitefish at the **Whitefish Grill,** 235 Central Avenue (406-862-3354), where you can order sandwiches or get homemade Belgian waffles and espresso. **Hennessy's Restaurant,** 1701 Highway 93S in Kalispell (406-755-6860), has been a local favorite for breakfast, lunch, and dinner for fifty years. Enjoy western dining in a log restaurant while viewing the breathtaking scenery at **Rawhide Restaurant and Steak House,** 1 mile west of West Glacier on Highway 2 (406-387-4999).

For More Information

Ski reports and travel information: (800) 541-1447

Road conditions: (800) 332-6171

Montana Department of Fish, Wildlife and Parks: 1420 East Sixth Avenue, Helena 59620; (406) 444-2535

U.S. Forest Service: Federal Building, Missoula 59801; (406) 379-3511

Glacier National Park: West Glacier 59936; (406) 888-5441

Bigfork Chamber of Commerce: Box 237, Bigfork, 59911; (406) 837-5888

East Glacier Chamber of Commerce: Box 260, East Glacier 59434; (406) 226-4403

Kalispell Chamber of Commerce: 15 Depot Park, Kalispell 59901; (406) 758-2800

Whitefish Chamber of Commerce: 6475 Highway 93 S, Whitefish 59937; (406) 862-3501

Assistance with facilities for the physically challenged: Northwest Montana Human Resources, First and Main Building, Box 8300, Kalispell 59903; (406) 752-6565

List of outfitters: Montana Board of Outfitters, Department of Commerce, 111 North Jackson, Helena 59626 (406) 444-3738 or Montana Outfitters and Guides Association, Box 9070, Helena 59604; (406) 449-3578

Emergency Numbers

Glacier emergency: 911

Hospital: Kalispell Regional Hospital; (406) 752-5111

Emergency Road Service: (406) 888-7800

COLUMBUS

Columbus will surprise you. The largest U.S. place named for the explorer, Columbus offers families a friendly and affordable urban destination within easy reach of the countryside. Among the finds are an impressive arts center, a high-technology, interactive children's science museum, and easy day trips that let you discover heartland history.

GETTING THERE

American, Continental, Delta, Midway, Trans World Airlines, and USAir offer international and domestic flights via **Port Columbus International Airport** (614-239-4000). **Port Express Shuttle,** 2509 Englewood Drive (614-476-3004 or 800-476-3994), transports visitors between Port Columbus International Airport and downtown Columbus.

Two major highways intersect in Columbus, making this city easy to reach. I-70 links the city with areas to the east and west. I-71 links Columbus with Cleveland the north and Cincinnati and other areas to the south. I-270 combines with I-670 to circle Columbus and its surrounding areas. The nearest **Amtrak** train (800-USA-RAIL) arrives in Cleveland. **Greyhound,** 111 East Town Street (614-221-5311 or 294-5100), provides bus service from Cleveland to Columbus.

GETTING AROUND

COTA (Central Ohio Transit Authority), 177 North High Street (614-228-1776), provides public bus transportation for the city. COTA offers normal and express fares, plus transfers for a minimal fee. Call ahead for information on routes, schedules, and hours of operation.

WHAT TO SEE AND DO

Museums

The Columbus Museum of Art, 480 East Broad Street (614-221-4848; www.columbusart.mus.oh.us). The museum has an impressive collec-

Columbus

AT A GLANCE

- ▶ Explore hands-on science exhibits at COSI
- ▶ See gorillas, elephants, manatees, and other animals at the Columbus Zoo
- ▶ Take a day trip to The Wilds to see rare animals running free and to SeaWorld Adventure Park to see whales, dolphins, sharks, and other creatures of the deep
- ▶ Greater Columbus Convention and Visitors Bureau, (614) 221-CITY or (800) 345-4FUN

tion of impressionism, German expressionism, cubism, American modern, and contemporary art. Highlights include the Russell Page Sculpture Garden (an oasis with some running room), the Ross Photography Center, and *Eye Spy:Adventures in Art,* an interactive exhibition area for children ages six to twelve and their families.

Allow time for the gift shop, which has the usual notecards and niceties, but also an interesting collection of jewelry by local artists.

Attractions

Columbus combines interestingly ethnic and all-American attractions. Columbus has The German Village—a restored area originally settled by German immigrants in the nineteenth century. The city also has a major university and one of the largest state fairs in the country, held every August.

The German Village is a restored area of approximately 233 acres. It features brick homes built by German immigrants between 1840 and 1880 and offers cobblestone streets, boutiques, historic walks, and lots of bratwurst and beer. The sturdy but small houses, built by workers, often feature hand-carved lintels, clay chimney pots, wrought-iron fences, and small yards. Interestingly, the area is the largest privately funded restoration of its kind in the United States. Stop by the **Meeting Haus** of the German Village Society, 588 South Third Street (614-221-8888), for brochures on restaurants and bed-and-breakfast lodgings.

If it's fall, plan on checking out the German Village's annual **Oktoberfest** (September); June brings a **Haus Und Garten** tour.

In the **brewery district,** adjacent to the German Village, the former breweries are now beer gardens, offices, or shops. The **William Gray-**

COSI on the Riverfront

Ohio's Center for Science & Industry (COSI), a top hands-on science museum for more than thirty-four years, is moving to a new riverfront facility with 300,000 square feet of space, more than double the size of the present building. When the new building opens in late 1999, COSI will reorganize its exhibits around **Learning Worlds,** the organizing concept for the popular COSI Toledo. Learning Worlds present many scientific disciplines in one gallery.

At press time, although exhibits were still being determined, it's likely the new COSI will keep some favorite COSI Toledo galleries. In **Sports,** pitch a fast ball, play virtual volleyball, measure your high jump, and time your 50-yard dash. In **Whiz Bang Engineering Learning World,** build a roller coaster and then ride Zing 2000, a motion simulator re-creating a coaster's steep dives. In **Kidspace,** a play area just for little ones under 48 inches tall, preschoolers can get more comfortable with doctors and hospitals by sitting in an ambulance and diagnosing injuries from X-rays. Babyspace, a part of Kidspace devoted to tots, stimulates crawlers with mirrors on the floor and different fabrics placed low on the walls.

In the new building's **Space Theater,** see laser shows, journey through the human body, and race through space via Digistar 3-D technology. In the **IWERKS Theater,** watch 3-D and 2-D movies on a screen six stories tall.

Until the new property debuts, the current COSI is open, but in flux as exhibits are dismantled and moved. Currently COSI Columbus is located at 280 East Broad Street (614-228-COSI).

stone Winery, 544 South Fourth Street (614-228-2332), is housed in an 1875 brewery that's open for tastings, tours, and breakfast in the vault—a cozy space of limestone arched walls and wooden chairs. Even though your kids can't taste the wine, they'll like this winery. For a unique souvenir, take home the William Graystone wines; each bottle is graced with a scene or symbol of Columbus. For more information on the Brewery District, call (614) 241-2070.

Parks and Zoos

The **Battelle Riverfront Park** on the Scioto River waterfront near City Hall offers a pleasant bit of greenery. Its fountain, created especially for children, has a rim of stone slabs that are the perfect size for skipping along. This is a good place to bring a picnic lunch, rest, and enjoy the river view.

Columbus Zoo

The Columbus Zoo, home to more than 700 species of animals, is a beautifully landscaped park. In the past several years, the zoo has built new, larger, and more naturalistic exhibits.

The **African Forest,** a new habitat for gorillas and bonobos, places the visitor in the world of a field researcher. Gorillas surround observers in the round indoor exhibit, where only 1½ inches of glass separate the onlooker from the animals. The bonobos three-quarter-acre outdoor habitat features a waterfall.

The Columbus Zoo is also home to the world's largest indoor **elephant habitat.** The 10,000-square-foot facility has artificial trees doubling as scratching posts, and a shower triggered by the elephants. The pachyderms' outdoor play yard has two pools. With the new **manatee exhibit,** the zoo becomes one of the first facilities outside of Florida to house these endangered marine mammals. The manatees swim in a landscaped area modeled after the Ten Thousand Islands wildlife area in southwestern Florida.

The walkway at the **cheetah habitat** literally gives you a unique perspective on these special cats. Peering down on them allows even preschoolers to get a good look at these sinewy animals stretched out on the grass.

Modeled after an African marketplace, the **food court** has several concessions: Sbarro's Pizza, Charley's Steakery, Graeter's Ice Cream, and Oscar Mayer hot dogs. Strollers and wheelchairs are available for rental.

If your family loves animals, this is a worthwhile trip. Consider combining this outing with a visit to Wyandot Lake Amusement Park (See page 198).

Columbus Zoo, 9990 Riverside Drive, Powell, northwest of Columbus (614-645-3550).

The area's main attraction is the ***Santa Maria,*** one of the more authentic, full-size replicas of Columbus's flagship. This one was built for the city's 1992 quincentennial celebration. On board you hear tales of a typical day at sea, find out why hot meals were rare (fear of fire) and where the crew slept (on deck), get a chance to ogle the signal cannons and touch the huge tiller, and find out why navigation was a shared responsibility (because there wasn't any way to see ahead and maneuver the tiller at the same time). Call (614) 645-8760.

Franklin Park Conservatory, in Franklin Park, 1777 East Broad Street (614-645-8733). At this indoor conservatory, stroll through acres of indoor gardens and several climate zones. Originally built in 1859, this facility was significantly enlarged for Ameriflora 92, the city's tribute to

Schiller Park

For a time-out romp, stop by **Schiller Park,** bounded by Reinhard, City Park, Deshler, and Jaeger Streets. It's a great green space in the heart of the village, perfect for the kids. In summer, come here for theater under the stars, usually two Shakespearean productions and one musical. Donations are requested.

the Columbus quincentennial. The tiny and intricate bonsai plants, the tropical rain forest, and desert areas are kid favorites. Avoid strolling through the park, as this area has seen some crime.

Wyandot Lake Amusement Park, 10101 Riverside Drive (614-889-9283), is next to the Columbus Zoo. Open May through September, your kids can cool off here with such wet thrills as a wave pool, water slides, and an inner-tube adventure that will take them through such "backcountry" scenery as a misty canyon, a waterfall, and a mill camp. Dry fun includes go-carts and miniature golf. There are locker and shower facilities.

Performing Arts

BalletMet, 322 Mt. Vernon Avenue (614-229-4860), performs a variety of classical to contemporary works, including a holiday favorite, *The Nutcracker.* **CAPA (Columbus Association of the Performing Arts),** 55 East State Street (614-469-0939), owns and operates the Ohio Theatre, 55 State Street; the Palace Theatre, 34 West Broad Street; and the Capitol Theater, 77 High Street, which traditionally attracts international jazz, pop, comedy, children's, folk, and classical entertainers. CAPA also offers a classic film series. Call (614) 469-1045 for information. **CATCO (Contemporary American Theater Company),** 512 North Park Street (614-461-0010), is a semiprofessional theater performing off-Broadway productions in an intimate 176-seat theater. The **Columbus Symphony Orchestra,** 55 East State Street, 5th Floor (614-224-5281, 614-224-3291 for tickets), performs symphonic and pops concerts and has a series for children. **Opera/Columbus,** 50 West Broad Street (614-461-0022), is Columbus's opera company. Dress rehearsals, held on Tuesdays before opening night performances, are open to students and senior citizens at discounted admission. **The Wexner Center for the Arts,** Fifteenth and High Streets (614-292-2354), presents a variety of contemporary groups and traditional concerts.

Ohio State, Capital, Otterbein, and **Ohio Wesleyan Universities** frequently hold theatrical, dance, and concert events. For information call OSU (614-292-2787), Capital (614-236-6801), Otterbein (614-898-1600), and Ohio Wesleyan (614-369-4431).

TicketMaster (614-431-3600) has full-price tickets to theater, dance, concerts, and sporting events. Call for booth locations and hours of operation. For more information on the arts, contact the **Greater Columbus Arts Council** at (614) 224-2606.

The **Wexner Center for the Arts** presents art exhibitions, recent and classic films, and dance, music, and theater performances in a landmark contemporary building. The most active season for performances is September through May. The site has a good bookstore and a cafe. The Wexner Center for the Arts, Ohio State University, North High Street at Fifteenth Avenue (614-292-0330; 614-292-3535 for tickets).

Sports

Columbus Clippers, Columbus Baseball Team, Inc., 1155 West Mound Street (614-462-5250). The Clippers, the top farm club of the New York Yankees, play AAA ball at Cooper Stadium, I-70 and Mound Street, from April through mid-September. **Columbus's Chill Hockey Team,** 1460 West Lane Road (614-488-4455), skates at the Fairgrounds Coliseum from November to March. **Columbus Crew,** a Major League Soccer team, plays at Ohio State University stadium. The city's professional women's basketball team, **Columbus Quest,** plays at the Greater Columbus Convention Center.

For golf enthusiasts, there's the **Memorial Tournament at Muirfield,** 5750 Memorial Drive, Dublin (614-889-6700). This Jack Nicklaus-designed course hosts the PGA for one stop of the tour during June. For college sports call the **Ohio State University Athletic Department,** 410 Woody Hayes Drive (614-292-2624), for information on all Buckeye sporting events.

Scioto Downs, 6000 High Street (614) 491-2525, 2½ miles south of I-270, offers harness racing from May to September.

Side Trips

Olentangy Indian Caverns and Ohio Frontier Land, 1779 Home Road, Delaware (614-548-7917). Only about a half hour away, these caverns and a cave house museum are filled with Indian artifacts and geological displays. Open 9:30 A.M.–5:00 P.M. from April to October. Kids under seven are admitted for free.

Hocking Valley Canoe Livery and Family Fun Center, 31251 Chieftain Drive, Logan (614-385-8685 or 800-686-0386). Located about an hour outside of Columbus off U.S. 33 at the Enterprise exit, this center offers canoe, kayak, raft, and go-cart rentals, miniature golf and a driving range, plus canoeing packages and a tour of points of interest. Open April to October; reservations are required.

Sea World Adventure Park of Ohio, 1100 Sea World Drive, Aurora (800-63-SHAMU). It's two hours northeast of Columbus on Route 43, near I-271 and I-480 (Ohio Turnpike exit 13). Open mid-May to September, the center features ninety acres of marine life, entertainment, and

Roscoe Village

The drive to **Roscoe Village,** about 90 miles from Columbus, takes you through Coshocton County, past farmland and fields. At the village, six restored nineteenth-century buildings are strung along two blocks and interspersed with nineteen shops, creating a sense of life circa 1830–1860, when the Ohio & Erie Canal brought goods, people, and prosperity to the area. Watch a blacksmith and a broom maker, tour the schoolhouse and the fashionable physician's residence, and browse the shops. Best bets include the duck carver, the basket maker, and the **Johnson-Humrickhouse Museum,** known for its collections of Oriental and Native American art.

Be sure to visit the **canal,** 2 miles away. From Memorial Day to Labor Day, barges pulled by draft horses take you along the canal as guides tell you anecdotes about the people and animals that made the trip. But in fall, allow time to walk the towpath. The brilliant foliage is a gift to the eye, and the soft peacefulness a welcome respite during any city tour.

Roscoe Village hosts a **Gingerbread House Contest** on the Fourth of July, a **Gay 1890s Celebration** in September, with banjo playing and barbershop quartets; and an **Apple Butter Stirrin' Festival** in October with demonstrations of rope making and chair caning, as well as hog-calling contests.

Roscoe Village has several bed-and-breakfasts, none of which welcome children, but the **Roscoe Village Inn** (614-622-2222 or 800-237-7397) welcomes children and has comfortable rooms and good food.

Roscoe Village, 381 Hill Street, Coshocton; (614) 622-9310 or (800) 877-1830.

a well-designed kids' play area—Shamu's Happy Harbor (named after one of Sea World's killer whales).

The Wilds, 14000 International Road (614-638-5030). This 10,000-acre preserve, a ninety-minute drive southeast of Columbus, is home to many endangered species from around the world.

Special Events

July. Celebrate the nation's birthday with food and festivities at Red, White and Boom! The Columbus Jazz and Rib Festival is an entire weekend of jazz music.

August. Cruisin' on the Riverfront, a weekend of classic cars and food.

Ohio State Fair

Columbus's biggest festival is in August when the city goes "whole hog" for the **Ohio State Fair,** one of the city's most popular attractions and a tradition since 1848. This is a special treat for city kids, who may get their first chance to pet a cow, cheer at the pig races, ogle the huge butter sculptures, watch a tractor pull, and browse through buildings of agricultural exhibits. The midway, with its rides and games of chance and skill, may be unavoidable; to avoid nagging, set a limit ahead of time on how much money the kids can spend here.

The two-week fair also features nightly entertainment, free music concerts held twice a day, a free Kiddie Park, a quilt show, baking contests, crafts, a daily parade, and a petting zoo. For more information call the administrative offices; (614) 644-4000 or (800) BUCKEYE.

September. The German Village hosts its own Oktoberfest festival, which includes the Kinderplatz (Children's Place) with free kiddie rides and family entertainment. The KidSpeak KidsFest is a full day of free street performances, music, and games at Franklin Park.

November. The Columbus International Festival features the song, dance, arts, and food of more than fifty cultures, and usually special activities just for kids.

For more information, call (800) BUCKEYE.

Where to Stay

Columbus offers a variety of lodging options in town and nearby. In town is **The Westin Hotel,** 310 South High Street (614-228-3800 or 800-328-2073), with a turn-of-the-century lobby and comfortable rooms. The **Hyatt on Capital Square,** 75 East State Street (614-228-1234 or 800-233-1234), is connected to the City Center and Ohio Theatre and is located across from the State Capitol. **Doubletree Guest Suites,** 50 South Front Street (614-228-4600), offers families extra space and in-room refrigerators. The **Crowne Plaza,** 33 Nationwide Boulevard (614-461-4100), is another family-friendly alternative.

Embassy Suites is near town at 2700 Corporate Exchange Drive (614-890-8600), located at I-270 and Cleveland Avenue. It offers suites and indoor and outdoor pools. The **Worthington Inn,** 649 High Street in nearby Worthington (614-885-2600), began as a stagecoach stop in 1831 and now features twenty-six rooms decorated with Victorian furnishings, small inn hospitality, and full-service convenience. Not the least of the niceties at this four-star lodging is the regional American cuisine. The seared salmon wins acclaim as among the best in the city, as does the duck sausage. Try the sour apple tart for dessert. Rooms, which are oversized, include a continental breakfast. Children are welcome; kids twelve and under stay for free.

Where to Eat

Head for these restaurants in the German Village and in the Brewery District: **Schmidt's Sausage Haus und Restaurant,** 240 Kossuth Street (614-444-6808). Among the more famous eateries, this restaurant, open since 1886, offers steins of brew and an array of sausages. The place is noted for the Bahama Mama—a spicy sausage—plus good German potato salad, sauerkraut, and applesauce. If you're still hungry, try the huge cream puffs for dessert. Kids will like the accordion music and the festive air. Children are welcome at **Jeurgen's,** 525 South Fourth Street (614-224-6858), a German restaurant known for its excellent pastry and unusual varieties of pretzels. **The Engine House #5,** 121 East Thruman Avenue (614-443-4877), offers traditional seafood, pastas, and steaks, Your kids will like the ambience of the renovated firehouse. Come here to celebrate a birthday and watch the waiters slide down the firepole with a cake. Worth a visit if you have older children and teens is **Handke's,** 520 South Front Street (614-621-2500). Noted chef Hartmut Handke offers such pleasing dishes as onion cream soup, grilled duck breast, and seared sea scallops.

Other Columbus eateries: **The Spaghetti Warehouse,** 397 West Broad Street (614-464-0143), serves pastas. **Morton's of Chicago,** 2 Nationwide Plaza, corner of Chestnut and High Streets (614-464-4442), is more expensive but offers fine steaks and seafood; share your plate with the kids, as portions are large.

For More Information

Ask for a copy of *Kids Connection* magazine, 572 City Park Avenue (614-224-3003), which lists items of interest to families. The magazine highlights hundreds of family-oriented programs. While some are geared to city residents, many are also of interest to visiting kids.

Ohio Council for International Visitors (614-231-9610) offers translation services. **City of Columbus Construction Hotline** (614-645-PAVE). For tourist information, contact the **Greater Columbus Convention and Visitors Bureau,** Monday–Friday 8:00 A.M.–5:00 P.M. (614-221-CITY or 800-345-4FUN). When in town, stop by the Visitor

Center on the second floor of the City Center shopping mall, 111 South Third Street. The hours are Monday through Saturday 10:00 A.M. to 9:00 P.M., and Sunday noon to 6:00 P.M. Visit the Ohio Internet site (www.travel.state.oh.us) or the Columbus Web site (www.columbuscvb.org).

Emergency Numbers

Ambulance, fire, police: 911

Children's Hospital: 700 Children's Drive; (614) 722-2000

Poison Control Center: (614) 228-1323

Police (nonemergency): (614) 645-4545

Twenty-four-hour pharmacy: Revco, 7660 Sawmill Road; (614) 889-5104

17 Ohio

SANDUSKY AND THE LAKE ERIE ISLANDS

Often dubbed "Ohio's summer playground," Sandusky and the Lake Erie Islands offer lots of family finds. Sandusky has miles of lake shoreline for boating and bathing, plus an old-fashioned amusement park with up-to-speed roller coasters. For island fun Great Lakes–style, visit the Lake Erie Islands, especially Kelleys Island, and South Bass Island famed for Put-in-Bay. These islands gained significance in 1813 as the site of Commodore Perry's victory over the British in the War of 1812. But now the islands offer much more placid pleasures such as sunning, swimming, fishing, and bicycling, all at affordable prices.

GETTING THERE

The **Cleveland-Hopkins International Airport** (216–267–8282), about 65 miles from Sandusky, is the closest major airport to the area. Car rentals are available at the airport. **Amtrak** (800–USA–RAIL) arrives at Cleveland's main terminal, Ninth Street and Cleveland Memorial Shoreway. Amtrak also offers service to Sandusky. The schedule, however, is limited, and the station is not in a convenient area. Anyone taking a train directly to Sandusky should arrange for a ride beforehand. Also, there is no staff in the depot, so it is best to buy your return ticket before you leave; otherwise, you end up paying more for it on the train. **Greyhound/Trailways** (216–781–1400) offers daily bus service between Sandusky, 6513 Milan Road, and Cleveland, East Fifteenth Street and Chester Avenue.

To reach the Sandusky area by car, take the Ohio Turnpike, I–80, to exit 7 and follow U.S. 250 north to the Sandusky area. If you're heading to Port Clinton, take U.S. 250 and then follow Route 163 to the Port Clinton exit. Marblehead is off 269 north. To reach Catawba take Route 53 north from Route 2. Each of these towns has ferry service to the Lake Erie Islands. Catawba and Port Clinton have ferry service to South Bass Island

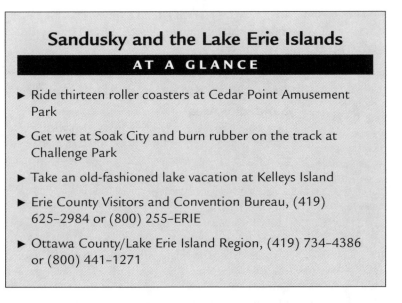

Sandusky and the Lake Erie Islands

AT A GLANCE

- Ride thirteen roller coasters at Cedar Point Amusement Park
- Get wet at Soak City and burn rubber on the track at Challenge Park
- Take an old-fashioned lake vacation at Kelleys Island
- Erie County Visitors and Convention Bureau, (419) 625-2984 or (800) 255-ERIE
- Ottawa County/Lake Erie Island Region, (419) 734-4386 or (800) 441-1271

and Middle Bass Island. Marblehead serves Kelleys Island. (See Getting Around.)

Getting Around

There are two things to remember when visiting the Lake Erie Islands: one, island hopping means living by the ferry schedule; two, don't think twice about leaving your car on the mainland. Getting around without an auto is easy. Most of the islands offer bicycle and golf-cart rentals, and guided island tours. Walking is also great fun in good weather. Kelleys Island and Put-in-Bay have narrated tram services. If you're adamant about bringing your car, call ahead to reserve ferry space.

Miller Boat Line (800-500-2421) serves South Bass Island and Middle Bass Island from Catawba Point. **Jet Express** (800-245-1JET) shuttles between South Bass (Put-In-Bay) and Port Clinton. **Sonny-S Ferry** (419-285-8774) serves Middle Bass from downtown Put-In-Bay with ferries departing on the hour. **Newman Boat Line** (419-798-5800 or 800-876-1907) and **Kelleys Island Ferry Boat Lines, Inc.** (419-798-9723 or 216-439-3555) both run boats between Kelleys Island and Marblehead. **Express Shuttle** (800-245-1JET), which departs from Port Clinton, provides service to both islands.

If you're only in the Lake Erie Islands area for a day, take an island-hopping cruise aboard the *M/V City of Sandusky* (419-627-0198), which originates at the Jackson Street Pier in downtown Sandusky and stops at the Casino Docks in Kelleys Island, Put-In-Bay, Lonz Winery, and Middle

Bass Island. **Emerald Island Express** offers seventeen different island-hopping, luncheon, and sunset-dinner cruises weekly.

Merry-Go-Round Museum

Were carousels a part of your childhood, and did calliope music always signal a good time? Share the pleasures with your kids at the **Merry-Go-Round Museum,** corner of Jackson and Washington Streets, Sandusky (419-626-6111). Take a spin on a merry-go-round and browse the carved animals, some caught in midprance. Check the schedule for carving demonstrations and hours.

What to See and Do

Sandusky Area

Combine two days in the Sandusky area with several days of island hopping for a sure-to-please, moderately priced family vacation that couples amusement park thrills with plenty of beach attractions.

Cedar Point

Life's little ups and downs are lots of fun at **Cedar Point,** P.O. Box 5006, Sandusky (419-627-2350; www.cedarpoint.com), an amusement park situated on the 364-acre Lake Erie Peninsula. This 128-year-old amusement park, which debuted its first roller coaster in 1892, offers up-to-date excitement. Best known for its thirteen roller coasters, the park bills itself as the largest ride park in the country, with sixty-seven rides. (*Rides,* the promoters say, not *attractions* as in Disney World.) Whether or not this phrase is a bit of hyperbole, the fact remains that there's lots to do here, and your kids won't be bored.

With thirteen coasters, Cedar Point has more up and down thrills than any other ride park. Some favorites:

Magnum XL200, one of the tallest and fastest coasters in the world, reaches heights of 205 feet and speeds of 72 miles per hour. Mean Streak, a 161-foot-tall wooden wonder, has dips and drops calculated to make you shriek with delight. Raptor blasts you through six inversions at speeds up to 57 miles per hour, all while your legs are dangling chair-lift style. Mantis features four upside-down inversions and one of the tallest vertical loops on any stand-up coaster. Disaster Transport zips you along a bobsledlike track in the dark.

The park hasn't ignored the little ones. **Camp Snoopy,** new for 1999, debuts with seven rides geared for young kids. Snoopy, Charlie Brown, Lucy, and others from the Peanuts bunch appear in the park, whose highlight is Woodstock Express, a 38-foot-tall family roller coaster—good for first plunges.

Berenstein Bear Country features sets from these favorite children's books. Come inside the Bear Family Treehouse, meet Papa, Mama, Sister and Brother bear, play at the Berry Bush Island clubhouse, and sit at the desks the bears use.

Additional pint-size attractions are Kid Arthur's Court, KiddyKingdom and the Gemini children's area which has a junior-size roller-coaster.

Soak City and Challenge Point

Adjacent to Cedar Point, **Soak City** and **Challenge Park,** One Cedar Point Drive, Sandusky (419-627-2350; www.cedarpoint.com), add more family fun.

Cool off on Soak City's water slides and inner-tube rides and by jumping the 3-foot waves generated in the 500,000 gallon wave pool. At Tadpole Town, Toddler River, and Choo-Choo Lagoon, little ones get wet with sprinklers, fountains, geysers, and wading pools. Race cars at Challenge Park's new Triple Challenge Racepark. Kids zoom along on a 160-foot course, older ones (rookies) try a 700-foot twisting course; and teens and adults burn rubber on a 1,200-foot track. You can also test your mettle on the rides. RipCord combines the thrill of skydiving and bungee jumping by launching riders from a 15-foot-tall tower. Tethered to a cable, you free-fall to within 6 feet of the ground. Challenge Golf, two eighteen-hole miniature courses, provide the quieter thrills of putting through caves, ramps, and waterfalls.

More Attractions

If you can get your kids out of the water and off the roller coasters, take them to **African Safari Wildlife Park,** 267 Lightner Road, Port Clinton (419-732-3606 or 800-521-2660). At this drive-through safari, you see tropical birds and camels outside your window. Kids get close to the animals with camel and pony rides, and a Turtle Taxi service (bring the cameras). At the pig races, root for your favorite porker. Let the wee ones work off some energy at the Jungle Junction playground.

The **Inland Seas Maritime Museum,** 480 Main Street, Vermillion (216-967-3467), details the nautical history of the Great Lakes. Step into the pilot house of a simulated 400-foot bulk-carrier ship, and view models, paintings, and photographs. Find out about some of the 10,000 vessels that were lost on the Great Lakes waters, from Sieur de la Salle's *Griffin,* which set sail in 1679 in search of furs, to the *Edmund Fitzgerald,* which sank nearly 300 years later.

The **Milan Historical Museum,** 210 Edison Drive, Milan (419-499-2968). This complex of six buildings takes you back to the nineteenth century. In the 1843 dwelling, once owned by Robert Sayles, see pressed glass, china, and doll collections. Other buildings to browse include a country store and blacksmith shop. It's open April through October.

Historic Lyme Village, Route 113, Bellevue (419-483-6052 or 419-483-4949), offers more nineteenth-century history. Tour restored homes, barns, shops, a post office, an 1880s mansion that serves as the village museum, a schoolhouse, and a general store. Call ahead for a listing of seasonal events, activities, and festivals. Guided tours of the village are available Tuesday through Sunday from June through August; and Sunday only in May and September. The rest of the year tours are by appointment only.

Train Tour of Put-In-Bay

For above-ground tours, little kids especially like a ride on the **Put-In-Bay Tour Train** (419-285-4855), whose one-hour narrated tour gives an island overview. What's also nice for families: for the same price, you can get on and off at different stops, which include all the island highlights—Heineman's Winery, Crystal Cave, Perry's Cave, and Perry's Memorial. Beginning in late May, the tram runs all week during the summer months from 10:00 A.M. to 5:00 P.M. From September through October the tram will run on weekends only, 10:00 A.M. to 5:00 P.M. Children under six ride free.

Lake Erie Islands

For top walleye fishing and hours of sailing, visit Kelleys Island and South Bass Island, two of the most popular Lake Erie Islands.

Less than 5 miles from Ohio's Lake Erie shore, **Kelleys Island** offers beaches, natural areas, and interesting archaeological sites. Busy in summer, but not bustling, the island's year-round (winter) population hovers at about 200. To find out what's happening, pick up a copy of the *Kelleys Island Funfinder* when you arrive.

Summer vacationers began arriving at this 2,800-acre island, the largest American island in Lake Erie, by steamer in the 1830s, and guests have been coming ever since. On Kelleys combine a beach vacation with a bit of archaeological history.

Take your kids to the prehistoric Indian mounds and petroglyphs, some of which date back to 12,000 B.C., while others portray Native American cultures. **Inscription Rock,** a large boulder on the south shore, is famous as having the most extensive and best-preserved prehistoric Indian pictographs in the United States. The animals, birds, and men that appear on Inscription Rock were created by Erie Indians between 300 and 400 years ago. The inscriptions, however, have not been well preserved and are difficult to see.

The Glacial Grooves State Memorial, on the north shore, offers another not-to-miss archaeological site. Among the finest glacial markings in the United States, this 400-foot-long trough, with its fossilized marine life, was pressed into Kelley's limestone during the Pleistocene Ice Age.

Kelleys Island State Park, with 661 acres, offers miles of hiking trails, relatively uncrowded beaches, campsites, and nature programs. Children may also enjoy searching for fossils throughout the island, especially along the trail that winds through an abandoned quarry.

The **Lake Erie Toy Museum** (419-746-2451), open Memorial Day through Labor Day, features more than 1,000 American and foreign toys dating from 1865 to 1980. Visitors can also stroll through the Butterfly Box, a garden where you can spot hundreds of butterfly varieties.

More developed than Kelleys Island, Put-In-Bay, on **South Bass Island,** features beaches, wineries, fish hatcheries, shopping, restaurants, and pubs. A bustling beach area, Put-In-Bay is famed for its tactical role in the Battle of Lake Erie, the War of 1812. On September 10, 1813, Commodore Oliver Hazard Perry and his troops sought much-needed shelter in Put-In-Bay. Here they rested before successfully battling the British. After winning, Perry sent his now famous message to General William Harrison: "We have met the enemy and they are ours." Today, the 352-foot **Perry's Victory and International Peace Memorial** stands in Put-In-Bay as a reminder of this historic event. The view from the top of the monument is one of the best in the area.

Near Perry's Memorial is a popular beach, called simply Bathing Beach. Stone Beach, part of **South Bass Island State Park** (419-285-2112), on the island's northwest, may be less crowded.

For some off-the-beach fun tour the **Heineman's Winery,** Catawba Avenue[(419-285-2811). Afterward, taste the wine or sample nonalcoholic grape juice. Even if your kids aren't excited by looking at crushers and storage tanks, they'll probably like the tour of **Crystal Cave,** included with admission to the winery. Inside, you see a giant geode discovered in 1897, whose largest crystal weighs about 300 pounds and measures 2 feet in length and 1½ feet in width. The cave is open from mid-May through late September. For more cave sites, go underground at **Perry's Cave,** 979 Catawba Avenue (419-285-2405), to see stalactites and stalagmites.

Another special ride is a spin on **Kimberly's Carousel,** Delaware Avenue, adjacent to the Carriage House, a children's clothing store. This restored 1917 carousel has thirty-six menagerie animals and a Wurlitzer organ. George Stoiber, a local businessman, bought the carousel in 1976, named it for his daughter, and spent eight years restoring this gem.

Shopping

On the mainland, near Sandusky, stop at the **Lake Erie Factory Outlet Center,** U.S. 250, ½ mile north of Ohio Turnpike exit 7 (419-499-2528). Scores of shops here advertise savings of 30 to 70 percent. As always with factory outlets, the quality and the price vary, but with a quick eye and some luck you could come away with bargains on brand-name clothing, housewares, and toys.

Performing Arts

On the Marblehead peninsula each summer, **Lakeside Associations,** 236 Walnut, Lakeside (419–798–4461), organizes a series of performances in this well-preserved Victorian town. In the past these have included ballet, folk music, international puppetry groups, acrobats, the Lakeside Symphony, and Shakespearean productions.

The Huron Playhouse, Ohio Street, Huron (419–433–4744). Ohio's oldest summer-stock theater offers performances Tuesdays through Saturdays, July through mid-August. Huron is a few miles east of Sandusky off U.S. 6. The **State Theatre,** 107 Columbus Avenue, Sandusky (419–626–3945), hosts concert pianists, ballet groups, drama, and popular musical groups. The **Playmakers Civic Theater,** Port Clinton (419–734–9089), also hosts plays.

Side Trips

For an interesting trip while visiting the Lake Erie Area, consider **Maumee Bay State Park,** 1750 Park Road #2, off I–280, 10 miles east of downtown Toledo in Oregon, Ohio, a great spot for fishing on Lake Erie. Aside from fishing the park offers golf, swimming, hunting, cross-country skiing (seasonally), a nature center, and lodging. Call (419) 836–1466.

Also consider **Sea World of Ohio,** 1100 Sea World Drive, Aurora (216–562–8101), which is thirty minutes southeast of Cleveland. See Shamu the killer whale in Shamu's Happy Harbor, a three-acre Caribbean-theme area, and thirteen "sea monsters and dinosaurs" at Monster Marsh, plus twenty geographically themed aquariums featuring a variety of sea life.

Teenagers and parents alike might be interested in the **Rock 'n' Roll Hall of Fame** in Cleveland.

Combine a visit to Sandusky and the Lake Erie Islands with a stay in Columbus, about 105 miles away (see the Columbus chapter) or Indianapolis, about 245 miles away (see the Indianapolis chapter).

Special Events

From May throughout September Port Clinton hosts the Summer Jazz program every Sunday at the Mon Ami Restaurant and Winery. Call (800) 774–4266 to find out who will be performing.

April. "Welcome Back" fish fry, Kelleys Island; performance of a children's play, Huron campus of Bowling Green State University.

May. Bed-and-Breakfast Tour of Kelleys Island; Walleye Festival, Water Works Park, Port Clinton.

June. Marblehead Lighthouse Tour, Marblehead; Tour of Homes and Bicycle Rally, Kelleys Island.

July. Fireworks at Lakeside, Port Clinton, and Put-In-Bay; Amish Quilt Festival, Put-In-Bay; Kelleys Island Islandfest.

August. Clam Bake, Kelleys Island; Croquet Tournament, Kelleys Island.

September. Celebrate the Battle of Lake Erie during Put-In-Bay's historical weekend.

October. Oktoberfest, Put-In-Bay.

WHERE TO STAY

Sandusky Area

Adjacent to the Cedar Point Amusement Park are two lodgings. The **Sandcastle Suites Hotel,** Cedar Point, P.O. Box 5006 (419-627-2107), offers two-room suites. Take a breather from the park to play tennis or lounge on Sandcastle's beach on the shores of Lake Erie. Sandcastle Suites offers shuttle service between the park and the hotel. For those who like historic properties and grande-dame hotels, there's the **Hotel Breakers,** Cedar Point, P.O. Box 5006 (410-627-2106). This landmark property has 650 rooms, some stained-glass windows, lots of wicker, and dates to 1905. The Breakers Tower, a ten-story wing, debuted in 1999. Impress your kids by telling them that former guests included Annie Oakley, Abbott and Costello, and John Philip Sousa. "Who?" they'll ask, but then you have something to talk about over lunch. The hotel has an ice-cream parlor, a swimming pool, and a beach, three kid-pleasing places.

Other possibilities include the **Holiday Inn,** Sandusky, 5313 Milan Road (419-626-6671 or 800-465-4329), which features an indoor pool and miniature golf. **The Econo Lodge,** U.S. 6, 1904 Cleveland Road (419-627-8000 or 800-424-4777), is a less-costly alternative and is across from the entrance to Cedar Point. **Camper Village,** also part of the Cedar Point complex, Cedar Point (419-627-2106), is a recreational vehicle campground with more than 400 sites. Each area has picnic tables, grills, electricity, water, showers, laundromat, and supply store.

Sawmill Creek Resort, off Route 13 North, Huron (419-433-3800), offers resort amenities within a reasonable drive of Cedar Point. With an eighteen-hole golf course, indoor and outdoor swimming pools, saunas, three restaurants, whirlpool, exercise room, tennis courts, gift shop, and marina docks, Sawmill has plenty to offer the family traveling with kids.

Kelleys Island

Kelleys Island has a number of bed-and-breakfast inns that more often than not prefer couples or families with older children. If you want to stay at a bed-and-breakfast, look in the *Kelleys Island Funfinder* for a list. Be candid about the ages of your children to be certain that your kids will feel comfortable at these properties.

More suitable family-friendly accommodations include **Sunrise Point,** P.O. Box 431 (419-746-2543 or 419-626-8779). They offer one-bedroom units and lakefront efficiencies, plus a play area for kids. A number of private homes are for rent as well. **Lake-Woods Edge** is on the lakefront. Contact the owner at 1036 Jeff Ryan Drive, Herndon, Virginia 22070 (703-435-6635). For the most up-to-date listings, obtain a copy of *Kelleys Island Funfinder.*

Put-In-Bay

Accommodations in the Put-In-Bay area include motels, resorts, hotels, and cottages. **Saunder's Resort,** Catawba Avenue (419-285-3917), offers fully furnished cottages a mile from downtown. The complex includes a pool as well as tennis, badminton, and shuffleboard courts. The **Perry Holiday,** 99 Concord Avenue (419-285-2107), has thirty-three rooms, each with a private bathroom, air-conditioning, and color television. One block from downtown, their facilities include a pool, laundry, picnic tables, and grills. **East Point Cottages,** Massie Lane (419-285-2204) offers eight furnished cottages from May through October for rental. Each cottage has its own kitchen. Fishing licenses, tackle, and bait are available at the cottages. **Parker's Inn,** Catawba Avenue (419-285-5555), has fifty rooms and a restaurant.

For more accommodations information, contact the **Ottawa County Visitors Bureau,** 109 Madison, Port Clinton 43452 (419-734-4FUN or 800-441-1271). Also contact the **Sandusky/Erie County Visitors & Convention Bureau,** P.O. Box 1639, Sandusky (419-625-2984 or 800-255-ERIE).

Where to Eat

Your kids may even come away from a vacation at Sandusky and the islands liking fish. At least have them taste the local specialties of Lake Erie perch and walleye.

The Sandusky Area

In Port Clinton, try **Mon Ami Restaurant and Historic Winery,** 2845 East Wine Cellar Road (419-797-4445 or 800-777-4266). Mon Ami serves perch, walleye, and Italian specialties. Just outside the Cedar Point

Amusement Park, the **Breakwater Cafe,** Cedar Point, Sandusky (419-626-0830), is a casual restaurant serving up a range of good eats from walleye to fajitas. **Damon's** in Battery Park (419-627-2424), offers great food and a 360-degree view of Sandusky Bay and Cedar Point, including the roller-coaster skyline. Take your older children to the **Tea Rose Tea-room,** 218 East Washington Street (419-627-2773), for afternoon tea and a reading of the tea leaves.

Kelleys Island

Head to the **Village Pump,** Water Street (419-746-2281). Here, the locals recommend the roast beef sandwiches, the hand-dipped onion rings, and the Lake Erie perch. The **Casino,** on the lakeshore off Lakeshore Drive (419-746-2773), has weekend entertainment and is known for its barbecued ribs, perch, and clam chowder. Sample wines made from a hybrid of European varieties and choose from an interesting selection of pasta and cheeses at the **Kelleys Island Wine Tasting Room and Gourmet Bistro** (419-746-2537). Close to the ferry docks and the downtown area, the bistro has a child's play area as well as an area for horseshoes and volleyball.

Put-In-Bay

The Boardwalk, downtown Put-In-Bay (419-285-3695), is the island's only waterfront restaurant. The food ranges from seafood to tacos to pizza. **The Village Bakery and Sandwich Shoppe,** at the Depot (419-285-5351), offers a variety of inexpensive choices and light meals. The **Bay Burger,** Village Center (419-285-6192), pleases kids with burgers and milk shakes. Try to get the tykes to try the walleye sandwiches. **The Snack House,** Delaware Avenue (419-285-4595), features homemade ice cream.

For More Information

Contact the **Ottawa County Visitors Bureau** for information concerning the Bass Islands and the Port Clinton/Put-In-Bay area, 109 Madison Street, Suite E, Port Clinton (800-441-1271; www.lake-erie.com). If you're looking for more information on the Sandusky/Kelleys Island area, contact **Erie County Visitors and Convention Bureau,** 231 West Washington Row, Sandusky (419-625-2984 or 800-255-ERIE; www.sanduskyohio.com).

Emergency Numbers

Ambulance, fire, and police: 911

There are no hospitals on Kelleys or South Bass Islands. For hospitals with emergency facilities, try Firelands Community Hospital, 1101

Decatur Street, Sandusky (419-626-7400) or Providence Hospital, 1912 Hayes Avenue, Sandusky (419-621-7000). Port Clinton does have a hospital, the Magruder Hospital, 615 Fulton Street, Port Clinton; (419) 734-3131.

Poison Control: (419) 626-7423

Twenty-four-hour pharmacy: Refer to the hospital emergency room facilities listed above. Rite Aid Discount Pharmacy has stores in Port Clinton and the Sandusky area, including one located at 220 Columbus Avenue, Sandusky; (419) 625-3801. Also located in Sandusky: Discount Drug Mart, 124 East Perkins Avenue; (419) 625-0733.

The Black Hills, The Badlands, and Mt. Rushmore

South Dakota's natural beauty and unusual geological features, plus its Wild West history and Native American presence, combine to offer families, especially city dwellers, an interesting landscape for a family vacation.

The Sioux Nation, despite being driven from the Black Hills after the discovery of gold in the area in 1874, still maintains a sizable presence in South Dakota. More than 70,000 Native Americans, most of the Lakota, Dakota, and Nakota tribes of the Sioux Nation, live within the state's boundaries, both on and off reservations.

Getting There

South Dakota has two major airports; the one in Rapid City provides better access to the Black Hills and Badlands areas. The **Rapid City Regional Airport** (650-394-4195), 9 miles southeast of town, is served by several carriers, including Northwest (800-225-2525), Skywest (800-221-1212), and United Express (800-241-6522).

Rental cars are available at the airport.

Jack Rabbit Lines bus company runs routes between Rapid City and Sioux Falls (605-336-0855). **Amtrak** does not provide any service to South Dakota. I-90 and I-29 are two of the major highways leading to Rapid City.

Getting Around

With a lot of wide open spaces, South Dakota is best seen by car. For those who prefer not to drive, **Gray Line** of Rapid City (605-342-4461) offers bus tours of the Black Hills and the Badlands.

The Black Hills, The Badlands, and Mt. Rushmore

AT A GLANCE

- Explore the peaks, canyons, and prairies of the Badlands National Park
- Peruse 20,000 artifacts in the Indian Museum of North America
- Visit Mount Rushmore National Monument
- Go spelunking at Jewel Cave National Monument and Wind Cave National Park
- Black Hills, Badlands, and Lakes Association, (605) 355-3600; www.travelsd.com

What to See and Do

The Black Hills

The Black Hills region, approximately 70 miles wide and 110 miles long, has much to offer families, including four national parks: Mount Rushmore National Memorial; Wind Cave National Park; Jewel Cave National Monument; and Devils Tower National Monument, which is just west of South Dakota in Wyoming. East of the Black Hills lies another not-to-be-missed site, the Badlands National Park.

The **Black Hills National Forest,** 10 miles west of Rapid City on U.S. 16, covers 1.2 million acres. In 1874 when General George Custer led a military expedition through the Black Hills, the region was sacred Sioux land. The Lakota Sioux named the region *Paha Sapa,* or "Black Hills," a place to communicate with *Wakan Tanka,* the "Great Spirit." Despite this, much of the land was taken from the Sioux after gold was discovered here in 1874. Among the Black Hills highlights are the following.

The **Mount Rushmore National Memorial,** P.O. Box 268, Keystone 57751 (605-574-2523), is about 23 miles southwest of Rapid City off U.S. 16A, and 2 miles southwest of Keystone. Mount Rushmore is what first comes to mind when people think of South Dakota. The chiseled faces of George Washington, Thomas Jefferson, Abraham Lincoln, and Theodore Roosevelt, carved by Gutzon Borglum in monumental scale, gaze out at the land. Each head is about 60 feet long, twice the size of the

Every member of the family will be awed by the epic faces of Mt. Rushmore.

Sphinx in Egypt. Borglum began sculpting this massive project in 1927 at age sixty, and he died in 1941 before completing the carvings, which were to feature also the shoulders, chest, and waist of each president. For the most spectacular light, arrive at dawn. Get a closer look at the memorial by following the Presidential Trail to the base of the monument. Up close it's easy to realize the enormity and complexity of the structure.

The thirteen-minute film at the visitors center details the crafting of the monument, as do the photographs and tools on display.

The interpretive center tells the history of Mount Rushmore. Visitors see the flag used in the unveiling of the sculpture and the tools used in the carving of the four presidents. The amphitheater hosts nightly ceremonies and special park presentations in the summer.

A huge visitor center houses the **Indian Museum of North America,** featuring more than 20,000 artifacts of North American tribes. A special wing is devoted to the Lakota, a majority of whom live in the Dakotas.

Providing a high-tech tour of Black Hills history, **The Journey Museum** is Rapid City's newest. Located near Mount Rushmore at 625 Ninth Street (605–394–6923), this $12.5-million structure explores 2.5 billion years of the area's history. Collections from the Sioux Indian Museum, the Minnilusa Pioneer Museum, the Museum of Geology at South Dakota School of Mines and Technology, the Duhamel Plains Indian Artifact Collection, and the State Archeological Research Center explores the geological history and cultural heritage of the Black Hill. Be sure to visit the outdoor geological field camp; watch the video wall puz-

Crazy Horse Memorial

Seventeen miles southwest of Mt. Rushmore, a fifth face takes shape in stone. Still being built is the **Crazy Horse Memorial** on U.S. 16-385 (605-673-4681). When completed, this tribute to the Lakota Sioux leader will be the largest mountain carving in the world—563 feet high and 641 feet long.

Lakota Chief Henry Standing Bear invited sculptor Korczak Ziolkowski to carve this monument because, wrote Standing Bear, "My fellow chiefs and I would like the white man to know the red man has great heroes, too." Ziolkowski began the project in 1947, and although he died in 1982, his family continues this monumental carving.

Ziolkowski, desiring not to depict a realistic image of this Lakota leader, but rather a rendering of the Native American spirit, portrayed Crazy Horse astride a steed, his arm extended, responding to the goading question "Where are your lands now?" asked by a white man after the Battle of Little Big Horn, when many Sioux were pushed onto reservations. The dramatic and dignified warrior points, answering "My lands are where my dead lie buried."

Once a year, during the first weekend in June, visitors can actually hike the mountain where Crazy Horse is being carved. At other times, visitors can view the memorial in progress from an observation deck, which offers an interesting look at the rare art of mountain carving. Admission is charged.

zle that, when solved, depicts a prehistoric woman; and tour the three teepees that allow visitors to touch items such as a buffalo hide and listen to a hologram-like image of a woman telling stories.

Forty-two miles north of Rapid City is **Deadwood,** an 1876 gold rush boomtown in the northern section of the national forest, off I-90 on U.S. 85 and U.S. Alt. 14 (605-578-1102). Although the city is a designated National Historical Landmark and many turn-of-the-century building facades along Main Street are preserved, the town is not exactly as it was in the gold rush days. Now more than eighty gambling establishments lure tourists. While these might contribute to the Wild West spirit of this frontier village where Wild Bill Hickok was murdered, the gaming also lends a somewhat tawdry air, which detracts from the family allure. Deadwood, however, has some family attractions, including an amusement park, the Sherman Street Trolley Station, and the Adams Museum.

One mile from the town the **Mount Moriah Cemetery,** known also as "Boot Hill," contains the graves of such western legends as "Wild

Bill" Hickok and Calamity Jane. If your kids crave wax museums, Deadwood's **Ghosts of Deadwood Gulch,** Old Towne Hall, Lee Street (605-578-3583), depicts eighteen scenes of pioneer days.

Gold Mine Tours

For some more gold rush days ambience, take an underground tour of the once prosperous **Broken Boot Gold Mine** on U.S. Alt. 14 (605-578-1876), where you can pan for gold. The mine brought up gold from 1878 until 1904. Explore the surface workings of one of the oldest and largest gold mines in the western hemisphere at the still-operating **Homestake Gold Mine,** Main and Mill Streets, in Lead, 3 miles from Deadwood (605-584-3110). Children under four are not permitted.

Custer State Park

Adjacent to the Black Hills National Forest is **Custer State Park,** 42 miles southwest of Rapid City on Highway 16A (605-255-4515). Featuring 73,000 acres of rolling grasslands and pine forests, the park is home to about 1,400 head of buffalo, one of the nation's largest herds. You're also likely to see deer, elk, pronghorn antelope, and bighorn sheep. In fall watch a buffalo roundup. Call for details.

For panoramic views, hike the 1½-mile trail to the top of Little Devil's Tower or follow the 2-mile trail to the top of Harney Peak in the adjacent Black Elk Wilderness. Both hikes require stamina and are best suited for older kids who like hills.

Pick up park information at the **Peter Norbeck Visitor Center,** 15 miles east of Custer on Highway 16A (605-255-4464). **Sylvan Lake,** 7 miles north of Custer on Route 87 and 89, is known for its setting amid massive rock formations, and for its fishing. **Legion Lake** has good fishing, swimming, and family-oriented budget cabins.

Along the 14-mile **Needles Highway Scenic Drive,** on Highway 87 from Legion Lake to the base of Harney Peak, the highest mountain in the Black Hills, you thread through the towering granite pinnacles, popular with rock climbers. On the **Iron Mountain Road,** which spans alternate 16 for 17 miles from Custer State Park to Mount Rushmore, you drive through granite tunnels, past Black Hills overlooks, and through stands of spruce and pine. You're likely to see buffalo, coyotes, prairie dogs, wild burros (the only wildlife in the park that it's okay to feed), and elk, especially in the early morning or at dusk along the **Wildlife Loop Road,** which forms an 18-mile loop passing the Wildlife Station and three of the park's resorts (see Where to Stay).

Wind Cave National Park

Wind Cave is the highlight of the 18,000 acres of grasslands of the **Wind Cave National Park,** 53 miles south of Rapid City, near Hot Springs and south of Custer State Park (605-745-4600; www.nps.gov). Wind Cave is a sure winner for kids fascinated by underground wonders. Said to be the

Jewel Cave National Monument

The Jewel Cave National Monument features more than 100 miles of accessible passageways, making it the second longest cave in the world. Unusual calcite formations hang from the ceiling.

Three tours, each covering about ½ mile, offer different views of the cave. The ninety-minute **Scenic Tour** follows a paved lighted path. (There are 723 steps, but not all at once.) The **Historic Tour,** conducted by candlelight, traces the route of the earliest cave explorers. The **Spelunking Tour,** more rigorous for ages sixteen and older, winds through undeveloped passages and caverns. You see clusters of hydromagnesite documented in only six caves in the world.

Whatever tour you choose, be sure to wear layers of warm clothing, as the average cave temperature hovers at a chilly 47 degrees Fahrenheit.

Jewel Cave National Monument, 59 miles southwest of Rapid City and 13 miles west of Custer on Highway 16; (605-673-2288; www.nps.gov).

world's sixth longest cave, this attraction offers more than 82 miles of mapped passages, with lots of boxwork ceiling formations. Rangers offer guided tours. These are easy walks, but there are steps. More difficult spelunking tours requiring crawling through narrow passages are available. Remember warm clothing and good walking shoes.

The Badlands National Park

The Badlands, 83 miles east of Rapid City (605-433-5361; www.nps.gov), exits 110 and 131 off I-90, will intrigue your family. Designated by Congress as a National Monument in 1939, and upgraded to a National Park in 1978, the Badlands has dense deposits of fossils from the Oligocene Epoch, the Golden Age of Mammals, including giant turtles, three-toed horses, and saber-toothed tigers. Once a saltwater sea, later a marsh, the area is now a remnant of one of the world's great grasslands, with jutting peaks, twisting canyons, and vast prairies. The formations reveal amazing colors as erosion has exposed the formations' layers of purple, yellow, tan, gray, red, and orange. Some of the best colors can be seen at sunup and sundown.

Wind and water created the wild assortment of pinnacles, cones, gorges, and other geologic oddities that caused the Lakota Sioux to label the region *Mako Sica,* or "Land Bad." French trappers and traders referred to the area as *Mauvaises Terres à Traverser*—"Bad Lands to Travel Across."

Hikes in Badlands National Park

It's a completely different experience to walk among the unusual knobs, pyramids, and points. Several developed trails cut through the Badlands.

- **The Fossil Exhibit Trail,** west of the visitor center on S.D. 240, south of Wall, is great for kids. This ¼-mile wheelchair- and stroller-accessible loop has replicas of area fossils.
- **The Cliff Shelf Nature Trail,** another ¼-mile loop just east of the visitor center on 240, passes through a juniper grove and a cattail marsh that attracts Badlands wildlife. While easy, a few steps make this not wheelchair accessible.
- **The Castle Trail,** northeast of the visitor center on 240, above the Cliff Shelf Trail, offers a 5¼-mile one-way stretch through rolling grasslands and Badlands formations, or a 6-mile loop when combined with the **Medicine Root Trail.**

Note: Weather changes can be sudden in the Badlands, so be sure to take proper clothing and provisions, including adequate food and water, when hiking any distance.

Soon after these trappers came soldiers, miners, cattlemen, and homesteaders who struggled with each other and the Sioux for the land. After the Wounded Knee Massacre, the Lakota were confined to reservations.

The park offers a variety of programs, including a Junior Ranger Program during the summer for ages five to twelve, which rewards kids with badges (parents pay a nominal fee) after answering questions about the park and the ranger-led programs they attended.

Look for deer, buffalo, and pronghorn antelope, but don't settle for just driving through the Badlands. Spend some time on foot. Obtain information about the hiking trails from the **White River Visitor Center,** open Memorial Day through mid-September, Highway 27 in the Stronghold Unit, 20 miles south of the town of Scenic. Hiking information is also available year-round from the **Ben Reifel Visitor Center at Cedar Pass,** off Highway 240, on the park's eastern side. Kids like the Touch Room with its fossils, rocks, and plants.

More Attractions

In Rapid City the free **Story Book Island,** 1301 Sheridan Lake Road (605-342-6357), is a good place to let little ones romp on replicas of popular storybook characters. A moat leads to a "fairy-tale castle."

Wall Drug Store

A stop at **Wall Drug Store,** 510 Main Street (605-279-2175), north of the Badlands on I-90, is a must. This small 1930s family drugstore got its boost by offering free ice water to hot and weary drivers during the Great Depression. Today the Wall Drug Store often serves 20,000 visitors each day. If you're wondering how a store in a town of 800 attracts so many visitors, you've never driven the highways of South Dakota, where signs relentlessly beckon you to come on by. This is the place for kids to stretch their legs, climb on the outdoor covered wagon, and get a photo with a 6-foot-tall rabbit. Inside they can search for souvenirs and admire the funky western decor. Although the food is plain, the atmosphere and collection of western art are not. While you peruse the murals and memorabilia, munch on a buffalo burger, and linger over homemade pie. A cup of coffee is still only 5 cents.

At **Bear Country U.S.A.,** off U.S. 16, 8 miles south of Rapid City (605-343-2290), roll up your windows and surround yourself with grizzly bear, timber wolves, mountain lion, buffalo, moose, bighorn sheep, and black bears as you drive through this 220-acre natural Black Hills habitat. After the drive, take the kids to see the young animals in the Welcome Center or go for pony rides.

In season two ski areas not far from Deadwood offer downhill fun. **Terry Peak Ski Area,** P.O. Box 774, Lead 57754, 3 miles west of Lead, is generally open Thanksgiving through Easter. Call (605) 584-2165 or (605) 342-7609; twenty-four-hour ski conditions, (800) 456-0524. The 20 miles of trails make this facility relatively easy to manage. There's also **Deer Mountain,** southwest of Lead on Highway 85, P.O. Box 622, Deadwood 57732; (605) 584-3230 or (605) 578-2141. It features 25 downhill trails, plus groomed cross-country trails and a ski school.

Shopping

In Rapid City, **Rushmore Mall** offers department stores and traditional mall shops. Stroll down **Main Street** and **St. Joseph's Street** for the specialty shops, including the Prairie Edge Galleries, Sixth and Main, for authentic Plains Indian arts and crafts.

Theater

Call the **Rushmore Plaza Civic Center,** 444 Mt. Rushmore Road (800-247-1095), to find out about upcoming performances and events.

Sports

The **Rushmore Plaza Civic Center,** 444 Mt. Rushmore Road (800-247-1095), has times and schedules for the **Rapid City Posse** basketball team.

More Great Family Adventures

- **Horseback Riding.** The born-and-raised Dakota cowboys at **Dakota Badland Outfitters** in Custer (605-673-5363; www.wordpros.com/dakota) guide you through the Black Hills wilderness and the Badlands on day or overnight trips. Ride horseback or, more suitable with young ones, sit in a mule-drawn ranch wagon as guides relate local history and legend, and provide picnic lunches. For more adventure, book an overnight pack trip into the Badlands backcountry.
- **Hot Air Ballooning.** Custer is also home of **Black Hills Balloons** (605-673-2520). Float over such scenic spots as Mount Rushmore, Crazy Horse Memorial, and herds of grazing buffalo. Check on minimum age and height requirements for children.
- **Bicycling.** Pedal along the 110-mile **George S. Mickelson Trail,** a former railroad bed that has been turned into a bicycle path. The trail winds through Black Hills forests and jagged cliffs and passes the Crazy Horse Memorial, Mount Rushmore, and Custer State Park. Several area cycle shops rent bikes. Nominal fee for trail passes for adults; ages 15 and under are free. Call (605) 773-3387.

Side Trips

Evans Plunge, in **Hot Springs,** just 9 miles south of Wind Cave, is a naturally heated, 87-degree mineral-water spring. This indoor-outdoor swimming complex features three water slides and a spa. Also in Hot Springs, visit the **Mammoth Site,** on Highway 18 (605-745-6017 or 800-325-6991). It has the world's largest concentration of Columbian and woolly mammoth bones discovered in their primary context.

For trout fishing go to **Spearfish,** 45 miles northwest of Rapid City on I-90 (605-642-2626 or 800-626-8013). Spearfish Creek and the area's lakes offer peaceful blue-ribbon trout fishing. A walk through the nearby canyon reveals waterfalls. The **Black Hills Passion Play** is another Spearfish event. Set on a stage two blocks long and peopled with 200 actors, this play recounts the last seven days of Christ's life.

Special Events

January. Black Hills Stock Show and Rodeo, Rapid City.

June. Crazy Horse Memorial Volksmarch, first weekend, the only time of year when the public can climb Crazy Horse Memorial.

July. Black Hills Heritage Festival, Rapid City, featuring arts, crafts, music, entertainment, and ethnic foods; The Black Hills Roundup, Belle Fourche, a top three-day rodeo; Gold Discovery Days, Custer, features a pageant, a parade, and a park festival; Days of '76, Deadwood, features reenactments of the gold rush, plus a rodeo.

August. Sturgis Rally and Races, a world-renowned motorcycle extravaganza.

September. Crazy Horse Open House and Night Blast, Crazy Horse Memorial, lights up the night with a actual dynamite blast of the monument; Deadwood Jam, Deadwood, bands play all day on Main Street.

October. Buffalo Round-up, Custer State Park, see a buffalo herd corralled by rangers and wranglers; Black Hills Powwow and Arts Expo, Rapid City, celebrates Native American dancing and art.

Where to Stay

A good base is Rapid City, which has lots of lodging choices. The **Radisson Hotel Rapid City/Mt. Rushmore** at Main Street, 445 Mt. Rushmore (605-348-8300 or 800-446-3750), has moderately priced rooms, plus a pool.

The **Holiday Inn–Rushmore Plaza,** 505 North Fifth Street (605-348-4000 or 800-465-4329), is another moderately priced lodging with a pool. At the **Best Western Town and Country,** 2505 Mt. Rushmore Road (605-343-5383 or 800-528-1234), there are both indoor and outdoor pools. The **Alex Johnson Hotel,** 523 Sixth Street, has a downtown location, a Native American and western decor, and often special family rates (605-342-1210 or 800-888-2539).

Keystone and Hill City are close to Mount Rushmore. In Keystone the **Powder House Lodge,** U.S 16 (605-666-4646), offers cabins and motel rooms. In Hill City, the **High Country Ranch Bed and Breakfast,** 12172 Deerfield Road (605-574-9003), provides some western flair with free half-hour horseback rides; family rates. The **Best Western Golden Spike Inn,** Highway 16-385 (605-574-2577 or 800-528-1234), is a moderately priced choice. The property has an indoor pool.

Custer State Park offers four lodges as well as campgrounds. **Blue Bell Lodge and Resort,** Highway 87S, has rustic cabins with modern amenities, plus horseback rides and chuck-wagon cookouts (605-255-4531 or 800-658-3530). The **State Game Lodge Resort** (605-255-4541 or 800-658-3530), where President Calvin Coolidge summered in 1927, offers lodge rooms, motel units, and cabins, as well as a restaurant and grocery store. Nearby Grace Coolidge Creek is noted for its trout. The **Sylvan Lake Resort** (605-574-2561 or 800-658-3530) overlooks—what else—Sylvan Lake. It's in the shadow of Harney Peak, the highest peak east of the Rockies. The resort has guest rooms, cabins, and a restaurant. **Legion Lake Resort,** Legion Lake (605-255-4521 or 800-658-3530), offers twenty-five rustic cottages; it's a good spot for swimming, fishing, and paddleboating.

You can also camp at one of the seven campgrounds in Custer State Park. Some sites are on a first-come basis, whereas others may be reserved by calling (800) 710-2267.

Shearer's Western Dakota Ranch Vacations, HCR1, Box 9, Wall (605-279-2198), 9 miles from Wall, features horseback and wagon rides, chuck-wagon suppers, and all the chores you want. Stay in the ranch home, log cabins, tents, or teepees.

Where to Eat

Try the **Flying T BBQ Suppers and Show,** on U.S. 16, 6 miles south of Rapid City (605-342-1905). Sample a cowboy chuck-wagon meal of barbecued beef, beans, baked potatoes, and biscuits served up in tin plates and cups. Live country-and-western music along with western decorations add to the atmosphere. Meals are moderately priced, and reservations are recommended.

A similarly themed dinner can be had at **Circle B Ranch Original Chuckwagon Supper and Western Music Show,** Highway 385 (605-348-7358 or 800-403-7358). The Circle B also livens things up with shoot-outs, trail and pony rides, gold panning, and mini-golf. **Casa Del Ray,** 1902 Mt. Rushmore Road (605-348-5679), serves Mexican fare. American burgers and a children's menu are available too.

In Custer State Park, check out the **Pheasant Dining Room,** U.S. 16A, Custer (605-255-4541). This **State Game Lodge** restaurant serves hearty fare and good homemade desserts at moderate prices.

For More Information

South Dakota Department of Tourism, 711 East Wells Avenue, Pierre, South Dakota 57501-3369; (605) 773-3301 or (800) 732-5682; www.travelsd.com

Black Hills, Badlands and Lakes Association, 1851 Driveway Circle, Rapid City; (605) 355-3600

Deadwood Visitors Bureau, 735 Main Street, Deadwood; (605) 578-1876

Wall Chamber of Commerce; (605) 279-2665

Rapid City Convention and Visitors Bureau, 444 Mt. Rushmore Road N., Rapid City; (605) 343-1744

Emergency Numbers

Ambulance, fire police: 911

Hospital: Rapid City Regional Hospital, 353 Fairmont Boulevard; (605) 341-1000 (emergency: 605-341-8222)

Pharmacy: Although there are no twenty-four-hour pharmacies in Rapid City, Albertsons, 855 Omaha Street, is open weekdays 9:00 A.M. to 9:00 P.M., and Saturday 9:00 A.M. to 6:00 P.M.; (605) 343-8542.

Poison Center: (800) 952-0123

19 Utah

Arches National Park and Canyonlands National Park

Arches National Park, just 5 miles north of Moab, features the world's largest concentration of natural red and golden sandstone arches. This is a sight your children will long remember. More than 2,000 majestic arches plus red-rock canyons, fins, spires, and balancing rocks give this landscape an extraterrestrial aura. The fascinating formations were created from the erosion of the Entrada Sandstone and Navajo Sandstone, thick layers of rock deposited as sand some 150 million years ago.

The park comprises 73,000 acres; you could easily get an "eyeful" after a few hours, but plan to spend at least a day, hopefully more, exploring. The early morning and early evening light are dramatic times to view the arches' red desert, with the peaks of the La Sal Mountains in the background. Open year-round, the park has a high season from mid-March to October.

Canyonlands National Park is quite close, and certainly worth a visit, although it's more rugged and not as accessible for families, particularly those with young children. (In fact, it's the state's least visited national park, albeit the largest.)

Getting There

Canyonlands Field Airport, 18 miles northwest of Moab on Highway 191 (435-259-7421), offers regular commuter service from Salt Lake City via Sunrise Airlines (435-259-7421). The nearest major airport is **Walker Field** in Grand Junction, Colorado, two hours east (970-244-9100), which is served by Mesa (a United Express connection), SkyWest (a Delta connection), America West, and Air 21. Major car rental companies are located at the airport.

The nearest **Amtrak** (800-USA-RAIL) is in the town of Green River, 50 miles northwest. By car, the park is 5 miles north of Moab off U.S. 191.

Arches and Canyonlands National Parks

AT A GLANCE

- Hike, raft, and take a jeep through red rock canyons
- See 2,000 majestic arches, spires, and balancing rocks
- Go hunting for dinosaur fossils and footprints
- Arches National Park, (435) 259–8161
- Canyonlands National Park, (435) 259–7164

Getting Around

A car is a necessity. Rental cars and jeeps are available in the area. A 45-mile (round-trip) paved road in the park leads to the major sights. There are also unpaved roads for four-wheel-drive vehicles.

What to See and Do

Arches National Park

The visitor center, just inside the park entrance, is open year-round and features exhibits and a slide program detailing the arch formations. Obtain a park guide here that shows the distances for hiking and the approximate times to allow.

Follow the paved road from the visitor center. While you can see a few of the major arches from the road, short trails (as well as more strenuous hikes) lead to many others. *Best Hikes with Children in Utah* by Maureen Keilty (The Mountaineers) details several trails in Arches, Canyonlands, and other Utah parks, and tells how to stimulate your kids' imaginations as you proceed. On your hike, take the opportunity to teach your children to respect the area's ecology, and remind them not to walk on the cryptobiotic crust, an important feature of the Colorado Plateau. This black, knobby surface frequently seen growing on the soil is composed of organisms that have an important function in the desert; they hold moisture, prevent erosion, and contribute nitrogen and carbon to the soil. They are easily recognized and shouldn't be stepped on or driven on. Stay on the trails and the roads.

Note: In the summer, temperatures can climb to 110 degrees Fahrenheit, so it's best to do your hiking early in the day or in the evening; carry and drink plenty of water, wear wide-brimmed hats, and use sunscreen.

Great Family Hikes and Drives: Arches National Park

- **Park Avenue Viewpoint.** The trailhead for this 1-mile hike (best with older kids) starts about 2 miles from the visitor center. The path along the red rock canyon bottom leads to **Courthouse Towers,** high vertical walls resembling a city skyline. Allow thirty minutes each way.
- **Balanced Rock.** Follow the road for approximately 10 miles along the base of the salmon-colored **Great Wall. Balanced Rock,** a massive 50-foot boulder appears to be precariously balanced atop a slim, 75-foot pedestal. The easy 0.3-mile loop that leads to the rock takes about fifteen minutes to walk.
- **Windows Section.** An easy 0.8-mile trail loop to **North** and **South Windows** and to **Turret Arch** takes about forty-five minutes.
- **Wolfe Ranch** and **Delicate Arch.** Continue along the main road for several miles to a spur that leads to **Wolfe Ranch,** an 1898 homesteader's cabin and corral. This serves as the trailhead for a 3-mile round-trip to a park landmark, **Delicate Arch.** The two- to three-hour moderately strenuous hike includes climbing up slick rocks to the arch. After crossing the steel frame bridge at **Salt Wash,** look for petroglyphs. Once you reach the arch, don't walk under it because the ground is quite steep.
- **Devils Garden.** The main road ends at **Devils Garden,** where there are about a dozen significant arches, some without names. The only one visible from the road is **Skyline Arch,** which can be accessed by an easy 0.4-mile hike. To get to **Landscape Arch,** one of the largest natural arches in the world at 306 feet across, follow the 1.8-mile trail.

Canyonlands National Park

Canyonlands is an immense 527-square-mile wilderness composed of three very different areas. The northern Island in the Sky district is a towering, level mesa between the Green and Colorado Rivers. The Needles district, southeast of the river's confluence, has the densest concentration of arches, rock spires, canyons, potholes, prehistoric Indian ruins, and petroglyphs—plus the Needles, enormous rock pinnacles of red and white. The Maze district, southwest of the rivers, is wild, remote, and accessible by four-wheel-drive vehicles only, with canyons, tall standing rocks, and colorful sandstone fins. Part of the Maze is **Horseshoe Canyon,** which is decorated by Native American rock art.

Great Family Hikes and Drives: Canyonlands National Park

Families who have visited Arches National Park, but who would like to spend at least a half-day exploring Canyonlands, should head straight to the Island in the Sky district and Upheaval Dome. Also interesting is the Needles District.

- **The Island.** This area, some experts say, has possibly the world's greatest exposure of red rock canyons. Particularly suited to families with younger kids and/or limited time, the district features short walks and spectacular overlooks of the **White Rim,** the **Needles,** and the **Maze.**

  Drive the 12 miles from the visitors center to **Grand View Point Overlook,** stopping at **Shafer Canyon** and **Buck Canyon overlooks,** or take the 1.5-mile dirt road to **Green River Overlook.** All provide different vantage points and superb vistas. You might see bighorn sheep, coyotes, or foxes on the ledges below.
- **Upheaval Dome.** This 2-mile-wide crater, one of the park's most spectacular formations, is filled with various colored spires and boulders. **Crater View Trail** and **Upheaval Dome Trail** offer easy to moderate hikes. There are two options: a 500-yard (one way) walk up slickrock to an unfenced view of the crater—good for young or beginning hikers—or a more challenging 0.8-mile (one way) hike to a second, fenced-in vantage point.
- **Needles District.** This area is 50 miles northwest of the town of Monticello and can be accessed via U.S. 191 and 211. **Newspaper Rock BLM Recreation Site,** 12 miles off U.S. 191 on Scenic Byway U-211, displays petroglyphs spanning 1,000 years.

  Although a paved access road leads to a number of viewpoints, some hiking or four-wheeling is required to see the attractions. The main road ends at **Big Spring Canyon Overlook,** which has an assortment of mushroom-shaped hoodoos.

Dating back to 1700 B.C. to A.D. 500, the intricate designs and life-size figures are perhaps the most famous prehistoric rock art in the United States.

Popular seasons in this park are from March to May and August to October. Services are very limited: You won't find food, gasoline, stores, lodging, or drinking water (except in the **Squaw Flat Campground** in

The Druid Arch is just one of the magnificent formations located in Canyonlands National Park.

the Needles). **Needles Outpost,** just outside the Needles park boundary, off U.S. 211, has gasoline, food, and limited supplies available spring through fall.

From Moab, the **Island in the Sky Visitors Center** (435-259-4712) is 32 miles north, then southwest, while the **Needles Visitors Center** (435-259-4711) is 75 miles southwest. Both are open seven days a week, with reduced winter hours. Rangers offer information, maps, brochures, and, during the summer, guided walks and evening campfire programs.

You can explore the park in several ways. Drive on paved and two-wheel-drive roads to the **Needles** and **Island in the Sky** districts, which lead to overlooks, trailheads, picnic areas, and developed campgrounds. There are also rugged four-wheel-drive trails throughout the park. These are steep and rocky sometimes, and in the park's own words, "tortuous."

Short walks and long hikes lead to some of the park's most outstanding features. Certain trails have wayside exhibits or brochures, available at trailheads or visitors centers. Because this is a desert area, *the park advises taking a number of precautions:* Carry a gallon of water per person per day (active people may require more); drink water frequently; protect yourself from intense sun by wearing a hat, sunglasses, sunscreen, long pants, and a long-sleeved shirt. Save strenuous activity for early morning or late afternoon. Be wary of climbing slickrock because it's often easy to climb up but impossible to climb down. Use special caution near cliff edges, and keep younger children in hand and older children in sight at all times.

Other Adventures

Moab, the only city in Utah on the Colorado River, is the headquarters for a number of jeep, raft, canoe, jet boat, and airplane tours of the region.

Horseback Riding. **Park Creek Ranch,** Mountain Loop Road, Moab (435-259-5505), operates two-hour horseback trips on the outskirts of Arches National Park from mid-March to the end of October. Kids under five can't ride alone. If doubled-up with a parent, then the pair can go out for a one-hour ride.

Hiking. Trek through the majestic canyons of the Green River with **Sheri Griffith Expeditions,** 2231 South Highway 191, Moab (435-259-8229 or 800-332-2439). Her family outdoor trips feature water games, hiking, bouldering, and camping along sandy beaches.

Rafting. Paddle the Colorado River on a raft and float through Canyonlands (minimum age six) with **Tag-A-Long Expeditions,** 452 North Main, Moab (435-259-8946 or 800-453-3292). You can also canoe the Green River, and then take a jet-boat back on the Colorado.

Canyonlands Field Institute (CFI), P.O. Box 68, Moab (435-259-7750 or 800-860-5262) features a variety of Eco-River Trips, including a two-day/one-night Colorado River journey to Westwater Canyon, on the Colorado-Utah state line near Moab. Spot bald and golden eagles as you float in an open canyon bounded by red sandstone cliffs, and ride one of the largest sets of rapids on the Colorado River. CFI also arranges a variety of programs custom-made for families. Sample programs include Arches National Park and/or BLM Wilderness Study Areas near Moab, and one-day naturalist-guided explorations.

Jeep Tours. Ride across the rugged terrain of the Canyonlands and the miles of jeep trails around Moab with **Tag-A-Long Expeditions,** Moab (435-259-8946 or 800-453-3292).

Dinosaur Tours. Explore significant dinosaur sites on the **Dinosaur Diamond Safari** (children must be sixteen years old), sponsored by **Dinosaur Discovery Expeditions,** 550 Jurassic Court, Fruita, Colorado (800-DIG-DINO). Visit sites in Grand Junction, Colorado, and Moab, Price, and Vernal, Utah (cities that form "The Dinosaur Diamond"). Dinosaur Discovery Expeditions offers a variety of family-oriented educational trips about dinosaurs.

Mountain Biking. Cycle down the popular **Slickrock Bike Trail,** which starts about 3 miles east of town and follows an extremely challenging, clearly marked 10-mile loop. This trail is not for beginners; be sure to pack plenty of water. **Rim Tours,** 1233 South Highway 191 (435-259-5223 or 800-626-7335), offers daily rentals and guided tours that include three- to six-day spring and fall outings to Canyonlands National Park.

Skiing. In the winter, slide down the snowy slopes of the La Sal Mountains with **Tag-A-Long Expeditions** (435-259-8946 or 800-453-3292) on their combination Alpine and Nordic ski trips.

Side Trips

Take some time to explore Moab, a pleasant town with some interesting attractions.

Dan O'Laurie Museum, 118 East Center Street (435-259-7985, closed Sundays). Archaeological, geological, and historical exhibits detail the area's history from the prehistoric Ute Indian days to the uranium boom of the 1950s.

Mill Canyon Dinosaur Trail, 13 miles northwest of Moab on U.S. 191, is an outdoor paleontological museum. Embedded in the landscape along this hour-long hike are dinosaur bones and fossils. Only a short distance from the trail are the remains of the **Halfway Stage Station,** a public rest area used from 1883 to 1904.

The Moab area has been a popular filming location since 1949. The information center provides you with a movie location guide. Locations are accessible with a two-wheel-drive vehicle. Inside **Arches National Park,** for instance, scenes for *Indiana Jones and the Last Crusade* were shot in the Park Avenue and Windows areas; in *Thelma and Louise,* the scene in which an officer is locked in his patrol-car trunk was shot at the Courthouse Towers area.

The small town of **Monticello,** 54 miles south of Moab on U.S. 191, close to the turnoff for the Needles section of Canyonlands, has a cinema, a strip of inexpensive motels, and several eateries. Situated on the edge of the **Abajo** or **Blue Mountains** at 7,050 feet, the town provides superb panoramas of the surrounding countryside. The **San Juan County Multi-Agency Visitor Center,** with information about all of southeast Utah, is at Highway 191 and 100 South. Represented here are the National Park Service, U.S. Forest Service, and Bureau of Land Management. For example, pamphlets about the many ancestral Pueblo (previously known as Anasazi) sites in southeastern Utah may be obtained from the **visitor's center,** 117 South Main (800-574-4386); the

National Park Service, (435-587-2737); or the **Bureau of Land Management (BLM)** (435-587-2141).

Special Events

The communities around Arches and Canyonlands offer a variety of year-round activities. Contact the **Utah Canyonlands Region** (435-259-8825 or 800-635-6622) for more information.

January. Winter Festival, Monticello.

February. Quarter Horse Show, Moab.

March. Canyonlands Half Marathon, Moab; U.S. Mail Trail Ride equestrian event, Green River.

April. Easter Jeep Safari; Bicycle Stage Race; Quarter Horse Show—all in Moab. Jeep Jamboree, Blanding.

May. Annual Arts Festival, Moab.

June. Rodeo; Butch Cassidy Days, Moab.

July. Frontier Days, Blanding; Pioneer Days celebrations, Moab/Monticello; Little Buckaroo Rodeo, Green River.

August. County Fairs, Moab/Monticello; Rodeo, Monticello; Dead Horse Point Square Dance Festival, Moab; Hispanic Folk Festival, Monticello.

September. White Mesa Annual Ute Indian Bear Dance, Blanding; Melon Days, Green River; Utah Navajo Fair, Bluff; Moab Music Festival.

October. Canyonlands Fat Tire Bike Festival; Rock, Gem, and Mineral Show, Moab; Jeep Jamboree, Blanding.

November. "Day of the Dead," community art show, Moab.

December. 10K Winter Sun Run, Moab; Canyonlands Christmas Festival, Moab.

Where to Stay

The park's **Devils Garden** campground is open on a first-come, first-served basis, with water available from mid-March to mid-October. Facilities include tables, grills, and flush toilets. Because the campground is normally full by late morning or early afternoon during peak season, plan to arrive early. The park begins supplying campground permits at 7:30 A.M. Often, in spring, the campground is full within an hour. In summer and fall, the permits are usually all snatched by noon.

Area accommodations are listed in the brochure *Utah's Canyonlands,* available from **Canyonlands Travel Region** at the visitor centers in Moab and Monticello, or call (800) 574-4386, and in the *Utah Travel Guide,* available from the Utah Travel Council (see For More Information). Lodging includes a variety of motels and several bed-and-breakfasts. One possibility is **Comfort Suites,** 800 South Main (435-259-5252 or 800-228-5150), with seventy-five rooms, a pool, hot tub, and kitchens. **Cottonwood Condos,** 338 East 100 South, is in a residential area right off Main Street (435-259-8897 or 800-447-4106). This former apartment house has eight one-bedroom units that come with stocked kitchens and a queen-size sofa in the living room. Linens and towels are provided.

Where to Eat

There is no food served or sold in the park. Moab is where you'll satisfy your appetite. **The Moab Information Center** supplies a restaurant guide. **Bar-M Chuckwagon,** 7000 North Highway 191, Box 724 (800-214-2085), serves hearty cowboy-type vittles, followed by a one-hour Western show with a live band, Native American dancers, and more. It's held every night except Sunday from June through September in an outdoor tent with a retractable canopy top. The restaurant is open Fridays and Saturdays, April through May.

Some local favorites include **The Rio-Colorado Restaurant and Bar,** 2 South 100 West (435-259-6666), which serves Southwestern cuisine, some Mexican, special desserts, and Sunday brunch with full buffet. "Come Taste the West" at the **Branding Iron,** 2971 South Highway 191 (435-259-6275). Open daily, this lounge offers Tex-Mex items such as tacos, chili, grits, and burgers. Entertainment is served on Friday nights with karaoke.

Golden Stake Restaurant, 540 South Main (435-259-7000), is a family-style restaurant that serves steaks, hamburgers, and home-style meals.

For More Information

National Parks: **Arches National Park,** P.O. Box 907, Moab 84532 (435-259-8161); **Canyonlands National Park,** 2282 South West Resource Boulevard, Moab 84532 (435-259-7164). Log on to the National Parks Internet site: www.nps.gov.

Area Tourist Information: **Grand County Travel Council** (Moab Information Center), corner of Main and Center, Moab (435-259-8825 or 800-635-6622); **San Juan County Travel Council** 117 South Main, Monticello (800-574-4386); **Utah Travel Council,** Council Hall/

Capitol Hill, Salt Lake City 84114-1396 (801-538-1030).

Emergency Numbers

The only phones are at the visitor centers. The park has qualified emergency medical personnel who can help the injured or can transport them to San Juan Hospital, 364 West 100 North, Monticello (435-587-2116), or Allen Memorial Hospital, 719 West 400 North (435-259-7191).

Pharmacies: Family Drug, 90 North Main, Moab; (435) 259-7771. San Juan Pharmacy, 148 South Main Street, Monticello (435-587-2302), is open 9:00 A.M. to 7:00 P.M. Monday through Saturday. Closed Sundays.

Poison Control: (800) 456-7707

Salt Lake City

Salt Lake City, the capital of Utah, takes its name from the 80-mile-long Great Salt Lake, 15 miles west of town. The lake features white-sand beaches, beautiful pink-streaked sunsets, and many species of migratory birds. The sprawling city, surrounded by the Wasatch Mountains to the east and north and the Oquirrh Mountains to the west, is a safe area where families can enjoy a relaxed vacation at a slower pace than in most other cities. The city is world headquarters of the Mormon religion, whose first settlers arrived in the valley in 1847. Today more than half of the city's population are members of the Church of Jesus Christ of Latter Day Saints (LDS). The city's Mexican American, Greek, and Japanese communities add some cultural diversity to this clean, inviting city. Currently, the city is preparing to host the 2002 Winter Olympics.

Getting There

Salt Lake City International Airport, 776 North Terminal Drive (801-575-2400), serves most major airlines and is ten minutes west of downtown. Car rentals, cabs, city bus #50 (with hourly departures), and courtesy vans from some of the better hotels provide transportation into the city.

The **Amtrak** station (800-USA-RAIL) is at 320 South Rio Grande. **Greyhound** is at 160 West South Temple (801-355-9589 or 800-231-2222). Interstates 15 and 80 intersect in Salt Lake City.

Getting Around

A car isn't absolutely necessary, thanks to the public transportation system and the fact that most of the main tourist activities cluster right in the heart of town. The streets run at right angles to each other, numbered in a grid scale starting at the center point of Temple Square.

The **Utah Transit Authority**'s bus system (801-287-4636) is extensive and runs throughout the valley. A free-fare zone helps visitors tour

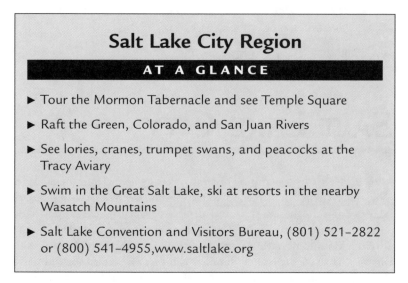

Salt Lake City Region

AT A GLANCE

- Tour the Mormon Tabernacle and see Temple Square
- Raft the Green, Colorado, and San Juan Rivers
- See lories, cranes, trumpet swans, and peacocks at the Tracy Aviary
- Swim in the Great Salt Lake, ski at resorts in the nearby Wasatch Mountains
- Salt Lake Convention and Visitors Bureau, (801) 521-2822 or (800) 541-4955,www.saltlake.org

the downtown area. Call the transit authority for information. An old-fashioned trolley, with pickup points at Trolley Square and Temple Square, circles downtown and major hotels.

What to See and Do

Historical Sites

The center of the city, and the heart of the Mormon religion, historic **Temple Square,** 50 West North Temple, encompasses ten acres enclosed within a 15-foot wall. Inside are the six-spired **Mormon Temple,** the **Tabernacle** (which is the concert hall), **Assembly Hall,** gardens, monuments, and information centers (801-240-2534). Several types of free guided tours are given throughout the day.

Completed in the 1890s, the Temple, constructed from granite and hardwood, took Mormon pioneers forty years to construct. The building rises more than 200 feet above ground at its highest point. Only faithful Mormons may enter the Temple, but millions of visitors are allowed in the adjacent Tabernacle.

The Tabernacle's unusual design catches attention with its domed roof and red sandstone piers. The building's acoustics are amazing; kids, seated in the rear, "ooh" and "aah" when they hear the "cling" of a pin as it hits the floor near the front podium. Public organ recitals take place daily. The public may attend Thursday evening rehearsals of the world-famous **Mormon Tabernacle Choir** and the Sunday morning performances at 9:30 A.M. (You must be seated by 9:15 A.M.) Visitors are also invited to the evening miniconcerts, scheduled throughout the week, by the Mormon Youth Choir and Symphony.

At the **Joseph Smith Memorial Building,** just east of Temple Square, 15 East South Temple (801-240-6738), sit down at one of the 150 family research stations and find out about your ancestors by accessing the computer database. It's open Monday through Saturday from 8:00 A.M. to 10:00 P.M. For more in-depth research, head a block west to the **Family History Library and Museum,** 35 North West Temple (801-240-2331). It has the world's largest collection of genealogical information, including registers, passenger lists, local histories, and much more. You do not need to be a Mormon to access these records or find them useful. The archives cover information on many generations of individuals in more than fifty countries.

Beehive House, 67 East South Temple, a block east of Temple Square (801-240-2671). Here, city-founder Brigham Young made his home in the mid-1800s. See how pioneers conducted their daily lives through displays that include hand-stitched quilts and rugs, butter churns, and iceboxes. Free twenty-minute tours take place regularly throughout the day. The beehive, a symbol of the Mormon work ethic (and the state symbol), is on the building's small tower and is also part of the Utah state seal.

The **State Capitol,** North State Street and Capitol Hill (801-538-3000), is quite impressive, with an ornate interior and great views from Capitol Hill. Admission is free.

Utah Museum of Natural History

Here are 200 million years of history under one roof, with skeletons of Jurassic dinosaurs, Native American artifacts, and an archaeological collection of more than 500,000 objects from 3,800 sites. **Paleontology Hall** is especially popular with kids, who can check out how they measure up to an Apatosaurus leg. In the **Quinney Dinosaur Discovery Hall,** touch real dinosaur specimens and watch staff in a paleontology lab demonstrate how dinosaur fossils are prepared for display. There are changing temporary exhibits and a museum gift shop. Utah Museum of Natural History, 1390 Presidents Circle, University of Utah (801-581-4303; www.umnh.utah.edu).

Museums

While not exactly teeming with museums, Salt Lake City has some kid-friendly places the whole family will enjoy.

At the **Hansen Planetarium,** 15 South State Street (801-538-2104; www.utah.edu/planetarium), you can explore the wonders of the night sky, enjoy 3-D OmniScan laser shows to the music of Led Zeppelin and Pink Floyd, and, using a heliostat, examine solar flares on the face of the sun. Kids love making their hair stand on end when they touch the Van de Graaf generator. Preschoolers enjoy Connie the Comet in the Planetarium's *Tales of a Comet* show. New in 1999 is Where

Salt Lake City's Temple Square holds much in store for visitors.

in the Universe Is Carmen Sandiego? Based on the popular television show, this interactive exhibit takes visitors through the solar system in search of the elusive Carmen.

Utah Museum of Fine Arts, 1530 East South Campus Drive (801-581-7332; www.edu/umfa). This fine collection at the University of Utah includes work by such masters as Jean-Baptiste-Camille Corot, Thomas Gainsborough, Sir Anthony Van Dyck, and Jan Brueghel the Younger, as well as art from North and South America, Asia, Africa, and Oceania, plus period furniture and seventeenth-century tapestries.

The Pioneer Memorial Museum, 300 North Main Street (801-538-1050), has thirty-eight rooms housing an extensive collection of pioneer artifacts. Step back in time to prairie days as you peruse old-fashioned dolls, wooden clocks, and hand-stitched clothing of the period. In the Carriage House is the covered wagon used by Brigham Young to cross the plains, as well as a mule-drawn streetcar. There's also a blacksmith shop, plus more than 50,000 pioneer histories on file.

The Children's Museum of Utah, 840 North 300 West (801-328-3383; www.childmuseum.org). Here kids can walk through an enormous dollhouse to learn about size and scale, experience what it's like to get around in a wheelchair, turn their energies to a climbing wall or being a 747 jet pilot, and visit a pioneer cabin. Regularly scheduled seminars and workshops explain things like how to make a clay pot and how a cow produces milk. There's also a mammoth skull dig and a new toddlers' section for really young adventurers.

Tracy Aviary

Located on eight wooded acres in the southwest corner of Liberty Park is **Tracy Aviary,** 589 East 1300 South (801-322-BIRD; www.tracyaviary.org). A leader in nature education and the oldest public aviary in the world, the facility features more than 1,000 birds, from vultures to eagles, trumpet swans to parrots. Peacocks and pheasants roam freely.

During the summer, a ***Birds of a Feather*** bird show is presented daily at noon and 2:00 P.M. In the **Lory Walk** (lories are small Australian birds), kids delight in feeding the birds apple pieces (under the supervision of trained personnel). And coming in 1999 is a **Red Crowned Crane** exhibit. This crane is the second most endangered crane in the world. It's hoped that the two coming to Tracy Aviary will breed in this bird-friendly environment.

The **Night Hawks** program allows children to spend the night in sleeping bags and learn more about their feathered friends.

Great Salt Lake

The 80-mile-long **Great Salt Lake** is quite marshy and somewhat sticky. Kids are fascinated by the tiny brine shrimp that live in the lake and the "thick" water, which has a salinity rate as high as 27 percent, though the salt concentration is not as high as it used to be. Floating in the lake is still a unique experience. Warning to kids: Don't get a mouthful of this water because it tastes terrible. And if you get water in your eyes, you'll wish you hadn't. The water stings. Be sure to wear eye goggles when swimming.

Catch a rare sight each November on the lake's **Antelope Island.** Modern cowboys employ jeeps and helicopters to round up herds of bison. As the name implies, there are antelope on the island, as well as elk and bighorn sheep, but these herds were introduced after the original animals died off.

One of the most accessible points on the lake is **Saltair Beach State Park,** 16 miles west of the city on I-80 (801-250-4400). Here you'll find white-sand beaches, picnic areas, paddleboats, food concessions, and a parking lot. At the **Saltair Pavilion,** summer concerts take place.

Amusement Parks

Cool off in the huge freshwater pools and on the thirty water slides of **Raging Waters,** 1700 South 1200 West (801-977-8300; www.citysearch.com/slc/ragingwaters). The park has Dinosaur Bay—themed with "active volcanos" and prehistoric playmates—Adventure Cove, a rope swing, Acapulco Cliff Dive, and the Waimea-H_2O Roller Coaster. New attractions

Water Adventures

- **Raft.** Several Salt Lake outfitters offer rafting trips on the Green, Colorado, San Juan, and other rivers from May to September. Try **Holiday River Expeditions;** (801-266-2087 or 800-624-6323; www.bikeraft.com). They also offer trips on the Yampa River in Dinosaur State Park. At **Moki Mac River Expeditions** (801-268-6667 or 800-284-7280), minimum ages vary with the trips. Trips range from one day to two weeks.
- **Cruise.** For a cruise on the Great Salt Lake, try **Salt Island Adventures;** (801-583-4400 or 888-725-8475; www.gslcruises.com). Trips also depart from Antelope Island and Saltair State Park.
- **Sound and Light Show. Canyonlands by Night,** (435-259-5261 or 800-394-9978; www.moab.net/canyonlandsbynight), takes you on a sound and light show on the Colorado River. The canyon walls are bathed in 40,000 watts of illumination.

include the Balboa River Expedition, Splash Island, and the Surfside Cafe.

Lagoon Amusement Park, 17 miles north on I-15 in Framington (801-451-8000; www.lagoonpark.com), is the largest amusement park between Kansas City and the West Coast. Get an all-day passport for access to 125 rides. Colossus the Fire Dragon takes you 85 feet in the air at 55 miles an hour—standing up. Pioneer Village has music, games, and food courts. Little ones like the Baby Boats and Puff the Roller Coaster. An RV park and campground are adjacent to the park.

The **Utah Fun Dome,** off 700 West (801-263-8769). This entertainment mall has an 80-foot bungee tower (but we don't recommend jumping; just watch), bowling, video games, laser tag, indoor and outdoor miniature golf, arcades, go-carts, roller skating, and rides. There's also a food court with lots of choices.

Ogden's Eccles Dinosaur Park, 1544 East Park Boulevard in Ogden (801-393-DINO), is thirty minutes from Salt Lake City on I-15, exit 347. This outdoor park, open from April through October, has more than one hundred life-size dinosaurs and flying reptiles. Coming in 1999, a Paleontology Lab, where kids can watch dinosaur bones being prepared for exhibit and can touch real dinosaur eggs. On site are a gift shop and the Raptor Cafe.

Parks and Zoos

Hogle Zoo, 2600 East Sunnyside Avenue (800-582-1631; www.hoglezoo.org), is home to more than 1,400 furry, feathered, and scaly creatures from

Special Tours

- **Trains.** One hour's drive from Salt Lake, in Heber City, is the **Heber Valley Railroad,** 450 South 600 West (435-654-5601 or 801-581-9980; www.hebervalleyrr.org), Utah's steam passenger railroad. The train crosses the farmland of Heber Valley, follows the Deer Creek Lake, and descends into the breathtaking, pine-filled Provo Canyon. Special events throughout the year include murder mysteries, bluegrass music, storytelling, and dances. There's a snack bar and a gift shop.
- **Beer.** Find out how beer is brewed by taking the free microbrewery tour offered every Saturday at noon at the **Salt Lake Brewing Company,** 367 West 200 South (801-538-2104), an award-winning microbrewery.
- **City Tour.** Take the time to try **Old Salty** (801-359-8677 or 800-826-5844), a two-hour summer tour of Salt Lake's main attractions aboard open-air railcars that leave from Temple Square.
- **Silver Mine.** Travel 1,500 feet down in a mine shaft to a 3,200-foot tunnel that in its heyday created twenty-two millionaires. **The Park City Silver Mine Adventure,** on Route 224, 1½ miles south of Park City (800-467-3828; www.netpp.com/pcsilvermine), is fun for everyone except the claustrophobic. Visitors learn how the mine worked, see where the horses were kept, and witness a simulated mine blast. Topside there are core samples and mining equipment on display, as well as a man-made drift where deposits of pyrite and other treasures can be dug for. And the Lunch Bucket Cafe and Tommy Knockers Sweet Shop provide meals and snacks. There's also a gift shop.

around the world. Those with special kid-appeal: The Great Apes exhibit, the African Savannah, and the polar bear cub twins born on Thanksgiving Day, 1998. Don't miss the hands-on Discovery Land, where kids experience what it feels like to be an animal, sliding down the middle of a hollow tree or "burrowing" under the earth. Tiny tots might like to touch the critters at the Small Wonders Barn, and everybody can enjoy a ride on the scale model of a CP Huntington Steam Locomotive that loops around the east end of the zoo, past a few zoo residents that can be seen close up. A new entry plaza is coming in 1999, with new attractions for the kids.

Stroll through thirty acres of gardens at the **Red Butte Garden,** the University of Utah, off South Campus Drive on the eastern edge of Fort

Land and Air Adventures

- **Ballooning.** Float above the city and surrounding countryside. **The Great Balloon Escape** (435-645-9400) offers flights for all ages—with or without champagne—over some of Utah's most beautiful terrain.
- **Gambling.** For daily luxury bus service from Salt Lake to the largest casinos in Wendover, Nevada, try **Casino Caravans** (801-685-9311 or 800-876-5825).
- **Dog sledding.** The **Wasatch Adventure Company** provides the dogs, sleds, and guides. You only need to hold on. This company also can arrange spelunking in caves, hang gliding and paragliding, rock climbing, scuba diving in geothermal caves, and snowshoeing in the Rockies.

Douglas (801-581-IRIS; www.utah.edu/redbutte). This is a pastoral, take-a-break place with duck ponds, water lilies, abundant floral displays, and rare plants. Outside the main garden, another one hundred acres remain in their natural state, except for the easy hiking trails that are open to visitors. These trails take you to a shady streamside canyon and ridge tops more than 500 feet above the valley floor for a spectacular view of the surrounding Wasatch Mountains and the Salt Lake Valley below. Throughout the year, educational and recreational programs are offered, including concerts and kids' programs; call ahead for schedule. Admission on the first Monday of every month is free.

Liberty Park, Seventh East between Ninth and Thirteenth South (801-972-7800), offers sixteen wooded acres of outdoor recreation, with tennis courts, walkways, concessions, a children's play/garden area, and a pond with paddleboats. At the Seven Canyons Fountain, visitors can "walk" Utah's mountains. The fountain is a topographical map depicting the Wasatch Front and its canyons, covering about an acre. Each canyon is labeled, and water representing the actual rivers flows down each one.

This Is the Place Heritage Park, 2600 Sunnyside Avenue (801-584-8391), below the mouth of Emigration Canyon on the east side of the city, marks the end of the Mormon Trail, used over a twenty-two-year period by 68,000 pioneers migrating from Illinois. Old Deseret Village is a re-creation of pioneer life in Utah between 1847 and 1869. Costumed hosts greet visitors in buildings (some reconstructions, most relocated original dwellings, including Brigham Young's Farmhouse) with authentic furnishings. At the visitors center, a mural and audio presentations detail the migration of the Mormon pioneers. An ice-cream saloon and carriage rides add to the fun.

The park is also the home of This Is the Place Monument, 2601 Sunnyside Avenue, commemorating the site where Brigham Young first declared, "This is the place," referring to a safe refuge for the Mormon people. The monument is 60 feet high and 86 feet long, making it one of the largest in the United States. From the monument, enjoy a breathtaking view of the valley below.

Go country at **Wheeler Farm,** 6351 South Ninth East (801-

264-2212). At this horse-powered seventy-five-acre dairy, visitors can help milk cows, feed chickens, gather eggs each afternoon, and afterward tour the restored 1898 farmhouse. Nature walks, wagon rides, farming and weaving demonstrations, songs, and pioneer stories are part of the fun. December brings Christmas on the Farm, with wagon rides, Santa, a nativity play, and homemade decorations.

Theater, Music, and the Arts

Salt Lake Convention and Visitors Bureau (801-521-2822 or 800-541-4955) provides information on cultural attractions, or consult the morning *Salt Lake Tribune* or evening *Deseret News*. The city hosts several theaters, including the **Pioneer Theater Company** at the University of Utah (801-581-6961 or 801-581-5682), a well-respected regional theater with equity actors in leading roles. **Salt Lake Repertory Theater** (City Rep), 148 South Main Street (801-532-6000), stages musical comedies. There is also the **Promised Valley Playhouse,** 132 South State Street (801-364-5696).

Ballet West (801-393-6901; www.balletwest.org), **Ririe-Woodbury Modern Dance Company** (801-328-1062), and **University of Utah's Repertory Dance Theater** (801-581-6702) all perform at the Capitol Theater, 50 West 200 South (801-534-4364), as does the **Utah Opera Company** (801-355-ARTS; www.utahopera.org).

The **Utah Symphony** gives concerts year-round at Abravanel Hall, 123 West South Temple (801-533-5626).

Sports

Salt Lake Buzz minor league baseball team plays from mid-June to Labor Day at Franklin Covey Field, 77 West 1300 South (801-485-3800; tickets, 325-BASE; www.buzz.fanlink.com.). The popular NBA **Utah Jazz** basketball games are held at Delta Center, 301 West South Temple (801-355-DUNK; www.utahjazz.com).

Utah's women's professional basketball team, the **Utah Starzz,** also play at the Delta Center (801-355-DUNK; www.wnba.com/starzz). The **Utah Grizzlies** professional hockey team, plays at the 'E' Center in West Valley City (801-988-8000).

Shopping

Trolley Square, 600 South 700 East, is a complex of fashionable shops, eateries, and theaters in buildings that used to house the town's electric trolleys. Just south of Temple Square, you'll find two enormous downtown shopping malls. **Crossroads Plaza,** 50 South Main (801-531-1799; www.crossroadsplaza.com), with four floors of shops and restaurants; and **ZCMI Center Uptown,** 36 South State (801-321-8743), with two floors of stores, including the ZCMI Department Store and a food court.

Gardner Village, 1100 West 7800 South, West Jordan (801-566-8903; www.gardnervillage.com). The village features old-style shops and the 1877 Gardner Mill, converted into a country store. In the village, **Archibald's Restaurant** (801-566-6940), a former grain silo, serves up teriyaki chicken, fish, salads, and other dishes. The builder of the silo, Archibald Gardner, was a Mormon during the time when polygamy was still accepted. Each booth has a portrait portraying one of Gardner's eight wives, along with a brief history of her life.

If you're a fan of the Sundance catalog, you'll want to stop by the **Sundance Catalog Outlet Store,** 1460 South Foothill Drive (801-581-9711), to see the unique collection of home furnishings, men's and women's fashions, and jewelry, all discounted from original catalog prices.

And in the spirit of the 2002 Olympics, there are three **U.S. Olympic Spirit Stores** to choose from. Call (801) 364-9994 to find which is closest to you. All three sell Olympic T-shirts, jackets, hats, and collectibles.

SIDE TRIPS

Salt Lake City is the gateway to nine ski resorts, all located within an hour of downtown. This is a skier's paradise, as the season runs from November until May or June. The UTA (801-BUS-INFO) provides daily buses to Alta, Brighton, Solitude, and Snowbird. (See the Wasatch chapter for additional information on Utah ski areas as well as the recreational opportunities of the Wasatch National Forest.)

In summer, these slopes offer families great hikes and a variety of recreational opportunities. **Snowbird** (801-521-6040) and **Solitude** (801-534-1400) offer weekend mountain-bike clinics for all levels. In addition, in summer take the aerial tram to the summit of Hidden Peak for splendid views of Heber Valley and the canyons of the Wasatch Mountains. Two trails lead back to the base, about a two-hour hike. Guided hiking tours can be arranged.

Kennecott's Bingham Canyon Mine, U-48, Copperton (801-322-7300). Located 22 miles west of Salt Lake City, the canyon is the largest man-made excavation on earth—2½ miles from rim to rim. A visitors center houses an exhibit explaining the pit's geology and open-pit copper-mining operations. A theater features a twelve-minute video on the mine. The center provides a bird's-eye view into the huge open pit where trucks and shovels appear to be toy-size. Open April to October, it's worth seeing.

Adventure

Salt Lake City is a good starting point for heading to the state's five national parks, all a day's drive away: Arches and Canyonlands (see the Arches chapter), Capitol Reef, Bryce Canyon, and Zion. Contact the Utah Travel Council for more information.

Originally constructed for the U.S. Ski Team, and slated to be one of the venues for the 2002 Winter Olympic games, the **Utah Winter Sports Park** offers ski-jumping facilities to the public. Certified instructors will teach thrill seekers aged three to eighty-three. Also available are ice rocket rides.

Special Events

Contact the Salt Lake Convention and Visitors Bureau for more information on the following events.

January. Sundance Film Festival, Robert Redford's outlet for independent filmmakers, held in Salt Lake, Park City, and Sundance (801-225-4107).

March. Music in the Mountains offers a variety of musical talents.

April. Mountain Man Rendezvous; Fielding Garr Ranch House (801-773-2941).

May. Cinco de Mayo Festival, Utah State Fair Park (801-359-2521); Asian Festival (801-271-4264); Sailing Celebration and Race Week, Great Salt Lake (801-250-1898); Utah Square Dance Festival (801-277-4132).

June. Utah Arts Festival with performing artists, crafts, children's art yard, and environmental exhibitions; Gina Bachauer International Piano Festival, with world-class international prodigies and performers competing (801-521-9200); Utah Scottish Association Highland Games, Fort Douglas (801-571-6212).

July. Jazz and Blues Festival, Snowbird (801-742-3300); Inter-tribal Native American Celebration (801-533-9503); The Days of '47 Celebration honors the arrival of the pioneers in 1847, with square dancing, fireworks, rodeos, and one of the biggest parades in the U.S.A.

August. Belly Dancing Festival, with Middle Eastern food and festivities; Nature Fair, Tracy Aviary.

September. Utah State Fair; Greek Festival, three days of dancing, performances, and plenty of baklava.

October. World of Speed finals, Bonneville Salt Flats (801-785-5364); Buffalo Round-up, Antelope Island; Latin American Festival, Gallivan Center (801-263-3001).

November. Historic Temple Square Christmas Lighting Ceremony electrifies 250,000 lights that decorate the square; a Dickens Festival with Christmas shops and entertainment operates from late November to mid-December at the Utah State Fair Park.

December. Candlelight Christmas Tour, This is the Place Heritage Park, features caroling and costumed pioneer families who welcome visitors to their period-decorated homes and share stories and cookies.

Where to Stay

The *Salt Lake Visitors Guide* has a comprehensive listing of lodgings, including several bed-and-breakfasts. Because tourism is Utah's number-one industry, expect a wide choice of reasonably priced accommodations. If you plan to visit on the first weekend in April or October, when Mormons from other regions congregate here, be sure to reserve well in advance.

Downtown. **Peery,** 110 West 300 South Street (801-521-4300 or 800-331-0073). The city's oldest lodging is an elegant, renovated seventy-seven-room hotel with in-room movies, free breakfast, free cribs, and two restaurants. **Doubletree Hotel,** 255 South West Temple (801-328-2000) is large and modern, with 495 rooms and nineteen suites (some with refrigerators), a pool, free airport shuttle, restaurant, and coffee shop. **The Quality Inn City Center,** 154 West 600 South (801-521-2930 or 800-521-9997), offers well-priced, comfortable accommodations.

Elsewhere. **The Residence Inn by Marriott,** 765 East 400 South (801-532-5511 or 800-331-3131), is 8 blocks from downtown and 1 block from Trolley Square. Suites sleep up to six, and there's an outdoor pool, complimentary continental breakfast, and free airport shuttles. **Embassy Suites Hotel,** 600 South West Temple (801-359-7800 or 800-362-2779), offers another suite option for families, plus an indoor pool.

Budget accommodations are available at **Travelodge,** 524 South West Street (801-531-7100 or 800-255-3050), and the **Shilo Inn,** 206 South West Temple (801-521-9500 or 800-222-2244). Both are near numerous restaurants, and the Shilo Inn has a pool.

Where to Eat

Salt Lake Visitor's Guide has a restaurant section with maps and descriptions. Here are some good family choices.

Ruth's Diner, 2100 Emigration Canyon Road (801-582-5807). About ten minutes from downtown, the diner is known for its great breakfasts (lunch and dinner also served) presented amid 1940s decor.

Right next door is the **Santa Fe Restaurant,** 2100 Emigration Canyon Road (801-582-5888), which has a romantic Southwest lodge setting and serves a Sunday brunch buffet, plus daily lunch and dinner.

Cafe Pierpont, 122 West Pierpont Avenue (801-364-1222). Located in a renovated school, this restaurant welcomes families with Mexican fajitas, enchiladas, fresh tortillas, and nachos. **Brackman Brothers Bagels,** 147 South Main (801-537-5033), the best place for New York-style bagels, also sells sandwiches and snacks.

Check out the elaborate setting, as well as the Mexican and American food, at **Totem's Club and Cafe,** 538 South Redwood Road (801-975-0401). Wooden pillars, wagon wheels, spouting fountains, and live entertainment add to the western-lodge feel. Because the restaurant is a bit out of the way, many of the downtown hotels provide shuttle service.

For More Information

Salt Lake Convention and Visitors Bureau, 180 South West Temple (800-541-4955 or 801-521-2822; www.saltlake.org). **Utah Travel Council,** 300 North State Street, Capitol Hill Council Hall, Salt Lake City 84114 (801-538-1030 or 800-222-UTAH). **Visitor Information Center,** Temple Square at South Temple Street (801-240-2534), has information on the Mormon church.

Emergency Numbers

Ambulance, fire, police: 911

Hospitals: Holy Cross Hospital, 1045 East 100 South; (801) 350-4111

Primary Children's Medical Center, 100 North Medical Drive; (801) 588-2233; main number 588-2000

Poison Control twenty-four-hour hotline: (801) 581-2151 or (800) 456-7707

Twenty-four-hour pharmacy: Located inside the grocery store Harmon's, 3200 South 1300 East; (801) 487-5461.

21 Utah

Wasatch-Cache National Forest and Ski Vacations

The Wasatch-Cache National Forest—more than a million acres of lakes, forests, canyons, and mountains located north, east, and southeast of Salt Lake City—provides families with a variety of year-round vacation possibilities. The Wasatch Mountains, part of the Rocky Mountain range, are home to several ski areas, some considered among the best in the country, with slopes for every age and ability. Many ski resorts stay open all year, offering hiking, mountain biking, and other fair-weather recreation.

Getting There

Salt Lake International Airport, 776 North Terminal Drive (801-575-2400), is served by most major airlines. Car rentals are available. Salt Lake City's **Amtrak** is at 320 South Rio Grande (800-USA-RAIL). **Greyhound** is at 160 West South Temple (800-231-2222).

Getting Around

On a ski vacation, you may not need a car if you plan to spend most of your time at the resort or on the slopes. Shuttle buses transport skiers from the airport and downtown Salt Lake City to the ski resorts. Call **Canyon Transportation** at (435) 225-1841 or (800) 255-1841. **Lewis Brothers Stages** (435-359-8677 or 800-826-5849) operates buses from the airport and downtown, plus **Canyon Jumper** buses from Park City to Alta, Snowbird, Solitude, and Sundance. **Share-A-Ride Van Services** is available upon request from the airport or downtown to all locations along the Wasatch Front. There's also **Park City Transportation,** 1555 Lower Ironhorse Loop, Park City 84060 (435-649-8567 or 800-637-3803). **Utah**

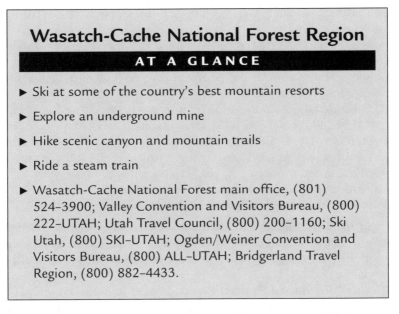

Wasatch-Cache National Forest Region

AT A GLANCE

- Ski at some of the country's best mountain resorts
- Explore an underground mine
- Hike scenic canyon and mountain trails
- Ride a steam train
- Wasatch-Cache National Forest main office, (801) 524-3900; Valley Convention and Visitors Bureau, (800) 222-UTAH; Utah Travel Council, (800) 200-1160; Ski Utah, (800) SKI-UTAH; Ogden/Weiner Convention and Visitors Bureau, (800) ALL-UTAH; Bridgerland Travel Region, (800) 882-4433.

Transit Authority's Ski Bus (801-287-4636) operates to and from most downtown hotels, with several stops around the valley.

What to See and Do

Skiing

The Wasatch Mountains, with an average of 500 inches of snow yearly, feature some of the country's best skiing. Utah's snow—a dry, light powder—has been dubbed by some "the greatest snow on earth." The U.S. Ski Team likes it—they're based in Park City. The area will play a significant role in the 2002 Olympic Winter Games.

Another bonus for families heading to Utah: several ski areas all within an hour's drive of Salt Lake City's airport. This proximity makes turning your vacation into a ski sampler easy to do. Stay at one or two areas and test the terrain at several more. In addition, companies such as **Ski Utah Interconnect Adventure Tour** (801-534-1907) lead the hearty and experienced on day-long ski explorations of as many as five of the region's ski areas. For brochures, contact (800) SKI-UTAH.

Big Cottonwood Canyon. **Brighton** is 30 miles southeast on Star Route 152 (801-532-4731 or 800-873-5512; www.skibrighton.com). Known as "the place where Salt Lake learns to ski." Brighton was voted number one for child/family-friendly terrain and best value by Utahns in the *Wasatch Parent* magazine reader poll. This is a great place for beginners, with 21 percent of the runs just for them. Kinderski classes lasting one-and-a-half-hours are offered for ages four to seven three times daily. Ages eight and older take group lessons and can also take snowboarding lessons. Two children up to ten years old ski free with one paying adult; seniors seventy and older also ski free. the Alpine Rose cafeteria is available for meals and snacks.

Solitude Mountain Resort is 28 miles southeast on Star Route 152 (801-534-1400 or 800-748-4754; www.skisolitude.com). Rated as one of the top forty North American ski resorts, Solitude has The Moonbeam Ski and Snowboard Academy offering instruction and full-day supervised skiing and snowboarding for kids four through twelve. (Kids also enjoy the troll-themed terrain garden.) Solitude's Nordic Center offers 20 kilometers of groomed trails through the canyons, forests, and fields.

Little Cottonwood Canyon. Little Cottonwood Canyon is our favorite place to ski in Utah. While Snowboard and Alta are just 1 mile apart, they are vastly different. Both are great for families and both offer world-class skiing.

Snowbird Ski and Summer Resort, 28 miles southeast on Utah 210 (801-933-2100 or 800-232-9542; www.snowbird.com). Snowbird, unlike Alta, is a big, bustling, modern resort designed with a pedestrian village of condominium and a luxurious hotel that flank the base area. Both Alta and Snowbird have great skiing and Little Cottonwood Canyon's famous 500-plus inches of snow, but unlike Alta, Snowbird welcomes snowboarders. The Gad II lift makes the entire mountain accessible to riders. For those who want to ski both areas (and you should), Snowbird operates a shuttle to and from Alta.

Some experts say Snowbird combines the best, most challenging U.S. terrain with the best lodging facilities. Interestingly, 50 percent of the mountain is designated beginner and intermediate. This combination of challenging, expert trails and varied and abundant runs for skiers of lesser abilities makes Snowbird a find for families with mixed-skill skiers. A high-speed tram whisks 125 riders at a time to the 11,000-foot summit, Hidden Peak, in eight minutes, doing a great deal to eliminate both lift lines and mountain crowding. From Hidden Peak, experts tackle the double-black diamonds of Peruvian Gulch ski area to the east (such as High Baldy and Silver Fox), plus an array of challenging steeps.

Intermediates and novices take the Gad Lifts to ski the blue and green trails of the gentler Gad Valley to the west. Fun runs include Lunch Run, Bassackwards, and Big Emma. Baby Thunder chair lift takes you to thirty acres of terrain, most of it tailored to beginners and intermediates. From the base area you can ride the shuttle bus to this lift. There are designated family ski areas where speed demons aren't allowed.

For Kids: For nonskiing children, Snowbird features child care for ages

The scenery in Wasatch-Cache National Forest's Logan Canyon is nothing short of spectacular.

six weeks to three years, as well as Camp Snowbird, a day-long child-care program for ages three to twelve. Located in a bright room in the Cliff Lodge, the Camp Snowboard Nursery is a state-licensed child-care facility. Only thirty-five little ones from infancy to three years can be accommodated so be sure to make nursery reservations when you book your lodging. From early January to mid-April, every Friday night from 6:30 to 10:00 P.M., ages three to twelve make friends, do crafts, watch movies, and eat dinner together. Participants should register one day in advance.

The ski school's Chickadees program for three- to four-year-olds guarantees personalized attention by pairing two children with similar ability with one instructor. These one-and-a-half-hour sessions are like semiprivate lessons, but at a reduced price. For older children, Snowbird features all-day and afternoon-only child/teen super classes for ages five to fifteen. Super classes, available for skiers and for snowboarders, include lessons, lunch, pizza parties, and "cookie" races.

For Teens: Along with super classes for teens, Snowbird lures this hard-to-please group with Wings. This six-hour mountain adventure, offered daily for all levels of teen skiers and boarders, provides group camaraderie and coaching in ski and riding techniques. Our young testers not only gave Wings rave reviews, but they liked the fact that teens are a significant (but not overwhelming) part of the Snowbird population. Snowbird takes care of teens off the slopes, with activities available at selected times. Teens climb the walls with Radical Rock, an evening outing to the nearby Snowbird Canyon Racquet Club; and meet each other at Saturday Fusion, a you-pick-it agenda of movies, swimming, mochas, and sodas. (Available certain Saturdays January through April).

Good deals: As part of its increased commitment to families, Snowbird frequently offers Kids Ski Free program throughout the season. Up to two children age twelve and younger ski all chairs free with each adult who purchases an all-day chair or tram ticket.

Alta, P.O. Box 8007 (801-359-1078 or 800-707-2582; www.altaskiarea.com).

Alta is an entirely different type of ski area. The experience reminds one of being at a European ski hideaway. Alta claims the distinction of being the second-oldest lift-serviced ski area in North America. Ever since 1939, when the chairlift began operation, Alta's mountain has been tempting recreational skiers.

The mountain is still the magic here. Unlike other ski areas, the Alta Ski Lifts Company operates the lifts, and the other businesses, whether restaurants or lodges, are owned individually. About a dozen small inns and hotels scattered nearby lodge guests. The atmosphere is low-key, almost funky. The base lodge is small and serviceable with an eatery, ski shop, and a children's area, and little or no apres-ski activities. At Alta nightlife is what you make it. There are no snowmobile companies or other nonski attractions.

This is a skier's mountain, pure and simple. Snowboarding is prohibited. Along with the well-suited destination skiers, Alta attracts its share of locals, many skiing in jeans or overalls, attracted by the combination of low lift prices and exceptional terrain. Alta keeps its mountain uncrowded by operating just eight lifts and no quads. If you are not staying at an area lodge, arrive early. When the parking lots are full, the ski area doesn't accept any additional skiers.

Expert runs predominate at Alta, but enough blue and a few green trails exist to keep less qualified skiers happy. Crooked Mile is a particularly satisfying green run, gentle, long, laced with tall pines, and wide. Tamer expert trails wind down Breeley Bowl, Westward Ho, and Wildcat Ridge.

For Kids: The Alta Children's Center takes care of nonskiers from ages two months to twelve years, although most of the children enrolled tend to be between three and six.

Mini-Adventures is a group program for ages four to six, providing two hours of skiing, plus lunch, and a half day of day care. Mountain Explorers offers skiing and group fun for ages seven to twelve.

Alta Lodge, one of the area's overnight choices, offers a free apres-ski program for children ages four to eleven. The evening activities begin at 4:00 P.M. usually with a craft.

For Teens. At busy times there are special teen classes that challenge and supervise knowledgeable skiers. Our teen testers gave a hearty thumbs up to a skills workshop on moguls. But remember: Alta doesn't allow snowboarders.

Good Deals: Lift tickets are low here; generally, almost half the price of Park City, Deer Valley, and other Utah ski areas.

Provo Canyon. Laid back, environmentally conscious, and just plain beautiful, **Sundance,** RR3, Box A4, Sundance (801-225-4107 or 800-892-1600), is on 6,000 acres of protected wilderness at the base of Utah's mighty 12,000-foot Mount Timpanogos. This relatively small resort offers 450 acres of downhill skiing and 14 kilometers of cross-country trails. About a half hour from the Salt Lake City airport, this retreat was created by Robert Redford in 1969. The property features ninety-three cottages and ten mountain homes tastefully accented with Native American crafts and Western hand-hewn furniture. Both Alpine and Nordic skiing are available, as is ski archery and snowshoeing. The Sundance Kids ski school has programs that include all-day supervision, lunch, and instruction. Group lessons are available for kids ages six and older. The restaurants use produce grown organically in Sundance's own greenhouse.

Park City. Located about forty-five minutes east of Salt Lake on I-80 and U-224, the former mining town of Park City is now home to trendy restaurants and boutiques. It also sports three resorts that offer something for every level of ability. The upcoming 2002 Winter Olympic Games will be held in Salt Lake City; the Park City area will be the site of a large number of the competitions, many of them held at the new **Utah Winter Sports Park** in Bear Hollow, 4 miles west of Park City on Route 224 (435-658-4200). The park has four Nordic jumps, a freestyle jump, an Olympic bobsled/luge track, and a snowboard half-pipe, and is open to the public.

Park City Mountain Resort, 1345 Lowell Avenue, Highway 224 (435-649-8111 or 800-222-PARK; www.parkcitymountain.com). This is Utah's biggest ski area, with ninety-seven designated trails, 750 acres of open-bowl skiing, and a mixture of beginner, intermediate, and expert terrain. Park City is also Utah's only real ski town. Once a rough-and-tumble mining camp where claim jumpers and shoot-outs were as common as the silver deposits that drew hordes of prospectors in the 1870s, Park City now charms skiers. Main Street, with its nineteenth-century frontier facades, is listed on the National Register of Historic Places, although what were once bordellos and saloons are now trendy restaurants and boutiques. This makes Park City the place to stay if your children, particularly your teens, crave shopping, people-watching and off-the-slopes fun. There's lots to do besides ski, especially important if yours is a "mixed" family of skiers and nonskiers.

Park City recently opened its slopes to snowboarders. Ski Adventure, for three-year-olds and new skiers ages four to six offers personal instruction and lunch. Kinderschule, for ages four to six with some experience, offers ski instruction, snacks or lunch, and fun kid-oriented activities. A Youth School provides group lessons tailored for kids seven to fourteen years of age. Mountain Experience classes draw many preteens and teens. Quick Carve (a new way to make the transition from skis to snowboards) and kids' Burton snowboard lessons are offered, as are Black Diamond Tours for advanced adventurers who want to try Jupiter Peak and the newly opened bowls on Pinecone Ridge. Park City Mountain Resort's **National Ability Center** (435-649-3991) arranges year-round sports and recreational opportunities for children and adults with disabilities, including a winter ski program. This has been rated the best of its kind in the nation.

The Canyons (formerly Wolf Mountain), 4000 The Canyons Drive (435-649-5400 or 888-CANYONS; www.thecanyons.com), is Utah's newest ski resort. Although the terrain is geared more toward intermediate and advanced skiers, The Canyons also has Kids Central for toddlers to teens. The "skiers in diapers" program offers private lessons for toddlers eighteen months to three years. The Perfect Kids program offers day care for kids eighteen months and older, providing ski and snowboard instruction, snacks and lunch, and fun activities. Friday and Saturday evenings there's a tubing park for families. The Canyons has Utah's largest half-pipe, the Launch Pad.

Deer Valley, 2250 Deer Valley Drive South, Highway 224 (435-649-1000 or 800-558-3337; www.deervalley.com). If you crave resort amenities and first-class pampering with your western ski adventure, come here; but remember, snowboarders are not allowed. The emphasis at Deer Valley is on service, which begins with the ski valets. (Yes, Virginia, there really are ski valets.) These cheery helpers remove your skis, poles, and other gear from your car before you park, eliminating one of the first burdens of family skiing: schlepping all that heavy equipment from a sometimes distant parking spot to the lift area.

Truly friendly hosts come over to chat with you at the base area and guide you on complimentary mountain tours. Even at lunch, the food is very good (don't pass up the turkey chili) and at dinner the entrees (smoked trout, blackened tuna, mussels in broth, and lots more at the unlimited seafood buffet) veer into the superb category. As a result, Deer Valley attracts its share of the rich and famous. But rest assured; we're told that the glitterati are treated as "just folks" and the atmosphere remains friendly. You and your family will feel welcome and comfortable, even if you're not famous and even if your ski attire is more put-together than pricey Bogner.

Just about 1 mile away from downtown Park City, Deer Valley offers you easy access (via car) to all of Park City's off-the-slopes attractions. Like the Park City Ski Area, Deer Valley will be the site of several of the events for the 2002 Olympic Winter Games. The big distinction between the two areas: ambience. Deer Valley's philosophy is to be a fine resort that just happens to be attached to a ski mountain.

The mountain was carefully thought-out, with runs following natural fall lines; this, combined with the expert grooming, makes skiing a variety of terrain easy. Ski aficionados say the slopes here are just a bit tamer than those at Park City. Known primarily for its intermediate trails, Deer Valley has added eight new runs of beginner and intermediate terrain. The Snowflake and Burns chairlifts service guests learning to ski. Success is for competent beginners; Last Chance is a wide cruising run for intermediates. On Lower Bald Mountain which features smooth beginner and intermediate terrain, is the blue-rated Big Stick. Bald Mountain sports steeper skiing. Experts like Morning Star and Fortune Teller, both black diamonds for those who want to ski trees. Flagstaff Mountain features quick cruisers such as Hawkeye and Lucky Star, as well as the difficult, double black diamond Ontario Bowl.

For Kids: The Children's Center offers day care and activities for infants and children two months old to twelve years old. (Reservations are strongly recommended.) For older children, there's the Adventure Club, with a variety of programs, including group lessons for kids in first grade through twelve years old. There's a full-day Bambi Special for ages three to four and a half- and full-day Reindeer Club for ages four and a half through kindergarten, with lessons, snow play, and indoor activities.

For Teens: Teen Equipe workshops for ages thirteen to seventeen, offered periodically throughout the season, feature a full day of challenging skiing. Deer Valley, alas, doesn't allow snowboarding.

Summer on the Slopes

Several of these area resorts also offer warm-weather pleasures.

Snowbird's aerial tram stops at the top of Hidden Peak, offering mountain bikers a spectacular 11,000-foot view of canyons and valleys. The tramway is open daily year-round except in May and from late October to late November. Golf, swimming, and biking are also offered. Snowbird's summer sizzles for kids with Camp Snowbird Day Camp for ages four to twelve, featuring activities such as panning for gold, hiking, tennis, nature studies, movies, and crafts. The camp operates weekdays from early June through the Friday before Labor Day. Overnight camps and workshops for older kids, held on selected dates, include swimming, tram rides, nature studies, and more. For further information and reservations, call (801) 521-6040, ext. 5026.

Snowshoeing and Snowmobiling

Nonskiing activities in Deer Valley include the **Norwegian School of Natural Life** (435-649-5322 or 800-649-5322), which has programs (including snowshoe tours) designed around the needs and abilities of the participants and **Snowest Snowmobile Tours** (435-645-7669 or 800-499-7600, ext. 2001), which rents snowmobiles. Dogsledding, sleigh rides, and hot air balloon rides are available through **ABC Reservations Central** (435-649-ABCD, ext. 2223, or 800-820-ABCD, ext.2223).

At **Sundance** summer's bonuses include hillsides of wildflowers, horseback trail rides and day trips, guided hikes, hot air balloon flights, fly-fishing forays, hayride dinners, waterskiing clinics, outdoor theater, free movies, and low lodging rates. The Sundance Kids Day Camp, from 9:00 A.M. to 4:00 P.M. Monday through Saturday for ages six to twelve, features Native American myths and crafts, hiking and horseback riding, and a theater workshop. There are also helicopter tours and a three-hour round-trip hiking and cave tour through the Timpanogos Cave.

Strap your mountain bikes to the chairs of **Solitude's Moonbeam Lift** for the ride that leads to 25 miles of trails for all levels of cycling. Bike and accessory rentals are also available. For kids four to twelve, there's Camp Solitude (801-536-5700), open from June to August. There's hiking, swimming, arts and crafts, and games, and kids are encouraged to have fun outdoors while learning about nature. Trout fishing and fly-fishing are available along Big Cottonwood Creek or Silver Lake nearby.

Deer Valley's Sterling Lift near Silver Lake Lodge carries mountain bikers up to thirteen trails totaling 20 miles for beginner to advanced rides (more terrain planned soon). Open Wednesday through Sunday afternoons, with extended hours weekends and holidays, the lifts can be accessed with an all-day pass. Bike and helmet rentals are available at the Silver Lake ticket office at the base; call (435) 645-6733 for more information. Children must be accompanied by a paid adult eighteen or older. The resort also has a 4.8-mile primarily singletrack course—the former site of World Cup mountain bike action. More summer fun: a swim and tennis club open Memorial through Labor days, where everyone is welcome; call (801) 649-1000 for information. Summer Adventure Camp (435-649-1000) for kids ages five to twelve, offers mountain trail exploring, weekly field trips, creative arts and crafts, and swimming from June to August.

Guided meal or trail horseback rides provided by Park City Stables leave from both Deer Valley and Park City resorts. For reservations and information, call Rocky Mountain Recreation (435) 645-7256. (This company operates fishing and pack trips and winter snowmobile tours; minimum age is six for all trips.) The horseback rides are offered from Memorial Day through mid-October, and there are pony rides for the kids in the summer. **Park City Resort** also has a pony corral for younger kids, an Alpine Slide (younger kids slide down with a parent), a Little Miners Theme Park, with scaled-down rides for ages six and under, and a terrific miniature golf course.

The town of **Park City** is part of a nationwide Rails to Trails program that converts abandoned rail lines for multiuse recreation. The town's 20-mile rail trail is great for biking as well as easy nature walks. To find out more about bike rentals from local shops and hotels, or to get a free Park City Bike Guide, call the Chamber Bureau at (435) 649-6100 or (800) 453-1360.

ABC Reservations Central, Park City (435-649-2223 or 800-523-0666), books a number of area adventures including hot air ballooning, historic tours, glider flights, and backcountry snowmobile tours; they also book lodging and transportation.

Aside from ski resort trails, the Wasatch Mountains have fat-tire trails, some as close as ten minutes from Salt Lake. The Wasatch Crest Trail, for instance, branches off Millcreek Canyon (3800 South and Wasatch Boulevard). This experts-only challenging trail features spectacular Alpine views, steep climbs, stream crossings, and rocky stretches. Call the Salt Lake Ranger District, 6944 South 3000 East, at (801) 943-1794 for maps and tips if planning a fat-tire trek through the Wasatch.

Something Different

- **Train ride.** The **Heber Valley Historic Railroad** (801-581-9980), a steam passenger railroad, crosses the farmland of Heber Valley, follows Deer Creek Lake, and descends into beautiful Provo Canyon.
- **Underground Mine Tour.** Go 1,500 feet underground with the **Park City Silvermine Adventure** (800-467-3828; www.netpp.com/pcsilvermine). Learn how the mine operated, where the horses (they operated machinery) were kept, and witness a simulated mine blast.
- **Scuba Dive.** For warm-water diving in a mineral-rich crater, try **Homestead Resort Scuba Diving** (435-655-7444 or 800-467-3828)

Backcountry Adventures

Wasatch-Cache National Forest also offers unlimited opportunities for family excursions. A great deal of planning should go into a backcountry outing. Even the forests get crowded on holidays and in summer. Wasatch-Cache is one of the country's most heavily used forests for recreation. To avoid crowds and temperature extremes, visit in autumn and spring. Contact a National Forest Service Office (see For More Information) for specific advice and information.

Logan District

Logan, home of Utah State University and about 90 miles north of Salt Lake, is just southwest of **Logan Canyon Highway,** U.S. 89, a National Scenic Byway, most of it traveling primarily through the forest's Logan

Music in the Mountains

- **Deer Valley** hosts the Utah Symphony, with guest artists such as Crystal Gayle, Roger Williams, The Preservation Hall Jazz Band, and the Kingston Trio. In August, there's a Bluegrass Festival and a Jazz Festival.
- **Park City** has concerts in the City Park bandstand every Wednesday evening, live entertainment every Saturday on historic Main Street, and an International Music Festival during July and August.

Ranger District. The byway, just over 39 miles long, runs from the mouth of Logan Canyon to Bear Lake.

The scenic byway tour starts at the **Logan District Ranger Office,** where you'll find information, rest rooms, picnic tables, and pleasant canyon views. Some highlights of the drive include the following.

Logan Wind Cave, 5 miles from Ranger Office, can be found high above Logan Canyon. A 1.5-mile trail, moderately difficult for kids, leads to the cave. Spring visitors are treated to clusters of blooming wildflowers, while fall brings spectacular autumn foliage. The cave is part of the rock formation you'll pass midway up the canyon wall, called the China Wall. *Best Hikes with Children in Utah* by Maureen Keilty (The Mountaineers) details this and other hikes in the Wasatch National Forest. On this hike Keilty advises that you watch out for rattlers.

At **Wood Camp Campground** and **Jardine Juniper Trail,** 10.3 miles from Lady Bird, campers find only seven individual family units with no water. The big attraction here is west of the campground, where the Jardine Juniper trailhead is located. This moderately strenuous and long (5 miles one-way) trail climbs more than 2,000 vertical feet through glacier-carved moraines and green forests. With older, hardy kids, it's worth the hike to the end to see the tree thought to be more than 2,000 years old—and one of the largest living junipers anywhere.

Accessed by a paved but winding 7-mile road that climbs 2,300 feet to the lake, at 8,100 feet elevation, is a popular thirty-nine-unit campground, **Tony Grove Lake Area,** 19.2 miles from the Ranger Office, usually open July 4 to October 1. From here try a self-guided nature trail around the perimeter of the lake, which passes ancient glacial deposits and fields of wildflowers. Spruce and fir trees stand in the wetter areas of the shore and spread into a thick forest beyond. See fauna such as mountain chickadees, ground squirrels, yellow-bellied sapsuckers, and muskrats. As for flora, the lake is home to gooseberry shrubs, pink coral-bells, tangled willows, and mountain sunflowers.

Beaver Mountain Ski Road Junction, 24.2 miles from the Ranger Office, leads to the ski resort (435-753-0921), via Road 243. From late November to mid-April, the resort has three chairlifts and a day lodge. The road leads to camping spots in the Sink Hollow and Beaver Creek areas. There's also a tubing hill families will enjoy.

The Limber Pine Nature Trail is an excellent spot for a family hike. The 1¼-mile loop, which starts from a picnic spot, is easy for kids and takes about an hour to complete. A guide available at the trailhead points out the geological history and different wildlife species. You'll hear (and maybe even see) the nuthatches, woodpeckers, and mountain chickadees that fly through the treetops, and you'll witness the quaking aspen trees, bent over in arches by heavy snows.

The scenic byway ends at **Bear Lake,** 20 miles long and from 4 to 8 miles wide, one of the state's most popular spots for water recreation. Half of the lake is in Utah, the other half in Idaho. Year-round fishing from shore is excellent on the east side. (Legend has it that the lake is home to the mythological Bear Lake Monster.) Raspberries grow wild all around the lake, and several small stands sell raspberry milk shakes.

Bear Lake State Park (435-946-3343), the final stop, comprises three state-operated facilities: **Bear Lake Marina,** 2 miles north of Garden City; **Rendezvous Beach,** which has a sandy beach and is 2 miles west of Laketown; and **Eastside,** 20 miles north of Laketown.

For a brochure detailing things to see and do on this scenic byway, stop by the Logan Ranger District at 1500 East and Highway 89, Logan 84321 (435-755-3620). For more information you can also contact Bridgerland Travel Region, 160 North Main, Logan (435-752-2161 or 800-882-4433). More than forty hiking trails are listed in the book *Cache Trails,* available at area sporting-goods stores.

Wasatch Mountain State Park

About 45 miles east of Salt Lake City, 2 miles northwest of Midway, and 22 miles from Park City, **Wasatch Mountain State Park** (435-654-1791) is a popular destination. It features a thirty-six-hole golf course, more than 135 camping/picnicking areas, modern rest rooms, hot showers, utility hookups, and plenty of recreation areas. For information about boating, call (800) OHB-RIDE; for camping, (800) 322-3770. Nature trails are used by cross-country skiers and snowmobiles (rentals available in the park) in the winter, and by hikers in the summer. This is Utah's most developed state park and, as you might expect, summers are crowded—and hot.

The Ogden District

A scenic byway, U-39, starts in **Ogden,** some 30 miles north of Salt Lake, and stretches for 44 miles through the narrow **Ogden Canyon.** The road climbs through the Wasatch-Cache National Forest to some of northern Utah's most breathtaking vistas. Along the way you may catch glimpses of wildlife such as mule deer, ground squirrels, and marmots. If you venture onto back roads that lead away from the traveled route, you find breathtaking overlooks, picnic areas, fishing, and campgrounds.

The byway also leads to a highlight of this district, the **Pineview**

Reservoir, a popular summer recreation area with two designated swim areas with lifeguards, two campgrounds, two boat ramps, and two trailheads, including the 22-mile **Skyline Trail** (also open to mountain and motor bikes). This is a part of the **Great Western Trail,** which, once completed, will stretch from Canada to Mexico, incorporating various hiking, biking, horseback, and vehicle trails.

This region features twelve developed campgrounds. For more on this area, contact the **Union Station Information Center,** 2501 Wall Avenue, Ogden (801-625-5306/TDD 801-625-5644). It has detailed recreation maps showing roads, trails, and campgrounds. Information is also available from Ogden Ranger District, 507 Twenty-fifth Street, Ogden, 84401 (801-625-5112).

Side Trips

The booklet *Utah's Scenic Byways and Backways* contains descriptions of popular touring routes in the state, including several in and around the Wasatch area. The drives last from forty-five minutes to several hours, and the routes are also denoted by rainbow-colored signs throughout the state. Included is one of the most popular mountain routes in the state, the **Mirror Lake Scenic Byway,** U-150 from Kamas through the Wasatch-Cache National Forest to the Utah–Wyoming border. Scenic viewpoints, picnic areas, lakes, meadows, and rugged peaks and cliffs can be accessed from this high mount byway, much of which parallels the Provo River.

For more day trip ideas, see the chapters on Arches and Canyonlands National Parks, near Moab, and Salt Lake City.

Special Events

See the Salt Lake City chapter for more festivities. For more information on the following, contact one of the visitor's bureaus listed under For More Information, or the individual ski area.

January. Treats await as you ski from station to station at Solitude Ski Resort's Chocolate Lover's Tour and Chocolate Tasting Extravaganza.

March. Winterfest Snow Sculpture; Music in the Mountains, both in Park City.

April. Easter Egg Hunt, Park City Ski Area.

June. Savour the Summit, Park City's food festival, features samples from more than thirty area restaurants; Cannondale Cup Mountain Bike Race, Utah Winter Sports Park.

July. The nation's best cowboys take part in the Oakley Rodeo; An Old-Fashioned Fourth, Park City.

August. Park City Art Festival; Summit County Fair, Coalville Fair Grounds.

September. Autumn Aloft, thirty hot air balloons ascend from Park City: Miner's Day Celebration, with parade down Main Street, fun, and games, Park City.

October. Oktoberfest at Snowbird Mountain features polka dancing, German beer, and live entertainers.

November. America's Opening, Main Street, Park City, kicks off ski season with Men's World Cup Ski Races, fireworks, on-snow parades, music, food, and more.

December. On Christmas and New Year's Eves, many ski resorts have visits from Santa complete with on-slope parades and more.

Where to Stay

The Utah Travel Guide, published by the Utah Travel Council, is a helpful reference that includes lodging and other state information.

A wide variety of accommodations exists in and around the Salt Lake City and Park City areas. Most of the major ski resorts mentioned previously offer their own lodging and/or chalet arrangements; ask for reservations when you call. *The Utah Winter Vacation Planner,* available from the **Utah Travel Council,** lists ski-area lodging. There are several reservation services that book entire packages, including **Park City Ski Holidays** (435-649-0493 or 800-222-PARK), representing more than 3,000 units in town including private homes and condos.

There are many lodging options in the the town of Park City. **Identity Properties** (800-245-6417) offers condominiums within driving distance and also at the ski base area. **Shadow Ridge Resort Hotel and Conference Center** (435-649-4300 or 800-451-3031) has hotel rooms and one-, two-, and three-bedroom condos located at the ski base. The **Radisson Inn Park City** (435-649-5000 or 800-333-3333) offers free shuttle service to Park City and Deer Valley's slopes, allows kids twelve and younger to eat free, and features an indoor/outdoor pool. **Marriott's Summit Watch Resort** (800-223-8245), located on Main Street near the Park City Ski Area town lift, offers two-bedroom villas with kitchens.

Moderately priced family lodging is available in Park City. Try **Best Western Landmark Inn,** 6560 North Landmark Drive (435-649-7300 or 800-548-8824). It features rooms with refrigerators, a twenty-four-hour restaurant, free shuttle to the slopes, and a convenient location just minutes from the mountain and next to a factory mall. You will find moderate rates at the **Snowshoe Inn,** 1450 Empire, only 150 yards from Park City Ski Area (435-649-8443 or 800-453-3812). Rooms have small refrigerators and coffeemakers. The **Edelweiss Haus,** 1482 Empire Avenue (435-649-9342 or 800-438-3855), offers moderate motel-style rooms, some of which are suites with kitchenettes.

The ten-room, renovated, 1893 former miners' boardinghouse, the **Old Miners' Lodge,** 615 Woodside Avenue (435-645-8068 or 800-648-8068), is fun. Families are welcome, and cribs are $5.00 extra. The **Inn at Prospector Square Hotel,** 2200 Sidewinder Drive (435-649-7100 or 800-453-3812), offers one- and two-bedroom condominiums, an indoor pool, and free shuttle service to the ski area. See the Salt Lake City chapter for accommodations in the city.

The Cliff Lodge is Snowbird's flagship property. This upscale ski-in/ski-out hotel features a child-care facility, a spa with a rooftop pool, and a wide range of pampering treatments. Three condominium properties—**The Lodge at Snowbird, The Inn,** and the **Iron Blossom Lodge**—let efficiencies and one-bedroom units with a loft, all of which have kitchenettes. Some even have fireplaces. Access to swimming pools, saunas, and exercise facilities is included in the room rates. Call (800) 453-3000.

Alta Lodge (801-742-3333) has an easygoing atmosphere. Its fifty-seven rooms are dorm-style, with bathroom-in-the hall accommodations. Others have fireplaces and glass walls that overlook the canyon. Meals are a great opportunity to meet other guests, as tables seat eight to ten. **Blackjack Condominiums** (800-343-0347), which provides transportation to Alta and Snowbird, lets studio and one-bedroom condos.

Near Deer Valley, **Stein Eriksen Lodge** (435-534-0563) is a splurge. Before dismissing this option based on its price, consider that this four-star hotel is consistently rated among the top ski lodges in the United States.

Shadow Ridge Resort Hotel and Conference Center (800-451-3031) has hotel rooms and one- to three-bedroom condos located at the base of Park City. A shuttle bus is run to Deer Valley and Park City from the **Radisson Inn Park City** (800-333-3333). The hotel also features a kids-eat-free program for those twelve and under, and an indoor-outdoor pool. **Marriott's Summit Watch Resort** (800-210-8200), just off Main Street, Park City, offers two-bedroom villas with kitchens.

For lodging in the Ogden area, contact the **Ogden/Weber Convention and Visitors Bureau,** 2501 Wall Avenue, Ogden (801-627-8288 or 800-ALL-UTAH). For the Logan area, contact **Cache Chamber of Commerce,** 160 North Main (435-752-2161 or 800-657-5353).

Some of the **National Forest** campgrounds can be reserved by calling (800) 280-2267 or TDD (800) 879-4496. Other sites book on a first-come basis. The most popular (read "crowded") camping areas are in Ogden and near Salt Lake City. A few choices: **Perception Park,** on the shore of the Ogden River, features about fifty sites, lots of nature trails, and good fishing. It's also one of the few campgrounds equipped with flushing toilets, and it's handicapped accessible. **The Spruces,** in the mountains east of Salt Lake City off I-215, is an expansive camping area with rest rooms.

Where to Eat

In Logan, typical American-style eats are served up at the **Blue Bird Cafe,** 19 North Main (435-752-3155). Kids love the almost 20-foot-long counter where the cafe's famous chocolates are displayed.

People come from miles around to the town of **Perry,** about 20 miles north of Ogden, to eat steak, prime rib, barbecue, and other tasty dishes at the five-star **Maddox Ranch House Restaurant,** 1980 South Highway 89 (435-723-8545 or 800-544-5474).

At Sundance, **The Foundry Grill** is a casual restaurant with a floor to ceiling view of 12,000-foot Mount Timpanogos.

In Odgen, dinner (steak, shrimp, prime rib) is an experience at the **Prairie Schooner,** 445 Park Boulevard (801-392-2712). Eat inside a covered wagon, with a campfire and howling coyote sounds.

Enjoy a local specialty, freshly harvested peach milk shakes, at the **Peach City Drive-In,** 306 North Main (801-723-3923). Located north of Ogden in Brigham City, this eatery also offers chicken baskets, steak sandwiches, and cheeseburgers.

Park City has more than fifty restaurants serving everything from continental cuisine to hearty western fare. **Baja Cantina** (435-649-2252) has a children's menu and perennial favorites such as tacos and burritos. **Ziggy's** (435-649-2776) features moderately priced pizza, pasta, sandwiches, and calzones.

Main Street offers up a variety of choices: **Cisero's Ristorante** (801-649-5044) offers Italian fare at good prices and has a kids' menus; **Burgie's** (801-649-0011) features specialty burgers and sandwiches; **Main St. Pizza & Noodle** (801-645-8878) has a selection of pizza and pasta; **Texas Reds Pit BBQ & Chili Parlor** (801-649-7337) has children's menus and take-out portions of its ribs and chili. Teens with more sophisticated tastes (not to mention their parents) might like **Mercato Mediterraneo** (801-547-0030), which offers such Mediterranean fare as paella, cassoulet, and lamb and chicken couscous, or the **Barking Frog Grill** (801-649-6222), known for its award-winning southwestern cuisine.

Around Snowbird, the **Forklift** (801-742-2222, ext. 4100) serves breakfast and lunch. **Pier 49 San Francisco Sourdough Pizza** bakes gourmet pizza on a sourdough crust. Less fancy varieties are available for finicky eaters. Contact the **Park City Chamber/Bureau** at (435) 649-6100 or (800) 453-1360 for dining information.

For More Information

Visitor Information: **Salt Lake Convention and Visitors Bureau,** 180 So uth West Temple (801-521-2868). **Utah Travel Council,** Salt House, 90 Salt Lake City Temple, Salt Lake City 84114 (801-538-1030). The Utah Travel Guide Internet site is www.netpub.com/utah/w. For a copy of the *Ski Utah Winter Vacation Planner,* contact **Ski Utah,** 150 West 500 South, Salt Lake City, 84101 (800SKI-UTAH; www.skiutah.com).

Forest Service and Ranger Districts: The USDA Forest Service (800-322-4100; TDD 801-524-6762) distributes a pamphlet called *Leave No Trace! An Outdoor Ethic,* which provides helpful advice and rules of the forest. The main office of the **Wasatch-Cache National Forest** is located at 8226 Federal Building, 125 South State, Room 8103, Salt Lake City 84138 (801-524-5030). You may also contact individual district offices, some of them listed above.

Contact the Wasatch-Cache National Forest's main office for information on handicapped-accessible campgrounds and trails.

Emergency Numbers

Ambulance, police, fire: 911

Hospitals: Salt Lake City—Holy Cross Hospital, 1045 East 100 South (801-350-4111); Primary Children's Medical Center, 100 North Medical Drive (801-588-2000). Ogden—McKay-Dee Hospital, 3939 Harrison Boulevard; (801) 627-2800. Park City—Park City Family Health and Emergency Center, 1665 Bonanza Drive; (435) 649-7640. Logan—Logan Regional Hospital, 1400 North 500 East; (435) 752-2050.

Poison Control twenty-four-hour hotline: (800) 456-7707 or (801) 581-2151

Smith's has twenty-four-hour pharmacies at 442 North 175 East in Logan, (435) 753-6570; and 4275 Harrison Boulevard in Ogden, (801)479-0700. In Park City a twenty-four-hour pharmacy is located inside Albertson's Food Store, 1800 Park Avenue; (435) 649-6134. In Salt Lake there's a pharmacy open until midnight inside a grocery store, Harmon's, 3200 South 1300 East; (801) 487-5461.

Door County

Sticking out into Lake Michigan like a long, skinny finger, Wisconsin's Door County peninsula is flanked by Green Bay on its west coast and Lake Michigan on its east coast. While only 13 miles wide and 42 miles long, Door County's orchard-graced interiors and lovely coastal vistas contribute to the relaxed atmosphere that pervades the county's four tourist seasons. Door County holds the distinction of being home to ten lighthouses, which is the most of any county in the United States.

Most of the picture-perfect towns are located either on the west or east coast, with the Green Bay coast providing the most family-friendly and prettiest villages. Towns such as Egg Harbor, Fish Creek, and Sister Bay, to name a few, are flanked by boats and yachts harborside and abundant flowers curbside in the summer.

Inland, the county is very rural, with apple and cherry orchards dominating the economy after tourism. Actually, Door County is the fourth largest producer of cherries. The apple and cherry orchards are part of the reason that Door County is a year-round destination, with the pink blossoms gracing the countryside in May, pick-your-own cherries in July, and apple picking and lovely autumn colors in the fall. While there are plenty of trails for cross-country skiing and snowmobiling in the winter, summer best affords families the opportunity to discover the lovely beaches, secluded coves, and rocky inlets of both Green Bay and Lake Michigan, as well as the biking and hiking trails in the five state parks. During the summer season, there are also many other family-oriented outdoor activities available, including petting farms, boat rides, miniature golf, and a small water park. Since July and August are peak season, reserve your accommodations early.

Getting There

Visitors flying to the region arrive either in the small **Green Bay Airport,** which is 43 miles by car from lower Door County (Sturgeon Bay), or the **Milwaukee Airport** (where there are more air connections) and drive north 140 miles on Route 43 to Green Bay, continuing to Sturgeon Bay

Door County

AT A GLANCE

- Participate in diverse four-season outdoor family activities
- Visit several lighthouses
- Ferry to nearby islands
- Explore small towns with abundant shopping and art galleries
- Play on tranquil beaches on Green Bay and Lake Michigan
- Door County Chamber of Commerce, (920) 743-4456, doorcountyvacations.com

via Route 57. Note that the quainter mid- to upper Door County towns of Egg Harbor, Fish Creek, or Sister Bay, are an additional thirty to forty-five minutes north of Sturgeon Bay. For those driving from the Windy City area, it is about 200 miles from Chicago to Sturgeon Bay.

Getting Around

A car is a necessity in Door County; however, bicycles are readily available to rent for closer exploration of the back roads and state parks in particular.

WHAT TO SEE AND DO

Farms

Door County, with its inland pastoral setting, offers numerous opportunities for children to get a taste of farm life. There are working farms that give tours, including **Lautenbach's Orchard Country,** Highway 42, ½ mile south of Fish Creek (920-868-3479). Orchard Country offers guided tours of its cherry and apple orchards, which tell you about growing, harvesting, and processing the produce. Tours also include samples of cider and wine. Orchard Market, where you can purchase apple, cherry, and other local products, is also on the property.

There are also a few petting farms, including **Vacationland Farm,** Highway 57, Sister Bay (920-854-2525), which offers year-round activities for children. In the warmer months, there is a petting zoo complete with llamas, buffalo, rabbits, and monkeys. Western-style cookouts are held every Wednesday evening from June through August. The Corral has guided trail rides, a pony ring, and horse-drawn hay rides in the fall. In the winter, sleigh rides are available.

The Farm, Highway 57, Sturgeon Bay (920-743-6666), is open daily from Memorial Day through Labor Day. Here children can enjoy petting, feeding, and giving bottles of milk to the very tame farm animals, along with watching hourly goat milking. The extensive grounds also have displays of old farm machinery and nature trails that wind through woods, a small pond, and prairie grasslands. Kids get to see what early pioneer homes looked like, since five log buildings have been moved to the property for you to explore.

Lighthouses

Door County, home of ten lighthouses, boasts the most beacons to sailors of any county nationwide. The only ones open to visitors on a regular basis, however, are **Eagle Bluff Lighthouse** in Peninsula State Park and **Cana Island Lighthouse**. Located about 4 miles northeast of Bailey's Harbor on Highway Q, the Cana Island Lighthouse was built in the mid-1800s and is accessible by wading from the mainland across a narrow channel with ankle-deep water. The others are located in Bailey's harbor, Washington, Plum, Pilot, Rock, and Chambers Islands, and there are two in Sturgeon Bay. Every year there is a Lighthouse Walk on the third weekend in May, when all lighthouses are open to visitors.

Beaches and Watersports

Since the waters of both Green Bay and Lake Michigan are generally tranquil, there are many beaches suitable for children. But, due to the sometimes rocky coastline, most of the beaches are very small. Note that Green Bay is a bit warmer than Lake Michigan.

The state parks all have sandy beach areas for swimming. **Nicolet Beach,** located in Peninsula State Park has bathrooms, showers, changing facilities, and food concessions. Since the beach is located on Nicolet Bay, on the Green Bay side of the peninsula, you can be guaranteed very tranquil waters. **Whitefish Dunes** has a very lovely beach on Lake Michigan (you must hike in about ten minutes from the parking lot to the beach), which is on a rather steep dune flanked by pine trees and offers only basic bathroom facilities. **Newport State Park,** Lot #3, is also on Lake Michigan, but is easier to reach, especially for little ones, and offers nicer bathroom facilities and a picnic area. **Potawatomi State Park** also has a sandy beach area as does **Rock Island State Park.** On Washington Island, **Sand Dunes Beach** and **Schoolhouse Beach** are also family friendly beaches. (See Side Trips for Washington and Rock Islands.)

Bailey's Harbor Ridges has a beach area that is separate from the Ridges sanctuary. Most of the towns have swimming areas, which tend to be small. These include Fish Creek, Egg Harbor's Frank E. Murphy Park, and Lakeside Park in Jacksonport.

While Ephraim does not have a sandy beach spot for swimming, its harbor is the perfect launching spot for exploring Green Bay by boat, since watersports rentals abound. **Wisconsin Water Wings**, 9993 Highway 42, South Shore Pier, Ephraim (920-854-9000), offers parasailing over Green Bay, which is dotted with tiny islands and picturesque coves. While Wave Runners are not suitable for little ones, motorboats and pontoon boats that seat up to twelve people are also available for rent at South Shore Pier; in Ephraim (920-854-4324).

State Parks and County Parks

There are five state parks scattered throughout Door County. **Peninsula State Park** juts out into Green Bay in Fish Creek; **Newport State Park** is located on Lake Michigan in Ellison Bay. **Whitefish Dunes State Park** and **Potawatomi State Park,** both of which are in Sturgeon Bay, are located on Lake Michigan and Green Bay, respectively. **Rock Island State Park** can be reached from the mainland via Washington Island. With the exception of Rock Island, which can only be reached in season, all the parks offer excellent hiking, biking, and cross-country skiing trails, as well as plenty of open space for snowshoeing.

Peninsula State Park (920-868-3258) is the county's largest and probably the best park for biking, since it has separate, wide trails for bikers and hikers. Nature programs and boat rentals are offered on Nicolet Beach. Also located in the park is a theater that stages summer performances, Eagle Bluff lighthouse, and an eighteen-hole golf course (920-854-5791) open from May through October. As you drive, hike, or bike through the 3,776-acre park, you will come upon a number of lovely vistas of the bay.

Newport State Park is the second largest park, with 2,400 acres of wilderness area offering 30 miles of hiking trails and 11 miles of Lake Michigan shoreline, featuring hidden coves and rocky headlands. While most of the coastline is not suitable for swimming, Lot #3 affords easy access to a fine, sandy beach flanked by tall pine stands. Birders should note that more than 175 species of birds have been recorded in the park.

Whitefish Dunes has the highest sand dunes in Wisconsin and therefore offers the most breathtaking and rugged vistas of Lake Michigan. You can climb the tallest dune, "Old Baldy," for a view of Lake Michigan and Clark Lake. There are more than 14 miles of hiking/skiing trails and a beautiful sandy beach area for swimming. The ranger station offers guided tours through this park, known for its wildflowers and outdoor displays of sites used by early indigenous people.

Potawatomi State Park is located on Green Bay in the town of Sturgeon Bay. The park has 6 miles of hiking trails, 13 miles of ski trails, numerous bike trails, campsites, an observation tower, a boat ramp, fishing, and adjacent downhill skiing.

Winter Fun

In the winter, the hiking trails in four of Door County's state parks become cross-country ski trails. For snow and trail conditions, call the Door County Chamber of Commerce at (920) 743-4456, ext. 3. This same hotline also lists the conditions of the more than 250 miles of snowmobile trails in Door County.

- **Downhill skiing.** Potawatomi State Park offers downhill skiing on weekends and on Wednesday evenings.
- **Sledding and tobogganing.** Peninsula State Park offers sledding and tobogganing.
- **Ice Fishing.** Call the Fishing Hotline at (920) 743-7046 for details on how and where they are biting.
- **Snowshoeing.** Snowshoes can be rented at Nor-Door Sport & Cyclery in Fish Creek (920-868-2275), Mac's Sport Shop in Sturgeon Bay (920-743-3355), and Sister Bay (920-854-5625).

There are a number of county parks too. Two of note are Cave Point and Bailey's Harbor Ridges. Located north of the village of Valmay off Highway 57, the highlight of **Cave Point County Park** is listening to the water whoosh in and out of the underwater caves that have been chiseled by the tides of Lake Michigan. There is a small picnic area. During the summer you may even be entertained by young adults jumping off the cliffs into the clear, cool waters below. (Since some of the cliffs reach up to 30 feet, we do not recommend trying this high dive.)

Bailey's Harbor Ridges Sanctuary is a nature and wildlife area on Lake Michigan offering independent and ranger-guided hikes. Some of the rarest wildflowers in Wisconsin can be found on the ridges. There is also a separate beach area for swimming.

More Family Fun

For those rainy days in Door County, visit **Hands On** art studio, 8499 Highway 42, Juddville (located between Egg Harbor and Fish Creek; 920-868-1822). Parents and kids will enjoy exploring their creativity by painting their own ceramics, tiles, T-shirts, greeting cards, birdhouses, and glassware. Prices are on an hourly basis in addition to the price of the piece you choose to paint. Hands On fires it, mounts it, or frames it for you to pick up the next day; they will ship it to you if necessary. While there is no minimum age, it is probably best if your child is kindergarten age or older, since there are mostly fragile items in the studio.

Door County has its share of outdoor family fun activities. **Thumb Fun,** Highway 42, north of Fish Creek (920-868-3418), is a small amusement and water park. There are five water slides, "Wet & Wild" bumper cars, high-speed go-carts, a haunted mansion, eighteen-hole miniature golf, a video game center, and rides for small children too. Another spot for miniature "adventure" golf is the eighteen-hole **Pirate's Cove,** 810 Bayshore Drive, Highway 42, Sister Bay. The course itself will entertain the kids with its pirate theme and waterfall.

For an unusual indoor visit, stop at **Collector Showcase,** 3910 Highway 42, Sturgeon Bay (920-743-6788). While a bit on the rinky-dink side with its rather musty displays, Collector Showcase will fascinate anyone who loves Barbie dolls or old and unique cars. There are twenty-eight cars, from a 1916 Maxwell to a 1983 DeLorean, old animated Marshall Fields Christmas displays, a huge collection of antique dolls, and more than 1,000 Barbies of all ages and nationalities. This eclectic little spot is a fun (and very reasonably priced) stop for families.

Side Trips

Washington Island

Door County peninsula is dotted with islands, many of which are uninhabited. While Chambers Island and Detroit Island have summer homes, Washington Island is the only one that is inhabited year-round. Perched on the northernmost tip of Door County, this tranquil island offers many family-friendly activities and is accessible by the **Washington Island Ferry Line.** The ferry carries passengers, bicycles, and cars from Northport Pier at the end of Highway 42. No reservations are necessary for the thirty-minute ride. For rates and schedules, call (920) 847-2546 or (800) 223-2094. Alternatively, you can sail the ***Island Clipper*** boat for a narrated cruise tour to the island. The boat leaves the mainland at Gills Rock; call (920) 854-2972 for information. The Washington Island Chamber of Commerce can be reached at (920) 847-2179.

Washington Island, with nearly 100 miles of quiet roads, is perfect for exploring by bicycle or car. You can bring your own bikes or rent them in Gills Rock near the ferry. To avoid paying extra to bring them aboard the ferry, you can rent your bikes on Washington Island right as you disembark, at **Harbor Bike Rental.** The bikes on the island, however, are only one speed and have foot brakes—luckily, the island is very flat.

Another way to explore Washington Island is via the **Washington Island Cherry Train** (920-847-2039). The narrated ninety-minute open-air tour leaves from both ferry terminals. The **Viking Tour Train** meets the *Island Clipper* from Gills Rock and also offers a similar tram ride. Since the "downtown" is 3 miles from the ferry, this island is not suited for walking only.

There are a number of family activities on the island. The **Washington Island Farm Museum** opened in 1998 to educate children and adults about the history of farming on the island and features old farming machinery and original log houses. A novel attraction is the **Double K-W Ostrich Farm,** where huge ostriches strut behind their cages (the male ostriches are not nice creatures) and frozen ostrich meat is sold. Children can buy feed for the other friendlier animals there, such as sheep and small pigs.

The **Art and Nature Center** (920-847-2025) is located in an old schoolhouse and features a gallery of local art as well as a nature room with exhibits and a naturalist available for hikes and classes. **Sievers Looms** (920-847-2264) features island-built and -designed weaving looms and offers classes through its Sievers School of Fiber Arts.

There are a few beaches tucked away on Washington Island. **Schoolhouse Beach** has calm waters, a rocky beach, and picnic tables. Picnic sites are available at **Percy Johnson County Park,** which also has a beach area. **Sand Dunes Beach** is a real gem, with its small sandy beach area flanked by evergreens. The lovely, clean, clear waters attract families, but there is a narrow rocky strip once you enter the water. The only facilities at the beach are outhouses.

Jackson Harbor Ridges is a State of Wisconsin scientific area and is a fine example of beach, dune, and shore meadow communities. While swimming is not available at The Ridges, there are nature trails and ranger programs offered in season.

Rock Island State Park

For those wishing to totally get away from it all, **Rock Island State Park** is a tiny island off of Washington Island. Due to its fragile ecosystem, cars and bicycles are not permitted on Rock Island. Instead, the 900-acre island offers hiking trails ranging from thirty-minute to three-hour loops. In addition to picnic and camping sites, you may want to check out the massive stone **Thordarson Estate,** listed on the National Register of Historic Places, and **Potawatomi Lighthouse,** which is the oldest lighthouse in Wisconsin. **Rock Island Beach** is a small sandy beach with bluffs behind it. Since this is at the northern tip of the peninsula, water tends to be colder here than on the west and east coasts of Door County.

Boats to Rock Island State Park depart seasonally from Jackson Harbor on Washington Island for the fifteen-minute voyage. For more information on Rock Island, contact the park staff from May to November 15 at (920) 847-2235; from November 15 through April contact the Newport State Park staff at (920) 854-2500. (Both parks have small staffs; you may have to be persistent in trying to reach them.)

Milwaukee, Wisconsin

Milwaukee sits on Lake Michigan and is a smaller, less hectic version of its larger Lake Michigan counterpart, Chicago, which is about 60 miles to the south. Milwaukee boasts well-kept waterfront areas flanked by green parks and playgrounds. The city has a twenty-four-hour park hotline for information on swimming pools, wading pools, and watersports; (414) 257-5100. To speak with someone concerning other park details, the parks information number is (414) 257-6100. In the summer, you may want to check out **Cool Waters** (414-321-7530), a family water park in Greenfield Park.

The **Milwaukee Zoo,** 10001 West Bluemound Road (414-771-3040), is open year-round and features animals in their natural environments, separated from visitors by moats. The zoo has a newly renovated aquatic and reptile center, and little ones in particular enjoy the zoo train and zoomobile tours.

One of the top attractions for younger children is the **Betty Brinn Children's Museum,** 929 East Wisconsin Avenue (414-291-0888). The hands-on museum is appropriate for toddlers through ten-year-olds. Highlights include arts and crafts projects, a human heart replica for little ones to crawl through, a television studio, a pretend apple orchard and juice factory, and store replicas. The facility has been cited by *Parent* magazine as one of the top ten children's museums nationwide.

Older children will enjoy the **Discovery World Museum,** The Milwaukee Museum Center, 712 West Wells Street (414-765-0777). As part of a $17.3 million Museum Center expansion, Discovery World recently moved into a new 45,00-square-foot facility. Preteens and teens will enjoy the plethora of interactive areas—140 in all—including Entrepreneurs Village with its Buy & Sell Area, Manufacturing Area, and R&D Cafe, where youths can choose projects off the menu, such as how to make paper; Area 51 Test Pilot Training Center; Weather 4Cast Center; and Lightwaves & Laserbeams laser show. Discovery World offers weekend "family fusion" workshops and live theater shows.

Other spots that children and teens will enjoy include the **International Clown Hall of Fame,** which is a one-of-kind display of memorabilia located in the lower rotunda of Plankinton Arcade in Grand Avenue Retail Center; **Humphrey IMAX Dome Theater,** with its giant wraparound screen; and **Riverwalk,** which winds along the Milwaukee River throughout downtown. Riverwalk takes you through the city's restaurant and pub area and is also the launching point for gondolas and water taxi rides.

Milwaukee is home to some of the country's best German restaurants, with venerable institutions like **Maders Restaurant,** 1037-41 North Old World Third Street (414-276-2720), and **Karl Ratzsch's Restaurant,** 320

East Mason Street (414-276-2720) topping the list. These famous restaurants have great old-world interiors. Maders especially will please little ones with its kids' menu and numerous rooms, some reminiscent of medieval banquet rooms where princes and princesses may have once dined.

Performing Arts

Door County offers a wide array of performing arts during the summer season. The **Door Community Auditorium,** P.O. Box 397, Highway 42 at Gibraltar School in Fish Creek, (920-868-2728), offers an impressive lineup from spring through Christmas. Stars who have performed here include Ray Charles, Rosemary Clooney, and traveling troupes such as the Minnesota Ballet and Alvin Ailey Ensemble. Every April and August, the **Peninsula Music Festival,** featuring northeast Wisconsin's only professional orchestra, is staged here. Call (920) 854-4060 for details.

For theater under the stars, check out a performance at the **American Folklore Theatre** in Peninsula State Park (920-868-9999). Seating is general admission and tickets are purchased on the night of the show; the box office opens up one hour prior to the performance.

The **Peninsula Players,** Highway 42, Fish Creek (920-868-3287), bills itself as the oldest professional resident summer theater in the country. It is located in a pavilion amid fourteen forested acres and gardens.

If you are staying in Door County for at least two weeks during the summer, your children can get involved in the local music scene at **Birch Creek Music Center,** 3821 County Highway E, Egg Harbor 54209 (920-868-3763). Birch Creek is a respected summer music school by day and a music performance center by night.

While not in the category of live entertainment, the **Skyway Drive In** movie theater, Highway 42 between Fish Creek and Ephraim (920-854-9938), offers new releases in a nostalgic setting.

Shopping

There are specialty shops and galleries galore in Door County. Some of the fine-arts stores may frown upon small children visiting, due to the breakable art object displays, but there are plenty of child-friendly stores. They include **Spielman's Wood Works,** 4075 Highway 42, Fish Creek (920-868-3130), which has a section of handmade wooden toys; **Teddy Bear's Picnic,** Founders' Square on Main Street in Fish Creek (920-868-3339), with its large collection of stuffed animals; the **Fish Creek Kite Store,** 3851 Highway 42 at Thumb Fun water slide, Fish Creek (920-868-3769), with its brightly colored kites, wind socks, and mail-order catalog; and **Murray's Irish House, Inc.,** Highway 42, Fish Creek (920-868-3528), which has a section of children's Irish knit sweaters and kilts.

Special Events

Door County is known for its good, clean fun which makes it perfect for families. May is the busiest time, due to the monthlong Blossomfest. The following is a sampling of the annual festivals and events in Door County.

January. New Year's Day festivities; Polar Bear Swim in Lake Michigan; America on Parade, Egg Harbor, anyone can march and anything goes in this goofy parade; Candlelight Skiing, all state parks except Rock Island

February. Candlelight Skiing, all state parks except Rock Island; Winter Games, Fish Creek, festival on frozen Green Bay with activities including ice golfing, ice bowling, and a cherry-spitting contest.

April. Peninsula Music Festival, Baileys Harbor.

May. Blossomfest's countywide events include Blossom Run, Lighthouse Walk, Blossom Ball, Maifest, Blossom Parade; Shipyards Tours, Sturgeon Bay.

June. State Park Open House Day, free admission to all state parks; Taste of Door County food festival, Sturgeon Bay; Fyr Bal Festival, Scandinavian festival including fish boils and bonfires, Ephraim; Kids' Fishing Derby, Sturgeon Bay.

July. Fourth of July festivities countywide, largest parade is in Baileys Harbor; Belgian Days, family event celebrating heritage of local Belgian community, Brussels.

August. Cherry Daze cherry harvest festival, Jacksonport; Maritime Museum Classic Wooden Boat Show includes children's model boat building contest, Sturgeon Bay; Door County Fair, Sturgeon Bay; Sons of Norway Norsk Fest, Sturgeon Bay.

September. Marina Fest includes boat parade, Venetian night, fireworks, Sister Bay; Baileys Harbor Autumnfest, lumberjack show, antique car show, wagon rides, flapjack fling contest; Harvest Festival, Sturgeon Bay.

October. Pumpkin Patch Festival, Egg Harbor; Fall Festival, features a parade, fireworks, crafts, and a helicopter that drops Ping-Pong balls with prizes inside, Sister Bay.

November/December. Christmas Walk with caroling, tree lighting, free movies for children, B&B tours, Sturgeon Bay; Holly Days, Egg Harbor; Capture the Spirit, tour festively decorated B&Bs and inns, horse-drawn sleigh or wagon rides, Sister Bay and Ephraim.

Where to Stay

The Door County Chamber of Commerce provides INNLINE, an excellent information system available in Door County that provides up-to-the-minute hotel and motel vacancies. Contact INNLINE via the Door County Web site, www.doorcountyvacations.com, or use the unique touch-screen computers once you get to Door County. INNLINE computers are available at each town's visitors information center.

While there is an abundance of accommodations providing all price ranges and styles—from basic motel rooms to family-style condominiums—here are a few that offer family-friendly accommodations or amenities.

Wagon Trail Resort, 1041 Highway ZZ, Ellison Bay (920-854-2385 or 800-99-WAGON). Situated on more than 200 wooded acres, Wagon Trail offers miles of hiking, skiing, and snowshoeing trails, along with numerous types of accommodations suitable for families. These include standard rooms with mini refrigerators; two- and three-bedroom suites with kitchenettes; and vacation homes and cottages with two or three bedrooms, one to two bathrooms, fireplaces, and fully-equipped kitchens. The resort has a game room, indoor pool, sandy swimming beach with adjacent playground, and marina for pontoon and kayak rentals. Wagon Trail also provides a list of local baby-sitters, upon request.

The Bridgeport Resort, 50 West Larch Street, Sturgeon Bay (800-671-9190), has a number of facilities that little and big kids will love. They include an indoor play area with tunnels and ball pits, a state-of-the-art game room, an indoor lap pool, a heated outdoor pool with waterfall, and, for the adults, a fitness center complete with whirlpool and sauna. There are also outdoor grills. The Bridgeport has one-, two-, and three-bedroom suites with full kitchens, fireplaces, and balconies.

Landmark, 7643 Hillside Road, Egg Harbor (920-868-3205 or 800-273-7877), offers Kamp Landmark for children ages five and older from Memorial Day to Labor Day. The program runs from about 9:30 A.M. to 8:00 P.M. with half-hour breaks between activities. Offerings include fishing in Egg Harbor, making earthworm observatories, outdoor activities, and evening pizza and video parties. Situated on a wooded bluff, the resort has some good views as well as a fine restaurant. Condominium suites have one, two, or three bedrooms with living room and dining and kitchen areas. Some of the amenities include an indoor and an outdoor pool, tennis courts, fitness and game rooms and adjacent golf course.

Evergreen Hill, P.O. Box 730, Fish Creek (920-868-3748 or 800-686-6621), is wonderfully situated by the entrance to Peninsula State

Park. The two-bedroom condominiums are fully equipped with two bathrooms, three televisions, complete kitchen, and fireplaces. All units have a deck facing the pool and nicely landscaped greenery. There is also a gas grill on the property. The Homestead (see below) is the contact for information and reservations for Evergreen Hill.

Beowolf, 3775 Highway 42, Fish Creek (920-868-2381 or 800-433-7592), is on ten acres of wooded inland property and features lodge rooms—some with kitchenettes—and suites. Kids will enjoy the large indoor pool, game room, playground, tennis courts, and the VCRs that are available for rent.

The Homestead, 4006 Main Street, Fish Creek (920-868-3748 or 800-686-6621), is a motel offering standard rooms with two queen beds and refrigerator, as well as newer one-bedroom suites in a separate building. The suites have a sofa sleeper in the living room, a fireplace, TV/VCR, kitchenette, and whirlpool tub. The lobby of the main building offers an indoor pool, whirlpool, sauna, fitness room, and free continental breakfast in a cozy public room.

Little Sister Resort, 360 Little Sister Road, Sister Bay (920-854-4013), is tucked into cedar woods along Green Bay. The resort offers one-, two-, and three-bedroom cottages and chalets suitable for families, and features fireplaces, televisions, and waterfront views. Resort activities include hiking to nearby Pebble Beach, playing tennis, boating, or enjoying a waterfront fish boil.

Where to Eat

Door County is known for its fish boils, a Scandinavian tradition that originated more than one hundred years ago. Children will enjoy watching the "show" as potatoes and fish are boiled outside in a huge cauldron over a wood fire. When the fish is cooked, kerosene is dumped on the fire, creating a spectacle of flames and a bubbling over of the fish oils. The whitefish is served with melted butter, potatoes, cole slaw, and Door County cherry pie. There are numerous restaurants specializing in fish boils, including **White Gull Inn,** 4225 Main Street, Fish Creek (920-868-3517); **Little Sister Resort,** 360 Little Sister Road, Sister Bay (920-854-4013); and **Square Rigger Galley,** 6332 Highway 57, Sturgeon Bay (920-823-2408).

If fish boils don't tempt your taste buds, there are several other family-friendly eateries in Door County.

Culvers, 5581 County Road BB, Sturgeon Bay (920-746-0870). Home of "butterburgers," frozen custard, and children's menu, Culvers serves fast food in a pleasant, clean atmosphere. **Al Johnson's Restaurant,** 700 North Bay Shore Drive, Sister Bay (920-854-2626). Al Johnson's provides a family atmosphere for breakfast, lunch, and dinner. Kids will love seeing the goats graze on the grass roof of this Swedish-style restaurant. Bring your camera! **Not Licked Yet,** Highway 42, Fish Creek (920-868-2617), is open seasonally for outdoor dining beside a nicely landscaped play area for children. Window service features burgers, salads, and ice cream—great for little ones who can't sit through an entire meal.

For More Information

Contact the **Door County Chamber of Commerce,** P.O. Box 406, Sturgeon Bay 54235 (920-743-4456; doorcountyvacations.com) for literature on the area. For information on Wisconsin, contact the state tourism board at (800) 432-TRIP or www.tourism.state.wi.us. For specific details concerning Milwaukee, contact the Greater Milwaukee Convention and Visitors' Bureau at (800) 231-0903; for Milwaukee hotel availability, call (800) 554-1448.

Emergency Numbers

Ambulance, fire and police: 911

Twenty-four-hour physician-staffed emergency service: Door County Memorial Hospital, 330 Sixteenth Place, Sturgeon Bay; (920) 743-5566

Upper Peninsula Clinics: Nor Door Clinic, Sister Bay, (920) 854-2347; Washington Island Clinic, (920) 847-2424

Poison Control: (800) 815-8855

Pharmacy: There are no twenty-four-hour pharmacies; instead contact WalMart, Sturgeon Bay, during daytime hours; (920) 746-0412.

23 Wisconsin

Northwoods Area

The vast Northwoods area of Wisconsin offers families an unspoiled, natural setting for a vacation of down-to-earth pleasures. Most northern Wisconsin communities were once lumbering centers, and the lore and legends of those days live on, although the logging industry declined by the early 1900s. Today the Northwoods is a sporting paradise and summer vacation retreat. Families come here for the scenic woodlands and lakes.

While there are no official boundaries for the Northwoods, the region is considered to be the north-central (north of Wausau) and northeastern (north of Green Bay) part of the state. Oneida County, where Minocqua, Woodruff, and Rhinelander are situated, and Vilas County, home to Arbor Vitae and Lac du Flambeau, are its tourist centers. Minocqua, called the "Island City," is one of the area's popular summer resorts, thanks to the lake that surrounds it and its proximity to more than 3,000 lakes and ponds, the largest concentration of freshwater lakes in the world. Pine-scented forests offer hiking and biking trails, and day trips lead to man-made and natural wonders. In winter this area (Minocqua and surrounding towns are referred to as the Lakeland area) is a top snowmobile destination, as well as home to Minocqua Winter Park, a cross-country ski facility.

Getting There

The **Rhinelander-Oneida County Airport** (715-362-3641), 25 miles from Minocqua, is served by major commercial carriers. Taxi service is available at the airport. The **Lakeland Airport,** 1545 North Farming Road, Woodruff, is available to private planes. Call (715) 356-4340. **Greyhound** (715-362-2737) also goes to Rhinelander. There are no nearby Amtrak stations.

Getting Around

Cars, boats, and bikes are the popular transportation modes around these parts. There's no public transportation.

Northwoods Area

AT A GLANCE

- Hike, ski, and snowmobile through pine-scented forests
- Learn about logging at the Rhinelander Logging Museum
- See birch bark canoes and Chippewa clothing and crafts at the George W. Brown Jr. Ojibwe Museum & Cultural Center
- Minocqua-Arbor Vitae-Woodruff Area Chamber of Commerce, (800) 44-NORTH, www.minocqua.org
- Rhinelander Chamber of Commerce, (800) 236-4FUN

What to See and Do

Parks

Torpy Park, downtown Minocqua, has a beach with approximately 340 feet of frontage on Lake Minocqua. The beach is safe for kids, as it has roped swimming areas, lifeguards, and a designated boat-landing area. The park has a diving area, a kiddie dock, tennis courts, a sand volleyball court, picnic tables, and grills, as well as a band shell for evening activities. In winter dress warmly and come here for ice skating.

Brandy Park, Arbor Vitae, off Highway 51N on Lemma Creek Road, has a beach/swim area with lifeguards, tennis courts, baseball diamonds, rest rooms, and a pavilion with picnic tables and grills. Shady Park also has an ice-skating rink in winter.

Bearskin State Park Trail is a wilderness trail that extends for 18.2 miles, from just north of the Lincoln and Oneida County line north to Minocqua. The trail, which you enter from behind the Minocqua Post Office, is a former railroad grade that's been surfaced with crushed red granite for hiking and biking. Deer, raccoon, otters, beavers, and other native wildlife can be seen. You cross the scenic Beaver Creek several times via rustic trestles. In winter snowmobiles are allowed to use the trails, although no other motorized vehicles are permitted. Midpoint on the shore of **South Blue Lake,** there's a rest area with toilets, picnic tables, grills, and drinking water. A pass is required for bicycling.

Minocqua is within striking distance of two forests, both offering wilderness recreational opportunities. It's about 13 miles from downtown Minocqua to the eastern part of the vast **Chequamegon National**

Minocqua Winter Park

In winter **Minocqua Winter Park,** Squirrel Lake Road off Highway 70 West, offers visitors 75 kilometers of groomed cross-country trails, a certified ski school, a ski shop that rents and sells skis and snowshoes, and special trails groomed for small children. The day lodge provides childcare on Tuesday, weekends, and holidays. Call (715) 356-3309. The facility is closed Wednesday.

Forest with nearly 850,000 acres of lakes, rivers, streams, northern hardwoods, pines, and meadowlands. There are twenty-four campsites; the **Chippewa Campground** in the Medford District is the only one with warm-water showers and flush toilets. It has a swimming beach and play area. For camping reservations call (800) 283-CAMP. The forest publishes a number of helpful brochures on different aspects of the park, including cross-country ski and hiking trails, scenic overlooks, wetland wildlife viewing areas, historic sites, and fishing and boating areas. Contact the forest headquarters, 1170 Fourth Street, Park Falls (715-762-2461), for more information.

Northern Highland-American Legion State Forest, Woodruff, is the other forest. It's about 5 miles north of Minocqua to the southwest fringe of the forest near the Woodruff area headquarters. This forest offers 222,000 acres with 900 lakes, plus woodland, nature, and hiking trails. Families also enjoy picnicking, swimming, and canoeing.

There are nine unsupervised beach and picnic areas throughout the park. The closest to Minocqua is **Clear Lake,** which also has a rustic campground (no flush toilets or running water) and a swimming area. For more information stop by or contact Woodruff Area Forest Headquarters, 8770 Highway J, Woodruff 54568 (715-356-5211).

Museums

George W. Brown Jr. Ojibwe Museum & Cultural Center, Peace Pipe Road just south of the Indian Bowl, in Lac du Flambeau (715-588-3333). The nearby village of Lac du Flambeau lies in the center of the 144-square-mile Lac du Flambeau Chippewa Indian Reservation. The French name, meaning "Lake of the Flaming Torches," was given by fur traders who saw Chippewas fishing in their canoes by torchlight. The Ojibwe Museum and Cultural Center, which is open late June through mid-August, appeals to kids. Exhibits include an authentic Indian dugout canoe, birchbark canoes, crafts and traditional clothing, ceremonial drums, artifacts, and an exhibit displaying Chippewa activities and clothing. Demonstrations take place regularly.

Minocqua Museum in downtown Minocqua at 416 Chicago Avenue (715-356-7666), displays the Island City's unique history. Open early June through Labor Day. Call for hours.

Rhinelander Logging Museum, Pioneer Park (715-369-5004). Rhinelander began as a supply center for the logging camps when logging was in its heyday. Today the museum, open from mid-May through mid-September, has a replica of an 1870s lumber camp, complete with bunkhouse, cook shanty, and blacksmith shop constructed of Norway pine logs. Logging artifacts on display include tools and equipment and fascinating photographs. On the grounds are early logging equipment, such as a narrow-gauge locomotive and a rare steam-powered snow snake used to haul sleds of logs over icy highways. A cage contains a black "hodag" (see Shopping for a description of this local mythical creature) and a miniature electric sawmill. Stop by the gift shop for a hodag souvenir or other Northwoods item. Most of these items are crafted by senior citizens who work at the museum.

Dr. Kate Pelham Newcomb Museum, 923 Second Avenue, Woodruff (715-356-6896), pays tribute to an extraordinary local woman who reached the sick in a special car outfitted with skis on the front wheels and tractor treads on the rear. To access more remote areas, she used snowshoes. Dr. Newcomb practiced until she died in 1956 at age seventy, and her story, told in this museum, is really an inspiration.

Powwows

- **Lac du Flambeau Indian Powwows,** Indian Bowl (715-588-3346), take place from late June through mid-August. Kids enjoy the ceremonial dances by authentic Chippewa performers.
- **Wa-Swa-Goning,** in Ojibwe means "the place where they spear fish by torchlight." The French fur traders named it Lac du Flambeau. See wigwams, willow fish traps, birch bark baskets, and handmade bows and arrows at this twenty-acre re-created Indian village. Call (715) 588-2615.

Attractions

Million Dollar Penny, the biggest penny in the world, stands on the Arbor Vitae-Woodruff grounds. It symbolizes 1,700,000 pennies (the net contribution collected during the Million Penny Parade for the building fund of the Lakeland Memorial Hospital).

Jim Peck's Wildwood, 2 miles west on Highway 70 (715-356-5588). This is primarily a petting zoo, where kids feed tame deer, pet a porcupine, and cuddle a llama. There's a bear, too, just to admire. Kids will also like the adventure boat rides and nature walk on this thirty-acre property.

At the **Lac du Flambeau Fish Hatchery,** on the Chippewa Reservation, Highway 47, there's a fishing pond open from May through August where the entire family can fish without a license and pay only for the trout caught. Call (715) 588-3307.

At the **Northwoods Wildlife Center,** 8683 Blumstein Road (715-356-7400), more than one hundred injured species are treated yearly. See eagles, deer, and other animals being nursed back to health and, hopefully, to the wild.

Special Tours

- **Wilderness Cruises.** From mid-May to mid-October, enjoy narrated tours aboard the ***Wilderness Queen.*** This boat cruises the unspoiled shoreline of the **Willow Flowage,** a man-made lake built as a reservoir for regulating the Wisconsin River. Sights along the way include wildlife (osprey nests, eagles, loons, and sometimes deer), plus islands and coves. Lunch, dinner, and Sunday brunch cruises are available. Wilderness Cruises is about 15 miles from Minocqua. Call (715) 453-3310 or (800) 472-1516 for more information.
- **Llama Hikes. Old Homestead Llama Treks** (715-453-3094) offers hikes through the Northwoods. With "Take a Llama to Lunch," you walk and the llama carries your picnic.
- **Guided Wilderness Adventures.** Paddle the Northwoods' lakes with **Chequamegon Adventure Company,** Minoqua (888-634-6630). The company creates custom canoe and kayak trips for a daily fee. In winter, their guides lead snowshoe, cross-country ski, and dog-sledding outings.

Circle M Corral, 2½ miles west of U.S. 51 on 70 West (715-356-4441). This amusement and theme park features water slides, kids' rides and splash area, bumper boats, go-carts, train and pony rides, miniature golf, horseback riding, batting cages, a shooting gallery, video games, and a food court.

The Min-Aqua Bats, one of the oldest amateur water-ski shows in the United States, presents a show at Minocqua's downtown Aqua Bowl every Wednesday, Friday, and Sunday night from mid-June to mid-August at 7:00 P.M. The show is free, though donations are requested. Call (715) 356-5266.

Performing Arts

Northern Lights Playhouse, 5611 Highway 51, Hazelhurst, 5 miles south of Minocqua (715-356-7173), presents different shows weekly from May to October, including Broadway smashes, musicals, comedies, and children's shows.

Shopping

There are lots of antique and specialty shops throughout the area. Don't miss the famous Wisconsin fudge at **Dan's Minocqua Fudge Shop,** 521 Oneida Street, downtown (715-356-2662). Loons—the symbol of the Northwoods—are the theme of the **Loon Land Trading Co. Twisted Root Emporium,** 207 Front Street, downtown (715-356-5179). Buy a loon souvenir; then take a look at the solid wood accessories and log furniture.

If you're in Rhinelander, stop by any gift shop for a souvenir "hodag," a dragon-like creature with white claws and white horns along its back. This mythical creature was "photographed" in 1896 by a local lumberman who claimed to have led a party of loggers to capture the monster in a cave. Later, of course, it was revealed as a harmless hoax—done "to get people talking." Today, hodag is the name of every local high school athletic team, as well as the name of a park, a weekly shopping guide, and numerous area events. (See Special Events for one example!)

Scheer's Lumberjack Show

Woodruff, which adjoins Minocqua, used to be a boisterous logging settlement, and, mid-June through August, brings back some of those colorful days. The kids love the chopping and sawing, canoe jousting, speed climbing, clown acts, and log rolling. It's great fun. **Scheer's Lumberjack Show,** Highway 47, Woodruff (715-356-4050.

Side Trips

Take an excursion aboard the **Laona and Northern Railway's** steam train, the ***Lumberjack Special.*** The train departs from the historic depot in Laona, about one and a half hours east of Minocqua. The train goes to the Camp Five Museum Complex from mid-June to late August, except Sunday, leaving at 11:00 A.M., noon, 1:00, and 2:00 P.M. Check ahead for times. Unless you arrive at boarding time, there's not much else to do in this rural area. Return trains leave at 11:20 A.M., 12:20, 1:20, and 4:00 P.M. Buy your tickets at the depot, about ⅓ mile out of Laona toward Rhinelander on Highway 8.

The museum complex, accessible only by train, is about 2½ miles from the depot. Here you'll find a logging museum with artifacts, active blacksmith and harness shops, a lumber company money collection, a thirty-minute video on how the steam engine gets going in the morning, and other exhibits.

Also onsite are an old-fashioned country store, an animal corral, an ecology walk, and a nature center. A half-hour forest tour by surrey is included in the admission fee, or take a hayrack/pontoon boat ride through a bird refuge and along banks of wild rice for a slight additional charge. Call (715) 674-3414 in summer and (715) 845-5544 in winter.

Special Events

Check with the Minocqua-Arbor Vitae-Woodroof Area Chamber of Commerce for special doings in the area. The Lakeland *Times,* published twice weekly, also includes local events. Some highlights:

February. Snowfest features ice sculpting, ice bowling, cross-country ski demos, snowman building, and hot air balloon demonstration flights.

March. Howard Young Cup in Minocqua Winter Park, the biggest cross-country ski race in Wisconsin after the Berkebiner. Call (715) 356-3309.

July. The Fourth Celebration; Hodag Country Festival, Rhinelander, a three-day celebration—the largest in the Northwoods—featuring an outdoor amphitheater with top country-music entertainment, camping on grounds, food, souvenirs (hodags, anyone?), and family fun.

Where to Stay

There are a variety of accommodations in the area, ranging from motel rooms to housekeeping cottages to luxury suites. The Minocqua-Arbor Vitae-Woodruff Area Chamber of Commerce has a visitors guide that lists all types of lodging. Here are a few selections for families.

Sandy Point Resort and Disc Golf Course, 1230 Sandy Point Lane, Lac du Flambeau (715-588-3233), has a beach disc (Frisbee) golf course and comfortable, basic cabins. **Black's Cliff,** Hazelhurst (715-356-3018), has a ¾-mile shoreline on Lower Kaubashine, a 200-acre lake. The resort has housekeeping cottages and a kids' tree house. **Aberdeen Lodge,** Twin Pines Road (715-543-8700), has modern log cabins and a location on Manitosh Waters chain of lakes.

The Beacons of Minocqua, 8250 Northern Road (800-236-3225), is on Lake Minocqua. Sixty units range from one to three bedrooms. Kid comforts include pontoon boats, game rooms, summer activities, and a beach.

The Point Resort Hotel, Highway 51S (715-356-4431), has sixty-nine studios and suites on Lake Minocqua. The resort has an indoor pool, a playground, terraces with gas grills, and docking facilities. It's only a short walk to family attractions, dining, and shopping.

Minocqua Shores, Island City Point (715-356-5101). One mile from town, this resort offers three- and four-bedroom lakeside condos with dishwashers and microwaves, one- to three-bedroom cottages. The property has a beach area, and pontoon and paddleboat rentals.

New Concord Inn, Highway 51 in downtown Minocqua (715-356-1800), has fifty-four rooms, an indoor pool, and a game room. The inn is across the street from Torpy Park Beach, 1 block from the Bearskin Trail, and within walking distance of the water-ski show.

Where to Eat

Hearty meals are the norm in the Northwoods. The Minocqua-Arbor Vitae-Woodruff Area Chamber of Commerce visitors guide lists a number of area restaurants. Here are several families will like.

Paul Bunyan's Lumberjack Cook Shanty, 8653 Highway 51 North, has an 1890s logging camp feel and specializes in hearty camp breakfasts—lunch and dinner served, too. Stop by for the Friday Fish Blast. (Note: Just about every restaurant in town has fish fries on Friday.) Call (715) 356-6270 for information.

Mama's Supper Club (715-356-5070), overlooking Curtis Lake, on Highway 70 West, has kid's menus and serves delicious Sicilian fare, including homemade pizza.

Pappy's Pizza Pub, 198 Highway 51 N, Woodruff (715-356-2140), serves Chicago-style pizza and sandwiches. Eat there or have them deliver.

For More Information

Contact the **Minocqua-Arbor Vitae-Woodruff Area Chamber of Commerce,** P.O. Box 1006, Minocqua 54548, for literature on the area, call (800) 44-NORTH; www.minocqua.org. For Rhinelander information call the **Rhinelander Chamber of Commerce** at (800) 236-4FUN. For free Wisconsin travel literature, including the excellent *Wisconsin Auto Tours Guide,* featuring the Northwoods and Minocqua, call (800) 432-TRIP. Or visit Wisconsin on the Internet at www.tourism.state.wi.us.

Emergency Numbers

Ambulance, fire, and police: 911

Twenty-four-hour physician-staffed emergency service: Howard Young Medical Center, 240 Maple Street, Woodruff; (715) 356-8000

Poison Control: (608) 262-3702 (Madison)

There's no twenty-four-hour pharmacy; the hospital will dispense an overnight supply of medicine after pharmacy hours. Joe's Lakeland Pharmacy, Save-More Plaza, Route 51N, Minocqua (715-356-3303), is open from 9:00 A.M. to 6:00 P.M. weekdays and 9:00 A.M. to 4:00 P.M. Saturday (closed Sunday); Wal-Mart pharmacy, Highway 70 West (715-356-1609).

Grand Teton National Park and Jackson

Snow-capped, jagged, and glistening in the sun, Grand Teton's mountain peaks, rising as high as 13,770 feet, fulfill the vision of the American West as both rugged and beautiful. The Gros Ventre and Shoshoni tribes called the 40-mile range Teewinot, a word meaning "many pinnacles." The mountains ascend sharply on the park's western side, above mirrorlike glacial lakes and a deeply forested valley. Grand Teton National Park, stretching for 310,521 acres across fields, mountains, and lakes and cut through by a river, is often bypassed on the way to the more famous, and more crowded, Yellowstone National Park to the north.

But don't pass this beauty by. While sharing much of Yellowstone's larger-than-life scenery, Grand Teton is less crowded and less well known. As a result, on a visit here, families leave the throngs behind. You can hike on quiet trails, float down the Snake River, canoe on pristine lakes, and enjoy the frequent sightings of moose, deer, and elk.

Getting There

The **Jackson Hole Airport,** 1250 East Airport Road (307-733-7682), hosts about fifteen daily flights from connecting Salt Lake City and Denver. The **Grand Teton Lodge Company,** Box 240, Moran 83013 (307-733-2811), offers a shuttle from the airport to Jackson Lake Lodge. Among the taxicab/shuttle services are **All Star Taxi** (307-733-2888), **Alltrans Taxi/Charter** (308-733-3135), **Buckboard Cab** (307-733-7372), **Gray Line of Jackson Hole** (307-733-3135), and **Jackson Hole Transportation. Jackson Hole Express** (SLC to JAC) can be reached at (307) 733-1719.

A car is important in order to get easily around the park at your own pace. Rental cars are available at the Jackson Hole Airport.

Grand Teton National Park and Jackson

AT A GLANCE

- Explore Grand Teton National Park where snow-capped mountains meet glacial lakes
- Enjoy breathtaking scenic drives, hikes on quiet trails, rafting down gentle rivers
- Ski on downhill and cross-country trails
- Attend the Jackson Hole Summer Rodeo
- Grand Teton National Park, (307) 739-3399, www.nps.gov
- Jackson Chamber of Commerce, (307) 733-3316

When driving to the Grand Teton National Park from the south, pass through Jackson and continue north on U.S. 26/89/191, a highway that is open year-round, covers the length of the park, and continues to Yellowstone. From the east, enter the park at Moran Junction, on U.S. 26/287.

Public transportation is minimal. **Greyhound** services Rock Springs, Wyoming (nearly 200 miles away) (307-362-2931). They also go to Idaho Falls in neighboring Idaho, about 100 miles from Grand Teton (208-522-0912). The nearest **Amtrak** station is in Pocatello, Idaho, about 150 miles away from the park.

Getting Around

A car is a must. If you want to tour the park by mountain bike or canoe, rent these in Moose, just outside the southern park entrance.

What to See and Do

Getting Oriented

Your first venture should be to the **Grand Teton National Park Headquarters,** Visitor Services, P.O. Box 170, Moose (307-739-3399). It's about 12 miles north of Jackson near the park's southern border. Talk to the rangers about trails, sites, and activities that appeal to your family. Pick up a free map, songbird guide, and the *Teewinot,* the park newsletter. The newsletter lists hikes, lodgings, and naturalist programs (including summer campfire programs and full-moon walks), ranger-led hikes, and children's programs. Be sure to obtain a copy of the *Young Naturalist,* a brochure that sparks kids' interest with park information, nature questions, and a list of activities necessary to earn a Young Naturalist souvenir badge. (While kids must earn this, parents must pay a nominal fee for this award.)

Browse the Visitor's Center bookstore. *Short Hikes and Easy Walks in Grand Teton National Park,* available for a small fee, is a great resource as it offers suggestions to families, especially those with small children, and those who want to experience the wilderness without the hard work. The parks department also has handouts with hiking information. *Day Hikes,* a free publication, contains a map of the trailheads and lists mileage and elevation. The publication lists less strenuous and time-consuming walks of thirty minutes to the more involved, and often more strenuous, treks that could keep you on the move for up to fourteen hours. *Teton Trails,* available for a moderate fee, includes detailed descriptions of hiking trails and details what you might encounter in the way of flora and fauna of the Teton Range.

Grand Teton's many wonderful recreational pleasures—from easy scenic drives to simple hikes, boat rides, and peaceful canoe trips to difficult backpacking treks—suit families with diverse outdoor temperaments.

Scenic Drives

If pressed for time on this family push, you could just drive through the park by entering at Moose and continuing north along **Teton Park Road.** This winding stretch continues for about 50 miles, becoming U.S. 287/191/89 near the park's northern border as the road heads into Yellowstone. Some scenic places to stretch your legs: about 8 miles north at **Cottonwood Creek** and **Lupine Meadows.** If your visit can only be brief but does allow for time out of the car—a necessity—continue north to pristine **Jenny Lake,** where a brief ferry ride and a short walk lead to a picnic spot by a waterfall. Be aware of the schedule for the return boat rides; after the last trip you must either spend the night or take a long hike back, about two and a half hours (see hiking section later in this chapter).

Back on Teton Park Road, the trip north leads you by the 7,593-foot **Signal Mountain** and **Jackson Lake,** an impressive stretch of clear waters with wooded shores. At **Colter Bay Visitor Center,** take time to check out the educational programs and to browse in the **Indian Arts Museum,** where Native American artists demonstrate their crafts daily from June through early September.

Autumn is a magical time among the majestic Grand Tetons.

Grand Teton National Park

Hiking and Canoeing in the Southern Park. After the ferry ride across Jenny Lake, follow the trail ¼ mile to **Inspiration Point,** 400 feet above the lake. Continue along the trail for 0.2 miles to **Hidden Falls.** While Hidden Falls is often crowded, the trail to **Cascade Canyon** usually isn't. From Hidden Falls continue 3½ miles along level ground to the glacier-carved boulders of Cascade Canyon, habitat of the yellow-bellied marmot and golden-mantled ground squirrel.

North of Jenny Lake are two nearly connected bodies of water offering easy hikes, easy canoeing, and scenic views. **String Lake Trail** circles String Lake for a flat 3½ miles (allow about three hours). **Leigh Lake Trail** (park at the String Lake parking lot) leads 2 miles (about one hour) to the lake's south shore. To get a scenic view of 12,605-foot **Mount Moran,** canoe to the northern edge of String Lake; then portage about 100 yards to Leigh Lake. Paddle along this lake, pausing to hike along the shores. You can picnic at almost any spot and be sitting pretty with a scenic view of Mount Moran. You can rent canoes from **Dornans' Moose Enterprises,** 10 Moose Lane (307-733-2522), as well as from several park concessions.

Hiking and Canoeing in the Northern Park. **Jackson Lake.** Is 20 miles long, dominating the northern section of the park. It is more heavily forested and generally quieter than the lakes in the southern section. **Signal Mountain Marina** on Jackson Lake (307-543-2831) rents canoes. You can find helpful information and nature programs, including slide shows about coyotes and bald eagles, at the **Colter Bay Visitor Center.**

Hermitage Point Trail loops for 3 miles around **Swan Lake** and **Heron Pond** through pine forests, meadows, wetlands, and lakes. You are likely to catch sight of beaver, otter, elk, and moose and hear the horn-like sounds of trumpeter swans. A round-trip hike of the entire 8.8-mile Hermitage Point trail takes about four hours. **Lunchtree Hill Trail** pleases young children and bird lovers. The ½-mile stroll begins at Jackson Lake Lodge and winds through marshy meadows, home to songbirds and hummingbirds. **Grand View Point Trail,** a 2.2 mile, two-hour round-trip trek suitable for older children, rewards you with a climb through woods to a summit with a panoramic view.

Swimming. Although it's allowed at **Jenny Lake, String Lake,** and **Leigh Lake.** most people opt not to swim in these glacier-fed lakes' waters that hover at about 54 degrees Fahrenheit. Only those impervious to the cold go for the plunge. String Lake offers the shallowest waters, and Leigh Lake invites with quartz sand and a beautiful view. While fishing is allowed on Bradley and Taggert Lakes, swimming is not.

River Float Trips. A float trip down the Snake River gently weaves you through the spectacular landscape, providing ample opportunity for wildlife viewing. Especially nice are the dinner trips. These leave from the Moose Visitor Center around 6:00 P.M. for a 10-mile drive upstream. Your float downstream on a twelve-person raft takes about three hours, including a stop for dinner at an encampment. Dress warmly.

While wildlife sightings are not guaranteed, you're likely to see animals at dusk. Often great blue herons dance above the water and eagles nest in the tall pines. You might even see a moose.

Outfitters include **Barker-Ewing Float Trips** (800-365-1800 for scenic trips and 800-448-4202 for white-water trips), **Grand Teton Lodge Company Float Trips** (307-543-2811), and **Triangle X Float Trips** (307-733-2183), which has trips with an overnight in a teepee.

Fishing Trips. Twenty-six Jackson Hole businesses offer guided trips, including **Westbank Anglers** (800-733-6483). The **Wyoming Game and Fish Bureau** (307-777-4600) has a list of outfitters and sites.

Mountain Biking. Rent some fat wheels from **Adventure Sports** (307-733-3307) for a self-guided scenic pedal. But be careful; don't bike along the often crowded park roads. Use the designated mountain trail.

Horseback Riding. The area east of Jackson Lake is a good spot for guided rides. With the **Jackson Lake Lodge Corral** (307-543-2811) saddle up for a guided breakfast or evening excursion. The **Grand Teton**

Off-the-Slopes Winter Adventures

- **Feed the Elk.** At the **National Elk Refuge** east of Jackson, thousands of elk come to feed during the winter. A sleigh ride through the refuge with **National Elk Refuge Horse Drawn Sleigh Ride,** Box C, Jackson 83001 (307-733-5386), is available from mid-December through April. The whole family, even little ones, will like seeing these majestic animals close-up.
- **Wildlife Safari.** The **Great Plains Wild Life Institute** (307-733-2623) has naturalist-led tours. Use the van's telescopes and binoculars for up-close looks at bighorn sheep, moose, and bald eagles. Wildlife Discovery tours include the extra fun of lunch at a local ranch plus a snowshoe nature walk. A half-day sunrise tour is offered too. Call ahead to book.
- **Dogsled trek.** This is a cozy and easy way to get into the backcountry. The huskies do the work while you savor the woodland peace and the wildlife. For this tour all you'll hear are the wind in the trees, the swoosh of the sled, and the panting of the dogs. Among the area's companies **Jackson Hole Iditarod Sled Dog Tours,** Box 1940, 83001 (307-733-7388), is led by Frank Teasley, a professional musher and veteran of Alaska's grueling Iditarod. His guided runs take you east to Granite Hot Springs, past wildlife trails and to a 108-degree hot-springs soak (wear a suit). Other routes go through Grand Teton National Park. **Washakie Outfitting Dog Sled Tours** (307-455-2616 or 800-249-0662) is another choice. Ask about the size of the sled. For most runs two smaller kids or one adult and one small child can usually snuggle in the sled, while another adult, if the guides permit, can stand on the back of the sled. Ask how many sleds will be required for your group.
- **Snowcoach tour.** The south entrance to **Yellowstone National Park** (see Yellowstone National Park chapter) is about two hours away. In winter, most of the roads are closed to public vehicles, but the animals are out. With young children opt for a tour by heated park snowcoach (a bus equipped for the deep snow). Call **Yellowstone Reservations** (307) 344-7311 or **Flagg Ranch Resort** (307) 543-2861, or (800) 443-2311.
- **Snowmobile Tours.** With teens or preteens try a snowmobile run from Yellowstone's south entrance to Old Faithful. Pass

(continued)

Off-the-Slopes Winter Adventures *(continued)*

by bison and elk, track coyotes, and watch out for the mule deer as you roar up to this steamy geyser surrounded by snow—quite a sight in winter. But be aware; it's an arduous trip, about 80 miles each way. Outfitters include **Rocky Mountain Snowmobile Tours,** (307-733-2237 or 800-647-2561), **Flagg Ranch Village** (307-543-2861 or 800-443-2311), **Heart Six Guest Ranch** (307-543-2477 or 888-543-2477), and **Jackson Hole Snowmobile Tours** (307-733-6850 or 800-633-1733).

Lodge Company (307-543-2811) operates one- and two-hour treks for riders ages eight and older.

Hot Air Ballooning. Float above the Sanke River and the Jackson Valley in a hot air balloon. Outfitters include the **Wyoming Balloon Company** (307-739-0900).

Jackson

On this vacation, allow some time to explore the town of Jackson (Jackson Hole is the valley), a cowboy town 12 miles south of Grand Teton National Park's Moose headquarters. Jackson's small-town, Old West flair and friendliness intrigue kids. With little kids, hop aboard the **stagecoach,** at the corner of the town square next to the ticket booth, for a short spin through town.

You'll notice right away that the town square differs from most local parks because it's adorned at all four corners with arches made of real elk antlers, which are collected by the local Boy Scouts after the local herd sheds them. Be around this square in the summer on a Monday through Saturday night at 6:30 P.M. when the town's good guys shoot it out with the bad guys, a special treat for elementary school kids. (Warn little ones of the guns' noise, and assure everyone that it's safe. No real bullets are fired.)

There's more rough riding at the **Jackson Hole Summer Rodeo,** Rodeo Grounds, Snow King Avenue (307-733-2805), every Wednesday and Saturday evening through Labor Day. Kids love the steer roping, barrel racing, and quick horsemanship.

The **National Museum of Wildlife Art,** 2820 Rungius Road (307-733-5771), features 250 works by well-known painters and sculptors, plus a private collection of big game wildlife art. The **Jackson Hole Historical Society and Museum,** 105 North Glenwood Street (307-733-9605), focuses on Jackson's history with archaeological artifacts, fur-trade exhibits, and mounted game heads (which often scare little kids and annoy environmentally concerned adults).

Golf. Jackson Hole sports two championship golf courses, both with scenic views: The **Jackson Hole Golf and Tennis Club,** P.O. Box 250, Moran 83013 (307-543-2811 in winter, 307-733-3111 in summer); and the **Teton Pines Golf Club** (307-733-1733). Apparently the high altitude (6,209 feet above sea level) carries golf balls 10 percent farther than at sea level. For younger kids **Alpine Gardens,** Snow King Resort (307-733-5200), offers eighteen holes of miniature golf.

Scenic Mountain Views. Get a bird's-eye view of the summer and fall scenery, even if you don't ski, by riding the **Snow King Resort Scenic Chairlift,** Snow King Resort (307-733-5200). If you hike up, the ride down is free. For a nominal fee **Teton Village's Aerial Tram,** Teton Village (307-733-2292), offers splendid views as well.

More Winter Fun

Alpine (Downhill) Skiing. The Jackson Hole area offers excellent skiing at three facilities. The slopes at **Snow King Ski Resort** (307-733-5200), Wyoming's original ski area, nearly swoop down into town. Open to skiers from mid-December to April, with night skiing available Tuesday to Saturday, Snow King has a 1,571-foot vertical drop and lots of beginner and intermediate trails.

On the sunny west side of the Teton mountains is **The Grand Targhee Ski Resort,** Box SKI, Alta, Wyoming, via Driggs, Idaho 83422 (307-353-2300 or 800-TARGHEE). The ski area offers 3,000 acres of terrain, about 70 percent of it intermediate.

Grand Targhee has nursery facilities for tots two months and older. Children ages three and four can have private lessons, while ages five to seven take a learn-and-play program. The ski school also has ski programs for ages five through twelve. Children five and under always ski free, and children fourteen and under generally ski free when one adult purchases a three-day or more lodging package. At Grand Targhee it's hard for kids to get lost since all trails funnel down into the same base area.

The **Jackson Hole Mountain Resort,** Box 290, Teton Village 83025 (307-733-2292 or 800-443-6931), is the area's most well-known resort. Twelve miles from Jackson, this ski area boasts a 4,139-foot vertical rise, the steepest in the United States. Jackson Hole, while offering some top-notch difficult terrain, also has more than 22 miles of groomed beginner and intermediate trails. Rendezvous Mountain is a challenge; most families start and even keep to the less demanding trails on Apres Vous.

At the Jackson Hole Ski School, classes are available for adults, kids ages three to five in the Rough Rider Ski Program, and six to thirteen in the Explorer Ski Program. A nursery is available for ages two months to eighteen months, and child care is provided for ages nineteen months to five years. Children five and under ski free. Call the ski school for new program information at (307) 739-2663.

Nordic (Cross-Country) Skiing. Ski-skating tracks are available at Jackson Hole Nordic Center, Grand Targhee Nordic Center, Spring Creek Nordic Center, and at Teton Pines Nordic Center.

For those who like the easy, gliding pace of cross-country skiing, the **Jackson Hole Nordic Center,** P.O. Box 290, Teton Village 83025 (307-733-2629), rents cross-country skis and offers several kilometers of groomed trails. A variety of cross-country programs are offered for children and families.

The Grand Targhee Nordic Center, Box SKI, Alta (307-353-2300 or 800-TARGHEE), has 15 kilometers of groomed trails. The **Teton Pines Nordic Ski Center,** next to the J.H. Racquet Club (307-733-1005), features between 10 and 13 kilometers of trails plus lessons for children and adults as well as day-care facilities and rentals. The **Spring Creek Nordic Center,** Box 3154 (307-733-1004), offers 14 kilometers of trails that wind through a nature reserve, making it likely you'll spot some deer, elk, maybe even moose. Rentals and lessons are available.

In **Grand Teton National Park,** check with the rangers for trail conditions, but generally when there's snow, favorite cross-country trails include the beginner's 3-mile **Swan Lake–Heron Pond Loop,** near the Colter Bay Visitor Center, and the longer 9-mile **Jenny Lake Trail.**

Theater and the Arts

Yes, Jackson has theater, but the fare tends to be good old Western family goings-on. From Memorial Day through Labor Day, check out the musical comedy at the **Jackson Hole Playhouse,** Deloney Street between Millward and Glenwood Streets (307-733-6994). The **Grand Teton Mainstage Theater,** P.O. Box 20264 (307-733-3670), at times, also sports what they call "elegant and rowdy family fun." The town also has a chuck-wagon show: **Bar J Chuckwagon,** Teton Village Road (307-733-3370).

Shopping

Boutiques, western-wear shops, more than thirty-five fine art galleries, and three museums specializing in western landscapes and paintings of cowboys and Native Americans, ring the town square and adorn the side streets. Pop in and out of the galleries until you find one that appeals to you; you won't have a problem. Other good bets: **Trailside Galleries,** Town Square and Center Street, Drawer 1149 (307-733-3186), and **Martin-Harris Gallery,** upstairs at 60 East Broadway (307-733-0350).

Many stores offer Native American jewelry and crafts. Know what you're buying and comparison shop. The **Valley Bookstore,** 125 North Cache, Town Square (307-733-4533), features a good selection of maps, mountaineering books, field guides, and children's books.

SIDE TRIPS

For more river adventures, contact **Barker-Ewing River Trips,** 45 West Broadway, Box 3032B, Jackson 83001 (307-733-1800 or 800-365-1800). They offer a white-water overnight raft trip down the Snake River, on a section that is scenic but not in the Grand Teton National Park. Minimum age is six. This trip is a delight, but remember to dress warmly and bring rain gear and gloves just in case. (You're not in Kansas anymore.)

Even with little tots you can re-create the pioneer days with **wagon train trips** lasting two to six days. Families ride in renovated wagons that have cushions to soften the bounce (an amenity not available to our stalwart pioneers). You can also ride horseback alongside. The trips include campfire cookouts and, with some outfitters, staged "Indian" attacks just to simulate the frontier fears and create some excitement. Among the outfitters: **Wagons West,** Peterson-Madsen-Taylor Outfitters, P.O. Box 1156A, Afton 83110 (307-886-9693 or 800-447-4711).

SPECIAL EVENTS

Check with the Chamber of Commerce for more specific information about these events in the Grand Teton and Jackson areas.

February. International Rocky Mountain Stage Stop Sled Dog Race; Cowboy Ski Challenge.

April. The Pole-Pedal-Paddle, a ski-cycle-canoe relay race starts at Jackson Hole and finishes at the Snake River.

May. The Elk Antler Auction, Jackson town square; Old West Days with Native American dancing, cowboy poetry, and Mountain Man rendezvous; Teton Village Mountain Man Rendezvous.

June–September. Wednesday and Saturday see the Jackson Hole Summer Rodeo near downtown Jackson.

July–August. Nightly concerts at the famed Grand Teton Music Festival, Teton Village.

August. Grand Targhee Bluegrass Festival with musicians from the Rocky Mountain region, children's entertainment, and crafts.

September. Jackson Hole Fall Arts Festival of gallery shows, artist's workshops, and dance.

October. Quilting in the Tetons, exhibits and workshops.

December–April. Ski races for amateurs.

WHERE TO STAY

Lodging is limited within Grand Teton but widely available in nearby Jackson. Within the park, one of the best lodges for families is **Signal Mountain Lodge,** Box 50, Moran (307-543-2381). They offer lakefront cabins, apartments, and motel units. **Jackson Lake Lodge,** Box 240, Moran, is also lakefront and a good family choice with motel-style units (307-543-3100 or 800-628-9988). **Colter Bay Village Cabins,** Box 240, Moran (307-543-3100 or 800-628-9988), rents log cabins.

Grand Teton National Park has five National Park Service campgrounds. **Jenny Lake,** with only forty-nine sites, is the most popular; this campground tends to fill before 8:00 A.M., so arrive early. Another popular spot is **Lizard Lake** with sixty sites; this tends to fill by 2:00 P.M.

Outside the park grounds there are several facilities. **Snake River KOA,** 12 miles south of Jackson Highway 89-191, Star Route Box 14A (307-733-7078), has showers and also arranges horseback riding and float trips. Trailers and tents are welcome.

For familiar chain lodgings, try **Best Western Lodge at Jackson Hole,** Box 7478 (307-739-9703 or 800-458-3866), or **Best Western Inn at Jackson Hole,** Box 328, Teton Village (307-733-2311 or 800-842-7666). **Days Inn,** which offers free continental breakfast, is a mile south of downtown Jackson, Box 2986 (307-733-0033 or 800-329-7466). The Jackson Hole Chamber of Commerce has a complete listing of all area accommodations.

Another option is **Teton Village,** Teton Village Property Management, Teton Village (307-733-4610 or 800-443-6840), 12 miles northwest of Jackson on Wyoming 390. The company has 125 condominiums spread out at the base of 10,536-foot Rendezvous Peak.

Snow King Resort, P.O. Box SKI, Jackson 83001 (307-733-5200 or 800-522-5464), has hotel rooms, suites, and condominiums. For more Jackson Hole accommodations, call **Jackson Hole Central Reservations,** Box 2618, Jackson 83001; (307) 733-4005 or (800) 443-6931.

Another ski resort that makes an ideal summer spot for families, especially those with tots, is **Grand Targhee,** Box Ski, Alta 83422, about an hour's drive from Grand Teton National Park (307-353-2300 or 800-

Wildflower Inn

In Jackson Hole the **Wildflower Inn** (307-733-4710), a bed-and-breakfast 10 miles from the park's south entrance, welcomes families. This hand-hewn log home sports pleasing country decor, a glass-enclosed hot tub, and friendly hosts. Stay here for a real western welcome. For additional bed-and-breakfast options, call the **Jackson Hole Bed and Breakfast Association** at (307) 542-2632.

TARGHEE). The Kids Club Day Camp has activities for ages four to ten from 9:00 A.M. to 5:00 P.M. Grand Targhee's accommodations include motels and condominiums.

Go western with a dude ranch stay. The **Triangle X Ranch,** P.O., Box 120T, Moose 83012 (307-733-2183), is a dude ranch complete with nature hikes, scenic float trips, western dancing, and cookouts. Winter activities include cross-country skiing and wildlife viewing. **Lost Creek Ranch,** 25 miles northeast of Jackson, P.O. Box 95, Moose 83012 (307-733-3435), has two-bedroom cabins, an outdoor heated pool, tennis court, and a children's program. Ride the range or head off to a secluded fishing spot. **R. Lazy S Ranch,** a mile north of Teton Village, P.O. Box 308, Teton Village 83025 (307-733-2655), has twelve cabins and separate riding programs for adults and kids over six, as well as pack trips, hikes, and boating.

Spring Creek Resort Hotel & Conference Center

Situated on a 1,000-acre nature preserve atop a butte, this casually upscale resort is both family friendly and rated four-diamond by AAA. Rooms and condominiums are available. Great views and some of the area's best dining make Spring Creek a treat. Kids especially like looking out the dining room windows to count the wildlife that roams by. The resort also provides transportation to the ski areas and has its own cross-country center. In summer the resort can arrange day forays, from whitewater rafting to hiking and horseback riding. **Spring Creek Resort Hotel & Conference Center,** Box 3154, 1800 Spirit Dance Road (307-733-8833 or 800-443-6139).

WHERE TO EAT

Before setting out to explore the park, stock up at **Dornans' Deli,** 10 Moose Street (307-733-2415), with muffins, sandwiches, and drinks, or sit down and eat at an outdoor picnic table as you gaze over the Teton peaks. In the park, take a meal break at the **Grand Teton Lodge Company,** Jackson Lake Lodge (307-543-2811).

Jackson, like any town that swells in season with tourists, serves up a variety of eateries. The tourist map of town lists most of the restaurants, including the familiar fast-food places just like the ones back home.

For some western pizzazz with your plateful of baked beef and chicken, go to the **Bar J. Chuckwagon and Original Western Show,** off Wyoming 390 (307-733-3370). After your meal, go country with a medley of cowboy singing, poetry, foot-stompin' fiddle playing, and dancing. In town, **Bubba's Bar-B-Que,** 515 West Broadway (307-733-2288), dishes up moderately priced ribs, chicken wings, and a salad bar. In winter go to dinner by horse-drawn sleigh with the **Bar-T-Five Outfitters,** P.O. Box 2140, Jackson 83001 (307-733-5386). Layer-up for this moonlight-and-stars ride to a pioneer cabin for barbecue and chicken followed by medleys performed by the Bar-T-Five Singin' Cowboys.

For More Information

The **Moose Visitor Center,** 12 miles north of Jackson Hole, is at the park's southern end. **Colter Bay Visitor Center,** near Jackson Lake (307-543-2467), is in the north area of the park. **Grand Teton National Park,** Drawer 170, Moose 83012. **Wyoming Division of Tourism,** I-25 at College Drive, Cheyenne 82002 (307-777-7777 or 800-225-5996). **Wyoming State Parks and Historic Sites,** 2301 Central, Barrett Building, Cheyenne 82002 (307-777-6323). **Wyoming Recreation and Parks Association,** Box 953, Rawlins 82301 (307-328-4570).

For a *Jackson Hole Vacation Planner,* call **Jackson Chamber of Commerce;** (307) 733-3316. Weather and road conditions, (307) 733-2220. Via Internet: info@jacksonhole.com.

Before your trip obtain a copy of the sixteen-page *The Kids Guide to Jackson Hole,* available from Nancy Brumsted and Jan Segerstrom, Teton County Schools, P.O. Box 568, Jackson County 83001. The guide, written by local schoolchildren, gives other kids inside tips.

Emergency Numbers

Ambulance, fire, police: 911

Local sheriff: (307) 733-4052

Local police: (307) 733-1430

Local fire department: (307) 733-2331

Hospital: St. John's Hospital, 625 East Broadway in Jackson; (307) 733-3636

Twenty-four-hour pharmacy: Albertson's Grocery Store, 520 West Broadway; (307) 733-9222

Poison Control Hotline: (800) 422-2704

YELLOWSTONE NATIONAL PARK

No family member will ever be bored in a national park as spectacular as Yellowstone. This important and impressive geothermal region continues to display some of the powerful forces deep within the earth. Old Faithful erupts spraying steam hundreds of feet into the air. But this well-known geyser, with a habit of spouting on schedule, is just one of many that mark the landscape. Yellowstone offers much more than geysers. Admire the canyon, hike through forests along trails that lead to waterfalls, take scenic boat trips on the lake, fish for trout, ride horseback, and just look out your car window to see bison, moose, and bighorn sheep in their native habitat.

GETTING THERE

The **Yellowstone Regional Airport** (307-587-5096), Cody, serves the Big Horn Basin and is serviced by SkyWest/Delta Connection and United Express. **Jackson Hole Airport** (307-733-7695) is larger and serviced by Delta, SkyWest, American Airlines, Continental Express, and United Express.

Greyhound (406-587-3110) offers bus service to Bozeman, Livingston, and West Yellowstone, Montana. **Karst Stage** (406-586-8567 or 406-587-9937) offers connecting bus service from Bozeman and Livingston to the park's north entrance. The **Rock Springs Busline** (406-669-3208) serves Jackson; **Powder River Bus Lines** (307-754-3914) serves Cody. From most of these towns you can take bus transportation to Yellowstone National Park. **Powder River Transportation** (307-527-6316 or 307-587-5544) provides bus service from Cody to Yellowstone's east entrance. There is no direct rail service to the park.

To enter Yellowstone National Park by car coming from Montana in the north, take U.S. 89; from the northeast, take U.S. 212; from Cody, which is east of Yellowstone, take U.S. 14/16/20 or the Chief Joseph Scenic Highway to the northeast entrance. If traveling from the south,

Yellowstone National Park

AT A GLANCE

- See geysers, hot springs, and pastel-colored water holes
- Ride a stagecoach or a horse
- Explore Yellowstone's canyon, 20 miles long and 4,000 feet across
- Look for elk, bison, mule deer, and bears
- Visit the Buffalo Bill Historical Center in nearby Cody
- Yellowstone Park camping, dining, lodging, and tours: AMFAC, (307) 344-7311, www.travelyellowstone.com

take U.S. 287/191/89; if arriving from the west, take U.S. 20 to the park's west entrance. The park's entrance fee is good for seven days. If you plan to stay longer, have a disability, or are over sixty-two years of age, look into an annual Yellowstone Passport, Golden Eagle, Golden Access, or Golden Age Passport.

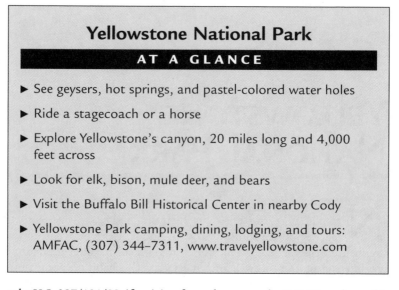

Getting Around

A Grand Loop Road that cuts a figure eight, stretching for 142 miles through the park, takes you by most of the major attractions. Those who prefer that others do the driving should contact **AMFAC,** the park's concessionaire, Yellowstone National Park 82190 (307-344-7311; www.amfac.com). They offer bus tours that cover the Grand Loop, or choose either the Lower Loop or the Upper Loop. These drive-by tours, however, don't do much more than literally allow you to "glimpse" Yellowstone.

The best way for families to experience Yellowstone is by spending time here. Be sure to get out of the car: Stroll, hike, horseback ride, and walk. Only by getting off the road can you truly gain a sense of Yellowstone's grandeur.

What to See and Do

Spring, summer, and early fall before the snows arrive are the best times for families to visit Yellowstone. To avoid the busiest times however, schedule your arrival by late spring or early June. Because Yellowstone is most popular for families in warm weather, particularly when school's out, the hiking, driving, and sightseeing information listed below applies to the warm seasons unless otherwise stated.

If you can get away in late spring or in early autumn, your visit may be more satisfying. Not only do the crowds dissipate at these times, but so does the heat. In spring wildflowers dot the meadows, and in fall the aspens turn the color of spun gold, creating fairy-tale vistas of mountains and ridges.

Winter in Yellowstone brings a special rustic peace. The park's vast fields of snow make Yellowstone a haven for cross-country skiers and snowmobilers. In places icicles arch over the falls, while elsewhere a meadow remains perennially green, thanks to the warmth of a nearby hot spring. Eagles float overhead, gliding on an updraft of air warmed by the boiling geysers. Winter does, however, make for some closed roads and deep snow. Snowmobiles are available, and the cross-country skiing on groomed trails or in the backcountry is superb—if you know what you are doing. AMFAC offers a day trip by heated snowcoach to accessible park highlights. (See Getting Around.)

Yellowstone can be divided into five different regions: **Geyser Country,** full of fumaroles, mudpots, hot pools, and home to Old Faithful; **Mammoth Country,** a thermal area of hot springs; **Roosevelt Country,** where the park offers stagecoach rides and rugged scenery; **Canyon Country,** made dramatic by the Grand Canyon of Yellowstone; and **Lake Country,** where moose, and sometimes bear, roam the shores of Yellowstone Lake, where the native cutthroat trout is plentiful.

Note: Beyond these five areas lies the backcountry. A permit is required if you plan to trek through this area, and you will have to inform the various ranger stations of your exact plans. The wilderness can be beautiful, but precautions should always be taken. Ask the rangers for information about campsites, trails, hiking guides, and bears.

Yellowstone Institute

Find out about grizzly bears, learn how to track animals, discover medicinal plants, and follow Yellowstone's wolves at special weekend family seminars. These are some of the topics covered by the Yellowstone Institute. Participants can bunk on site in log cabins or camp. Reserve these popular programs well in advance.

Call the **Yellowstone Institute** at (307) 344-2294; www.nps.gov/yell/yellinst.htm.

Geyser Country

Old Faithful, named for its regular schedule of eruptions, is the star. Check the chalkboards at the Visitors Center, the local shops, and ice-cream parlors for the "expected" time or simply watch the crowd getting thicker. Although Old Faithful won't disappoint—splashing steamy water 100 to 180 feet into the air, a reminder of earth's primal forces—the area around Old Faithful is disappointing, overbuilt, and overcrowded. With all the parking lots, lodging, eateries, and traffic jams, this bit of the park often seems more reminiscent of a mall than a majestic natural wonder.

Midway Geyser Basin, on the road from Old Faithful toward Mammoth Hot Springs, has colorful pools. At the **Three Senses Trail** visually impaired visitors (and everyone else) can focus on the sounds and feel of the geysers and hot springs. **Fountain Paint Pot** is a must. Allow at least a half hour to walk through this area, where the algae and bacteria surrounding these muddy water holes have turned them to shades of pastel pinks and blues. **Gibbons Meadows,** on the road north from Geyser Country to Mammoth Country, is a favorite grazing spot for herds of bison.

Family Hikes in the Upper Geyser Basin. These easy boardwalk trails wind past forty steamy geysers and hot, bubbling pools. The **Geyser Hill Loop,** a 1.3 mile-track, takes you to **Beehive Geyser,** which can spray more than one hundred feet in the air, but alas, not as predictably as Old Faithful, and **Doublet Pool,** which has a beautiful blue color.

Let your kids use their imaginations to figure out why each geyser was given its particular name. Guess about Turban Geyser, Morning Glory Pool, Mirror Pool, and Sapphire Pool. Listen to the bubbling, watch the grayish white smoke rise, and smell the sulfur (you do become acclimated).

Keep an eye out for Old Faithful, which looks even more dramatic when you are not shoulder-to-shoulder with other tourists. Be careful of the bison; some like to sit near the boardwalk. Admire them from afar. However peaceful these animals may look, they are wild, unpredictable, and can be dangerous.

Note: Be careful to stay on the boardwalk. Do not walk on the ground because the crust around these thermal areas can be dangerously thin. Visitors have been burned, and some killed by the scalding water. Also tell your kids ahead of time to resist the urge to throw pennies, sticks, or anything else into the boiling springs. This is not good for them or the thermal attractions. Hold little ones by the hand, or put them in the stroller; the boardwalk makes for a perfect pathway.

Mammoth Country

Near the northern border of Yellowstone and just minutes away from Gardiner, Montana, is **Mammoth Hot Springs,** where even in high season, the crowds thin out a bit. We prefer staying here for its rustic but serviceable lodging and because this area is less crowded than some others. Look at the films and photographs of the park at the **Albright Visitor Center** (307–344–7381, ext. 357). The acidic waters of Mammoth Hot Springs pass through the limestone calcium carbonate remains, eventually causing these unusual shaped terraces. Walk around these colorful formations. The springs continue to grow, now covering an entire hillside.

Beaver Ponds Trail is an interesting hike, but not for beginners. The trail puts you to the test, gaining 500 feet in elevation.

Horseback Riding. Try an early morning ride when the animals may be more active. With luck, you may come upon a herd of elk as you ride through the sagebrush and aspen groves. Even a brief foray off the road does much to enliven your sense of Yellowstone's wonders.

Roosevelt Country

Roosevelt Country drew the first tourists to Yellowstone, since the area had lodging facilities. Less dramatic than the geyser or canyon areas, Roosevelt Country has the simple serenity and peaceful good looks of forests, meadows, streams, lakes, and marshes.

Tower Fall Trail is a rewarding and not too difficult half-mile hike that leads to **Tower Fall,** a waterfall that cascades 132 feet. Deer often rest on the rocks at the river bottom, where the tumbling waters create a thunderous display.

Horseback and stagecoach rides can be arranged through the Roosevelt Lodge. Minimum age for riding is generally eight. Younger kids can sample a pioneer journey in a scenic but short jaunt in a replica of a Concord stagecoach. These depart June through August.

If you continue from the center of Roosevelt Country toward the northeast entrance of the park, you'll see the **Lamar Valley** and **Lamar River,** known for its good viewing of bison, elk, and mule deer. Small ponds for fishing are nearby.

Canyon Country

Don't miss Canyon Country; many think of this as Yellowstone's most dramatic feature. The canyon, 20 miles long, stretches 4,000 feet across. The canyon walls have dramatic striations of pink, yellow, and orange. Two waterfalls, the **Lower Falls** and the **Upper Falls,** cascade into the misty canyon. Bypass Canyon Village, a touristy spot, but check out the **Canyon Visitor Center** (307-344-7381, ext. 6205), which has maps.

The **Clear Lake Trail** is a moderate hike that goes through large rolling meadows and forested areas to Clear Lake. Just a few miles south of the canyon lies the **Hayden Valley,** an expanse of wild grass and sage that attracts elk, bison, and bears. Be careful; you are in bear country.

Scenic Overlooks. Both **Inspiration Point** and **Grandview Point** afford spectacular canyon views. Along the South Rim, stop at **Upper Falls Overlook,** which is handicapped accessible.

Lake Country

More than 100 miles of shoreline surrounded by tree-covered mountains and blue skies make Yellowstone Lake not only North America's largest mountain lake, but another park highlight. Look for Canada geese and trumpeter swans. At the **Fishing Bridge Visitor Center** (307-344-7381, ext. 6150) find out about fishing areas and permits.

Elephant Back Mountain Trail is a 4-mile hike to a panoramic view of the lake and into Pelican Valley.

At **Lake Yellowstone Hotel** from June to September, you can sign up for a one-hour narrated scenic cruise. Watch for bear and moose that graze along the shoreline and bald eagles as they swoop down to catch trout.

Sunset Views. **Steamboat** and **Lake Butte** are excellent spots for views of Lake Yellowstone and are prime locations for a sunset picnic and photos for the scrapbook.

Winter Adventures

Covered with snow, Yellowstone serves up a special kind of peace. In winter, park roads are restricted to over-the-snow vehicles. The elk, bison, deer, and coyotes still roam the park, but the majority of tourists do not. From the **Mammoth Hot Springs Hotel** (see Where to Stay), you can rent snowmobiles, go ice skating, or rent skis. If cross-country skiing is your prime interest, book a stay at **Old Faithful Snow Lodge,** near the famous geyser. The ski shop rents equipment including snowshoes, and nearby 40 miles of relatively short trails glide through the Old Faithful area, taking you past steaming hot springs, shooting geysers, and some big game—elk and bison. Additional short trails are available in the Blacktail Deer Plateau area and the Lamar Valley. To get to some of the trailheads, hop aboard a snowcoach or the van shuttles. Warming huts are spaced throughout the park for snowmobilers, skiers, and snowcoach passengers. Dress appropriately. **The Heart Ski Ranch,** Moran (307-543-2477), offers family-friendly snowmobile trips in winter.

Snowcoach and snowmobile tours. Yellowstone's south entrance is about two hours away from Jackson Hole. In winter most of the roads are closed to vehicles, but the animals are out. With young children, you can take a tour of the park by heated snowcoach (a bus equipped for deep snow). Contact **AMFAC reservations** (307-344-7311).

Teens and preteens might like a guided snowmobile tour from Jackson Hole to Old Faithful. It's a difficult trip—about 80 miles each way—and you'll pass many other snowmobiles, but in winter bison often congregate near Old Faithful. Outfitters include **Jackson Hole Snowmobile Tours** (307-733-6850 or 800-633-1733) and **Rocky Mountain Snowmobile**

Tours (307-733-2237 or 800-647-2561). Contact the Jackson Hole Chamber of Commerce (307-733-3316) for more outfitters.

SIDE TRIPS

Cody

President Teddy Roosevelt called the stretch of road from Yellowstone National Park's east entrance to Cody, Wyoming, the "most scenic 52 miles in the U.S." The land along what became the **Buffalo Bill Scenic Byway,** Route 14/16/20, hasn't changed much since Roosevelt's era.

The drive parallels the river and pulls you through the Shoshone National Forest and the Wapiti Valley. The steep granite walls of the Shoshone Canyon reflect the sunlight. Cottonwoods line the river banks and the road cuts through gorges surrounded by yellow-and-pink mesas, buttes, and bluffs with names like the Slipper, Laughing Pig, and Chimney Rock. Look carefully and you might see bison grazing and bighorn sheep and elk clattering over the boulders. This is the west of pioneer treks and movie vistas.

A car is really a necessity if you are continuing from Yellowstone to Cody. A scenic drive brochure is available from the Cody Chamber of Commerce, outlines routes to and through such scenic sites as the Chief Joseph Scenic Byway, Thermopolis and Hot Springs State Park, Red Lodge, Montana, and the Bighorn Mountains.

Spend the night in Cody, as there are some worthwhile attractions. The first one you'll come to is **Historic Trail Town,** Highway 14/16/20, 2 miles west of the Buffalo Bill Historical Center (307-587-5302), open mid-May to mid-September. Set on a strip of land just off the main drag, Historic Trail Town looks like a cowboy movie set, but this is the real thing. On this site near where western legend Buffalo Bill Cody and friends first surveyed "Cody City," archaeologist Bob Edgar has collected and placed twenty-six authentic nineteenth-century log buildings that face each other on two sides of a "street." Scores of wagons and wheels line the middle.

The weathered wood and simple furnishings create a haunting feel, evoking the West as it really was. The structures offer up such legends as the Hole in the Wall Cabin where Butch Cassidy and the Sundance Kid plotted, a saloon with bullet holes in the door, and Trail Town Cemetery, where, among others, Jeremiah "Liver Eating" Johnston, a mountain man, hunter, and trapper whose life became a movie legend, lies buried. As you peer in these fragile-looking homes and feel the wind in your face, you can imagine the toughness of pioneer living.

Take a family-friendly raft trip through the **Shoshone National Forest.** Most of the trips combine easy paddling with just enough rapids for

Buffalo Bill Historical Center

Buffalo Bill Historical Center, 720 Sheridan Avenue, Cody 82414 (307–587–4771 or 800–553–3838) is the "Smithsonian of the West." Spend an afternoon at this facility's four museums, and you'll come away with an enhanced sense of both western myth and reality.

- **Buffalo Bill Museum** presents artifacts of Showmen Buffalo Bill Cody and his Wild West Show. From these you understand the larger-than-life panache of mountain men, rodeo riders, and sharpshooters such as Annie Oakley.
- **Cody Firearms Museum** includes muskets dating to 1590, as well as eighteenth-century flintlock rifles, Civil War pistols, and nineteenth-century percussion revolvers.
- The **Whitney Gallery of Western Art** collection presents the land and its people, sometimes idealized, through the eyes of such artists as Frederic Remington, Charles Russell, and Albert Bierstadt.
- **Plains Indian Museum** presents the clothing, religious objects, and daily artifacts of the Sioux, Crow, and twenty-five other tribes who lived from the Mississippi River to the Rocky Mountains, and from Texas to mid-Canada. Children delight in the intricately beaded moccasins, shirts, and dresses. Take time to sit in a real tepee with your kids and discuss its symbolism and practicality, and experience the world from this vantage point.

  At the Plains Indian Powwow, one of the nation's largest gatherings of Plains tribes from the United States and Canada, members sing and dance in competition wearing tribal dress, Buffalo Bill Historical Center; Frontier Festival.
- **The Cody Nite Rodeo** is the event that has earned Cody its nickname "Rodeo Capital of the World." After dinner follow the crowds to the rodeo grounds (307–587–5155). Every evening from June through August cowgirls rope calves and race barrels, and cowboys ride broncos. Purchase tickets in advance at the ticket booth wagon, City Park; from the Cody Country Chamber of Commerce, 836 Sheridan Avenue (307–587–2297); or at the gate after 7:00 P.M.

some thrills, but always ask about the suitability given the ages of your children. With **Wyoming River Trips** (307–587–6661), excursions range from ninety-minute floats through scenic red-rock canyons to half-day (up to five hours) wildlife viewing trips on which the rapids and the wildlife add excitement. Additional outfitters: **River Runners** (307–527–

A llama trek is a fun and unique way to experience Bighorn National Forest.

RAFT), **Cody Boys River Trips** (307-587-4208), and **Red Canyon River Trips** (307-587-6988).

Bighorn National Forest

The **Bighorn National Forest,** 23 miles east of Cody on Alternate Route 14, encompasses more than a million acres in north-central Wyoming near the Montana border. The activities here are as great as all outdoors: fishing; hiking, camping, and exploring the backcountry. As some areas restrict vehicles, park the car and hike in to sample this forest.

Along Route 14, you drive through canyon and forest. The cliffs along the roadside may seem intimidating, but this is the most manageable road, especially for trailers or during winter weather. Highway 14A is a more open, alpine route with great overlooks, but the 10-percent grade makes this road difficult for some vehicles and drivers.

On the way to Bighorn is **Powell,** in the heart of the Shoshone reclamation area. An agricultural center, Powell grew green as a result of the Buffalo Bill Reservoir irrigation project. Look west for a glimpse of **Heart Mountain**—a geological phenomenon because the mountain's top is older than its base.

Just beyond Lovell, which is at the junction of U.S. 14A and 789/310, stop by the **Bighorn Canyon National Recreational Area Visitor Center,** U.S. 14A (307-548-2251). It's open daily in summer, and on Saturdays and Sundays other times. Ask about summer guided hikes and nature talks, and obtain a copy of *Canyon Echoes,* the forest newsletter. For more western canyons and wildlife, turn north on Route 37 just before the visitors center for views of **Bighorn Canyon** and the **Pryor Mountain Wild Horse Range,** where more than 120 wild horses roam free. About 17 miles from the turnoff, enjoy the viewed from the **Devils Canyon Overlook** of Bighorn Lake below and the many-hued canyon walls.

While hiking, you might see bighorn sheep and black bears, although the latter are rarely seen by tourists. No grizzlies reside in the Bighorn.

Medicine Wheel, 27 miles east of Lovell, is a controversial attraction within Bighorn National Forest. This prehistoric 74-foot stone circle, with twenty-eight spokes radiating from a central cairn, is said to be a sacred place of worship for Native Americans. Although tourists are not supposed to enter the area, non-Native Americans often park in a nearby lot and hike the mile to the observation area. Because the trail is strenuous, a shuttle is available in summer to transport people who may have difficulty making the climb. The information booth provides literature about the significance of this area to Native Americans.

Continue on 14A to **Burgess Junction,** where this road joins U.S. 14. About 5 miles south of this junction, take Forest Road 26 to the **Big Goose Falls Ranger Station.** From here continue on route 296 to **Big Moose Falls.** This 5-mile one-way hike from the ranger station crosses the East Fork four times, providing wonderful views, plunge pools, and water-sculpted rocks. But beware: The 10-mile round-trip may be best for older children and teens who are hearty hikers (parents, too, should be in shape). As always, bring plenty of water, food, and appropriate clothing—T-shirts, sweatshirts, and rain gear.

An easy hike is the 2.4-mile **Blue Creek Loop Trail.** The trailhead begins at Sibley Lake, Highway 14, near the campground. Follow the creek and, if you like, venture onto another loop, the **Deadhorse Park Loop.** While the terrain remains easy, the two loops together amount to 6 miles. Bring your camera for some photographs of the often-seen moose, deer, and elk in the meadows and the lodgepole pines.

On Route 14, the **Shell Falls Trail** in the Paintrock district offers some more easy hiking. Walk through the forest on a path that treats you to some wonderful views of the falls. Spend time at the novelty shop you'll pass, managed by a couple who give a singing/talking introduction to the falls. After hearing the stories and fun facts, the falls are even more fun. Look around for the bighorn sheep, who like the steep cliffs and fresh water.

More Day Trips

Include time in your Yellowstone vacation to explore nearby, and often less crowded, **Grand Teton National Park,** Wyoming. While it's possible to sample the park in a day, try to at least spend one overnight. In season the Jackson area, the southern gateway to Yellowstone, offers good skiing with short lift lines on relatively uncrowded slopes. (See the chapter Grand Teton National Park and Jackson.)

Where to Stay

Yellowstone National Park

Book your park accommodations as soon as you know the dates of your stay. Especially in season, Yellowstone is busy, and lodgings fill up fast. For reservations, call (303) 344-7311. The park cabins and lodges offer a range of family-friendly rooms for a variety of budgets. There are ten accommodations in six locations within the park. Most of these are basic, without televisions, radios, and telephones; some are without private baths.

Mammoth Hot Springs Hotel, open December to early March and late May through late September, offers hotel rooms and cottage-style cabins, some with full bath, and some without. This is the only park lodging fully accessible by automobile in winter. From here you can rent snowmobiles.

Roosevelt Lodge and Cabins, open June through the end of August, has rustic charm and simplicity. Limited number of family cabins.

Canyon Lodge and Cabins, open June through the end of August, is ½ mile from Yellowstone's canyons, and cabins are simple but have private baths.

Fishing Bridge R.V. Park, open from the end of May until September, allows RVs up to 40 feet in length, hard-sided only—no pop-ups or tents. Electric, water, and sewer hookups and laundry and shower facilities are available.

Lake Yellowstone Hotel & Cabins, open mid-May until the end of September, is among the park's best. Suites are available, but rooms in the annex building are less expensive.

Lake Lodge Cabins, open from June until September, offers cabins. The property has laundry facilities and a restaurant.

Grant Village, open June 1 through September, is situated on the shore of Yellowstone Lake and provides the southernmost overnight accommodations in the park. Rooms have private baths; there are laundry facilities and a steak house on the property.

Old Faithful Inn, open early May through early October, is a National Historic Landmark standing near Old Faithful. This stately log hotel has a dining room, lounge, and gift shop.

Old Faithful Lodge Cabins, open late May through mid-September, also has a view of Old Faithful and accommodates visitors in simple cabins with or without private baths.

Old Faithful Snow Lodge, open mid-May through mid-October, and

Family Dude Ranch

Whether you're a greenhorn beginner or a saddle savvy wrangler, **Paradise Guest Ranch** has a ride to suit you. This ranch offers custom rides twice daily for adults and kids six and older. Feel free to choose a scenic, slow-paced trail ride through the woods, a trot across a ridge top, or an adventuresome all-day trek that has you jumping ravines and galloping across high mountain meadows. Unlike many other guest ranches, Paradise allows you to ride with your kids or send them on with their own group.

When not on horseback, kids six and older and preschoolers ages three to five enjoy nature-oriented children's programs from 8:30 A.M. to 5:00 P.M. Nonriders (and the saddle-sore) can join a guided mountain walk, fish for trout, or soak in a hot tub. Evening activities bring the family together at talent shows, chuck-wagon barbecues, and square dances. The accommodations are first-rate in modern cabins with kitchen, fireplace, and laundry facilities. Paradise Guest Ranch, Buffalo, Wyoming (307-684-7876).

again in winter, is popular with skiers. While the rooms do not have baths, the cabins do. In winter this lodging is accessible only by over-the-snow vehicles. AMFAC's snowcoaches arrive here daily for excursions.

All reservations can be made through the Reservations Department, AMFAC, Yellowstone National Park, Wyoming (307-344-7311). Rooms at Yellowstone book quickly, so it's best to make reservations at least four months in advance. About twelve campgrounds are also available, most on a first-come basis.

Cody

Near the eastern entrance to Yellowston National Park is Buffalo Bill's original lodge (with a few modern changes). **The Pahaska Tepee,** 183 Yellowstone Highway, Cody 82414 (307-527-7701), has cabins, and offers fishing, overnight pack trips, and trail rides.

The historic **Irma Hotel,** 1192 Sheridan (307-587-4221), a town grande dame that has lost a bit of her "glow," offers forty original rooms in the historic hotel, plus annex rooms in a motel. The **Buffalo Bill Village Resort,** Seventeenth and Sheridan Avenue (800-527-5544), is a complex of three hotels: a Holiday Inn, a Comfort Inn, and the Village. There's a pool as well.

For a listing of eighty bed-and-breakfasts in the Wyoming area, contact Bed & Breakfast Western Adventure, P.O. Box 20972, Billings, Montana 59104 (406-259-7993).

Bighorn National Forest

Camping areas within the forest are divided into five districts: Buffalo, Tensleep, Paintrock, Medicine Wheel, and Tongue. Each has picnic grounds, grocery facilities, cabins or motels, and restaurants. **Bear Lodge** on 14A (write 1643 Seventeenth Street, Sheridan 82801; 307-655-2444) and **Arrowhead Lodge** (P.O. Box 267, Dayton 82836; 307-655-2388) are two good picks. Both offer modern motel units and rustic cabins. (Be sure to specify which type of lodging you prefer.) Bear Lodge has a stock pond for fishing, and snowmobiling in winter. Arrowhead has nearby rivers and streams for fishing, as well as snowmobiling and skiing in the winter.

WHERE TO EAT

Yellowstone National Park

Yellowstone offers a variety of dining choices. Dress is always casual, and cafeterias and fast food are easy enough to find. The restaurants at **Mammoth Hot Springs, Lake Yellowstone Hotel, Old Faithful Inn, Grant Village,** and **Canyon Lodge** offer a variety of choices on their menus, including children's meals. Breakfast and lunch are served, and reservations are required for dinner; call (307) 344-7901. Family-style restaurants are located at **Roosevelt Lodge** and **Old Faithful Snow Lodge.** Roosevelt Lodge offers an Old West Barbecue. **Lake Lodge, Old Faithful Lodge,** and **Canyon Lodge** all offer cafeterias with choices of salads, sandwiches, pasta, chicken, and more. If your stay is short and every minute counts, fast food is available at **Mammoth Hot Springs, Old Faithful,** and **Canyon Lodge.** As a convenience for hikers and fishers, box lunches can be ordered from any dining room or cafeteria and can be picked up the next morning.

Cody

Dine at the **Buffalo Bill Bar** and the **Irma Restaurant,** the Irma Hotel, 1192 Sheridan (307-587-4221), a hotel built in 1902 by Buffalo Bill Cody, and named for his daughter. Belly up to the elaborate cherrywood back bar, a gift to Cody from an appreciative Queen Victoria, who delighted in Buffalo Bill's Wild West Show. Despite the tin ceiling and ornate bar, this place is far from fancy. Locals with muddy boots and dusty chaps come here for the prime rib.

The Sunset House Family Restaurant, Sunset Motor Inn (307-587-2257), serves three meals daily and has take-out lunches. Kids like the piano music. **Franca's Italian Dining,** 1421 Rumsey Avenue (307-

587-5354), requires reservations. Try the house specialty, *Tortelloni Verdi al Mascarpone,* prepared by Franca herself. For a free dining guide, call (307) 587-2297.

For More Information

Yellowstone National Park

For park camping, dining, lodging, and tour information, contact **AMFAC** (307-344-7311). For information for the physically challenged: Handicapped Access, Yellowstone National Park, Wyoming 82190 (307-344-7381, ext. 2108). Log on to the National Parks Internet site: www.nps.gov.

Cody

Buffalo Bill's Yellowstone Country, Cody; (307) 587-2297

Bighorn National Forest

Bighorn National Forest, 1969 South Sheridan Avenue, Sheridan 82801; (307) 672-0751.

General

Wyoming Division of Tourism, I-25 at College Drive, Cheyenne 82002; (307) 777-7777 or (800) 225-5996.

Emergency Numbers

Yellowstone and Cody

Ambulance, fire, police: 911

For rangers in Yellowstone: (307) 344-7381

Hospital, emergency room, and pharmacy: In Yellowstone National Park, Yellowstone Medical Services offers twenty-four-hour emergency room and ambulance service from the end of May through mid-September at Lake Clinic in Lake, on Yellowstone Lake; (307) 242-7241. Other medical facilities are located at Old Faithful Clinic, Old Faithful area (307-545-7345), from the end of May through mid-October and at Mammoth Family Clinic, Mammoth Hot Springs (307-344-7965), year-round, Monday through Friday. West Park Hospital, 708 Sheriden Avenue, Cody; (800) 654-9447 or (307) 527-7501.

Pharmacy: Cody Drug, Eastgate Shopping Center, 1813 Seventeenth Street, Cody (307-587-2283), provides an after-hours emergency pharmacy and has a delivery service.

Poison Control: (800) 442-2702

INDEX

D

I

J

K

S

T

U

V

W

Y

Z